W9-AOP-825

FLORIDA STATE
UNIVERSITY LIBRARIES

JUN 2 6 2001

TALLAHASSEE, FLORIDA

Japan and the enemies of open political science

'This is an ambitious, controversial, ground-breaking and timely book . . . It deploys a cross-disciplinary scholarship of exceptional range and depth to argue a position of considerable importance – that the Japanese achievement warrants making a significant revision of western social science so as to correct the Eurocentric biases that are inherent in its dominant methodologies . . .'

John Gray, *Fellow, Jesus College,*
University of Oxford

The central argument of *Japan and the Enemies of Open Political Science* is that Eurocentric blindness is not a moral but a scientific failing. In this wide-ranging critique of western social science, Anglo-American philosophy and French theory, Williams works on the premise that Japan is the most important political system of our time. He also explains why social scientists have been so keen to ignore or denigrate Japan's achievements. If social science is to meet the needs of the 'Pacific Century', it requires a sustained act of intellectual demolition and subsequent renewal.

David Williams is Senior Research Fellow in Japanese Politics at the School of East Asian Studies, University of Sheffield. He is the author of *Japan: Beyond the End of History* (Routledge 1994).

Japan and the enemies of open political science

David Williams

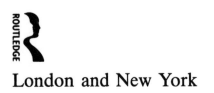

London and New York

H
6l
.W557
1996

First published 1996
by Routledge
11 New Fetter Lane, London EC4P 4EE

Simultaneously published in the USA and Canada
by Routledge
29 West 35th Street, New York, NY 10001

© 1996 David Williams

Phototypeset in Times by Intype, London
Printed and bound in Great Britain by Mackays of Chatham plc.

All rights reserved. No part of this book may be reprinted
or reproduced or utilized in any form or by any electronic,
mechanical, or other means, now known or hereafter
invented, including photocopying, and recording, or in any
information storage or retrieval system, without the
permission in writing from the publishers.

British Library Cataloguing in Publication Data
A catalogue record for this book is available from the British Library

Library of Congress Cataloguing in Publication Data
A catalogue record for this book has been requested

ISBN 0–415–11130–7(hbk)
ISBN 0–415–11131–5(pbk)

This book is, and has been since my youth,
more precious than country and kin and public
advancement – indeed, for me, it *is* these things.
Arrian, *The Campaigns of Alexander*

For my parents
and for
St Antony's College, Oxford
where this book began to take shape

Contents

x *Contents*

Part III On classic ground

Preface

Cultural outposts, like railway stations, stimulate the imagination. They encourage the projection of thought. Romanticizing exotic places may be a prelude to scientific conquest. To have been born, as I was, on the Western world's Pacific frontier with the Asian colossus, to have been raised in a California community where the heirs of Asia and Europe had learned, with difficulty, to cultivate a fruitful domesticity, was the rarest of privileges. It was to begin a lifetime exercise in the weighing of contrasts and similarities between cultures and continents. But the continent that has mattered has been Asia.

Even more than the utopian promise of the New World, it is Asia that has provided the millennial touchstone for European self-awareness and identity. It is against Asian failures that we measure the fineness of our moral and intellectual discriminations. It is against Asian achievements that we test the sinews of our organizational and technological powers. It is no accident that the study of politics in the West began with an act of comparison between Greece and Asia.

Our shifting attitudes towards Asia provide an unrivalled barometer of our confidence in Western civilization. In modern times, the commanding place of Europe and the West in the making of global history has been such that episodes of Asiatic-inspired doubt have been remarkably few. The classic European moments of critical self-examination include Voltaire's witty celebration of Confucian reason at the expense of European obscurantism and Montesquieu's sardonic exploitation of the contrast between Turkish virtue and European folly in *The Persian Letters* (1721).

Today such confident self-appraisal no longer governs the Western response to Asian success. Among some Westerners, this Oriental provocation has sparked a crisis of belief in Western values, practices and institutions. In other Europeans, North Americans and Australians, it has excited paroxysms of anti-Asian criticism and contempt. To those Westerners with a gift for generous wonder, our contemporary condition is more acutely mirrored not in the cultural condescensions of the Enlightenment but in Marco Polo's unresisting celebration of the wealth and power of Kublai Khan's court. Unlike modern Western man, medieval Europeans such as Polo were taught by both history and contemporary reality, as reflected in the glories of Islamic civilization or the overwhelming martial superiority of the Mongols, to cultivate a pronounced inferiority before the achievements of Asia. In this sense, if in no other, Polo's vision of Asian power housed little surprise for the fourteenth-century European mind. Six hundred years later the idea that Chinamen would one day equip the English household with the most advanced of technical necessities would have struck John Stuart Mill, and most of nineteenth-century Europe with him, as a bizarre fantasy. The fact that this Taiwanese prospect no longer strikes Westerners in this way offers evidence that, after half a millennium of European ascendency, Western sensibility has come full circle.

In this era of mounting Asian excellence in manufacturing, commerce and technology, politics has persisted as a redoubt of Western confidence. Democracy remains our forte. This has encouraged a sustained European meditation on the failings of Asian forms of governance that is as old as Herodotus and as fresh as our recoil against the 1989 massacre in Tiananmen Square. When we describe contemporary Chinese politics as 'barbaric', we speak Greek. When we confront the collective darkness of Asian misrule with the Western imperatives of freedom and democracy, we echo Pericles' rejection of Persian slavery and authoritarianism. A pronounced Western urge to censure contemporary Asian political values and habits has resulted. So has a certain hubris. The bruised conviction of European superiority locates its compensatory heaven in the Asian political condition. The confident ethical posture at work in our reaction against the terrorists' cellars of Lebanon, the spoiled ballot papers of Indian democracy, Confucian paternalism in Singapore, the bloodstains on Beijing's central square, and the rape of Kuwait, offers us neither moral, nor intellectual, nor political challenge.

The example of Japan is entirely another matter. Indeed it may be unique. Across a dozen concerns and disciplines, the Japanese model has, since the late 1970s, come to cast a formidable shadow. In a way true of no Asian nation since the vigorous prime of the

Ottoman Empire, Japan looms large today in the practical affairs and speculative cares of the contemporary Westerner.

Japan's status as the world's pre-eminent industrial, commercial and financial power has transformed the history of comparative civilization. The hazards of the 1990s have not altered the weight of this claim. Quite the contrary, this Japanese achievement should serve as a forceful reminder that the technological and organizational advantage of the modern West over the rest of the world is less than four centuries old. Joseph Needham's *Science and Civilisation in China* offers no more potent antidote (if such still be needed) for European complacency than when he insists that Asia, not the West, has been the world's traditional generator of fresh ideas and technical innovations.

Despite the labours of many Japan specialists, most Western social scientists still deny that the Japanese experience of government raises fundamental questions about Western political practice and theory, about the relationship between the polity and society, the individual and the nation, and the state and the marketplace. The grounds for this intellectual consensus must be re-examined. It is my conviction that Japan's experiment with modernity illuminates, in a way unrivalled by any other episode in world history, the flaws and limitations of Western political, social and economic theory. It may be time, therefore, to rethink some of the epistemological axioms of Western social science. With this potential harvest in mind, this book seeks to survey the political foundations of 'the social science and the philosophy of the Pacific Century'.

THE AIM AND NATURE OF THE BOOK

To peruse any serious newspaper is to discover ample recognition of Japan's importance in the contemporary world. Similarly in academe, a chair or lectureship in Japanese studies is now an accepted measure of a university's commitment to non-European studies. How, then, is one to explain the fact that Japan casts hardly a shadow on the core of the curriculum, the Euro-American mainstream? Western students of political thought concede no ground to modern Japan, which in turn has left hardly a trace on the methods and ideas of the post-war economist. Courses in theory, methodology and philosophy, as branches of the social sciences, have maintained, with rare exception, a studied indifference to the achievements of non-Western societies, including Japan, and to the particular difficulties of writing and thinking about such societies in a Western language. Nowhere is this more evident than in the great universities of the heartland of the Western world, Britain and Continental Europe.

I seek to call into question this indifference. My objective in writing this book is to deposit something resistant and Oriental beneath the skin of the Western tradition of political reflection. If this ambition is to be achieved, then the philosophic underpinnings of Western social science must be examined afresh. We must break with the ruling monist orthodoxy in social science, and its insistence that all true scientific problems have one and only one answer. An explicit pluralism – philosophies rather than philosophy – must be embraced if Japan and its place in the modern world are to be properly understood.

In this book I analyse some of the central questions of the philosophy of social science, but I am not a professional philosopher. Indeed it is my suspicion that no philosopher or methodologist would either care to or be able to write a book in the mode of *Japan and the Enemies of Open Political Science*. This is in fact an even bolder claim that it sounds. In recent decades research priorities among many Western philosophers have been significantly reordered. Under the impact of world events, there has been a re-orientation towards the problems of the 'subject', communal identity, nationalism and multi-culturalism in the work of philosophers as different as Jacques Derrida, Charles Taylor and Richard Rorty. Their labours should be regarded as compelling versions of the post-imperialist liberal doctrine of 'openness' or cultural relativism. In their varied ways, these philosophers insist that a certain tolerance should be extended to non-Western societies within the framework of the European sciences. But their dissent from Eurocentrism is argued entirely in European terms.

To acknowledge an intellectual void is not to fill it. In the writings of such advocates of philosophic 'openness', it is rare to encounter an Asian idea or thinker. Such encounters demand a certain intimacy with an Asian society, its tradition of thought and language. This, I believe, I am able to bring to a philosophic study of modern Japan.

In theme and approach, *Japan and the Enemies of Open Political Science* flows naturally from my earlier book, *Japan: Beyond the End of History*. That book also had an explicitly philosophic dimension. In the earlier study, I sought to identify the Japan-shaped hole in the discourse of Western social science. Here, I have laboured to reduce this gap, thereby pushing my critique of the European sciences to its radical and necessary conclusion.

To my knowledge, no Japanese project in the precise mould of *Japan and the Enemies of Open Political Science* has previously been attempted by a Western scholar. I have sought to capture fresh ground on several fronts. First, I have attempted to demonstrate that Japan, as an object of study, cannot be adequately grasped by Anglo-American positivist methods alone. It is my conviction that area studies, as a branch of Western learning, must defend its own methodological approaches and philosophy. Where these are lacking, we must develop our own methods even when this means rejecting social scientific orthodoxy. The conscious aim here is to lay the philosophic and methodological foundations for a new approach to area research which I call 'Euro-Asian studies'.

Second, I am determined to breach the sturdy wall that isolates Japanese studies from the Western academic mainstream, while at the same time forcing mainline scholars to take Japan more seriously. If this means we must abandon our comfortable academic ghetto, so be it.

Third, and finally, *Japan and the Enemies of Open Political Science* is one of the first efforts by a Western scholar to apply the rigours of European philosophy to the study of contemporary Japanese government and politics as a body of thought as well as a system of institutions. This is to address a long-neglected scientific problem. Political philosophers such as Oxford's John Gray have perceptively argued that methodology is the great weakness of the social scientific approach to the study of modern Asia, just as Edward Said insists that the neglect of methodological questions subverts the labours of the Western Orientalist. Here, I have sought to ease the scientific vulnerabilities of what is one of the most compelling of mental endeavours: the attempt to master a culture other than one's own.

POLITICAL SCIENCE: OPEN OR CLOSED?

No branch of the social or human sciences better illustrates the potential of Japan to transform our fundamental philosophic and scientific assumptions than political science. The first and most important reason is that Japan's modern achievement is, at numerous points, political in nature. The second is that many political scientific concerns – area studies, political theory, comparative analysis, political economy, public administration and methodology – are vulnerable to the claims of a strongly argued case for Japan's contemporary importance. The third reason is that political science, *as a science*, straddles the boundary between the empirical and positivist sciences.

Sitting on the methodological fence has made political science vulnerable to attack from several directions. Thus far, the forces of postmodernism have largely been repelled. Positivism is another matter. Indeed, Western political science, and the political science of Japan in particular, highlights the secret dilemma of modern social science: the tension *between* empirical and positivist approaches. This tension defines the choice between open and closed political science.

In his essay 'Science as solidarity', Richard Rorty observes that

> any academic discipline which wants a place at the trough, but is unable to offer the predictions and the technology provided by the natural sciences, must either pretend to imitate science or find some way of obtaining 'cognitive status' without the necessity of discovering facts.[1]

Rorty is surely right about the pretensions of scientism or the uncritical application of scientific or quasi-scientific methods to inappropriate fields of research. Dogmatic scientism is the great bane of modern social science. Despite the impact of French students of the natural sciences such as Gaston Bachelard, who died in 1962, or Thomas Kuhn's *The Structure of Scientific Revolutions* (1962) or Paul Feyerabend's arguments gathered in *Farewell to Reason* (1987) or even the writings of Rorty himself, the attractions to the political scientist of objectivist science, in the Newtonian mould, remain strong.

This Newtonian fallacy cannot be satisfactorily addressed unless the problematic nature of positivism is grasped. Even Rorty's own formulation cited above mis-states the fundamental problem. The danger is this: scientific status is being denied to political scientists *despite* the fact that they are busy discovering new facts.

This is the methodological issue at the heart of the recent row that has flared up over the application of rational choice methods to the study of Asian politics.[2] Advocates of social scientific prediction, economic positivism, behaviouralism and rational choice, and some schools of quantitative research methods all suffer from empirical bad faith: they extend lip service to empirical methods while denying to people who practise them the status of social scientists. They do not, in their methodological heart of hearts, believe in empiricism. As a result, they threaten to deny jobs and research funding to some of the best-known names in the Western political scientific study of Japan and their students.

Equally as damning, close empirical examination of the Japanese model suggests that positivism has failed in its exaggerated

ambitions not because it is immoral or unfair or politically conservative, but because it has often been, even by its own biased standards,
not particularly good science.

In the name of scientific dogmatism parading as rigour, positivists
have repeatedly sought to close political scientific departments to
the pure empiricist. This makes the political positivist into the often
unwitting ally of the enemies of open political science and area
studies who dominate economics, psychology and cultural theory.
This is not science as solidarity. In some ways, it is not science at
all.

UN-AMERICAN ACTIVITIES

In the theatre of ancient Rome, it was a convention for actors to
proceed onto the stage conspicuously carrying, rather than wearing,
their masks (*Larvatus prodeo*). In the most famous essay in *Mythologies*, the one titled 'The World of Wrestling', Roland Barthes
indulges this impulse to expose, boldly and without apology, the
contrived character of stage-craft illusion. Here I reinterpret this
Roman gesture as a bow both to the need for clarity about first
principles and to the very human urge to know something of the
truth about the person and the theoretician who stands behind every
theory.

This is a European book. It is also, in some ways, a rather Japanese
one. As a result, an explanation may be owed to my North American
readers. As British readers share many of the values of their American colleagues, they, too, may be puzzled by the 'look' of *Japan and
the Enemies of Open Political Science.*

In *The Open Society and its Enemies*, Karl Popper gave the word
'enemies' a specific ballast and consequence. Despite its publication
near the end of the Second World War, Popper and his publishers
took the chance of perplexing some potential readers with his title.
Why did he not speak of 'free' or 'liberal' societies rather than use
the novel and therefore obscure expression 'open society'?

The title of Popper's 1945 masterpiece can be defended on the
grounds of the book's content. This was more than a political tract
supporting the right cause at the right time. In censuring the vulgar
determinism of the Soviet apparatchik and the half-educated party
hack outside the Soviet imperium, Popper was advocating a certain
'openness' towards tomorrow and its possibilities. He urged Europeans to reject the iron laws at once positivist and dialectical which
he believed formed the core of Hegelian and Marxist philosophy

because they close the door on an indeterminate future. For Popper, 'openness' touches on more than political values. It is a specific posture that the enlightened man and woman adopts towards time, progress and methods of doing science. In this sense only, *Japan and the Enemies of Open Political Science* sails in the wake of Popper's great work.

Marx and the history of ideas

The kind of political philosophy embodied in the Popperian *oeuvre* demonstrates why the history of ideas is taken so seriously in Europe, and why it should be taken more seriously in America and Britain. The Italian thinker Galvano della Volpe made his way from Hegel to Marx via Hume. By contrast, Marx helped me, when I was younger, to free myself of the grip of Hume and his epigone so as to come home to Hegel. A rich repertoire of ideas is essential if one is to reach one's philosophic destination. That is the point of tradition.

The European tradition of philosophy merits the closest attention. Despite my endorsement of this truth, I was taken to task by one of my acutest critics for neglecting Marx in *Japan: Beyond the End of History*. I think such criticism was misplaced because that book was unapologetically Hegelian in thrust and also because I think that Marx's hour has passed. If, during much of the twentieth century, Hegel was read as an essential backdrop to Marx, today there has been a reversal of roles: Marx should be understood as an arresting reader of Hegel who has assumed a new primacy.

My call for a return to Hegel here is neither eccentric nor foreign to the Anglo-American tradition. Less than a century ago, Hegelian idealism was a force with which to reckon at Oxford and Harvard. That this climate of feeling is almost incomprehensible to most undergraduates reading philosophy in the English-speaking world today is a monument to the rigour and prejudice of the analytic and ordinary-language schools. But the roots of Anglo-American disdain for European philosophy after Hegel remain puny and dubious. Indeed, philosophic openness in Britain and America demands that such contempt and bias be banished. Importantly, there are signs that openness is finally starting to bloom again.

Such openness should be extended to Hegel, but should Marx similarly benefit? In discussing this book with a Jesuit-trained Thomist who teaches philosophy in Hawaii, no issue prompted greater incomprehension than the suggestion that Marx might have a place of prominence here. This admirer of Václav Havel pronounced Marx 'dead'. Is this not the main philosophical consequence, he asked, of the demise of the Soviet Union? The answer is 'yes, but'. The present pontiff carried a Marxist text into the conclave which elevated him to the papacy in 1978. Given what happened during his reign to European communism, a certain nervousness may result if his successor is discovered to have taken a copy of *The Wealth of Nations* into the conclave that makes him Pope. Nevertheless, more was at stake in Cardinal Wojtyla's selection of reading material than 'Know thy enemy'. Marx and Marxism have mattered here in Europe. This is a view to which many Western Europeans cling, whatever Poles may feel. The Western European outlook is beautifully captured in the stance of the Marxist proofreader who appears in George Steiner's novella *Proofs*.

This response to reading Marxist texts in Western Europe implies no approval of Stalinist tyranny. Such readers accept that Hungarian Cardinal Jozsef Mindszenty is still regarded as an anti-communist hero by many. The oppression of Catholics in Eastern Europe only added to the long list of the victims of Lenin's state. This list is unfortunately where the story of Marxism ends for most Americans. Here, too, is found still another reason that Marx is largely unread in the United States and why indifference to this German philosopher, along with ignorance of the history of ideas, philosophically divides one side of the Atlantic from the other.

The story, however, does not end there. Steiner's argument that the prime motive in the intellectual labours of Georg Lukács, the Hungarian Marxist philosopher, was 'to make the world safe for Shakespeare and Pushkin' justifies the cultural conservative's generous reading of the Marxist tradition. As a German philosopher, Marx helped this Hungarian arch defender of European high culture to reach *his* philosophic goal. The point is that Marx was, in a manner comparable to St Augustine and St Thomas Aquinas, a master thinker who has left an indelible mark on posterity. This recognition explains why it is possible at Oxford to speak of the canonic tradition of political philosophy reaching from Plato to Marx without raising the faintest flicker of a don's eyebrow.

Marx established intellectual standards that will survive the demise of the Soviet Union and European communism. This confident assessment looks back to Daniel Bell's conclusion that 'Given the protean scope of his knowledge, and the extent of his interests and influence, Max Weber is the single major figure in twentieth-century social thought who can be compared to Marx'.[3] But it is

Steiner who delivers the *coup de grâce*: 'the pressure of presence throughout the world of the mind and of moral feeling exercised on civilization by a Marx, a Freud, even a Lévi-Strauss, is of a calibre which American civilization does not produce'.[4] Such classicism, this great un-American activity, forms the leitmotif of *Japan and the Enemies of Open Political Science*.

European texts; Japanese context

When I was an undergraduate in a Japanese university, I was confronted with the uncompromising claim that to study philosophy in Japan demanded intimacy with Kant, Hegel and Marx. Digests or summaries or reworkings of Marx and Engels by the Japanese equivalent of C. Wright Mills or T. B. Bottomore were judged insufficient. To take Marxism seriously in Japan meant immersing oneself in the *1844 Manuscripts, The German Ideology*, the *Grundrisse, A Contribution to the Critique of Political Economy* and *Das Kapital*. Ideally, one read these texts in German.

Such memories come flooding back when the historian Carol Gluck complains that in *Japan: Beyond the End of History* I dealt with the Japanese-language literature 'only glancingly'. Given the number of Japanese texts quoted or discussed in depth in that book, her remark makes no sense unless one resides in the West where one's 'Japan' may be reduced entirely to a set of published sources. For those of us who make Japan our home, that nation is the context of our thinking lives. It may safely be assumed to be ever present. Japan is more than a printed object which one excavates in search of exotic treasure or Orientalia.

The balance between Japanese and European texts in this book decisively favours Europe. This is in perfect keeping with the balance of citations throughout Iwanami's two new series: the twelve volumes of *Shakai Kagaku no Hoho* (The methodology of the social sciences) and the sixteen volumes of *Gendai Shiso* (Contemporary thought) published between 1993 and 1995. During the twentieth century, the Japanese mind has consistently sought to achieve an ever closer marriage between European texts and Japanese context. This is the strategy that I have followed here. It is very Japanese.

Literature and freedom

The most radical departure from Anglo-American scholarly practice here has, however, little to do with Japan. This is my absolute refusal to take any notice of the scientistic wall that some have sought to erect between the social sciences and the humanities. Such barriers are intolerable. Reality is so difficult to grasp that one must exploit every resource. The literary criticism of George Steiner and Edward Said, to cite two cardinal examples, has been indispensable to my work.

This open stance towards the riches of art and the humanities derives from my early schooling and sense of tradition, and has no connection whatever with Derrida's dreary attempt to deconstruct science in favour of rhetoric and semantic play. It strikes me as entirely natural that Sartre and Valéry wandered across the frontier between philosophy and literature in perfect freedom. When Rorty concedes that this is an enviable condition but says that it is unthinkable in the United States because philosophy departments will not permit it, one is forced back on the hoariest of Tocqueville's clichés about the lack of respect for intellectual freedom in the American sensibility. It is time for this to change.

Acknowledgements

The issues raised in this book were first treated in a series of lectures that I gave at Oxford during the Michaelmas and Hilary terms of the 1990/91 academic year. It was on that occasion, in discussing the various features of Japanese government in outline, that I began to feel the renewed press of more fundamental questions, what in German are usefully known as *die Grundprobleme* of a discipline.

Japan: Beyond the End of History was my first attempt to expose these philosophic conundrums to fresh scrutiny. Here, they are addressed in a more direct and sustained manner. I am grateful to Professor Arthur Stockwin for making my Oxford stay possible. I must also thank all my colleagues and students at Oxford who generously gave of their time and energy to furthering this project during my year at St Antony's. I must also thank Mr John Gray of Jesus College, Oxford, and Professor Marius Jansen of Princeton University for timely encouragement during crucial phases of the writing of this book.

A word of appreciation is due to Sir Ralf Darendorf and the Fellows of St Antony's College for maintaining the unique atmosphere and status of the college, for it was at St Antony's that this study took a decisive turn. Professor Albert Hourani, the late and much-admired student of Arab society, encouraged me to return to Edward Said's *Orientalism*.

I wish also to thank Professors Arthur Stockwin, Ian Gow, Glen Hook, Maurice Wright and Ian Neary, and all the participants of the annual conference of the Japan Politics Group at the University of Sheffield before whom I presented selections of *Japan and the Enemies of Open Political Science* in September 1994.

It is a special pleasure for me that Chapter 1 ('Japan and the European political canon') appeared, in slightly altered form, in Heiner Timmermann (ed.), *Die Kontinentwerdung Europas: Fest-*

schrift für Helmut Wagner zum 65. Geburtstag, Berlin, Duncker &
Humblot, 1995.

Finally, I must acknowledge my debts to all those who helped
with the final stages of publication. In particular, I would like thank
Mr Robin Reilly for his editorial advice and assistance. Mr Kenneth
Jones of Teikyo University gave generous amounts to time to this
project. I am also grateful for the cooperation and encouragement
that I received from Mr Gordon Smith, Ms Victoria Smith, Mr
James Whiting and Ms Angie Doran of Routledge and the freelance
editor Ms Frances Dedrick.

Glossary

area studies The social scientific study, either interested or disinterested, of the world by geographic region.

canon A set of texts of unqualified excellence that have been tested by time, and which forms the foundation of a religious, literary or scientific tradition.

classic A book that has won an established place in a canon.

economics The study of economic behaviour in accordance with an elaborate system of positivistic laws.

empiricism A method of social research that concentrates on the facts about human institutions and behaviour with little or no reference to positivist laws.

essentialism The doctrine of cultural studies that holds that cultures have an identifying essence which precedes and governs any factual or textual manifestation of that culture.

Eurocentrism The doctrine that holds that Europe is the centre of the world. In the wake of decolonization, this view tends to be confined to the intellectual, cultural and scientific spheres of global life.

hyperfactualism The condition of scientific indigestion that arises from the truth that the number of facts relevant to the understanding of any social phenomenon may be almost infinite.

logical positivism A school of early twentieth-century Austrian and British philosophy. Regarded as a term of abuse by some, philosophers remain divided about the meaning of the term 'logical positivism'. Here it is used with special reference to social science, and is blamed for a double failure. First, it has fanned a fawning naivety which has discouraged scrutiny of the precise meaning and actual practice of empiricism. Second, it has imposed intolerable constraints on political philosophy in the name of unattainable scientific standards and inflated expectations for philosophic certitude.

monism The philosophic or scientific belief that genuine philosophic or scientific problems have one and only one solution. The contrary position is here termed 'pluralism'.

nominalism The philosophic and linguistic doctrine which argues that words are only labels or names for things which exist in a way that words do not.

Ontology/ontology The study or delineation of what exists. The term 'Ontology' here refers to an ideology or religious doctrine that is disciplined by reason or a leaven of objective truths (Thomistic theology or Marxist socialism is an Ontology, while astrology and racial suprematism are not). By contrast an 'ontology' is a doctrine about reality that manifestly embraces scientific or philosophical rigour, such as logical positivism or Hegelianism.

open/closed political science The distinction is about research methods. Closed political science denies any role for pure empiricism, as prevails in area studies, in favour of positivist, universalist and mathematical (as opposed to statistical) research methods. Open political science recognizes the positivist achievement but refuses to accept the claim that positivism alone qualifies as true science.

Orientalism The academic school of textual study of the Orient or Asia by Westerners that predates the consolidation of social science between *c.* 1870 and *c.* 1930.

'Orientalism' The Western doctrine that holds that Asians are racially and culturally inferior to Westerners, and are best understood in an essentialist way.

political correctness A Western ideology, with roots in the 1950s and 1960s, that insists that minorities or the disempowered must be compensated for the discrimination that they have suffered by symbolic respect and deference in the public sphere.

political economy Traditional name for economics (e.g. Marx's *A Contribution to the Critique of Political Economy*).

positivism A scientific and philosophic idea that holds that facts are only comprehensible, that is real, when understood within a framework of universal laws. Examples of such laws include the Laws of Thermodynamics or the Law of Supply and Demand.

relativism The political belief that the advocacy of the superiority of Western values, practices and institutions should be banned from any discussion of non-European cultures.

science Any body of knowledge organized in a systematic or rational manner. An English rendering of the German term *Wissenschaft*.

text A printed object that is worthy of close study and reflection, particularly if it is a classic.

theory Abstract knowledge or reasoning that may be empirical, positivist or conjectural.

Japanese conventions and English usage

Throughout this book, Japanese names are given in their proper order, with the surname first and the personal name second. With names of Westerners of Japanese descent, Western order is preserved.

Macrons have been dispensed with. They are irrelevant to those who do not understand Japanese and unnecessary for those who do.

To avoid charges of modishness, I have sought to conform to the rules of English usage set out in the standard authorities, especially *The Concise Oxford Dictionary* (1990), recommended by Routledge, and *Collins English Dictionary* (1991). Both dictionaries endorse the view that the pronoun 'he' may refer to 'a person of unspecified sex, esp. referring to one already named or identified (if anyone comes he will have to wait)'. Words such as 'mankind' are used in their normal English sense, that is 'the human species' regardless of gender.

Part I

Japan: the splendour of its prime

Another Athens shall arise,
And to remoter time
Bequeath, like sunset to the skies,
The splendour of its prime
                                Shelley

1 Japan and the European political canon

What is important is not what other people make of us,
but what we ourselves make of what they have made of us.

Sartre

A PLACE IN THE PANTHEON

The twentieth century has given the Japanese a unique taste of greatness. Nothing in that Asian society's thirteen hundred years of recorded history matches what it has accomplished in recent times. This achievement has universal reach. It qualifies Japan for a place of honour in the world's pantheon of political systems or polities. With proper recognition, post-war Japan will remain an object of mature thought long after the present golden age has passed. We will remember it, as we remember Athens, the Roman Republic and Renaissance Florence.

In each of these canonic examples, be it a city-state or an empire, the polity embodies a triumph of experience mediated by a supreme example of textual reflection. Classical Athenians, Republican Romans and Renaissance Florentines all made history, but this making was enhanced because within the walls of these communities could be found a Plato, a Cicero and a Machiavelli. Thought confirms the deed. What Plato achieved for the Athenian polis, or Hobbes for the England of the Civil War, or Alexander Hamilton for the new American republic must now be wrung from the post-war Japanese miracle.

To seek to win a place for modern Japan in the canon of Western political philosophy is no small undertaking. Indeed this venture will succeed only if many minds become convinced that the European tradition of political theory, initiated by Thucydides and Plato, will remain incomplete without the ingestion of the Japanese experience of government. But if we are to deposit something resistant and Oriental beneath the skin of the Western tradition of political thought, then we must first banish the obscuring hubris of 'Orientalist' assumption that prevails in Western social science. The limitations of a vast discourse must be overcome. But the most invidious of these limits is the axiom of Asian quiescence.

> Without significant exception the universalizing discourses of modern Europe and the United States assume the silence, willing or otherwise, of the non-European world. There is incorporation; there is inclusion; there is direct rule; there is coercion. But there is only infrequently an acknowledgment that the colonized people should be heard from, their ideas known.[1]

The force of Edward Said's censure is in no way diminished by the fact that the Japanese narrowly escaped colonization. Japan's classic moment has been denied; its silence has been assumed. Science is at work in this hubris. Western assumptions of civilized superiority are grounded in our methods of grasping the truth. These encourage us to ignore the fact that the non-European world has generated no other political system that presses upon Western sensibility with as much ontological weight as that of modern Japan. Such willful European blindness lends credence to Jacques Derrida's provocative suggestion that philosophy – that elaborate structure of thought, nursed into glory over the past twenty-five centuries – is merely 'White metaphysics'. Derrida is mistaken; but the only way for the Western student of Asia to prove that Derrida is wrong about philosophy and social science is to grind a fresh set of lenses through which to peruse the theories and institutions that have nourished the Japanese miracle. One claim can, however, no longer be resisted. The time for Japanese ideas to be heard has arrived.

Even here, a dark note must be sounded. It is almost impossible for an educated European to imagine the depth of emotion that this Japanese apotheosis may spark among alert non-Europeans. The hitherto unrivalled excellence of European political philosophy has depressed Asian political thinkers even when it has spurred them to greater effort. Sakai Naoki has observed that Japanese writers on the intellectual history of their country (*Nihon shiso-shi*) are haunted by a spectral presence that is almost always an absence: the idealized Western reader.[2] For the striving Japanese intellectual it is the Western reader who has embodied the highest standards. It is he who must be appeased.

Such dependence not only breeds anti-European resentment, it also subverts the pursuit of Asian excellence. But the hurt is real. It encourages Asian thinkers on politics to mimic the psychology of a son of a father who neglects his child's small victories. The paternal recognition that is sought is never given. The superiority of European tradition has spawned an apparently callous complacency, which has littered the Western canon of philosophic and political analysis with traps and humiliations for the thoughtful Asian. The confident assertion of European centrality suggested in the epigram of Léon Brunschvicg, the French neo-Kantian philosopher, that 'The history of Egypt is the history of Egyptology' exasperates the non-Western sensibility. It is one of those confident observations that lends persuasiveness to Sakai's charge that Eurocentrism would deny the non-Westerner his own subjectivity.

A Japanese apotheosis today would send a quiet surge of pride through the non-European world of thought and letters, much as the triumph of Japanese arms over Russia in 1905 bolstered the still fitful confidence of anti-colonial nationalists when the star of European imperial supremacy still reigned. But Japan's triumph is not a matter of significance for non-Europeans alone. It offers a classic occasion for Western thinking of the first rank. Any European willing to examine the Japanese achievement, fairly and openly, will find the geography of his spirit enhanced and enriched. This is in no small part because the recognition of Japan's success demands, as was true of Locke, a two-pronged effort: substantive political theorizing and a fresh assault on methods. Only by curbing the claims of the dominant methodological schools of Western social science will a place be won for Japan in the pantheon of classic political systems.

The dialectic of deed and thought, phenomena and text, should urge us to ponder afresh the ways that the political and economic trajectory of modern Japan defies some of Western social science's most cherished epistemological and ontological postulates. The Japanese experiment should encourage a revolt against key aspects of twentieth-century science and theory. But the first target of any such critique should be the governing assumption of Japanology: a European studies Japan to understand only Japan. Rather one should study Japan to understand the totality of human experience, not because Japan is part of the whole, but because the Japanese example illuminates the whole.

THE CANONIC WOUND

Japan stands at the spear point of a larger endeavour. The modern phase of this enterprise begins, for many, with Johann Gottfried Herder (1744–1803). This German Romantic thinker sought to give the search for a bond 'between a people and the majestic projects of philosophy, literature, and the arts' primacy in the ambitions of the intellect.[3] In his essay 'African-American philosophy?', K. Anthony Appiah identifies the injury that such ambition would heal:

> Few black philosophers are undisturbed when they discover the moments when Africa is banished from Hegel's universal history and when Hume declares, in the essay on 'National Characters', that blacks are incapable of eminence in action or speculation (likening in the same place Francis Williams, the Jamaican poet, to a 'parrot who speaks a few words plainly.').[4]

The remedy for such humiliation lies in practical and mental achievement. The claims of shared identity motivate this drive to 'find something in Africa that *deserves* the dignity; that warrants the respect that we have been taught (in our western or westernized schools and colleges) is due to Plato and Aristotle, Kant, and Hegel'.[5] Japan's modern century merits such dignity, certainly in the contest of mind that is political philosophy.

The main currents of twentieth-century social science and philosophy, both Anglo-American and French, are unsympathetic to this non-European quest for canonic dignity. Positivists, behaviourists and post-structuralists have all sought to throttle Herder's crusade by disembowelling the political canon just as the non-Westerner would take the field. But unless we would conspire to drown our community in the waters of oblivion, the post-structuralist celebration of 'the death of the author' must be judged as an act of collective self-mutilation.

Pedagogic necessity and the weight of tradition have fortunately blunted this attempt to 'dethrone' the great texts of Europe's sustained meditation on government and politics since Pericles.[6] Despite the doubts that logical positivists have fanned about the methodological purity and philosophic rigour of the traditional pantheon of Western political theory, the centre has held. As a result, there is a wide consensus, even among those who would bury the political classic, about which texts find their natural place in this canon. Plato's *Republic*, Aristotle's *Politics*, Hobbes' *Leviathan*, Locke's *Two Treatises of Government*, Rousseau's *Social Contract*

and Hegel's *Philosophy of Right* are all masterpieces in this tradition, where the word 'tradition' highlights, for example, the web
of influence that links John Rawls to Rousseau, and Rousseau to St
Augustine.[7]

In labouring to redress the imbalance between the classical centre
and the intellectual bankruptcy of underdevelopment, the cultural
nationalist brings a sharp reading to bear upon this tradition. To
stanch what Sir Isaiah Berlin calls a 'wounded cultural pride', the
nationalist strives to elaborate a 'philosophic-historical vision', and
thus create 'an inner focus of resistance'.[8]

This precise economy of need rightly seizes on the communal or
nationalist dynamic at work in the canon. To the degree that the
towering monuments of European Romanticism are the products of
a cultural revolt by Germans – 'the first true nationalists' – against
French classicism, Romantic philosophy offers a decisive demonstration that competitive rivalry between communities can also feed
creativity of the first order.[9] National schools, in philosophy, painting
and scholarship, are the contentious fruit of this current in thought
and feeling.

Herder's nationalist dream of cultural autonomy unites the
communal need for reasoned self-regard, even collective survival,
with the creative compulsion towards mastering excellence in the
individual thinker. It is no accident that the canon of Western
political philosophy radically privileges the pivotal relationship that
binds the polity to the political thinker. Thus, the flux of Athenian
politics may be the immediate occasion of Plato's prescriptions, but
we remember Athens and assign to it a strict canonic pre-eminence
because Plato made it an object of classic political reflection. The
greatness of the polity shines through the text that outlives it, just
as *The Republic* has outlived the greatest Athenian of the greatest
age of Athens.

The radical dependence of the thinker on his polity and of polity
on the thinker is the defining dynamic of canonicity. Thus Hobbes
viewed English royal prerogatives as a solution to his philosophic
problem while Locke saw such absolutism as a danger to be resisted,
but the state of English politics – the Civil War has been called 'a
forcing house of European significance for political theory' – provided an indispensable context and occasion for their political and
philosophic meditations.[10] No doubt a complex lap of wave upon
wave, across the centuries, links the shores of English politics today
with those of the Civil War, but over the huge expanse of historical
cause and effect, *The Leviathan* and *Two Treatises of Government*

shine their canonic messages like the distant signals of a powerful lighthouse.

To become a classic, a text must transcend its original context. But to begin life at all, the text must be born in the full exploitation of its surroundings. Rawls' *A Theory of Justice* is inconceivable outside the philosophic ambit of American-style liberalism.[11] The impact of the Vietnam War on the final phase of the composition of Rawls' masterpiece was decisive. Indeed there are grounds to argue that the intellectually most bracing response to the bloody contest of national character that America endured in Indochina is to be found not in film or reportage – not in Francis Ford Coppola's *Apocalypse Now*, nor Oliver Stone's *Platoon*, nor Michael Herr's *Dispatches* nor David Halberstam's *The Best and the Brightest* – but rather in the core section of *A Theory of Justice* which addresses the vexed question of civil disobedience and resistance to the military draft. American politics of the 1950s and 1960s has proved to be textually fertile. Rawls' classic, this canonic nomination, must now face the test of the centuries. *A Theory of Justice* may yet prove to be the one great monument of unageing intellect to be born from the agony of the Vietnam War.

A canonic triumph demands that the political thinker and the polity fuse in rare mental congruence. Just as *A Theory of Justice* may be twentieth-century America's leading candidate for a place in the pantheon, the summits of which extend from *The Republic* to *Das Kapital*, so a parallel quest must be set in motion to generate a text capable of responding fully to Japan's twentieth-century accomplishments as a polity. The ultimate goal is to produce a classic on Japan worthy to grace the company of *The Politics*, *The Leviathan* and *The Social Contract*.

None of the mainstream disciplines that form the bulwark of social science have sought to contribute to the fulfilment of this textual ambition. In the name of methodological certitude and factual hunger, certain branches of Western positivism and empiricism would urge us to ignore Japan's canonic potential. Anglo-American economists, in particular, have persuaded an entire generation of Japanese social scientists that Japan's modern century is, in canonic terms, derivative and marginal. Even in the political science of Japan, one of the few Western disciplines where the contrary case has been argued, the canonic impulse has been quickly smothered by misdirected empiricism. Such occultation must be resisted.

If Japan's canonicity is to be fully mastered and properly honoured, then a clearing – Heidegger's pregnant word is *Lichtung* –

must be opened in the midst of this thicket of methodological and scientific obstacles. The resulting 'site', to adopt an idea of Derrida, will be bounded by several well-established academic disciplines but must be a colony of none of them. Such freedom is essential if the fetid air of our positivist and empiric slumbers is to be cleared so that a fresh scientific beginning may be made. Kant spoke of a *Kampfplatz*, a place of philosophic battle, and in its first methodological phase – its *Methodenstreit* – a genuine Japanese classicism will require such a battlefield. A perspicuous grasp of our post-positivist condition is indispensable. Two conflicting psychologies are at work in our need for a conceptually liberating horizon. One impulse is French and speaks the language of Gaston Bachelard when he insists that science progresses only by making total epistemic breaks with the reigning orthodoxy. This would have us strike out, with force and precision, at the philosophic enemies of Japanese canonicity, whether they be European, American or Japanese. But the second impulse is different, and might be called 'English' in its insistence that quiet reform is the truest, because most lasting, remedy for an occulted Japan. The English school reminds us that we are doomed by time and circumstance to be influenced by our well-established, if hostile, academic neighbours. They include, most notably, positivist political science; the classical school of British political economy, from Adam Smith to Alfred Marshall; philosophic positivists such as John Stuart Mill, Auguste Comte and their followers; and French structuralists and deconstructionists, who contend, with Edward Said, that area studies in the West is the perverse outcropping of the 'Orientalist' ideology.

Successful navigation around these continents of discourse will be a formidable exercise of mind. Like the Sirens, as Cicero warned, the powers of fatal attraction of these sciences are to be found not 'in the sweetness of their voices or the novelty and diversity of their songs, but in their professions of knowledge'.[12] At the outset, therefore, a certain deafness is in order if we are, in the words of Walter of Chatillon, to 'seek out those who dwell under another sun'.[13]

ANCIENT WORLDS, MODERN TEXTS

Paul Mus, the French student of Indochinese societies, used to recount an anecdote to illustrate the philosophic sources of Vietnam's impotence before the assault of European technology. 'When a French steamship was sighted off the shores of Vietnam in the early nineteenth century, the local mandarin-governor, instead of going to see it, researched the phenomenon in his texts, concluded it was a dragon, and dismissed the matter.'[14] The lesson of the story is not to be found in its literal truth, as an episode of history; it is probably apocryphal. Rather this is a parable that sets canonic blindness ('he researched the phenomenon in his texts') against empirical clear-sightedness ('instead of going to see it'). Here is a warning against the neglect of the 'real'. Such neglect left much of Confucian East Asia prostrate before the great lunge of Western imperialism; Japan's unflinching realism saved it. Such clarity defines the central thrust in European philosophy and social thought from the time of Francis Bacon (1561–1626) to the present. Empiricism, the tireless striving to discipline our actions with the facts, may explain why modern world history has been largely Western history.

Yet a double paradox rules even here. Reality, it would seem, is so obvious to sight that we can ignore it; textual canons are essential to ordered perception, but they may obscure social reality. The opacity of the real, no less than the indispensability of the canon, press on the ruling doctrine of social scientific inquiry: that facts or occurrences exist independently of the observer.

Contrary to the gospel of cultural relativism and structural anthropology, societies and cultures vary in their ability to 'read' reality. Such literacy allows one to distinguish between 'primitive' and 'advanced' societies. Whether a community's language helps to clarify or obscure reality depends significantly on the soundness of its canon, where a canon is defined as a congealed ontology, in textual form, of enabling ideas, to be tested by experience.

'The distance between "speech signals" and reality in, say, Biblical Hebrew or Japanese court poetry is not the same as in Jacobean English.'[15] Nor was it the same in nineteenth-century French and Sino-Vietnamese. Clear vision ensured that one language mapped reality decisively better than the other. For a nation to allow the distance between language and reality to grow too great is to invite disorder, even destruction.

The modernizer must narrow the gap between language and reality. This task has a canonic dimension. China's inability to modernize during the nineteenth century, in contrast with Japan's success in the face of the same European provocation, may be explained, in part, by the fact that the Chinese were less skillful than the Japanese at eluding the canonic blindness that the Chinese classics inflicted on ruling elites across East Asia. To modernize is to see.

Yet, if reality is so readily apparent, why did the Chinese mandarinate find the task so daunting? Cultural hubris and the claims of identity contributed to the débâcle that overwhelmed Chinese and Vietnamese Confucianism in the nineteenth century. But it is the 'opacity of the real' that makes the struggle to narrow the gap between speech signals and reality so arduous. The task is, further-more, unending because reality is subject to endless change. Thus, *Thought and Behaviour in Modern Japanese Politics* by Maruyama Masao may be read as another empirical parable which highlights how the obscurantism of Japanese ultra-nationalism so dimmed the vision of an otherwise emphatically clear-sighted, modernizing nation that it plunged into a hopeless and irrational war.[16] The mastery of social and economic reality reflected in Japan's post-war miracle paints the opposite picture. The distance between reality and perception has been narrowed so effectively that Japan has outstripped its old Western rivals.

If asked, anthropologists such as Claude Lévi-Strauss would deny this Japanese achievement. By insisting that the mental universe of a Brazilian Amerindian is no less complex and arresting than that of a modern Frenchman, the notion of a gap between language and reality is effectively abolished. French structuralism is uncompromis-ing in its central dogma. There are no primitive societies because there are no advanced ones. Everywhere comparable mythologies reign. Modernization is just our myth.

French theory reduces the Vietnamese struggle to master the military technologies and combat tactics necessary to defeat their French rulers and American protectors to a benighted semantic game. It ignores the profound sense of disorientation that must have overtaken North Vietnam's communist elite when, having defeated the American expeditionary force, it had to watch the cutting edge of modernizing progress in Southeast Asia pass to such un-Spartan city-states as Singapore and Hong Kong. Having conquered a vast distance between language and social reality to win two nationalist wars, Vietnam has been condemned by history to labour to close another gap between anti-colonial militarism and the demands of Pacific-Basin take-off. Having triumphed in one revolutionary struggle, Vietnam is now confronted with another. About such struggles, neither the structuralist nor the post-structuralist has any-thing useful to say because French theory since Lévi-Strauss has abandoned the empiricist spirit that helped to break the hold of the medieval scholastic cosmology and to usher in the modern world and its successive scientific revolutions.

The lessons of the Renaissance should not be discarded. In *New*

Worlds, Ancient Texts, Anthony Grafton describes how the European encounter with the Americas during the age of Columbus, what he calls 'the shock of discovery', threatened the world-view of Renaissance man, thus challenging the 'power of tradition'.[17] Grafton offers another caveat about the dangers of neglecting the real. Like Mus, he extols empirical clear-sightedness over canonic blindness. But unlike Mus, Grafton warns of flawed perception not among the discovered, explored and scientifically scrutinized, but among the explorers, discoverers and scrutineers. Europeans also may suffer handicapped perception. Herein lies a moral for the Western student of other climates and cultures.

The main victim of Grafton's research is naive empiricism: the vulnerable doctrine that to look is to see.

> The intellectual who sets out to describe another culture embarks on a task as difficult and elusive as it is fascinating. The would-be ethnographer must make a whole series of strategic and tactical decisions: he or she must adopt an attitude toward both the society to be described and the informants who describe it; select a limited number of topics to cover, since no general description of a society can ever be complete; and choose a literary form to convey the results to a public.[18]

So it is not simply a question of 'going to see it', be it a new world or a steamship. Indeed the business of mere description is not simple at all, but 'difficult' and 'elusive'. At every stage in the series of decisions that confronts Grafton's ethnographer, ancient models must be tested for their ability to cope with new facts. For Renaissance man the ancient models that mattered were drawn from the classical bedrock of biblical and pagan tradition, the high canon of post-medieval European civilization.

Thus, Christopher Columbus and Amerigo Vespucci 'observed with open eyes and recorded what they saw with active pens'.[19] But consistent with the European approach to life, both men were 'active readers' who viewed the novel facts of a new world through 'tightly woven filters of expectation and assumption about the past'.[20] Where Columbus 'used his texts to make the new familiar ... Vespucci – like Herodotus and Mandeville – did the reverse'.[21] It was the European canon, in its ancient and modern guises, that made these two models available. What this subtle dialectic between high learning and new fact denies is the myth of ready sight.

Columbus' detailed log of his observations swarms with efforts to describe a world that seems simply new, inaccessible to European analogies. The most eloquent of these take the form of simple confessions that he cannot describe what he sees – the now ancient strategy of marvel.[22]

The social scientist who is also an ethnologist must accept the historicism of the eye. The canon we inherit tightly organizes our perceptions. This is true not only of the Renaissance explorer but also of the best-trained eyes of all Western tradition, those of the master painter:

Even the greatest artist – and he more than others – needs an idiom to work in. Only tradition, such as he finds it, can provide him with the raw material of imagery which he needs to represent an event or a 'fragment of nature'. He can re-fashion this imagery, adapt it to its task, assimilate it to his needs and change it beyond recognition, but he can no more represent what is in front of his eyes without a pre-existing stock of acquired images than he can paint without the pre-existing colours which he must have on his palette.[23]

Vision is a sophisticated act of faith in one's civilization: seeing is believing. At work in the arts and sciences are not simplistic oppositions – practical men versus learned, facts versus books, science versus the canon – but a dialectic (tradition in vital tension with iconoclasm) in which the moderns complement, by renovation, extension and, where required, destruction, the project of the ancients. We see through tradition (in both senses). The empirical imperative of the social sciences permits no other conclusion; we are not philosophers who would toy with the fundamentals. But the dense, resistant complexities of reality bring enormous pressures to bear on the notion of naked, innocent vision.

Faced with Japan, a complex, literate civilization with ancient roots, the Western explorer-scholar must struggle afresh with the Renaissance dilemma: should one retrofit a traditional system of European ideas – positivism from Galileo to Keynes, for example – to match the new facts about Japan? Or should we bend Japan, our 'new world', to the old European system? Or might we try to devise some radically new patterns of thought and expectation worthy of our exploratory enterprise? What truths in the West's modern canon

are thrown into radical doubt by the accomplishments of this formidable Asian society?[24] Such questions press on us today with no less
force than they did on our Renaissance ancestors. Indeed they are
at issue whenever worlds collide.

2 Where are the masters?

Fame is the spur.
Milton

Fame is the spur – and ouch!
James Baldwin

I

Contemporary science and sensibility would reduce our canonic dreams for Japan to ash. We may be losing our ability to nourish a classic culture, that complex blend of values, ideals, practices and standards by which our civilization has tensed its mental and spiritual resources so as to be ever vulnerable to the 'anarchic shock of excellence'.[1] This new condition conspires against the writing and reading, production and consumption of texts of classic stature.

Textual classicism is rooted in a gamble on transcendence. The foe is death. This enemy threatens a community's hopes for collective survival no less than mortality would extinguish the ambition for classical glory in the individual thinker or artist. Increasingly unable or unwilling to generate the kinds of textual densities demanded by a classical culture, the mind of Europe may now face a metamorphosis unparalleled in its turbulent and epochal past.

In this inventory of loss, the price that emerging non-Western cultures may pay for the decay of textual classicism has rarely been calculated. In an unrivalled way, this burden falls on Japan and its modern political achievement. Indeed, the implications of Japan's failure, as a culture, to produce works of political reflection of classic stature for that nation's place in human history are as much ignored as they are serious. Thus, where Hegel, with his unforgiving clarity, memorialized the 'world historical significance' of the ancient

Persians and Greeks, Rome and medieval Christendom, the Reformation and the French Revolution, today Japan's miracle and its
claims to world-historical significance are wrapped in classical
silence. This is a kind of defeat, one provoked by the recession of
textual excellence.

FROM KANT TO AREA STUDIES

Japan is an Oriental polity. Its tradition of politics sets it apart from
the European experience. For many in the West, Japan is an alien
presence in the world, embodying what Sartre, after Hegel, might
have called *L'autre* (the Other). So to claim that 'Japan is an Oriental polity' is to assert what it is not: Japan is not a European political
system, nor an Anglo-Saxon one, nor, for that matter, a Western
one. It furthermore makes a great deal of difference, to paraphrase
Polish philosopher Leszek Kolakowski, whether we simply know
that Japan is an Oriental polity or whether we interpret its political
evolution and present status in the world in the light of that fact,
which then takes on a significance of its own.[2] This approach, often
neglected in Western political scientific writing, forces us to ask a
decisive question: is the political science of Japan, as currently practised in the West, adequate to the task of addressing the fact that
Japan is an Oriental polity?

Writing about the European encounter with the New World, Peter
Conrad has artfully observed that 'Before America could be discovered, it had to be imagined'.[3] Such is the cast of the human mind
and the weight of canonic expectation. But the transformation of
the study of Japanese government during the past two decades
should encourage us to reverse Conrad's proposition, and insist that
if Japan is to be understood, then it has to be un-imagined. If the
European canon is to be reformed, then Japan must cease to be
the object of dreamy projections, be they of good or evil, of fabulous
wealth or fabulous defeat. Certainly the Western student of modern
Japan must learn to set to one side his expectations, his ideology,
his values, perhaps even some branches of his science, before
embarking on his own voyage to the East, this trans-cultural exercise
of mind. Failing this, he must learn to keep the intrusive effect of
such expectations and values firmly in hand.

Alive to the importance of canonic tradition, Conrad concludes
that 'Columbus knew what he hoped to find before he left Europe'.[4]
Such civilized constraints should excite the ambitions of the Western
student of Japan. On him has fallen the supreme burden and oppor-

tunity to transmute his encounter with the Orient into the stuff of a canonic revolution. Francis Bacon, the great English painter, sought 'to take "shocking" and "unheard-of" material and deliver it in the European grand manner'.[5] This should be our goal.

This trans-cultural exercise calls upon our every resource. The powers of imagination, as Coleridge urged and many physical scientists acknowledge, are indispensable to this endeavour. But to stress the dangers of imaginative essentialism when writing or thinking about the Orient is to emphasize the intellectually resistant character of Japan's apartness. One could have alternatively seized on the modern or democratic or liberal dimension of the Japanese political system. But to interpret post-war Japanese politics solely in the light of that country's undeniable modernity, its democratic constitution and voting system or its relatively liberal legal code, is to sidestep the issue of cultural difference, and therefore to understate the problem of the perceiver and the perceived in any province of political science that is also a branch of area studies.

The distinction between the 'subject' and the 'object', between the student and what is studied, is vital in philosophy; it is just as important in the study of the non-European world. Without a sharpened awareness of the ways that Japan is a non-Western polity, we may misapply the often brilliant methods and insights developed by Western thinkers and social scientists since the Enlightenment. To repeat, the core difficulty is the gap between the perceiver and the perceived. How does what a Western political scientist brings to his study of Japan influence what he sees?

To pursue this line of reasoning is to urge that proper attention be given to Kant's plea for toleration of the defining pluralism of the Western tradition of science. Greater heed must be paid to a cardinal distinction drawn by the German philosopher in the Appendix to the Transcendental Dialectic of *The Critique of Pure Reason*:

> The logical principle of genera, which postulates identity, is balanced by another principle, namely, that of *species*, which calls for manifoldness and diversity in things, notwithstanding their agreement as coming under the same genus, and which prescribes to the understanding that it attend to diversity no less than to the identity.[6]

According to Kant, the principles of identity (the assumption that nature or the genus is uniform) and specification (the view that nature is composed of unrelated parts or differences or singularities) have generated contending camps among 'students of nature' and what will be termed here 'reality', natural or otherwise:

> This twofold interest manifests itself also among students of nature in the diversity of their ways of thinking. Those who are more especially speculative are, we may almost say, hostile to heterogeneity, and are always on the watch for the unity of the genus; those, on the other hand, who are more especially empirical, are constantly endeavoring to differentiate nature in such manifold fashion as almost to extinguish the hope of ever being able to determine its appearances in accordance with universal principles.[7]

Kant's examples of this divide are drawn from the positive natural sciences, chemistry in particular, but the gloss of this passage from *The Critique of Pure Reason* by Maruyama Masao in *Thought and Behaviour in Modern Japanese Politics* underscores its relevance to the social sciences:

> Immanuel Kant once remarked that all students of nature can be divided into two groups, those who were more concerned with the principles of homogeneity, and those who leaned towards specification. One group, according to Kant, seems to be 'almost averse to heterogeneousness and always intent on the unity of *genera*'; others 'are constantly striving to divide nature into so much variety that one might lose almost all hope of being able to distribute its phenomena according to general principles.'[8]

In what should be regarded as a liberating gesture, Maruyama goes on to observe that:

> If the same classification may be applied to social scientists, I must own my membership of the latter [heterogeneous] category. But as Kant himself goes on to say, both approaches are necessary. The exponents of neither approach can claim a monopoly of the truth; they should supplement, rather than arrogantly reject, each other.[9]

Kant's insight and Maruyama's gloss should resonate powerfully in contemporary social science, especially in view of the tendency among students of politics and government in Britain, America and elsewhere since the late 1970s to yield to the claims of universal science and economic positivism. The arrogant claims made for universalism need to be balanced against merits of the opposite, more heterogeneous, approach: one that is more responsive to concrete particulars, to empirical detail, and to non-Western values and perspectives. Such pluralism should aim for 'value-free', objective insights. It must be aware of the corrupting impact of ethnocentricity (Eurocentrism or Japanism, for example) or ideological advocacy (liberalism or neo-conservativism or political correctness). Pluralism is grounded in the belief that one methodology or set of technical constraints, even one generated by a so-called 'strong' philosophy of science, is inadequate to the task of describing or formulating abstractions about a complex Oriental society in Western terms.[10] Here, to borrow from Kant's terminology, the 'species' must be preferred to 'the unity of the genus'.

A sceptic could argue that Kant is not talking about social science and that his insight is therefore not applicable here. Thus we must recognize the possibility that such a counter-critique may provoke a line-by-line battle over the text of the Appendix to the Transcendental Dialectic, and its relationship to the main body of Kant's *Critique*. Given Kant's undeniable preference for universal science and the positivist approach, for Galileo and Newton, this battle might be lost by the supporters of pluralism and open social science. For our purposes here, however, Maruyama's reading will be judged as sound.

Kant and Japanese political economy

Anglo-American political science must awaken from the dogmatic slumbers of economic positivism. Our watchwords must be philosophical balance and methodological tolerance. Indeed such tolerance is indispensable if students of Japanese politics, public policy and political economy are to address some of the field's most troublesome issues, the greatest of these being the challenge and burden of the particularistic character of Japanese political life. Nowhere are the dangers of scientific positivism more apparent than in the growing interest among students of Japanese government in the subject of political economy.

Political economy, as a body of research methods, is not a neutral notion. Indeed, properly understood, political economy conspires to *divide* political scientists from economists. The Kantian difficulties inherent in this complex issue are captured in *The Political Economy of Japan*, the massive three-volume study, which more than any other text has brought home the importance of the concept of 'political economy' to students of Japanese society.[11] Breaking with normal English usage, the authors of the first volume unfortunately use the term 'political economy' to refer to an entity ('Japan's political economy') rather than to a science or set of research methods. But even before the appearance of Ricardo's *On the Principles of Political Economy, and Taxation* in 1817, the term 'political economy' had served as 'the former name for economics, as a discipline or science'.[12] For purposes of clarity, the term 'political economy' will be used here in its correct sense, to describe a discipline which remains even now dominated by the assumptions and methods of positive economics as given canonic formulation by John Stuart Mill, Alfred Marshall and their modern heirs.

No amount of prevarication can disguise the fact that *The Political Economy of Japan* is decisively coloured by economic positivism: an approach to the study of economic activity dominated by positivistic law-making. But does positivist economics subvert the cross-disciplinary promise of political economy as a new field of research? Does such positivism encourage, in Maruyama's usage, the 'arrogant rejection' of other approaches, including that of the political scientist?

As defined by economists working in the tradition of Mill and Marshall, political economy is a positive science. Such economists tend, in Kant's words, to be 'hostile to heterogeneity, and are always on the watch for the unity of the genus' (as positive economists define it). Economic positivism is logically committed to methodological monism: the belief that all significant problems have one, and must have only one, solution. In economics, this means that all human behaviour can be satisfactorily explained by reference only to economic positive laws.

As a result, economists tend to regard political science as, at best, an inferior empirical science or, at worst, a body of whimsical mumbo-jumbo. Most economists reject the idea that experts on the political science of Japan have anything useful to say about economic behaviour. True, a latent academic ecumenicalism has sought shelter in the recent revival of the concept of 'political economy', but this in practice has meant normal positive economics with a window-dressing of concern for empirical political science.

Positivist economics or political economy will always pose a threat to the sound understanding of Japanese society as long as it dogmatically rejects the cardinal distinction that Kant draws between these two very different schools of (human) nature. A measure of scientific and philosophical tolerance is required of economists. In essence, they must accept that economic behaviour may be legitimately interpreted without capitulation to the positivist doctrine of methodological individualism: the axiom that only individuals, not groups, exist.

Without such tolerance, any embrace of the rubric of 'Japanese political economy' will always risk confusion. It is one thing to say, as Kant does, that both approaches, universal science and particularistic empirical science, are necessary, and quite another to seek to arrange a marriage between these two rootedly incompatible approaches. Yet this is exactly what is attempted by the editors of *The Political Economy of Japan*.

Part of the problem lies in the sustained pressure exerted on the multi-volume study of *The Political Economy of Japan* by 'Japanese' ideas. Japanese tradition is more comfortable than its Western equivalent with intellectual eclecticism and cultural explanations (a dismissive attitude towards such explanations being one of the few prejudices that unite Western political scientific and economic writers about Japan). Japanese thinking is also more attuned to non-empirical strategies (e.g. futurology). It exhibits a general conceptual fuzziness (sometimes useful, sometimes not) as well as a practised complacency in the face of intellectually frayed edges. This approach is rooted in the habits of Japanese intellectual culture.

Beyond positivism

With this realization, we arrive at the clearing that forms the heart of *Japan and the Enemies of Open Political Science*. Two questions are paramount. *How* should one study Japanese politics? *Why* should one study Japanese politics? The answers to both questions house a plea for the merits of what might usefully be called the 'anthropological approach'.

First, there is the question of method. The 'anthropological approach' breaks with many of the ruling assumptions of Western social science, as formulated by the great nineteenth-century positivists, who worked, like Kant, in the long shadow of the Newtonian Revolution. Natural science must be put in its place. The work and thought of Jacques Lacan captures one key dimension of this counter-revolution in method:

> Biology not only provides unreliable models for the mental scientist but invites him to misperceive the very objects of his enquiry. If his intention is to explore that which is distinctly human in the human mind, he will attend to cultural rather than to 'natural' determining forces ... and [he] will have the anthropologist and

the sociologist rather than the biologist among his closest co-workers.[13]

Second, there is the question of motive: why study Japan? The answer must reach beyond *ad hoc* relevance and the pressures of today's economic headlines. Quite the contrary, the rise of the specifically Japanese political economy, as a body of thought, should be seen as a key development in the long *durée* of human history. Modern Japan offers a unique occasion and ground to bring the European age, with all its truth and grandeur, to a meditated close. Properly grasped, Japan's post-war achievement should encourage Westerners to strike a decisive blow against any would-be universal science that would deny that 'Japan is an Oriental polity'. This 'epistemic break' would help to overthrow the scientific paradigm which has discriminated for far too long against marginal disciplines, such as Orientalism and area studies, in favour of the positivist and monist intellectual mainstream. To take Japan seriously, in a manner worthy of Europe's classic past, will require an exercise in trans-cultural communication of extraordinary power and brilliance. But this is an opportunity as well as a provocation.

Has post-war Japan, as an experiment in political and economic action as well as thought, achieved world-historical significance? The mere suggestion that the Western mind might one day be decisively influenced by a kind of Japanese classicism, by Japanese thinking of the first rank, hints at a possible rupture with the sovereign splendours and certainties of the European mind since the Renaissance. Such a break has methodological implications. Indeed, without a methodological counter-reformation, tradition cannot be renewed. Initially this search for a method should aspire to a vigorous, anti-positivist empiricism. Only then might the way be opened to a classicism that would stand as the finest realization in Western thinking about modern Japan of Blake's commitment to 'the holiness of minute particulars'.

THE ANTHROPOLOGICAL APPROACH

Blake's Ontology and the prospect of significant Japanese influence on the methods and ambitions of a Western science – this classic opportunity – compels a return to the first principles of the great anthropologists of the European tradition. They teach us that we must bend to the truth. Bronislaw Malinowski, regarded by many as the pioneer of field research as a technique of Western anthropology, insisted that:

> The ethnographer's goal is to grasp the native's point of view, his relation to life, to realize his vision of the world, and out of this process, there may emerge [in the investigator] a feeling of solidarity with the endeavors and ambitions of the natives.[14]

Then there is the observation of Sir Edward Evans-Pritchard that the anthropologist

> must live as far as possible in their [the natives'] villages and camps, where he is, again as far as possible, physically and morally part of the community. . . . By living among the natives – as far as he can like one of themselves – the anthropologist puts himself on a level with them. Unlike the [colonial] administrator and missionary, he has no authority to maintain, and unlike them he has a neutral position. He is not there to change their way of life but as a humble learner of it; and he has no retainers and intermediaries who obtrude between him and the people, no police, interpreters, or catechists to screen him from them.[15]

Both of these modern masters conducted their field work before the Second World War. The use of the term 'native' is out of step with the pervasive liberal sensibilities of contemporary Western society, but these kernel statements of the anthropological method are relevant. Thus we might rephrase Malinowski's argument in this way:

> Our goal as Orientalists is to grasp the Japanese point of view, his relation to life, to realize his vision of the world, and out of this process, there may emerge [in the Orientalist] a feeling of solidarity with the endeavors and ambitions of the Japanese.

Or, the Orientalist

> must live as far as possible in the cities and villages of Japan, where he should try to become, again as far as possible, physically and morally a part of the community. . . . By living among the Japanese as far as he can like one of themselves, the Orientalist puts himself on a level with them. Unlike the diplomat or businessman or missionary, the Orientalist has nothing to sell, no policies to influence, no minds to change, no authority to maintain, and unlike them he has a neutral position.

The importance of personal experience in the field cannot be overstated. Owen Lattimore, perhaps the twentieth-century's greatest Western expert on Mongolia, embodied the true spirit of the field worker.[16] From a lifetime commitment to his 'tribe' Lattimore achieved an extraordinary reputation as an Orientalist. One accolade in particular stands out. When he attended a Leningrad conference of Orientalists in 1960, Lattimore

> made friends among scholars from the Mongolian People's Republic participating at Leningrad. They knew who he was. They had read his books and felt that his descriptions of life in Inner Mongolia in the 1930s rang true. One of them told him, 'Your Mongols are *real Mongols*.'[17]

The scrupulous observance of such precepts offers a sounder method to understand Japan as an Oriental polity than any interpretation that derives solely from the application of positivist laws, such as we find, for example, in Anglo-American economics. This is the lesson of the field-work methodologies, the seminal contribution of Malinowski and Evans-Pritchard to the overthrow of nineteenth-century positivistic armchair methods in anthropology.

Malinowski won international fame as an anthropologist as the result of a four-year stint among the Trobriand Islanders during the First World War. Evans-Pritchard built what was perhaps an even more sterling reputation as the result of six major anthropological expeditions, particularly twenty months among the Azande and twelve months among the Nuer. Regardless of what harvest contemporary anthropologists choose to make of this legacy, it contains a valuable lesson for the student of area studies, in this case the Orientalist. Japan is a vast, complex society, and the longer a professional researcher spends *in situ*, studying, observing and thinking about Japanese politics, culture and history, the more he will find in the methodology of Malinowski, Evans-Pritchard and Lattimore his preferred approach.

Such considerations bring us to the issue of language. The anthropologist rightly insists that only long residence in the host culture can provide the informing intimacies necessary for genuine intercultural understanding, and that a profound grasp of the language of the people and culture under study was therefore indispensable. A sound understanding of Japanese society will be grounded in a sound understanding of the Japanese language. No knowledge of positive laws, however universal in their claims, can substitute for such linguistic expertise.

The burden of proof for the quality of one's readings of Japanese social reality falls on the Westerner without Japanese. The illiterate must demonstrate that his science is unimpaired by the consequences of his illiteracy. On this count, positivism offers no dispensation for the field worker. This is particularly true where intercultural understanding is viewed not only as a kind of cognitive penetration or capture but rather as a form of critical audition. The deaf never hear the truth.

The shallow linguistic training of economists who attempt to study Japan may explain culture-bound applications of positive law-making to the Japanese economy. The view that an economist needs only sufficient Japanese to pick his way through statistical tables is unpersuasive. Whether this critique would reduce the native Japanese who are also economists to the role of what Evans-Pritchard dismissively calls 'interpreters' and 'catechists' is a different matter.

Empirical neglect and linguistic ignorance are old positivist failings. In the name of a universal science, Comte and other armchair positivists devised laws of human development and hierarchical schemes of civilizing progress during the nineteenth century. Field research was neglected; the empirical grounding of one's ideas, given that they were already, in Comte's portentous phrase, 'sufficiently matured', could be left to the public for their 'verification and development'.[18]

Positive law-making may be a revolution in other sciences, but not for anyone engaged in the disciplined scrutiny of a non-Western society. The contemporary armchair specialist has, too often, surrendered to the scientistic habits of the nineteenth-century European mind: positivist law-making at the expense of empirical field work. The great sins to be avoided are ethnocentricity and an undilute confidence in the maturity of one's own ideas, both attributes and failings of the armchair positivist of whatever century.

The serious study of non-Western societies requires rather different attitudes and approaches. The bare-bones summary of the anthropological method as the unadorned collection of empirical data, its ordering, abstraction and testing, understates the formidable difficulties involved. These challenge the modern tendency to belittle the laborious business of describing, accurately and fully, any complex dimension of an alien society. The excesses of post-war behaviourism and the systems approach have encouraged political scientists always to 'analyse', never to 'describe'. Such verbal scruples suggest a failure to understand that the accurate grasp and description of what is actually happening in the theatre of life of any society, familiar or foreign, verges on a philosophic provocation. Even the initial stage of the anthropological approach – the collection of data – bristles with conceptual and methodological obstacles.

Unless the Westerner is superbly acclimatized, has profoundly penetrated the semantic field (the linguistically coded horizon of meaning), has toughened himself against the dangers of empirical fatigue (the temptation to yield to what is immediately plausible when analysed in English, rather than in the referent language, in this case Japanese), is schooled in a wise passivity before the intellectual vertigo of hyperfactualization and empirical scatter (i.e. the resistance of reality to pattern), and is practised in scepticism towards his own assumptions (including an appropriate humility towards the status and scientific contribution of his 'natives'), then his efforts at mere description of any political or social phenomenon may go disastrously wrong.

Anthropological ideals demand that the student of other cultures struggle at every phase of his project to 'bracket' his beliefs, ideology and scientific dogmas. The German phenomenologist Edmund Husserl taught twentieth-century philosophers to heed the dangers of unexamined 'pre-knowledge' in any exploration of mind. For Husserl, this meant 'neither an elimination of nor a prescinding from other interests. Rather, it simply puts them into "brackets", thus retaining them, but allowing them in no way to influence theoretical considerations'.[19]

In ordering one's data, all the constraints and demands that apply to the gathering of data apply with equal rigour. The bane of the second phase of the anthropological approach might be termed the problem of 're-entry'. At this stage, the anthropologist must not only corner his 'truths', he must bring them home. He will normally lose the guiding hand of his native informant against whose mind he will test his theories and interpretations. He will also be buffeted by the demands of 'scientific sense'. The anthropologist's native language will begin to press with renewed force on how he interprets his carefully gathered data. The problem of language will emerge in so serious a fashion as to encourage the suspicion that all research findings on Japanese politics should be written in Japanese. Here will loom large the challenge of choosing an appropriate literary model to give form to one's findings. The Western researcher may have to answer not to one but to two sets of canonic precedents, those of the native and Europe.

Greater tangles lie in wait. Abstraction compels the anthropologist to be original. Complex conceptual difficulties will confront the student of any Asian society when he attempts to unravel the cats-cradle of fact, value and intention. The scope of the difficulty is phenomenal. It recalls I. A. Richards' suggestion that the most complex linguistic act that any human being may undertake is the translation of a classical Chinese text into English.

Even more seriously, the anthropologist may have to struggle with a theoretical void. Abstraction produces the sense that one is creating nothing out of something because the resulting conceptual construction appears to float somewhere between the truth of one's data and the epistemological demands of one's own scientific culture. Alfred Reginald Radcliffe-Brown's tussle with biological organism and notions of 'social system' illustrate the resistant character of the task. There is no obvious place where one should begin to divide the semantic continuum of human experience. An ontological shudder or metaphysical free-fall may result from a vigorous encounter with an alien totality, as dreamily captured in Gauguin's 1897 Tahitian masterpiece, *D'Où venons-nous? Que sommes-nous? Où allons-nous?* (Where are we from? What are we? Where are we going?).

Finally, and most arresting of all, cross-cultural understanding may penetrate the researcher's womb of native assumption and belief. Certainly, when the object of the anthropological approach is an advanced industrial society, as is most emphatically the case with Japan, the research process may exhibit a kind of 'feed-back' loop, in which spokesmen for the object culture will scrutinize how the Westerner or other researcher has collected and ordered his data, and what abstractions he has drawn from them. Completing this conceptual circle may be as intellectually bracing as any stage in the unfolding of the anthropological method. It is here that the initial shock of first-rank thinking by the 'natives' will be felt by the researcher. At the conclusion of this circle of demanding reflection will be harvested any of the truths of a particularly Japanese classicism. At native invitation, a European may learn to think himself free of the intellectual chains of an ancient heritage.

This kind of intellectual *engagement* between the perceiver and the perceived exhibits affinities with the anthropological labours of Claude Lévi-Strauss. Often criticized for his relative indifference towards field work, he was nevertheless encouraged by French intellectual tradition, especially under the impact of Rousseau, to expect great thoughts from his natives. When he concludes that native thought demonstrates a mental sophistication and depth that matches the reach and complexity of European civilization, Lévi-Strauss reveals his appetite for the *frisson* of Ontological perturbation which may accompany any disciplined encounter with the 'primitive mind'. But the most formidable of such encounters will not confirm the structures and conceits of the anthropologist's world-view, as is the case with Lévi-Strauss as a product of French tradition. Rather it will overturn them.

This is uniquely so in the case of modern Japan. A specifically Japanese school of political economy, as a body of theory, should now be taking shape. Over time, such a school may offer the richest ground for nurturing a genuine Japanese classicism, one richer than even the modern novel or theoretical physics or molecular biology, long suspected to be the fields where the Japanese mind would produce its greatest achievements.

As nowhere else, this provides the supreme occasion for taking Japan seriously. If, in his uncertainty principle, Heisenberg gave scientifically legal form to his discovery that the objects of research may be altered by the very process of examining them, then the anthropological approach can be shown to reverse the proposition: the object of research may, in the end, alter the subject (i.e. the mind and social condition of the researcher). There is no more radical formulation of the issue of 'perceiver' and 'the perceived'. The key moment will come when, in Western studies of Japanese government, Japanese thinkers and researchers begin to develop a strong theoretical counter-view to the high orthodoxies of Western intellectual and philosophical tradition and to the research paradigm which is grounded in this tradition.

The issue transcends scientific concern. In the contrast drawn here between the 'ontological' and the 'Ontological', the Western encounter with a Japanese classicism should be seen to bring the anthropological approach to ripe conclusion. Such matters carry a philosophic edge. Thus, the study of Japanese political and social reality may, via the feedback loop, not only result in significant alterations to the totality of Western research practice, its ontology, but may also change the Ontology, the self-conscious grasp and intellectual identity, of the Western researcher himself.

In his *Prison Notebooks*, Antonio Gramsci, the Italian Marxist theoretician, insisted that 'The starting-point of critical elaboration is the consciousness of what one really is'. Gramsci is merely asking us to abide by Socrates' imperative: 'Know thyself'. For Gramsci, the researcher should understand himself as 'a product of the Historical process to date, which has deposited in you an infinity of traces, without leaving an inventory, therefore it is imperative at the outset to compile such an inventory'.[20]

The starting point of any Orientalist science is to be found in a double process in which the scholar comes to know his own mind, and as a result takes an epistemological stand *vis-à-vis* his own habits of thought and those of the object of his study. Nowhere is this of more consequence than when the Orientalist is confronted with a 'native' classicism of revolutionary potential. Japan's canonic potential demands that we hammer out a Gramscian-style inventory. Much of this book is an attempt to organize such an inventory for the political scientist of Japan. The central ambition of this programme is to describe 'Japanese who are *real* Japanese'. The first step towards this goal will be taken when we recognize that Japan is an Oriental polity.

II

Carthage lacked political flair. Its constant concern for profit
prevented it having that prudence which goes with higher ambitions.
A galley anchored on the Libyan sand, it maintained its position by
sheer hard work. Nations, like waves, roared around it, and the
slightest storm rocked this formidable craft.

Flaubert

CLASSICAL EVASIONS

We are left with one knot to untie. Let us assume, as we can confidently assume of twentieth-century America, that post-war Japan embodies a genuine canonic phenomenon: a revolutionary reworking of the social, political and economic cosmos. But what becomes of our pantheonic project if Gramsci's inventory has been meticulously executed, if our researcher has nursed a persuasive degree of intellectual caring (what Kierkegaard and Heidegger called *Sorge*), and if he waits, in expectation, for that radical astonishment or *thaumazein* which canonic greatness alone can provoke only to discover that there has been no classic moment, that the shelf is empty? It is then that the hunt must begin for those who, in Nietzsche's unsparing phrase, have sought to 'unhitch the bow' of creative excellence.

For at least two generations, the Japanese nation has laboured with wonderful energy to change our world. The Japanese have made history; the phenomenon – the social fact – has been generated. But we appear to have the phenomenon without the text. Why has no canonic revolution followed? Is an unacceptable classical evasion at work here? Any inventory of this loss must take issue with the self-defeating ambivalence that too many of the most influential shapers of Japanese culture have displayed towards the classics. An unwholesome consensus has congealed which holds that Japanese sensibility has decreed, at least since Murasaki Shikibu proclaimed her ignorance of the formal brilliance of classical Chinese forms and genres, that classicism is not a native art.

When the canonic need has registered, the Japanese have turned to China or Europe rather than to native sources. This habit of cultural dependence may explain the lacquered depth of some of the solemn lists of would-be major writings that national pride has, on occasion, demanded. Behind the ambivalence and the lacquer lurks a pained and unnecessary intellectual and cultural inferiority. In a manner not unlike that of Americans, the Japanese have been too ready to concede that whatever they have achieved or may yet achieve as a nation, classicism is not their *métier*.

Japanese editions of the classics reflect this failure of nerve. The multi-volume collections of famous Japanese thinkers (*Nihon no Meicho*) paint a strained contrast, in intellectual force and imaginative reach, with editions of 'world classics' (*Sekai no Meicho*).[21] A distinction of language is at work here: all texts by native Japanese thinkers were written in Japanese or *Kanbun*; no world classic has been.[22] Language demarcates a textual frontier which secures a *cordon sanitaire*, insulating native values and sensitivities from foreign influence and contamination while shielding native talent from overwhelming foreign competition. Some comparisons are not to be borne. That the most serious examples of Japanese thinking with words have yet to yield a text that can be confidently set against Confucius' *Analects* or Kant's *The Critique of Pure Reason* or Adam Smith's *The Wealth of Nations* is beyond question. But it does not follow that no work of Japanese classic thought will ever cross this invisible barrier of genius to become a world classic. The notion that the Japanese are incapable of producing a canonic monument to their modern success must be rejected out of hand.

The history of modern Japan since 1945 should deal a decisive blow to native hesitation before the demands of classic excellence. The first revelatory lacunae have already appeared. Chalmers Johnson observes, for example, near the beginning of *MITI and the Japanese Miracle* (1982), that the student of the role of the state in the rise of the Japanese economy will find 'no set of theoretical works, no *locus classicus* such as Adam Smith or V. I. Lenin, with which to start'.[23] This intolerable condition offers the Japanese thinker a classic opportunity. It is time to incarnate, in a text, the full weight and significance of the Japanese miracle. The ambition must be to set forth, in the Japanese language, the rational under-pinnings and main intellectual consequences of Japan's post-war advance. In like manner, the foundations for Japan's modern ascent to be found in the Tokugawa canon of native political reflection, perhaps the supreme Japanese intellectual achievement of the past four centuries, demand the fullest textual harvest, again in Japanese.

The satisfaction of this classic need does not exhaust Japan's significance. If the Japanese prove unwilling and unable to rise to this challenge, then the ambitious Westerner will be tempted to apply to the non-European world Marx's damning observation in *The 18th Brumaire*: 'they cannot represent themselves; they must be represented'.[24] It is obvious that the Western textual tradition – mercantilist thought, for example – has exerted decisive impact on modern Japan. This suggests that the Japanese miracle may also offer the non-Japanese an occasion for classic excellence. In such matters, European expectations and standards, like those of the Chinese, are uncompromising.

For Westerners, the institutional accomplishments, the premised political verbalism and the sheer complexity of scale of Japanese civilization make it a unique mirror of our failings and achievements. To develop a theory of 'thinking nationalism' or 'motivated bureauc-racy', to digest inwardly the profoundest of Japanese insights, will require the fullest teasing of the intellectual resources of both Japan and the West in a sustained season of thought.[25] Such seasons are infinitely precious because they have been, by tradition, the occasion for textual creation of the first rank. Such proud projects will necessitate the demolition of a great wall of philosophic blindness and cultural prejudice. In the West, this anti-classicist barrier is built from positivist stone. In Japan, the offending material is nationalist obscurantism.

Japan must set its face against those who would have it shirk its classic responsibilities. Like advocates of political correctness in the West who urge Afro-Americans to borrow the phantom canonicity of ancient Egypt, there are those who insist that modernity has not defeated Japan, but rather that the Japanese have effortlessly outflanked it. In their different ways, Karatani Kojin, the literary critic, and Alexandre Kojève, the French Hegelian, proclaim the view that Japan has calmly tasted the postmodern condition since the eighteenth century, the middle of the Edo period.[26] In other words, Japan has not needed to overcome modernity because it is already postmodern. Caught in a cultural vacuum, an asphyxiating 'now' bereft of both a canonic past and a future to dream forward, the Japanese bathe freely, as it were, in the unearned postmodernist luxury of a creatively dead Shangri-la unburdened by the need for the liberating excellence of classicism.

Maruyama Masao is rightly sceptical of this attempt to finesse the provocation of modernity. In his essay 'How to learn from the classics', he takes issue with those Japanese cultural critics who argue that Japan's current 'retreat from the classics' is an exclusively contemporary phenomenon for which his nation pays no price.[27] Maruyama believes that two factors are at work in Japanese classical ambivalence today. One is the decline in the 'real presence' of objective standards of creative excellence and the established genres that give them life. The other is the nervous strain in Japanese sensibility, almost certainly the result of an inability to confront ageing and death, which has burdened that society with a tireless pursuit of novelty and a profound dread of being thought out of date (*jidai okure*).

Whatever implications such inconstancy has for the failure of Japan to produce a political classic worthy of her modern miracle, anti-classicism is not a novel strain in Japanese culture. It has been exacerbated by ancient Japanese fears for their national or racial identity, and by the cultural inferiority complex that has fed on such antiquated anxieties.

Maruyama's observations are bold in their general spirit. As a historian of Japanese thought, he is manifestly uncomfortable with the inexhaustible character of cultural dispute. Certainly such rancour invites both sterile contentiousness and invidious comparisons. But on this subject, Maruyama can speak with rare authority. He has explored the depth of his country's response to the canonic triumph of Chinese neo-Confucianism.[28] He is one of the editors of the volume by Ogyu Sorai, perhaps the greatest of all Japanese political thinkers, in Iwanami's monumental *Nihon Shiso Taikei* (The System of Japanese Thought).[29] Furthermore, Maruyama has made a sustained case for the contemporary relevance of Fukuzawa Yukichi, the Meiji political writer, in his three-volume *'Bunmeiron no Gairyaku' o Yomu*.[30]

No one is more aware than this Japanese political scientist and historian of the characteristic near-greatness, of a strength just below best, that Japan has already displayed in the field of political philosophy. The foundation stones for intellectual glory have already been laid within Japanese thought. The labours of Ogyu Sorai, of

Fukuzawa Yukichi and, indeed, of Maruyama himself, offer a radical challenge to those Japanese still inhibited by the demands of genius.

Maruyama demonstrates a clear Japanese grasp of the unmatchable rigour of classic creation. He readily concedes that the unfulfilled dream of a Japanese classicism must be weighed against the fact that throughout the entirety of Japan's thirteen hundred years of documented history, standards of cultural excellence and the formal genres that give them expression have been imported: in pre-modern times from China; in the modern age from Europe. Indeed, the very notion of canonic excellence is a Chinese invention. Confronted with this fact, nationalist sensibility falters.

> In other words, because such objective forms and canonic rules are originally of foreign provenance, the intellectual and artistic betrayal of such forms and maxims in Japan is inevitably caught up in, indeed made synonymous with, what is logically a completely different problem: the contest between native creativity and foreign importation.[31]

The results are damning. In Japan, the motion of the spirit which is originality, having never been made her own, has been lost sight of, and the Japanese creative impulse has all too often been dissipated in amorphous energy or in that current of heightened emotion that precedes true creation.[32]

'Betrayal of form' was, as Maruyama acknowledges, a central strategy of European Romanticism in its revolt against neo-classicism.[33] In contrast, the Japanese experience of high culture has fatally sought to reverse this natural order. One betrays from the outset. For Murasaki Shikibu, Maruyama concludes, 'In the beginning was Romanticism'.[34] However much some Japanese have been keen to seize on Murasaki's *oeuvre* for textual evidence of the superiority of Japanese civilization over the creative thinness of contemporary American culture, more than irony is at issue in the way that the author of the *The Tale of Genji*, much like Mark Twain, produced an extraordinary *oeuvre* while slighting canonic standards.

In Maruyama's view, the global trend in all literate societies towards the decay of established genres and 'the destruction of objective standards' during the late twentieth century merely conspires with this tendency that Japanese high culture has manifested from its earliest phase.[35] Such ambivalence has decisive implications for Japan's potential for achievement of the first rank. Maruyama appears wary of drawing the obvious conclusion from the Chinese and European experience of classicism, which teaches that the deeper the canonic roots of a society, the greater the certainty that any 'betrayal of form' will be, for that society, an adventure that engages the spirit with total demand; and the very opposition at work in this betrayal will link, inevitably, with the effort to reform, and thus renew, the canonic order.[36]

Less confident in their classical standards, American post-structuralists have not understood that this is the central ordering impulse at work in Derrida's re-reading of Rousseau and Nietzsche. Thus, Barthes pored over Racine, just as Baudelaire did before him. But, in the shallow soil of Japanese and American classicism, where, in Maruyama's view, 'canonic forms are casually worn and discarded', anti-formalism is a superficial affair, less a state occasion than 'a strip show'.[37]

Where some might see such anti-formalism as the expression of a preordained postmodernism, Maruyama stresses the role of national pride and prejudice. Throughout much of its conscious history, Japan has sought to catch up with and overtake the advanced nations that have dominated its cultural horizon. But the resultant hunger for foreign ideas and texts has reflected less the desire to nurse canonic excellence than to import what was, for current sensibility, the latest cultural mode or intellectual model. The dominant system of values is what Maruyama terms *saishin-ryuko-shugi*, or that weakness for mere fashion that only novelty can feed.[38] Japanese culture is caught in an imprisoning 'now-ism' (*genzai-chushin*), a stultifying immanence of the spirit which seeks to evade the glories of tradition, glories which are the work of centuries and which flower completely only in the purest classicism.[39]

The diverting demands of collective identity have, in the Japanese case, been allowed to pervert, subtly and unnecessarily, the canonic need, not only for textual excellence but also for the elaboration of the demands of universal reason and ethics in the political sphere. This double evasion dominated Japan's intellectual agenda even during the Edo period (1600–1868), when the privileges of canonicity, as reflected in the fierce debates over the character of the *Genji*, were probed with unprecedented seriousness. During the Edo era a kind of 'formal betrayal' was sustained by proponents of the National Learning Movement (*Kokugaku Undo*), but such betrayal did not declare itself in a set of texts to match the Chinese canon. Rather nationalist thinkers sought to betray canonic forms by excluding foreign ideas and values, and thus 'to exorcise the spirit of China' (*Karagokoro o kiyosaru*).[40]

This slogan is often associated with Motoori Norinaga

(1730–1801), the nationalist philologist and neo-Shintoist, whose ideas have had extraordinary impact on both conventional Japanese nationalist feeling and militant ultra-nationalism. Norinaga's system sought to appeal to emotion and pure sentiment over rationality and ethical imperatives. At its worst this descends into anti-foreign obscurantism. Norinaga, like Herder, was more scrupulous about this danger than his less intelligent, if more chauvinist epigone. But whatever may divide the ideological outlook of Maruyama, the cosmopolitan defender of high culture, from that of Karatani Kojin, the literary nationalist, they concur on the anti-intellectual thrust of Norinaga's teachings. In his essay 'History and the Other' (*'Rekishi to Tasha'*), Karatani writes:

> Before Meiji, Chinese learning and literature always embodied the cultural standard that mattered for the Japanese intelligentsia. Nationalism was the natural reaction against such Chinese influence, but even features of native Japanese culture such as Shinto manifested a genuine dependence upon Chinese ethics and theory. No Japanese thinker was more aware of this dependence than Motoori Norinaga, the scholar of the National Learning Movement, but he rejected [*shirizoketa*] not only Chinese theory, but 'theory' itself.[41]

Like Rousseau, Norinaga regarded himself as the uncompromising foe of civilized artifice and sophistication, especially if they were of Chinese or Indian inspiration. The fact that Norinaga saw high civilization, and the burdens of reason and enlightenment, as ideas to be liberated from, a sentiment Karatani would tragically echo, has undermined Japan's canonic potential. The contrast between Norinaga's rather secondary *oeuvre* and Rousseau's canonic achievement points to a crucial failure of nerve. It is not to Norinaga but rather to the intellectual vigour that may be found in Ito Jinsai, Ogyu Sorai, Yamazaki Ansai and Fukuzawa Yukichi that the advocate of Japanese classicism should look for enabling precedents.[42]

Norinaga preached the xenophobic dogma that ideas should be judged not by their quality or intellectual force but by their provenance: whether they were of Japanese origin or not. The urge to exorcise the spirit of Europe (*Oshu seishin o kiyosaru*) is the unmistakable impulse at work in Karatani's attack on Hiromatsu Wataru, the Marxist philosopher and author of an ambitious two-volume bilingual commentary, in German and Japanese, on a key part of the manuscript of *Die Deutsche Ideologie*.[43] Echoing Norinaga's xenophobia, Karatani censures Hiromatsu's *oeuvre*, particularly his Marxist writings, for not being Japanese enough ('*hontodo Nihon-teki na bunmyaku o motte inai*').[44]

This same parochial posture is at work in the attack on the formidable body of theoretical work produced by Yoshimoto Takaaki, another influential Marxist intellectual, by Asada Akira.[45] Such critiques reflect Japanese nationalist resentment not only of left-wing ideas, but of foreign thought itself. Once again it would appear that the betrayal of intellectual forms in Japan is caught up in 'the contest between native creativity and foreign importation'. The great danger is that such criticism may finally issue in the cultural nationalism of the second rate. A genuine Japanese classicism demands more.

CLASSICISM VERSUS POLITICAL CORRECTNESS

Japan's long struggle with the temptations of canonicity is one of the great neglected themes in the contemporary global debate over the related issues of Eurocentrism, the classical canon and political correctness. A corrosive moralism is at work in this neglect. Such moralism explains why the traditional Eurocentrist, who resists Japan's claims for a place in the Western canon of political philosophy, has a surprising ally in the advocate of non-European liberation. In the name of an obscurant morality, the champions of political correctness also deny Japan's right to intellectual dignity. This is a perilous posture because there is no salvation outside cultural success.

Saul Bellow's remark that 'When the Zulus have produced a Tolstoy, then I shall read him' speaks to the heart of the matter. Because human sensibility bends to canonic achievement, the overwhelming need is to produce a text capable of winning a place in the canon. The Japanese miracle demands canonic attention. Unfortunately, some spokesmen for the non-European world would rather rationalize defeat than rise to the challenge of creation of the first rank. This stance tends to blunt resistance to the enfeebling demands of parochial ethnocentricism. The writings of Karatani Kojin illustrate the danger.

Nevertheless, modern Japan, and much of East Asia with her, would today greet with blank incomprehension the lament contained in Aimé Césaire's poem which begins 'who and what are we?':

Eia for those who have never invented anything
for those who have never explored anything

for those who have never subjected anything[46]

This poem has been read as a powerful non-European rejection of the technical, cultural and imperial achievements of White civilization, but it may also be seen to nurse the ache of defeat and failure.[47] But it is not the ache of defeat that *finally* needs to be nursed, but the urge to create and to achieve.

Obscurantism can overwhelm true culture. When the history faculty at Stanford University voted to topple some of Europe's greatest minds from their canonic places in the academic pantheon, a *Japan Times* editorial urged the creation of a Stanford niche for the author of the *Genji*: an Oriental and a woman who was a creative writer, if not a thinker, of the first rank. One may be fully alive to the ambiguities in such as nomination, but still insist that this proposal carried conviction *if*, and only if, the primary goal of political correctness was the discovery and elevation of minority and non-Western talent, and the celebration of their achievements. This, however, is sadly not the case. Rather, political correctness represents at root a self-destructive rejection of achievement by anyone, whether European or non-European, White or non-White, male or female, heterosexual or homosexual.

Canonic excellence is a community's lifeline. The survival both of the individual and his collectivity are at stake in such liberating elitism. Any form of political correctness that undermines the pursuit of classicism is an enemy of those among the ranks of the marginalized of history who still thirst for personal and shared dignity in the intellectual sphere.[48] A thoughtful grasp on collective identity (an 'Ontology') can only be secured by sure purchase on reality (an 'ontology'). To have endured the humiliations of patriarchy or the tyrannies of heterosexualism or the horrors of the New World conquest or the 'Middle Passage' was to have displayed a special kind of heroism. That is beyond question. But it is not journey's end (having survived, to what end is life to be lived?). It is not enough to endure reality; one must change it. Somewhere in this testing process, a canonic stamp must be left on the world.

Both the defenders of Japanese exceptionalism and anti-European political correctness ignore the fact that the West's cultural achievement, the summits, if you will, have, at many points, been a consequence of a sustained response to identity-threatening or submerging cultural excellence, beginning with the classical Greeks. Jasper Griffin sets out the implied dialectic of identity and literary creation with precision:

In the words of Lytton Strachey, 'Greek art is, in every sense, the most finished in the world; it is for ever seeking to express what it has to express completely and finally; and when it has accomplished that, it is content.' On most of the peoples with whom the Greeks came into contact the effect of that formal perfection was deeply demoralizing. Lycians, Lydians, Etruscans, they all came under the spell of Greek form, and in most of the languages of the Mediterranean world no literature ever came into existence. . . . And so, in the end, their languages were doomed; Etruscan, Oscan, Messapian and many others simply withered away.[49]

The results of the encounter of Mediterranean cultures with the formal excellence of classical Greece should make clear the crucial link between the survival of a linguistic community and its capacity to nurture perfection of form in the arts, in this case literature. In the ancient world, the question was stark: match the Greek achievement or 'simply wither away'. In this sense, formal perfection may be seen as no mere civilized ornament, no empty reflection of an elitist bathos, but rather the very stuff of communal identity and survival. This profound interplay between a poetic ontology and a communal Ontology offers the most powerful gloss possible on the assertion of Osip Mandelstam, the great Russian poet and master of poetic form, that 'the people need poetry no less than bread'.

Advocates of political correctness have not begun to grasp the importance of this cultural dynamic. Instead their assault on the canonic glories of tradition should be judged to be fundamentally misconceived. A community should seek not to abandon or neglect or despise tradition but to match it. Griffin describes how the task is done:

It would turn out that Rome would take a unique course; not that of simple surrender to Greek superiority, nor that of pretending that Greek literature did not exist or presenting no problem, but the heroic task of creating in Latin a literature fit to stand beside that of Greece. That meant taking over the Greek forms, epic, tragedy, comedy, history, oratory, lyric, and producing in them works of classic style and stature. We see that Roman literature was the first to go in the direction that was taken, after the Renaissance, by all the literatures of Europe, which in turn set out to create works in all the classic genres.[50]

The challenge is unambiguous. There is more than literary

capriciousness at work in the fact that Derek Walcott chose to call his West Indian epic cycle 'Omeros', the Greek name for Homer.[51] In their different ways, Walcott and V. S. Naipaul may be seen to have brought to a kind of formal close the tradition of pastoralist and anti-pastoralist meditation on the 'bitter constraint' (Milton) that would mobilize poetic creation to overcome artistic mortality. In *The Enigma of Arrival* (1987), Naipaul wins a signal place for the prose narrative in a classic genre that reaches back to Theocritus and the Greek poets of ancient Egypt who invented pastoralism.[52]

It was by recourse to this same sanctified tradition that Milton and Gray created English verse, in the pastoral mode, to match the formal achievements of Greece and Rome. The result is clear. The ripple of cultural and creative challenge and response remains unbroken: Rome rises to the challenge of Greece; Italy and France to Rome; Germany to France; Britain and Russia to Europe. And with Naipaul and Walcott, West Indians rise to the cultural challenge of ancient Greece and post-Renaissance Europe – and meet it.

Japan has sought to meet the creative challenge of the European arts and sciences. It is the story of Roman creative brilliance, achieved in the face of the overwhelming authority of classical Greek forms, that provides the most telling precedent, because it is irresistibly sovereign, of Japan's twentieth-century cultural and intellectual achievements, in the novel, in the film and in architectural design. In the wake of a profound demoralization at the hands of Victorian science, Japanese scholarship has girded its loins: five Nobel Prizes (three in physics, one each in chemistry and biology) have been the result. *Oo-bei ni oikose* ('Overtake Europe and America'): this Meiji cry should decorate the banners of every endangered Ontology, in the developing world or anywhere else.

This is perhaps even more relevant because such perfection of form may be sought in interested and politically committed Ontological forms as well as disinterested ontological ones. It should be obvious why Frantz Fanon found it supremely useful, in the strongest ontological and Ontological senses of the word, to think about racism, colonialism and capitalism through the prism of European high culture. The force of Fanon's thought, as reflected in *Black Skin, White Masks, The Wretched of the Earth, Studies in a Dying Colonialism*, is reinforced at numerous points by a sustained encounter with Descartes, Hegel and Jean-Paul Sartre.[53] These White European males, living and dead, provided Fanon with access to 'the technique and style of Europe', to distinctive forms of philosophical expression and self-understanding, that is to a kind of creative perfection, which he exploited to hammer out his own Ontology without which he knew no people will flourish with intellectual honour.

A victim's anger must never rob him of his reason. The spokesmen for the dispossessed of three continents have memorialized such historic benchmarks as the five-hundredth anniversary of Columbus's arrival in the New World with a bitterness at once sincere and deep. But rage can conspire against liberation. This is the true message of that notorious verbal exchange from Naipaul's *In a Free State*. Here, two White Europeans ponder the beauty of a lake-side scene not so remote in time or place from the Belgian Congo shortly after independence:

> 'It's funny,' Linda whispered, 'how you can forget the houses and feel that the lake hasn't even been discovered.'
>
> 'I don't know what you mean by discovered,' Bobby said, not whispering. 'The people here knew about it all the time.'
>
> 'I've heard that one. I just wish they'd managed to let the rest of us know.'[54]

'Let the rest of us know'. This is the problematic that anti-European anger would have us ignore. Any successful defence of an endangered identity must address the external community as well as the wounds to the pysche. The dialectic of victimhood offers no other path to liberation. The victims will, in any case, always know their own poets ('Every brother on a rooftop can quote Fanon'). But what of the great world outside one's immediate communal orbit? The more endangered an Ontology, the more it must embrace an ontology capable of engaging the world beyond, even if that world is *L'autre*.

The point is that history's victims, unlike the poor, need not always be with us. Canonic success is the outward sign of an inward liberated state. Indeed the literary accomplishments of Walcott and Naipaul demonstrate what is at issue in the writer's ambition to achieve formal perfection. They have demonstrated that West Indians are capable of artistic creativity of the first order. Regarded by many 'metropolitan' or London critics (to borrow a key word from Frank Kermode's Eliot memorial lecture, *The Classic*) as the finest living writer of the English language, Naipaul may be seen to have redefined the essence of what it is to be a West Indian because he has revolutionized the scope of the possible in what a West Indian may achieve and has achieved.[55] This constitutes the most powerful rejection conceivable of Césaire's impotent lament for those 'who have never invented' or created anything.

This brings us to the heart of the contradiction of political correctness because it underlines the enabling fact at work in the unfolding of Naipaul's genius; the complicity of the European mind in this flowering. In the creation of the high tradition of the great English novel, from Fielding to Conrad, dead White British men and women have fashioned the indispensable vehicle for Naipaul to achieve a formal and substantive excellence. This is why, as Fanon and Walcott, Naipaul and Maruyama all recognize, the European achievement in the arts and sciences is infinitely precious to any non-European who seeks communal liberation, creative mastery and intellectual *amour-propre*. In this sphere of human endeavour, the centrality of Europe is no racist fiction:

> However accusingly, with whatever penitential hysteria, the argument is put, the fact of Western dominance during two and a half millennia remains largely true. *Pace* Joseph Needham, whose orientation of the cultural and scientific map in favour of China and, possibly, India, is itself among the most fascinating, imaginative of modern *Western* intellectual adventures, the manifest centres of philosophic, scientific, poetic force have been situated within the Mediterranean, north European, Anglo-Saxon racial and geographic matrix.[56]

This quotation should be affixed above the study door of every proponent of political correctness. George Steiner's summation of the Western achievement should not be the point where the political correctness debate ends, but where it should begin. This is because the high places in Europe's cultural achievement have so often been a consequence of a sustained response to identity-threatening or submerging cultural excellence, beginning with the classical Greeks.

Without an ontology, one cannot save an Ontology. Fanon knew this. Hence his unflinching engagement with the masters of European philosophic tradition. There are no grounds to doubt that Fanon would have regarded political correctness, however sympathetic he would have been with its anger, as a self-mutilating act. The upshot should be clear: the final stage of non-European liberation is non-European classicism.

JAPAN: WHERE ARE THE MASTERS?

In his essay titled '*Bunka no Hiteisei*' (Culture as negation), Aoki Tamotsu, the Japanese anthropologist, has sought to explain the growth of anti-Japanese criticism, especially among American and

European intellectuals and policy-makers since the 1970s.[57] Aoki laments the passing of what might be called the 'Ruth Benedict era of good feeling' in Japanese studies, particularly in America, the main object of Aoki's inquiry. In his view, research on modern Japan has benefited decisively from the growth of cultural pluralism in the West. Thus the Japanese, who had been regarded as an uncivilized and backward people, have come, during the twentieth century, to be appreciated in their own right, despite the fact that they are not Christian, European or White.

Mindful of the chill that descended on US–Japan relations during the 1980s, Aoki looks back with nostalgia to earlier, less strained decades. This stance ignores the consequences, political and otherwise, of the growth of Japanese power. Today Japan is no longer a weak, marginal nation seeking crumbs of respect and understanding from the tables of the rich men of the West. Quite the contrary, the representatives of the Japanese nation now occupy a place of pride at those very tables. The critical scrutiny that Japan now receives from the Western media and intelligentsia reflects the contemporary *devictimization* of Japanese culture in the global context. Japan's new power precludes the necessity for the often patronizing generosity of cultural relativism, with its taboos on hostile value judgements.

Proponents of political correctness have also sought to revoke the old relativist dispensations, in order to denounce Japanese majoritarianism and imperialism, to ascribe to Japan a new 'Tigeritude' (to adopt Wole Soyinka's expression) that was once thought to be the exclusive privilege of White cultures. Yet it remains an unambiguous fact that Japan has hitherto stood outside the privileged hub of history, outside Steiner's 'matrix' which has generated the 'manifest centres of philosophic, scientific, poetic force'. But rather than welcome the triumph of a non-Western 'coloured' nation in the face of stiff Euro-American economic competition, the defenders of political correctness have been keen to condemn Japan precisely because it has rejected the moral high ground of victimhood. Instead, Japan has striven to become the first non-White culture to break free of the nightmarish world of nineteenth-century underdevelopment and the despair that gripped what we once called 'The Third World'.

Such politically correct blindness aside, Japan now stands as the most powerful contemporary indictment of Césaire's poem on the lack of achievement by non-White societies. But true to its perversity, political correctness will grant Japan no quarter. The joys of apparently eternal victimhood are too satisfying and the demands of genuine achievement too great. But if the proponent of true non-European liberation did want to turn to Japan, as Fanon did to France, what would he find there? Could contemporary Tokyo provide the kind of creative apparatus and classical incentives that Paris provided to colonial intellectuals and poets earlier in this century or that London offered to the motion of the spirit so alive in Naipaul's literary ambitions? In *Black Skin, White Masks*, Fanon wrote: 'I am a Frenchman, I am interested in French culture, in French civilization, the French people. We [the Blacks] refuse to be considered "outsiders", we have full part in the French drama'.[58] After a lifetime of bitter struggle with French colonialism and racism, this statement will still stand true of Fanon as a thinker.

So, even if Japan were willing to play the role that France and Britain played *vis-à-vis* the creative excellence yielded up by their old colonies, could Japan do so? If not, who is to blame? Japan has something of true canonic worth to articulate, but why have its writers and thinkers yet to give this achievement canonic form?[59] With such questions, one might begin to draw up an inventory of what Japan has had to endure for its inward-looking character and for the rejection of universalist ambition in favour of the dubious blessings of uniqueness.

Against such failings must be set the fact that Japan, by its economic and technological achievements, both as an expression of public policy and private enterprise, has redefined several spheres of social and mental reality. So where are Japan's modern masters? Where is the seminal text setting out the principles of Japan's economic miracle? Amid the phantasmagoria of business biography and managerial tracts, where is the major *oeuvre* that captures, ontologically, the essence of Japan's triumph in business, management and the fostering of national power? Are we all to stand mute in witness to what Japan has achieved?

Aoki blames the new Western disenchantment with Japan not on his nation's rise but on Western decline. He points to the Vietnam War as the turning point in the rebirth of anti-relativism as an intellectual doctrine among educated Americans. The suggestion is that the death or severe deflation of the American dream is nurturing a new chauvinism.

The rubric of 'decline and fall' is valuable, but not for the reasons that Aoki suggests. If Japanese commentators have long sought to focus attention on the relative decline of British fortunes during the first half of the twentieth century and of American power since 1945, then the bursting of Japan's economic bubble in the 1990s invites the extension of this rubric to Japanese power itself.

There are sound reasons for thoughtful Japanese to brood on the Anglo-American dance with history. Assessing with a cold, clear eye the imbalance in power between London and Washington that accompanied Britain's post-imperial twilight, British Prime Minister Harold Macmillan observed that perhaps it was time for Britain 'to play Athens to the American Rome'. Macmillan was suggesting not only that the British had something to teach, but that Americans might be hungry to learn, a perception underwritten by the artistic and cultural sophistication of the Kennedy court. But as a product of the unself-conscious classicism of Edwardian public school education, Macmillan knew also that many of his countrymen would recall Horace's observation that having been conquered by Rome, the Greeks proceeded culturally to enslave their conquerors.

The pervasive classicism of British intellectual life has enabled it, again and again, to produce minds of the very first rank and allow Britain, as a consequence, to stand shoulder to shoulder (Voltaire thought that Britain stood head above shoulders) with all its European neighbours, ancient or modern. From this tradition of almost matchless excellence – in the sciences, literature and philosophy – it would appear that Britain has derived a kind of poise and confidence, a ballast, with which to face the uncertainties and dangers of the present, prophesied by Keynes in 1919 as that

> less happy day when the industrial labour of Europe could no longer purchase on such easy terms the produce of other continents, and when the due balance would be threatened between its historical civilizations and the multiplying races of other climates and environments . . .[60]

The United States may now be facing that 'less happy day'. Reflecting on the Macmillan analogy, it is impossible to imagine a US president announcing that the moment had arrived for America 'to play Athens to an Asian Rome'. The analogy would not be invoked because it would not be believed. There is no classical achievement, certainly outside political philosophy, for Americans to fall back upon.[61] Where there has been a substantial American contribution to the European ontology, this has cast hardly a shadow on the American Ontology. Even where genius has attempted to flourish on native ground – the example of the philosopher Charles Pierce comes to mind – the population at large has been systematically schooled to ignore it.

The result is damningly summarized in George Steiner's observation that 'The [European] inheritance of ontological astonishment and systematic response remains unbroken from Heraclitus to Sartre's *Les Mots*. It runs through Aquinas, Descartes, Hume, Kant, Hegel and Nietzsche. There is no American membership in that list.'[62] On the contrary, the apex of American cultural success, in architecture, the film and popular music, would appear to be entirely immanent in character: it exists only 'now'. When a Japanese investor buys the film studio or the famous building or the record company, he acquires the achievement. Shakespeare, Newton and Darwin are immune to such purchase. Hence the hurt and anger in the American response to Japanese intrusiveness on the US cultural scene during the late 1980s. This discomfort paints a sharp contrast with Macmillan's confident ease. Culturally, philosophically, mathematically, there will always be an England.

Which brings us to the central question at issue here: how well equipped is Japan for that 'less happy day'? On the cultural and intellectual front, Japan would appear to be even less well prepared than America. Japanese cultural achievements today are also immanent in character. More astonishing still, in the one sphere where Japanese success has the potential to revolutionize the paradigm of global social science, the Japanese mind has not begun to leave its great mark. Hardly anything is being stored up for that 'less happy' tomorrow. Wiser cultures, which have not forgotten the classical standards of achievement, order things more carefully.

Part II

Japanese greatness and the European inheritance

The difficult thing is to keep open the line to the
ancestral European imagination while at the same time
producing something that comes across as entirely new.
John Russell

Science

3 Positivism

Orientalism depends for its strategy on this flexible *positional* superiority, which puts the Westerner in a whole series of possible relationships with the Orient without ever losing him the relative upper hand.

Edward Said

The two greatest dangers posed by Western social science to the sound understanding of modern Japan are positivist procrustianism and empirical hyperfactualization. Positivism has evolved a set of scientific laws which may distort the truth; empiricism legitimates a search for factual knowledge which is in principle unending and thus subversive of any conclusion that the researcher might draw. That Kant judged the thrust towards positivist tyranny and empirical anarchy as the defining impulses of European science only underscores the crucial nature of the problem at issue. In this chapter, the challenge of positivist procrustianism will be confronted.

CLOSED MINDS

Invisible Japan

Japan is the most important political system of the late twentieth century. Its only rival for the rank of the world's most consequential polity, now that the Soviet Union has disappeared, is the United States of America. But the collapse of Soviet-style central planning also fans the suspicion that the whipping-boy status of Lenin's state in English-language textbooks on economics should probably be judged, whatever its heuristic uses, as an unfortunate ideological fetish which has conspired against taking Japanese capitalism seriously. Today economists can no longer rely on such mystification.

Indeed the scale and intensity of Western reporting on the Japanese economy – and the greatness of Japan's political system cannot be properly assessed without scrutiny of its economic structure – rightly recognizes the centrality of this Oriental society's experience of government in human history.

Western journalists have often praised the Japanese system for its unique achievements. This was particularly true during the brief period of enthusiasm for the apparent skills of Japanese policy-makers and businessmen in the wake of the second great oil crisis at the end of the 1970s. As such journalistic ebullience was matched by the first important harvest of scholarly theory and evidence about Japan's potential for economic ascendency, this may have been the most precious hour yet in the modern Western discourse on Asian society. It was certainly the most positive Western assessment of the non-Western world since the Enlightenment's celebration of the Ming and Ottoman Empires.

If one looks, however, beyond this massive turn to East Asia by the Western print media, one discovers a curious flaw. In contrast to Japan's well-deserved prominence in news reporting and analysis, European scholarship, outside the ghettos of business and Japan studies, has been strikingly indifferent to Asia's new giant. Evidence of this neglect may be found in articles about Japanese thinkers, statesmen and intellectuals in some of the more respectable reference works and teaching tools on political theory and economics. The academic mainstream of Western social science and philosophy has not only ignored the assertion that Japan is the most significant political system of our time, but it has also rejected Japanese claims to importance of any kind. Indeed for these thinkers and writers, scholars and editors, Japan is less than marginal: it is invisible.

Blindness and insight

Although the Japanese miracle has unfolded in vigorous spurts since the nineteenth century, it is perhaps best to seek evidence of Western indifference from more recent publications, when even the most cloistered European thinker should no longer have been able to ignore the fact of Japan's modern triumph. *The Encyclopedia of Philosophy*, published in eight volumes in 1967, offers a useful benchmark for comparison.[1] This massive reference work appeared three years before the publication of Herman Kahn's provocative study, *The Emerging Japanese Superstate*, but five years after *The Economist*'s pioneering article 'Consider Japan'.[2] What is clear is that by 1967 Japan's importance had begun to register on Western consciousness but few students of social thought were as yet willing to explore the intellectual foundations of modern Japanese political and economic success.

Nevertheless, the editors of *The Encyclopedia of Philosophy* aimed for generous breadth in their coverage of Asia. Thus, there are long entries on Islamic, Indian and Chinese philosophy and many articles on representative Asian thinkers. But these traditions tend, with certain exceptions, to be treated as either importers of Western ideas or as essentially pre-modern in scope and relevance. *The Encyclopedia of Philosophy* includes twenty-four articles specifically on Japanese thought, including separate entries on 'Buddhism', 'Zen' and 'Japanese philosophy'. Articles are devoted to nineteen individual Japanese philosophers, ranging from Hayashi Razan to Miki Kiyoshi. With modern philosophers, the absorption of Western ideas is stressed as well as the thinker's place in the evolving native tradition. Only in the case of Nishida Kitaro of the Kyoto School is a thinker judged to have appeal outside the immediate orbit of parochial Japanese interest. Nor is politics, as a factor in twentieth-century Japanese philosophy, neglected, especially as it touches on the questions of nationalism, Marxist influence and the country's involvement in the Second World War. But none of these entries attempts to ground Japan's post-war economic rise in its intellectual traditions. There are no articles on any twentieth-century Japanese political philosopher or theorist. Nevertheless, the impulse in post-war Western sensibility to recognize the existence of non-Western schools of philosophic reflection has left its stamp on *The Encyclopedia of Philosophy*. But there is scarcely a hint that Asian thought matches the rigour of Western philosophy, let alone surpasses it.

More telling is how, after 1967, serious Western interest in Asian ideas and thinkers has been confined to the scholarly margins. In the academic mainstream, in Europe and elsewhere, ignorance of the significance of post-war Japan remains the rule. This does not reflect a total obtuseness to the tumultuous changes that have shaken East Asian politics during the twentieth century. Even the 1973 edition of *A History of Political Theory*, by George H. Sabine and Thomas L. Thorson, includes a seven-page section on China and Mao Zedong in its chapter on communism, but only as a response, the editor notes, to a larger discussion of 'the penetration of the non-Western world by Western political theory'.[3] But between the 1961 and 1973 editions of this classic textbook, Japan overtook Britain,

France and Germany to become the world's third largest economy, an advance unmatched by any non-Western society in modern times. Surely this development demanded a response from political and economic philosophers? Yet, as late as 1987, neither Japan nor any Japanese thinker figures in the third edition of the *History of Political Philosophy*, edited by Leo Strauss and Joseph Cropsey.[4]

The recession provoked by the second oil shock of 1979 was a turning point. The publication of a series of revisionary studies by Western scholars of Japan such as *Theory Z* (1981) by William G. Ouchi, *Japan as No. One* (1979) by Ezra Vogel, and *MITI and the Japanese Miracle* (1982) by Chalmers Johnson, signalled a growing recognition, even in academe, that Japan had achieved the kind of importance true of no Asian polity since the Ming, Mogul and Ottoman empires.[5] Philosophic and economic works published after this period become increasingly vulnerable to the charge of studied apathy towards one of the most consequential developments of the post-war world.

During this crucial transition in global affairs, Frank Kermode began commissioning, from the 1960s, selections for the prestigious 'Modern Masters' series. He initially included works on such Third-World revolutionaries as Frantz Fanon and Che Guevara, but, of the twenty-one titles avaliable in 1995, not a single contemporary Japanese or East Asian thinker was judged to merit inclusion. The criteria applied by the editors of the Oxford University Press's 'Past Masters' series, which as of 1995 included fifty-five titles on individual authors, have been even more astringent. No East Asian philosopher, thinker or intellectual from the past twenty-five centuries, with the exception of Confucius – not Menicus, Chu Hsi or Wang Yang-ming, nor Dogen, Ito Jinsai or Ogyu Sorai – has been thought worthy of a volume. Such European indifference gives the false impression that the Asian colossus, intellectually at least, sleeps still.

A publishing dilemma is at work here. An introductory text on an Asian thinker is unlikely to be be produced if Western readers have no appreciation of this thinker's influence. But no readership for such philosophers can be nourished if their reputations remain uncelebrated. In America, scholars such as Wm. Theodore de Bary have laboured for a lifetime at the task of making the Confucian political tradition intelligible to Western readers, most recently in *East Asian Civilizations: A Dialogue in Five Stages* (1988) and *The Trouble with Confucianism* (1991).[6] Tetsuo Najita painted a vibrant picture of the astonishing vigour of Tokugawa political discourse in

Japan: The Intellectual Foundations of Modern Japanese Politics (1974).[7] The broad Western receptiveness to such difficult Oriental thinkers as Lao Tzu hint at the potential harvest.

The daunting task of winning a place for East Asian reflection within the European pantheon remains. The Orientalist who is also a modernist must demonstrate, as Allan Bloom demonstrated the importance of Nietzsche for thousands of readers in *The Closing of the American Mind* (1989), that Japan 'somehow *matters*' in the realm of ideas no less than in that of fact.[8] We need an East Asian answer to books such as Quentin Skinner's *The Return of Grand Theory in the Human Sciences* (1985), which sought to prompt a critical response from the British intelligentsia and its readership by introducing some of the most influential Continental European and American thinkers of our time. In her *Conversazioni americane* (1991), Giovanna Borradori has sought to provoke something similar from her Italian readership by interviewing nine of America's most prominent philosophers.[9] The success of such ventures points to a cardinal imperative. The East Asian contribution to classical and contemporary political, philosophic and economic reflection must be argued on *European* ground. Having achieved so much, endured so much, invented so much, the Japanese now require only a thinker worthy of their triumph.

The failure to generate the requisite textual densities may explain why, as late as 1987, *The Blackwell Encyclopedia of Political Thought*, edited by David Miller and others, could appear without a single entry in which post-war Japan's experience or intellectual tradition was even mentioned.[10] In 1991, Scott Gordon published a substantial volume titled *The History and Philosophy of Social Science*, the index of which contained multi-entries under 'Germany', 'France', the 'United States' and other important national traditions, but the entry for Japan included only a single reference: 'Spencer's influence in'.[11] In 1992 *The Routledge Dictionary of Twentieth Century Political Thinkers* was issued. Among the 159 entries, four Japanese were treated: a pre-war ultra-nationalist (Kita Ikki), a pre-war socialist (Yoshino Sakuzo), an economic historian (Otsuka Hisao) and a Marxist economist (Uno Kozo).[12] This represents the slightest bow to the significance of modern Japan, but it is revealing that Germaine Hoston's article on Otsuka concentrates entirely on his response to Karl Marx and Max Weber. Otsuka's penetrating analysis of Friedrich List and other proponents of neo-mercantilist *kokumin keizai* (national economy), a body of policy insights that has underwritten the miraculous advance of Japan, and much of East Asia with her, is passed over in silence.[13]

Such silence should be unthinkable among economists. Paul Samuelson, in the various editions of his best-selling textbook *Economics*, extended early recognition to Japan's economic importance. Writing during the final thrusting phase of Japan's age of rapid growth (*kodo seicho no jidai*), Samuelson concluded, in the ninth edition of *Economics* (1973), that 'The most remarkable phenomenon of economic development in the last century [the twentieth century] and this last decade [the 1960s] has undoubtedly been the Japanese'.[14] Such generous perception makes this edition of *Economics* a benchmark in Western awareness of post-war Japan's growing importance. It compares favourably with *The Encyclopedia of Philosophy*, which confined its recognition of East Asian achievement largely to the pinnacles of medieval and classical glory.

Even among Western economists, who almost by definition had less cause to neglect Japan than political philosophers, Samuelson's degree of interest in Japan reflects both the strengths and weakness of his intellectual guild. The point may be illustrated by comparing Samuelson's ninth edition and the 1991 edition of *Economics* by David Begg, Stanley Fischer and Rudiger Dornbusch. Samuelson's textbook, a larger if less demanding work, includes eighteen-page references under 'Japan' in its index. Begg, Fischer and Dornbusch list just seven.[15] But, reflecting the massive reporting on the Japanese economy of the late 1980s and early 1990s, Japan is occasionally used as an illustrative example by Begg, as in 'Japan sells automobiles to America; America sells wheat to Russia'.[16]

The content of such references raises a sharper issue. If we examine Samuelson's eighteen references to Japan, subtracting the three that overlap, we find that Japan's achievement, specifically praised in two places, is entirely numerical or statistical. What the Japanese have accomplished in the economic sphere may be explained by a body of theory formed *prior* to Japan's modern rise. The Japanese miracle has generated no phenomenon that challenges, let alone undermines, the main dogmas of economic positivist thinking. Positivism defines Japan; the reverse is untrue. In theoretical terms, Japan is nothing. On this Samuelson and Begg are in perfect accord.

In Samuelson's ninth edition there is a chart on the inside cover of the overseas edition which traces 'growth trends of real per capita GNP between 1870 and 1973'. With the exception of one brief interval during the 1890s, when Germany closed the gap between it and the United States, America leads this century of global economic expansion. In 1973, Japan still trailed both Germany and Britain. The table offers an emphatic demonstration of the key assumption of Samuelson and, to a degree, Begg as well: that the United States is the world's reference economy. This invites positivist neglect of Japan because the impact of economic positivism on policy-making in the United States, as in Britain, has been so great. Writing in the early 1970s, Samuelson's confidence in positivist lawmaking and in the economic supremacy of the United States reflects his trust in historic fact.

Samuelson's chart would have to be radically redrawn today. Japan has not only overtaken Germany and Britain but America itself. The new chart would offer a revolutionary challenge to the orthodox certainties of the 1970s. The difference between the 1970s and 1990s is that national achievement no longer bolsters the positivist's confidence in his system of laws. Science, not reality, has become the economist's redoubt.

Race, reason and science

Is such neglect racist? Advocates of political correctness have directed prickly attention towards the absence of women and people of colour from the lists of canonic tradition. In the works thus far cited, dead White European males exert a near-total monopoly on the privileged places in the pantheon of Western thought which continues to set the global standard. One might furthermore observe that the sexual orientation of thinkers such as Socrates, Keynes and Wittgenstein tends to be assiduously ignored. But the claims of political correctness do not form the only nub of sensitivity.

In the preface to the fourth edition of *A History of Political Theory*, Thomas L. Thorson equates the terms 'pre-Greek thought' and 'pre-philosophic thought'.[17] Greek thought has been, by tradition, judged superior not because it is Greek or White or male or European, but because the Greeks cultivated reason. Leo Strauss has argued that the Greek doctrine of natural right is grounded in the quest for reason. The fact that the ancient Chinese or Indians did not pursue this course of thought with as great a rigour as the Greeks does not impair the universal claims of reason. As Leo Strauss observed in *Natural Right and History*:

Some of the greatest natural right teachers have argued that precisely if natural right is rational, its discovery presupposes the cultivation of reason, and therefore natural right will not be known universally: one ought not even to expect any real knowledge of natural right among savages.[18]

The language is harsh but there is a direct link between the defence of reason by Plato, Hobbes and Locke against relativist criticism of the doctrine of natural right and the implicit denial by positivists of the importance of non-Western thought. Whatever Japanese scholars may argue, Western researchers tend to be united in their insistence that the writings of Yamaga Soko, Ogyu Sorai and Yamazaki Ansai are not philosophy or thought but mere ideology.

In the first volume of his monumental three-volume study titled *Black Athena*, Martin Bernal has described in detail what he believes to be the 'fabrication of Ancient Greece' by the Western academic community during the past two centuries.[19] The goal of the protagonists of what he calls 'the Aryan model' of classical studies has been to scour the pristine 'Whiteness', as a racial category, of ancient Greek thought from 'Coloured' contamination from the Levant and ancient Egypt. He contends that the impact of Near Eastern thought on ancient Greek society has been systematically denied to maintain the myth of classical Greek, that is White European, creative originality and genius. Does race provide the key to explain the widespread indifference to Japan by Western social scientists and philosophers?

If not, then what is the explanation? This tendency to ignore Japan may indeed be fuelled by cultural hubris, Eurocentrism, nationalist jealousy and even racist ideology, but reason also plays a role. In the sphere of disciplined analysis, the main barrier to the Western acknowledgement of the importance of the Japanese miracle, as fact and model, can be found in the doctrines of philosophic and economic positivism. This body of thought, so pivotal to our tradition, from David Hume and Adam Smith to Sir Alfred Marshall and Rudolf Carnap, stands firmly in the way of recognizing that Japan is today the most important political system in the world.

Grounded in the scientific and philosophic doctrine of empiricism, the conviction that truth is defined by experience and sense perception alone, positivism casts a shadow on all the disciplines that might otherwise urge us to reflect more deeply on the political and economic dimensions of the Japanese national achievement. Political philosophy in the English-speaking world has yet to free itself from the corrosive impact of logical positivism. The logical positivist dogmatist dismisses all Japanese reflection on the science of nation-building as 'meaningless' because it consists of statements other than those of simple fact or logic.

Prisoners of historicist constraints, textual positivists forbid the creative re-interpretation of Japan's political tradition. Positivism *rules* the methodology of modern economics. Economic positivists reject the possibility of an economic miracle. Confronted with claims for the importance of the Japanese experience of government, the positivist rebuke is unambiguous: there was no miracle and therefore there can be no significance. At every turn, the main impulse of positivism is to deny Japanese greatness in the name of science and truth.

The stranglehold of positivist doctrine on economics conspires against any alternative approach or methodology. It is nearly imposs-ible to study the economic behaviour of any society in the modern university, especially in the English-speaking world, without taking an oath of allegiance to economic positivism. This fact of academic life has momentous implications for the empiricist, working in politi-cal science, for example, who wishes to study Japanese public policy or any other dimension of political life which intrudes on the eco-nomic. The fact that students of other branches of Western social science, such as sociology and anthropology, have freed themselves of this positivist straitjacket may explain why the revolutionary importance of the Japanese struggle to modernize was first given serious recognition by sociologists such as Ronald Dore and Ezra Vogel. Many sociologists, anthropologists and historians would find these positivist chains, at this late date, an intolerable, if not risible, burden that is demonstrably out of phase with the needs of the social scientist who is also a student of non-Western societies.

One conclusion seems irresistible. On four of the branches of human knowledge that are indispensable to any proper assessment and appreciation of Japan's rise to the status of the first modern non-White economic superpower – economics, political science, Western political philosophy and Japanese political thought – positivism exerts an influence that is as decisive as it is pernicious.

The limitations of social science, in the positivist mould, for the political scientist are deep-rooted. One of the most damaging errors has been the unwise equation of positivism with empiricism. Positiv-ism is rooted in empiricism; the reverse is not true. Over-reliance on vulgar versions of Newtonian physics and scientific logic has encouraged the imposition of methodological hierarchies that have been largely ignored by the front-line researcher. There is something fundamentally amiss with a scientific approach that has nothing

better to offer the practising political scientist than the sterile judgement that the methodological core of Japanese research is at best a
body of low-level empirical generalizations.

Such criticism points to the central flaw of modern positivism,
especially in the eyes of the political scientist committed to adapting
empirical strategies to the needs of cross-cultural understanding.
The ruling concern of the orthodox mainstream of European philosophy since Descartes has been the quest for certain knowledge.
This crusade has pressed philosophers, especially those working in
the Austrian and British positivist tradition, to draw the net of
critical enquiry too narrowly for the purposes of the student of other
cultures, and then to tyrannize over this narrowed sphere in such a
way as to preclude all but the most scientistic modes of social
research.

This quest for certainty means that pristine positivism sets the bar
of achievement for the social scientist too high. Aggressive positivists, with their scientific pretensions, obscure both the practical needs
and the workaday achievements of the empirical researcher. But
positivism is damaging in another way. It has frustrated the effort
of political scientists who seek to demonstrate, in Hegel's phrase,
'the world-historical significance' of post-war Japan. That positivism,
this rigorous body of clear methods and powerful insights, should
conspire so effectively against the proper recognition of modern
Japan's status as a canonic polity, is one of the great contradictions
of contemporary social science. But the problem is genuine and cuts
deep. It encourages the conclusion that for the student of Japanese
government, positivism, at least for the moment, is dead. Or should
be.

POSITIVIST CHAINS

Bergson did not simply react to what he believed was wrong with the
European mind. He wanted to absorb the entire body of science which
had been built up in the preceding decades and free it from arbitrary
philosophical ingredients.

Leszek Kolakowski

Liberation.

Jacques Maritain, on
first reading Bergson

The impact of positivist thought on the European sciences of nature

and society, especially in English-speaking countries, has been profound. Few theoretical issues in the physical sciences or in the study
of philosophy and social life can be discussed without reference to
this body of discourse, with its roots in classical Stoic thought, about
the nature of science and truth. The early history of American
political science, certainly from the time of Charles Merriam's work
in the 1920s, demonstrates the contemporary force of this
judgement.

Nevertheless, there are important reasons to believe that positivism's influence on what John Stuart Mill called 'the social science'
– which today includes the study of Japanese government – has
often been excessive. The core difficulty is a leap of logic. Because
positivism forms the air that a natural scientist breathes, it has been
insisted that students of society breathe nothing else. This has
been, to adapt J. L. Austin's famous remark, 'a first-water, ground-
floor mistake', the making of which has required a 'form of philosophical genius'. Such genius commands respect. But if positivism's
overweening ambitions are to be curbed by the student of Asia,
then this formidable scientific doctrine, in its classic European form,
must be understood with precision.

Positivism is a complex word. In *An Introduction to Modern
Political Theory*, Norman P. Barry assigns positivism two meanings:

> First, a positivist believes in the clear separation of fact and value
> and argues that theoretical and descriptive accounts of man and
> society can be made which do not involve evaluative
> judgments. . . . In the second and more extreme sense, it is the
> theory that only phenomena which are in principle capable of
> being observed are of any significance for social science.[20]

Barry's first meaning draws the vital distinction, so dear to the
founders of late nineteenth-century social science, between 'facts'
and 'values'. But in a British context, Barry's formulation is inevitably coloured by the assault of logical positivists on the truth claims
of statements about values and morality.

Barry's second meaning reflects a habitual move in British philosophy: the assigning of overlapping definitions to 'positivism' and
'empiricism'. Granted, an insistence on 'sense certainty' unites the
positivist and empiricist. But it is crucial for the student of Asian
politics who writes and thinks in the English language, and who is
therefore vulnerable to the pressures of Anglo-American philosophic tradition, to understand that positivism and empiricism reflect
different approaches to science. Indeed for the modern student of

non-Western cultures in particular, it is essential that one distinguish, radically, *between* these two methods.

A full grasp of this distinction requires the addition of a third meaning to Barry's definition – positivism: a school of thought that holds that science advances solely by the elaboration and testing of universal laws. Empiricism, unlike positivism, involves no commitment to such scientific law-making. It is nevertheless a genuine science. Nowhere are the constraints of social science's positivist chains more restricting or more damaging than in the positivist's rejection of the scientific status of pure empiricism.

In *Auguste Comte and Positivism* (1865), Mill isolated the various strands of argument that link and divide empiricism and positivism. He identified the central tenet of Comte's 'Positive Philosophy' in the following manner:

> We have no knowledge of anything but Phaenomena; and our knowledge of phaenomena is relative, not absolute. We know not the essence, nor the real mode of production, of any fact, but only its relations to other facts in the way of succession or similitude. These relations are constant; that is, always the same in the same circumstances. The constant resemblances which link phaenomena together, and the constant sequences which unite them as antecedent and consequent, are termed their laws. The laws of phaenomena are all we know respecting them.[21]

In this passage, Mill comes close to ascribing to Comte the view that facts are not real facts (their relations are not constant) unless they are ordered within a framework of scientific laws. Where does this leave the isolated empirical fact, the building block of so many of the social sciences?[22] In discussing the differing hierarchies of knowledge proposed by Comte and Herbert Spencer, Mill accused Spencer of failing to 'distinguish between the empirical stage of the cultivation of a branch of knowledge, and the scientific stage'.[23]

The contrast that Mill draws between 'the empirical' and 'the scientific' is what today would be between 'the empirical' and 'the positive'. At their core, history, political science, anthropology and sociology are empirical, while economics and a few other disciplines are committed to positivism. The two approaches are methodologically distinct. In practice, contemporary scholarship denies a hierarchy of 'stages', with the empirical yielding, with progress, to the positive. In theory, however, some contemporary social scientists, following in Mill's footsteps, continue to insist on the hierarchic approach which sets positivism above empiricism. This conflict between theory and research practice has been the stuff of repeated strife between social scientists for much of the past century, particularly in post-war America. Mill and Comte are the source of the problem. This is how Mill characterizes the empirical approach:

> The commencement of every study consists in gathering together unanalysed facts, and treasuring up such spontaneous generalizations as present themselves to natural sagacity. In this stage any branch of inquiry can be carried on independently of every other.[24]

Humanity's stock of unscientific observation, mediated by the more 'elementary sciences', forms the rockface for positivist labour. The key point is that Mill does not regard such empiricism as scientifically rigorous.

> But though detached truths relating to the more complex order of phaenomena may be empirically observed, and a few of them even scientifically established, contemporaneously with an early stage of some of the sciences anterior in the scale, such detached truths ... do not constitute a science. What is known of a subject, only becomes a science when it is made a connected body of truth ... and each particular truth can be recognized as a case of the operation of wider laws.[25]

The intellectual consequences of Mill's view are unambiguous. *Pace* the way the pursuit of knowledge is actually organized in the modern university, Mill and his heirs, if consistent, hold that political science, anthropology, sociology and history are not sciences as long as their research findings do not generate universal positivist laws. Rather these would-be sciences stand as the inferior products of natural sagacity, unscientific empirical observation and unanalysed facts. The implicit rejection of the cultural sciences, which, for more than a century now, have borne the main burden of examining non-Western societies, is damningly clear. Such rejection must be kept in mind by the empiricist who studies Asian societies when he reads Mill, Comte and Emile Durkheim, the greatest of all French sociologists. Positivism offers clearly no quarter to the thinker who sees Japan as a 'text' (*tekusuto toshite Nippon*) or who is committed to an empiricist-inspired classicism.[26]

Comte's rules

Auguste Comte has been called the father of social science. He invented the word 'sociology' and gave the term 'positivist philosophy' something of its modern meaning. He has been described as the most widely known but perhaps least read of the positivists, but his impact on the orthodox definition of the scientific method has been formidable. Comte's rules are of particular value to anyone who would distinguish precisely between classical positivism and practical workaday empiricism.

In *Knowledge and Human Interests*, Jürgen Habermas summarizes Comte's influential set of methodological rules in the following manner:

1. All knowledge has to prove itself through the *sense certainty* of systematic observation that secures intersubjectivity. (*le réel*)
2. *Methodical certainty* is just as important as sense certainty... the reliability of scientific knowledge is guaranteed by unity of method. (*la certitude*)
3. The exactitude of our knowledge is guaranteed only by the formally cogent construction of theories that allow the deduction of lawlike hypotheses. (*le précis*)
4. Scientific cognition must be technically utilizable.... Science makes possible technical control over processes of both nature and society... the power of control over nature and society can be multiplied by following rationalist principles – not through the blind expansion of empirical research, but through the development and the unification of theories. (*l'utile*)
5. Our knowledge is in principle *unfinished and relative*, in accordance with the 'relative nature of the positive spirit'. (*le relative*)[27]

It is my view that empiricism and positivism, properly understood, share only two of Comte's rules: *le réel* and *le relative*. Whatever the importance of *la certitude* and *le précis* to the advance of positivist philosophy and some forms of scientific knowledge, their application to pure empiricism is limited. Any attempt to enforce a positivist orthodoxy grounded in these two rules should be rejected by the empirical researcher as scientistic dogmatism. As for *l'utile*, it is not a crucial concern of the empiricist, but the search for technically utilizable knowledge must rest on a sound empirical foundation.

As *la certitude* and *le précis* form the linchpin of positivist thinking about science, the scholarly implications of these two rules demands closer scrutiny. The scope and limitations of Comte's rules are well illustrated by G. H. von Wright's version of the central tenets of the positivist doctrine. According to Wright, the fundamental principles that underwrite the positivist approach to science are:

1. *Methodological monism*, or the idea of the unity of scientific method amidst the diversity of subject matter of scientific investigation.
2. The exact natural sciences, in particular mathematical physics, set a methodological ideal for all other sciences.
3. Causal scientific explanation which consists in the subsumption of individual cases under hypothetically assumed general laws of nature.[28]

What is the status of such ideals in the actual practice of the modern student of Japanese politics and society? First, the writings of most twentieth-century political experts on Japanese politics evince not a hint of recognition that mathematical physics or symbolic logic constitutes a workable theoretical model, let alone the sole ideal method, for political scientific research. Second, methodological monism – which for Wright means that only the mathematical model is legitimate, and that all scientists worthy of the name must observe it – is rejected, in practice, by almost all contemporary Western students of Japanese government. The notion that political science is in some useful sense 'immature' but on the road towards becoming a 'hard' or physical science has had little impact on the contemporary academic understanding of the workings or institutional arrangements or theoretical underpinnings of modern Japanese government (I discuss the recent controversy over rational choice and Asian studies at the conclusion of Chapter 4). Third, aside from the odd dabbler in rational choice or market theory, the goal of formulating general positive laws, such as pertain in positive economics, has had no obvious influence on the evolution of political scientific research on Japan. This was true even in the 1960s during the greatest flowering of the Modernization School.

If, however, the political science of Japan is not a positive science, then what kind of science is it? One answer might be that the political science of Japan is an empirically grounded word science; not a mathematically grounded positive science or an underdeveloped version of positive economics. To assert as much is to attempt to right an ancient wrong: the nominalist fallacy or the pronounced tendency among social scientific positivists to take 'the linguistic character of their knowledge for granted, as if language were nothing more than a transparent and unproblematic medium'.[29]

The theoretical framework that underwrites the work of political scientists who study empirical reality reaches beyond the positivist's insistence that his method alone provides a secure foundation for the growth of scientific knowledge. This is not to deny the huge contribution of positivists to the Western intellectual tradition, but is to acknowledge that it is sometimes necessary to curb the ambitious excesses of scientistic positivism. Such rebellions against positivist dogma have been a persistent feature of European intellectual life. At the turn of the last century, for example, when Jacques Maritain and Charles Peguy first encountered Henri Bergson's critique of the scientism of the French historian Hippolyte Adolphe Taine (1828–93) and the Orientalist Ernest Renan (1823–92), they spoke of a 'liberation' from the dead hand of positivism.[30] Bergson was seen as freeing French intellectual life:

> From scientism and Taine's or Renan's 'religion of science', from the belief that natural science, as it was constituted in the second half of the nineteenth century, had provided us with an unsurpassed model of genuine knowledge, that all criteria of validity and truth had been established in the procedures of empirical and mathematical science and that all cognitive results worthy of the name derive their legitimacy from the correct application of these criteria.... From mechanism, that is, from the belief that all events that occur in the universe consist of the spatial displacement of material particles according to the laws of Newtonian mechanics and that, consequently, it is the natural ideal of all sciences – in particular of the life sciences – to explain by those laws all the phenomena they study, and so ultimately to reduce all branches of knowledge to physics.[31]

So, once again, at the close of one century and the beginning of another in the unbroken millenial quest of European science for truth and knowledge, positivism must be challenged for reasons old and new. Again, much of the criticism made here echoes that of Bergson. So, in one sense, this is an attempt to continue the long dance of the Western mind, the repeating cycle of the rise and fall of positivist influence on European thought. But the pattern of this motion of the spirit is not a circle but a spiral. Natural science has moved on, at many points, from the unimaginative rigidities of late nineteenth-century positivism and the unhappy impact of Newton on Enlightenment social theory.

Today the scale must be tipped once more, away from positivistic dogma toward less scientific forms of knowledge and thought. This is necessary because twentieth-century social science, and not only in Britain, has been kept off-balance by the imperious thrust of nineteenth-century science *mediated by logical positivism*. Kolakowski himself has seen the logical positivism of Russell and the Vienna Circle as an alarmed intellectual response to an endangered civilization.[32] The horrors of the First World War gave credence, for many, to Julien Benda's assault on what he saw as the dangerous irrationalism at work in Bergson's philosophy. An empirical critique of positivism now proposes no return to the vitalism of D. H. Lawrence. More important, it is real changes in the real world – the rise of Japan and much of East Asia with her – that encourages a revolt against positivist doctrine. This larger picture means that no empiricist engaged in thinking and writing about non-Western societies, given the actual practice and authority of the political scientific study of Japan today, should be thwarted by the positivist strictures reflected in Comte's insistence on the indispensability of *la certitude* and *le précis*.

Comte's commitment to *le réel* is a different matter. When the French thinker demands that 'all knowledge has to prove itself through the *sense certainty* of systematic observation that secures intersubjectivity' then the practical empiricist would certainly agree that intersubjectivity is important. But neither sense certainty nor intersubjectivity (the ability of one scholar to reproduce the findings of another) functions as a scientific guarantee in social science as the natural scientist might expect (see Chapter 4). But, regardless of these problems, it must be understood that intersubjectivity is not a matter of shared opinions but of shared judgements by comparable authorities, who, as a result of their training and experience, can collectively assess the truth claims of a piece of research or reasoning. In this sense, Ibsen was right: 'Truth is with the few'.

A sceptic might argue that intersubjectivity mediated by training and guild-like standards of assessment dilutes any claim to objectivity because research findings are validated only by other scientists. One must live with such dilutions. Science is not a democracy where the truth is determined by votes, but rather a semi-closed community of comparable authorities, and must, in this sense, be unabashedly elitist. To paraphrase Bayle, it is the quality of one's mind and ideas, not civic equality, that determines one's status in what the seventeenth century termed 'the republic of letters' and we today call the global scientific community.

It must furthermore be conceded that Comte's demand for intersubjectivity does not make clear at what point in the research process the claims of intersubjectivity should apply. It is one thing for the Anglo-American critic of European introspectionism, after

Descartes, to insist that the insights of the probing mind must finally submit to the test of intersubjectivity – the reproducibility of experimental tests or empirical findings – and quite another for the social scientist to cultivate an occupational prejudice against disciplined reasoning by the individual scholar with himself.

To give birth to a major theory, such as Weber's Protestant ethic thesis or Durkheim's theory of suicide or even Chalmers Johnson's notion of Japan as a developmental state, one must think through a set of taxing conceptual difficulties. Such theories are not, in essence, the fruit of intersubjective debate. Quite the contrary, intellectual creativity begins with the thinker. He is the prime mover in this process of mental invention. Testing a scientific thesis, or indeed a positive law, is another matter. But a committed empiricist should never encourage opposition to theorizing: thinking about one's evidence, its implications and its suitability for empirical testing. The dangers of factless theorizing in the social sciences are much exaggerated; superficial *ad hoc* reasoning about empirical data is all too common.

In short, the empiricist, especially in a branch of area studies such as Japanese politics, must know how his own mind works. The music of thought is first heard from within. It is no accident that some of the most powerful insights and ideas in the whole tradition of European thought, from Archimedes in his garden to Keynes in his bath, have been the product of a distinct 'apartness' or meditative solitude. The claims of intersubjectivity do not mean submitting to 'group think'. Any scholar who believes otherwise needs to brood harder on the life and intellectual methods of Ludwig Wittgenstein. However defined, empiricism must not be a conspiracy against thought. Certainly the mental demands of the objective penetration of another society or polity – the cardinal intellectual move in cross-cultural understanding that defines every branch of area studies – means that 'unthinking empiricism' should be a contradiction in terms.

Comte's first rule also touches on another key empiricist concern: sense certainty. The vehement orthodoxy of the modern heirs of the medieval empiricists will not be understood unless one recalls that they were rebelling against rationalism: the great metaphysical tradition of reasoning from first principles. Rationalism is allied with the powers of introspection and logic; empiricism with observation or what Comte called 'sense experience'.

Factual knowledge is the fruit of the senses and experience. If a fact is defined as 'an event or thing known to have happened or existed', then the sceptic's question is: how does one *know*? In what sense, for example, does sitting in the senior common room of an Oxford college reading about the results of a recent Japanese election constitute an empirical act? The data in the article in *The Times* or *The Independent* will have come either from a Western wire service or the paper's correspondent in Tokyo. As almost no foreign correspondent working in Japan actually reads Japanese, the reporter in question will probably have gleaned his information from either one of Japan's English-language newspapers, such as *The Japan Times*, or a press agency translation, which will rely on the labours of their own reporters or on compilations from the Japanese-language press. But at no point in this information chain has anyone actually 'observed' a Japanese voter voting (an issue complicated by the fact that the Japanese use a secret ballot system) or has been involved in the vote count which generates the data. This would be true even if the Oxford don in our example were somewhat flamboyantly reading the election results as reported in the *Asahi Shinbun*.

What is empirical about this whole process is the conviction that, at least in theory, a trained observer *could* have stood in every Japanese voting booth on election day or that a researcher could actually go through every ballot, after the fact. Otherwise the whole system works on trust. One assumes that almost every Japanese voter has signed the correct politician's name to his ballot and that the count itself has been proper and reasonably accurate. The methodological vulnerabilities of electoral analysis must be stressed, however, because behaviouralism and other extreme forms of quantitative empiricism have lent a suspect glamour to psephology.

If measurement and systematic observation form the heart of the empiricist's endeavour, then the political scientist does very little of either in election reporting. Analysis of the raw or filtered data is another matter. Some tough-minded empiricists are less compromising. They insist that one must do one's own measuring and systematic observing, and not leave it to non-scientists, however professional. In other words, the strict empiricist does his own field work.

Field work looms large in research about a society other than one's own. For early twentieth-century anthropology, the pursuit of sense certainty and intersubjective truth has been the stuff of an anti-positivist revolution. The anti-positivist character of this revolt against Comte has been misunderstood. In *The Quest for Mind: Piaget, Lévi-Strauss and the Structuralist Movement*, Howard Gardner observes that before the rise of field-work methodology,

small coteries of dedicated scholars were ensconced in the libraries of London, Oxford, Cambridge and Edinburgh, poring over
the records made by missionaries, travelers, and adventurers of
their encounters with primitive people all over the 'uncivilized'
world and the British empire.[33]

Their method was grounded in the positivist systems of Comte
and Herbert Spencer that Mill endorsed. These systems posited a
hierarchy of stages in the progress of the human species, from
primitive savagery to the high civilities and liberal culture of nineteenth-century Europe. These 'armchair anthropologists' defined a
niche for each newly discovered tribe, consistent with its relative
state of development in the vast tableau of human progress. It was
in reaction to such pseudo-positivist laws of human advance that
the twentieth-century concept of field work came into being, most
notably in the empirical-based anthropology of Franz Boas. In transforming anthropology's paradigm, Boas, together with Bronislaw
Malinowski, destroyed Comte's positivist programme. What were
the sources of this revolution? This is how Gardner explains it:
'Following the example of the physical sciences, Boas inspired a
whole generation of American anthropologists to make careful eth-
nological investigations "in the field" and to eschew *a priori* generalizations about matters which could not be verified empirically'.[34]

Here is another example of the unfruitful elision of empiricism
and positivism. To the degree that the physical sciences offer empirical resistance to '*a priori* theorizing', Boas was following the
example of the physical sciences; to the degree that the physical
sciences derive their central methodology from the Newtonian
agenda of universal laws, Boas and Malinowski were *not* sailing in
the wake of the natural sciences.

Certainly from the standpoint of the Western student of non-
Western societies, it is obvious that Boas and Malinowski were
breaking with the entire Comtean paradigm and its complex inter-
weaving of the laws of progress and positive law-making. Again,
when the programme is viewed from the vantage-point of the
empirically trained Orientalist or area student, what is striking about
the classical anthropologists is their rejection or dilution of the *a
priori* assumptions of positivist laws which reflect the universal
ambitions of the Enlightenment project, from Newton and Smith to
Comte and Walras.

This is how we should understand Malinowski's claim (discussed
in Chapter 2) that 'The ethnographer's goal is to grasp the native's

point of view, his relation to life, to realize his vision of the world . . . there may emerge [in the investigator] a feeling of solidarity with the endeavors and ambitions of these natives'.[35] Whether the social scientist's 'tribe' be Trobriand Islanders, French Catholics or Japanese voters, the goal of 'grasping the native's point of view' stands at the heart of research in area studies. This makes the pursuit of 'sense certainty' an infinitely subtle exercise of mind. One must not overstate the importance of the contribution of the physical sciences, as positive sciences, to this enterprise.

Indeed the positivist sciences may be seen to have conspired against this endeavour. The dismissive Anglo-American attitude towards Dilthey's insistence on the importance of the intuitive grasp of an alien epoch or society is but one legacy of this conspiracy. The legacy of Dilthey should encourage one to ask which method is more consistent with Malinowski's call for 'empirical grasp': Newtonian mechanics or the German schools of hermeneutics, social phenomenology and the philosophy of *verstehen* (understanding)? The answer is not Newtonian physics if the goal is to meet the anthropologist's need for emphatic immersion in an alien community.

The cardinal impulse of positivism is conquest. Reality is to be subdued or, in Bacon's portentous phrase, to be put to the question (that is, to be tortured). The stance of the anthropologist tends to be rather different. He listens. He heeds the truth of his reality. He bends to it. The key rubric is responsion, not penetration.[36]

This issue is central to any discussion of how to analyse data from another culture. Take the example posed above of interpreting Japanese election results. The need to understand the foreigner's point of view, in this case the *Weltanschauung* of the Japanese voter, demands not only a knowledge of the Japanese language and the structure of values that influence how votes are cast but also how Japanese commentators assess such voting behaviour. This is the empirical shore that must be hugged. Intersubjectivity must refer not only to the communication between authorities of comparable competence but also between the researcher and the person or community that he is studying. Is there a better way to fight the entanglements of a flawed Orientalism?

The second and third of Comte's methodological rules are not taken seriously by most political scientists working in area studies. The majority feels little compulsion to pursue either *la certitude* supposedly guaranteed by methodological monism, or *le précis* promised by deductive law-making. In contrast, the fourth rule, 'scientific cognition must be technically utilizable' (*l'utile*), acquires special meaning when focused on modern Japan. Japanese achievements in the field of technology require no elaboration. But the problem of the utility or practicality of research results has also a Darwinian dimension. Darwin's late nineteenth-century earthquake transformed the thrust of Comtean utility. Not only did Darwinism threaten the dominant position of Cartesianism and Kantianism in European thought, but it also imposed the radical view that the validity of human knowledge is determined by its 'biological usefulness' (Kolakowski). The resulting pragmatic turn in Western thought and ideology, as reflected in social Darwinism, reflects that same bundle of late nineteenth-century influences that formed what I have termed the 'thinking nationalism' that has stimulated Japan's modernization programme.[37] This is not only because Japan entered 'modernity' when social Darwinism and the doctrine of the 'survival of the fittest' dominated the intellectual and political horizon of the imperialist West, but also because a pronounced tendency in pre-Meiji nativist thought had laid the groundwork for ready Japanese absorption of this alien idea. Indeed, Japan's establishment ethos may be uniquely attuned to the kinds of knowledge that qualify for the status of what Comte called '*l'utile*'.

Durkheim's Catholics

A divided intellectual inheritance haunts the student of modern Japan. The post-medieval empirical tradition, from Francis Bacon to Bronislaw Malinowski, underwrites the research methods of most political scientists, historians, sociologists and anthropologists who study Japan. For the political scientist, in particular, the shift in European sensibility that stands behind modern print journalism, forms another pillar of his approach.

For the empirical political scientist who would free his discipline from the demands of the positivist ontology, the most striking fact about the positivist tradition is its formidable staying power. Hegel, Marx, Darwin, Nietzsche, Weber, Pareto and Freud have all left their mark on mainstream political science. But for almost the entire course of the twentieth century, the century that gave birth to political science, it has been the positivist tradition, much as Mill and Comte understood it, that has offered the most sustained challenge to political scientific practice, especially in the United States. Positivist discontent with the merely empirical has been at the heart of this crusade. Outside the protected ghetto of Japanese political studies, the climate has often been cold, even bitter.

Given the evident attractions of positivist laws, why has the empiricist resisted the call of these scientific sirens? The brief answer is that the empiricist and positivist seek radically different kinds of knowledge. The point will be lost on any proponent of the 'Anglo-American' tradition of philosophy and social research who insists that empiricism and positivism are merely alternative terms for the same school. The difference may be illustrated by reference to the positivist interpretation of Emile Durkheim's classic study of why Protestants commit suicide more often than Catholics.

In *Social Theory and Social Structure* (1949), Robert Merton offered his famous restatement of Durkheim's insight: 'It has long been established as a statistical uniformity that in a variety of populations, Catholics have a lower suicide rate than Protestants'.[38] With an eye to the potential of Durkheim's insight to yield a positive law-like statement of some predictive power, Merton set out the Durkheimian thesis in the following formal manner:

1. Social cohesion provides psychic support to group members subjected to acute stresses and anxieties.
2. Suicide rates are functions of *unrelieved* anxieties and stresses to which persons are subjected.
3. Catholics have greater social cohesion than Protestants.
4. Therefore, lower suicide rates should be anticipated among Catholics than among Protestants.[39]

The focus of much discussion in the literature on methodology in the social sciences, Merton's formulation has been regarded as a masterpiece of interpretative reasoning. It is the kind of mental exercise that has encouraged generations of sociologists to believe that their subject is making progress toward the still distant goal of becoming a natural science.

The gloss of Richard J. Bernstein in *The Restructuring of Social and Political Theory* sets out the scientific goals embodied in Merton's formulation:

Merton is alert to the close connection between scientific explanation, precision, testability, and prediction. A well-formulated scientific theory is one that explains by showing how empirical phenomena and regularities can be derived from theoretical assumptions and appropriate initial conditions. But it must be stated with sufficient precision so that it is testable. Otherwise we would be unable to distinguish it from *post factum* explanation, since these pseudo-scientific explanations can also satisfy the criterion of derivability.[40]

Bearing in mind Bernstein's warning about 'pseudo-scientific explanations', it might be useful to set out an example of how purely empirical knowledge may or may not affect Merton's formulation of Durkheim's suicide thesis. In Catholic religious doctrine, certainly at the time of the publication of Durkheim's *Le Suicide* (Paris, 1897), the notion of 'sins against the Holy Ghost' formed part of the curriculum of Catholic education of primary-school children. Sins against the Holy Ghost were regarded as particularly grievous because they were unforgivable, where the term 'unforgivable' was not a loose use of language but referred to sins that were beyond the reach of priestly absolution in the confessional. Given the pivotal place of the sacrament of penance in Catholic belief, the notion of sins against the Holy Ghost was unsettling, even terrifying for the late nineteenth-century Catholic believer. Violation of this ban guaranteed eternal damnation. Among the most censured sins against the Holy Ghost was suicide.

This is the kind of knowledge that the anthropologist who makes pre-1963 French Catholics his tribe will know. Durkheim was, of course, familiar with such religious doctrines. But the implications of such tribal knowledge for Merton's formulation are also obvious. His scientific insight might be restated in the following manner:

1 Social cohesion provides psychic support to group members subjected to acute stresses and anxieties, but such social cohesion (i.e. religious discipline) may also be the cause of stress and anxieties as well as a remedy.
2 Suicide rates are functions of unrelieved anxieties and stresses to which persons are subjected; some of these stresses increase the suicide rate; others reduce it.
3 French Catholics may have greater social cohesion than Protestants (an intuitive insight at best), but live under moral prohibitions against suicide of the strongest form possible under Catholic religious discipline.
4 Therefore, lower suicide rates should be anticipated among Catholics than among Protestants.

Bernstein praises Merton's schema for the way it nicely incorporates Popper's demand for scientific theories which are stated in a such a way as may be disproved:

Merton also recognizes that in systematic theory there is explicitly or implicitly the need to employ laws – or, more cautiously, lawlike statements. Such laws must be carefully distinguished from mere empirical generalizations. . . . This is illustrated when Merton tells us that Durkheim's theoretic assumptions would enable us to predict that, if there should be a decrease in social cohesion among Catholics, then (*ceteris paribus*) we would expect in this group a tendency toward increased suicide rates.[41]

A student of tribal knowledge might argue that a decline in religious faith among Catholics, if it extended to a lapse in belief in doctrines such as sins against the Holy Ghost, might be more to the point than the vague notion of 'general social cohesion'. But for the empiricist, the real issue is otherwise.

The point that must be stressed is not how an anthropologist's tribal knowledge of late nineteenth-century French Catholics might further a Mertonian scientific campaign, but rather whether such tribal knowledge falls under the damning category of 'pseudo-scientific or *post factum* explanation' or 'mere empirical generalization'. This matters because Durkheim is keen to argue that the Christian ban on suicide was essentially the same for both Protestants and Catholics during the late nineteenth century.[42]

Bernstein's summary offers telltale signs of a crucial misunderstanding. His chapter that deals with Merton is titled 'Empirical Theory'. But is its subject matter empiricism or positivism? The implied dismissal of pure empiricism is forthright and confident. Confronted by Durkheim's research, the pure empiricist will seize on facts such as the Catholic belief in sins against the Holy Ghost. For him, this is one of those single, isolated (in Mill's sense) but also decisive facts that illuminate the whole intellectual horizon at issue in Durkheim's research. It is the sort of fact that forms the Holy Grail of the pure empiricist. By comparison, the issues of testablity or predictability are interesting diversions. The challenge of Popperian falsibility may be resolved by sampling Catholic religious belief and practice for the period in question. Once this is done, however, that question is closed. What the empiricist will seek to confirm or deny is whether claims about prohibitions on suicide were indeed uniform across different Christian communities (Catholic as well as Protestant). Whatever the positivist may claim, this empirical quest is not pseudo-science.

The positivist reading of *Le Suicide* only highlights a broad issue which affects social science as a whole. Let us examine three examples of such 'decisive facts' from Japanese politics in the late 1980s and early 1990s. Take, first, the resignation of Watanabe Michio as Japanese foreign minister in the spring of 1993. Watanabe served as a pillar of the Miyazawa government in part because he was an obvious candidate to succeed Miyazawa as president of the ruling Liberal Democrats. His departure weakened the Miyazawa government, which fell shortly thereafter for failing to carry out political reform. But Watanabe's withdrawal from the government and stage centre of party politics also undermined the cohesion of his faction. If he was not going to stand for the party presidency, what was the faction's *raison d'être*? Watanabe's resignation also called into doubt his future in party politics. It signalled to all his friends and opponents that power, real or potential, was slipping from his grasp. His vulnerability on this count vividly demonstrated the reverse side of the coin of traditional Japanese veneration for age: the sharp dismissal of the impotent of any age. The question was: why did he resign?

The official reasons were vague or forced. Imprecise references to illness and age were made in the quality press. The hospital that admitted Watanabe after his resignation refused all comment on any rumours of serious illness for fear of destroying Watanabe's career.

Two years later, after Miyazawa and his ruling Liberal Democratic Party had been swept from power in the summer of 1993, there was a flurry of speculation that Watanabe might succeed Prime Minister Hosokawa. Failing that, strenuous efforts were made by Ozawa Ichiro and his allies in the Shinseito party to get Watanabe to quit the LDP and join the anti-LPD ruling coalition. Again, rumours about Watanabe's health were rampant. If and when Watanabe, who has not looked well for years, does die of a wasting disease, then the truth about the final phase of his political career will be clarified. Until then political analysts will not know whether Watanabe's health was the vital issue or not. But the larger point is that such facts, and not testability or prediction or falsifiability, are what the pure empiricist is in search of. Are positivists saying that such facts are not worth knowing?

In the Toyo Shinkin affair, some of Japan's most reputable financial institutions were involved in huge loans, secured with forged deposit certificates, to an Osaka restaurateur. The following scandal resulted in the collapse of Toyo Shinkin, an Osaka-based bank, which allegedly issued some $2.6 billion in forged certificates of deposit (CDs) to Ms Onoue Nui, a remarkably well-connected businesswoman and stock-market speculator. She used these CDs to borrow 179 billion yen from other financial institutions, apparently to manipulate the market. Her victims included such pillars of the Japanese financial system as Fuji Bank and the Industrial Bank of Japan (IBJ). When Toyo Shinkin went bankrupt with reported debts of 260 billion yen, the Ministry of Finance and the private banking sector were forced to mount a huge rescue operation.

How did a bank such as IBJ fall foul of Onoue? A variety of explanations has been offered. But one in particular depends on knowledge of a single, decisive fact. If Tokyo press corps rumour, current at the time that the story broke, was accurate, then a key moment in the Toyo Shinkin scandal came and went when the IBJ's loans at issue were challenged at a board meeting of the bank. A single board member raised his voice, and declared that he would take responsibility for the matter. Consistent with Japanese corporate culture at this most senior level, the probing of the matter at board level ended there.

The answer to many questions that the scholar studying the Toyo Shinkin scandal would pose hangs on the 'fact' of that single boardroom action. What exactly was going on in the heads of the members of the IBJ board on the day in question? The scholar may never know the truth of the matter with certainty. Indeed the rumour may have been false. But what is beyond dispute is that this is the sort of fact that the empirical scholar seeks to learn the truth about. For such an empiricist, teasing out the true story of the Toyo Shinkin affair is more important than any competing claims for facts that are testable, predictable or falsifiable in Popper's sense.

The Recruit scandal of the late 1980s illustrates the point with even greater force. As part of its campaign to win friends and influence policy at the privileged heart of the Japanese establishment, Recruit-Cosmos, the giant media firm, reportedly distributed company shares to a long list of politicians and even to a few bureaucrats. The resulting influence-peddling scandal brought down the government of Prime Minister Takeshita Noboru in 1989. The affair was thought by many to demonstrate how closed the post-war alliance of the Japanese elite remains to penetration by new firms and industries, both foreign and domestic.

The Recruit affair may have contributed significantly to the divisions that ended the long unbroken reign of the LDP in 1993. But if press instincts were correct, then this business was important in an entirely different way. Media gossip insisted that one of the key players in the scandal was a member of one of Japan's caste minorities. If this were true, this 'fact' would force scholars to recast their view of post-war Japan's social make-up and the ways by which Japan's minorities have effectively subverted majoritarianism. Such 'facts' might even help to shatter a major Japanese social taboo. Yet, this is precisely the kind of fact that positivism tries to bury.

Whatever positivists may argue about the methodological naivety of pure empiricism, political science must embrace such empirical knowledge. It must borrow from news reporting and analysis. For the Japanese political scientist, tribal knowledge is tacit, intuitive as well as empiric. It consists of a vast accumulation of facts, insights, interpretations, arguments and educated guesses. Many of these facts – election results, for example – form part of a recognized body of public knowledge. But many others consist of what an anthropologist might call the 'knowledge of his tribe'. Most important of all, the positivist must learn to appreciate how the isolated facts uncovered by the pure empiricist may humble the proudest systems of positivist reasoning.

ECONOMIC POSITIVISM

> Economists: recycled Orientalists
> Edward Said

No creation of the European mind has contributed more to the neglect of Japan's canonic achievement than positivist economics. The procrustean tendencies in Western economic analysis of Japan are rooted in the economist's commitment to positivist laws. Positivist law-making forms the indispensable groundwork for all the main schools of contemporary economic theory: neo-Keynesianism, monetarism, the New Classical School and the branch of Marxism that remains loyal to Engels despite Lukács' famous 1923 dissent. If Japan's post-war miracle, and East Asia's with it, calls into question, in any significant way, the elaborate structure of positivist laws which underpin economic analysis, then the way that economic theory is taught and economic policy implemented will need to be rethought.

To urge this huge endeavour is to recall the sustained intellectual and moral assault on classical economics which Marx developed in *A Contribution to the Critique of Political Economy* (1859). The Marxist analogy speaks to the project proposed here in two important ways. First, Marx's programme failed. In a way untrue of Kuhn's narration of the scientific revolutions which we associate with Newton or Faraday, the Marxist example presents a picture of conscious challenge and defeat in which many Marxists have rethought their intellectual positions in the face of contrary scientific evidence. But the larger point must be that classical political economy is an astonishing achievement of the human intellect that not even the genius of Marx could overturn. So in the Marxist precedent we have a powerful reminder of the formidable nature of the task at hand.

Second, Marx was a positivist. In contrast, the critique proposed here is empirical. Exploiting the empirical evidence, my aim is merely to plant seeds of doubt. To this end, I ask in what ways do three recent examples of *empirical* dissent by economists from the orthodox analysis of economic policy in Japan, South Korea and Taiwan invite the social and political scientist to rebel against the claims of economic positivism?

Doubting positivists

Since the publication of *MITI and the Japanese Miracle* in 1982, scepticism about the soundness of the positivist approach has spread in the face of many obstacles. Perhaps inevitably, most of the progress to date has been empirical, not positivist. But, despite the well-established division of scholarly labour between economists and political scientists, the most consequential demonstrations of a new understanding of economic behaviour have been produced by economists themselves. If Japan's world-historical significance is to be affirmed, then the work of such doubting positivists will prove indispensable to the reform of economics. Sydney Crawcour, Robert Wade and Laura d'Andrea Tyson have in different ways hammered fresh cracks into the edifice of positivist economics as it influences our understanding of modern Japan.

These three economists are positivists to their fingertips. They see the scientific problem posed by Japan's rise through the lens of classic liberal economic orthodoxy. What is striking in the writings of all three economists is that the system of positivist laws which structures orthodox thinking has not prevented them from grasping some of the central truths about Japanese economic reality that empirical analysis would teach. Most important of all, they are as clear as positivism allows about what is at stake in East Asia's modern ascent.

Thus Crawcour, the Australian economic historian, stresses the surprising advantages of economic backwardness. It is precisely because the West offered Meiji Japan a model of development that 'a government with the will and the means to carry out or coordinate investment in new industries can play an important role'.[43] Crawcour believes that leaders of Meiji Japan

> had the knowledge, the will, and the means to play such a role, and they had no ideological inhibitions about doing so. They had a working model, as it were, of an industrial economy acquired from observing Britain, France, Germany and the United States.[44]

What then of the positivist position that government is, by definition, no competition for the unhindered flowering of market forces? Crawcour accepts that 'some economists oppose state intervention on the grounds that it cannot raise total output above the level that would be produced by the operation of competitive markets'.[45] But he insists also that:

> Free competitive markets are not, however, necessarily the best strategy for long-run dynamic growth. Specifically, market forces do not maximize long-run growth when the returns from an investment depend on other developments outside the investor's control. . . . A coal mine might not be profitable without a railway to carry its product to the market, but a railway might not be economical without the development of both the coal mine and other industries along its route. Yet all of these might be highly productive investments as parts of a state-supported development program.[46]

Crawcour's assessment of state-led industrialization by the Meiji regime is unambiguous and inevitably crowds positivist dogma. Contrary to free-market reasoning, the Japanese government did not simply provide an infrastructure or merely secure a favourable business climate, thus leaving investment and production decisions to be determined by market forces. Indeed, the evidence suggests that in a number of important economic sectors, the Japanese authorities acted to pre-empt investment and production decisions by the private sector, in the process overriding such considerations as relative factor prices and demand conditions. As is true of no other modern polity, the Meiji state confounds the positivist logic of economic theory after Adam Smith. When Crawcour suggests that state intervention by the Japanese government may have brought more growth than would otherwise have occurred, he knocks at the door of the world-historical significance of modern Japan.

Crawcour's stress on institutional factors in Japan's modern rise has resulted in his being labelled as an 'institutionalist', in contrast with the pure positivism of the free-market theorist. But Crawcour is better understood as an economic empiricist. He exploits the historical facts about Japan to restrain the procrustean tendencies at work in theoretical concepts such as 'the invisible hand', 'demand conditions' and 'relative factor prices', all of which derive their explanatory efficacy from the places that they occupy in the elaborate intellectual system of academic positivism as practised by the modern economist. The 'proof' of the Japanese economic miracle will be found in such empiricism and perhaps nowhere else.

Whatever its flaws, economic positivism is powerful science. But because of its normative ambitions, positivism is also open to ideological abuse. This defect has subverted the sound understanding of East Asian politics by Western social scientists since 1945. This is the chief warning that Robert Wade offers the student of Japan in *Governing the Market: Economic Theory and the Role of Government in East Asian Industrialization* (1991).[47]

The quest for proof of the effectiveness of Japanese industrial policy has always been a two-pronged effort. Economists have not established, on empirical grounds, the contrary view that industrial policy must be inferior to unregulated markets. The positivist critique of East Asian industrial strategies is rooted not primarily in the *facts* of the case (although many respectable facts are cited), but in a complex *theory* of economic behaviour derived from studying non-Asian societies, particularly Britain and America. Wade is unambiguous on this crucial issue:

> The question of whether measures designed by a well-meaning bureaucracy can achieve results superior to those which a more liberal market system would produce is impossible to answer conclusively; what would have happened in the absence of intervention is always unknown. Nonetheless, economists from Adam Smith onwards have not hesitated to make strong assertions, both positive and negative, about the effectiveness of government intervention without offering serious evidence to support their claims.[48]

In the absence of what Wade calls 'serious evidence', economists have offered an elaborate theory, at once mathematically elegant and factually impoverished. Their 'strong assertions' follow, as night the day, from a commitment to positivism as a method. For this commitment, East Asian studies have paid a heavy price. Nowhere has this been more true than in the study of the economies of

Taiwan and South Korea. Wade's review of the relevant academic literature paints an unhappy picture. It would appear that for the past half century the positivist Procrustes, stimulated by cold-war anti-communism, has systematically falsified the economic portrait of two of East Asia's most important polities.

This is a grave charge, but Wade does not flinch from carrying the battle to the positivist lines. Economists have long insisted, for example, that South Korea, like Japan, operates on free-market principles. But, according to Wade, 'the locus classicus of the view that Korea has had a relatively free trade regime, the study by Larry Westphal and Kwang Suk Kim (1982), suffers from serious methodological problems and uses data from one year only'.[49]

Blinded by positivist theoretical expectations, economists have tended to confine their research to confirming evidence. As a result of such efforts, Taiwan, for example, 'seems to meet the neoclassical growth conditions unusually well'.[50] But Wade goes on to observe that 'other evidence shows that the government has been intervening for decades, often quite aggressively, to alter the trade and industrial profile of the economy in ways that it judged to be desirable'.[51]

In economic studies of Taiwanese and South Korean development, there has been a pronounced tendency to neglect the importance of the pre-war and inter-war periods. The relative underdevelopment of both countries during the 1950s, for example, has been stressed, in Wade's view, in order to give an exaggerated weight to the supposed more liberal policies of the 1960s and afterwards. But this is only half the story. Concerning Taiwan, Wade concludes that 'The move toward more liberal trade and price policies was at most a necessary condition for the high-speed growth that was to follow (in the sense that growth would not have been so fast without it)'.[52] But it was not 'even remotely' the sufficient cause for such explosive growth.[53]

Wade is a cautious scholar. He cites Rodrik's warning that trade liberalization, as IMF analysts have been urging on the developing world for over a decade now, 'cannot be shown on theoretical grounds to enhance technical efficiency nor has it been empirically demonstrated to do so'.[54] But he is gentle almost to a fault with some of the obscurant tendencies of his fellow economists. Nevertheless, he argues that there are three distinct theories of East Asian success: the free market, the simulated market and the governed market.

The free-market theory holds that the workings of the free market *alone* explain the rapid growth of Japan, South Korea,

Taiwan, Hong Kong and Singapore. Thus, Hugh Patrick, perhaps the most influential advocate of the pure market theory approach within Japanese studies, insists that Japanese economic performance is 'due primarily to the actions and efforts of private individuals' responding to free markets (the word 'primarily' is the slightest bow to the institutional approach).[55]

Another advocate of the market-alone approach is Edward Chen, who insists that in capitalist East Asia state intervention is largely absent. David Aikman offers a comforting conclusion, at once patriotic and complacent, that Taiwan and Hong Kong demonstrate 'how faithfully, consciously or not, the rulers of these two countries have been to American conceptions of free enterprise'.[56] On the controversial trade question, John Fei would have us believe that

> the basic causation of success of the [East Asian] NICs on the policy front, can be traced to the lessening of government interferences in the market economy during the E-0 [export-oriented] phase. In Taiwan and Korea, interference with the market was considerably less as compared to other worse offenders in the near NICs and the Latin American countries.[57]

All three economists implicitly endorse the view that government cannot accelerate economic growth.

The second thesis that Wade has identified is the 'simulated free market model' of East Asian growth. This thesis denies the claims of free-market determinism. This school accepts the fact that the governments of Japan and the Asian newly industrializing countries (NICs) have successfully intervened in the domestic economy over the whole period in question. According to Frederick Berger,

> the crux of the Korean example is that the active interventionist attitude of the State has been aimed at applying moderate incentives which are very close to the relative prices of products and factors that would prevail in a situation of the free market.... It is as though the government were 'simulating' a free market.[58]

Wade believes that Garry Saxonhouse traces a similar approach when he insists that Japan's distinctive institutional features function as near equivalents of arrangements elsewhere: in the United States, for example. If Japan were a more advanced country, with well-developed capital markets, it would not need an industrial policy, but as it lacks such sophisticated institutions, it may need an industrial policy. Jagdish Bhagwati concedes the legitimacy of what he calls 'export promotion' strategies to offset the economic distortions of any protection of the domestic market.[59] Where free-market theory excludes all possible alternatives to a pure free trade regime, simulated market theory stresses the effectiveness of the neutral trade regime. But Wade acknowledges that simulated market theory 'can be considered a variant of the core neoclassical theory, which links economic success to self-adjusting markets'.[60]

The governed-market theory, Wade's third school, emphasizes the role of the state in driving East Asia's economic miracle. Writing of South Korea, Parvez Hasan states that 'the government seems to be a participant and often the determining influence in nearly all business decisions'.[61] On the nature of state planning in South Korea, Edward Mason concludes that 'the hand of government reaches down rather far into the activities of individual firms with its manipulation of incentives and disincentives'.[62] Even Henry Rosovsky concedes that Japan 'must be the only capitalist country in the world in which the Government decides how many firms should be in a given industry and sets out to arrange the desired number'.[63]

Wade sets out a complex theory of the governed market (GM), which involves three levels of causation. The first and best-known chain of cause and effect highlights three 'proximate causes' for the superiority of East Asian economic performance:

(1) very high levels of productive investment;
(2) more investment in certain key industries than would have occurred in the absence of government intervention; and,
(3) exposure of many industries to international competition, in foreign markets, if not at home. These are the proximate causes.[64]

These policy 'causes' may be seen, according to Wade, to be themselves the result of government policies. At this second level of causation, government 'incentives, controls and mechanisms to spread risk' have allowed the Japanese government to guide or govern or manipulate the way that resources are allocated, thus generating production and investment outcomes rather different from those that might have occurred under the operation of either free markets or simulated free-market policies.[65]

Behind this stands a third level of causation or explanation. This, Wade argues, casts a spotlight on the way that persistent policies and national goals 'have been permitted or supported by a certain kind of organization of the state and the private sector'.[66] Focusing on the Japanese miracle as it unfolded before the First Oil Shock

(1973–74), Wade calls attention to seven types of government policies which typify the East Asian governed-market approach: (1) post-war agricultural reform and land redistribution; (2) the manipulation of the financial system to ensure that private financial capital was made to serve the ends of industrial capital; (3) firm policy commitments to guarantee stability of 'long-term investment, especially the exchange rate, the interest rate, and the general price level'; (4) the insulation of the domestic Japanese economy from foreign competition in the domestic market, while maintaining clear priorities in the use of scarce foreign exchange, especially during the late 1940s and 1950s; (5) exports expansion; (6) the import of foreign technology and the nurturing of a national technology system; and (7) the targeting of particular industries for national purposes.[67]

This interpretation of post-war public policy-making stresses the importance of exchange rate markets, bank interest rates and price stability to Japanese success. But Wade comments that the key contrast between the 'free market' (FM) and 'simulated market' (SM) theories and the governed market (GM) idea is that the former 'are silent on the political arrangements needed to support their policies'.[68] But from the standpoint of science and method, there is another crucial distinction to be made between FM and SM theories and the governed-market theory. That is simply this: FM and SM are wholly dependent on positivist logic; GM is firmly grounded in non-positivistic empiricism.

Methodological tension, recognized or not, enlivens Laura d'Andrea Tyson's often harsh criticism of what she calls 'traditional market theory' in *Who's Bashing Whom: Trade Conflict in High-Technology Industries* (1992).[69] Tyson is that rare positivist-trained economist who dissents from some of the central doctrines of her school, and she exploits empirical methods to sustain her assault. When she concludes that 'technology-intensive industries violate the assumptions of free trade theory and the static economics that are the traditional basis for US trade policy', she cites empirical evidence, not positivist laws.[70]

When she assesses the strengths of anti-liberal positivism, as reflected in the 'new trade theory' of economists such as Paul R. Krugman, her positivist scruples re-emerge.[71] Indeed this methodological ambivalence hampers Tyson's ability to set forth her case with conviction. Tyson is haunted by the spirit of Friedrich List. Only her loyalty to Adam Smith prevents her from saying, with Hamlet, 'Stay, illusion'.

In a manner analogous to Wade's, Tyson divides the intellectual combatants over trade theory into three camps: 'free market traditionalists', 'moderate free traders' and 'cautious activists'. As with Wade's free-market, simulated-market and governed-market theories, Tyson's three approaches move from rigid liberalism, to dilute liberalism, to a level of effective state intervention undreamt by Smith and his followers. Tyson's 'cautious activism', like Wade's 'governed market', owes more to empiricism than to positivism, and more to List than to Smith. Thus, according to Tyson:

> Traditional free traders contend that if the Japanese restrict access to their market, whether intentionally through overt trade barriers or unintentionally through regulatory policies, they will pay higher prices and reduce their own economic welfare. True, the United States and Japan's other trading partners will suffer some loss of efficiency, because the gains from trade will be reduced.[72]

This is traditional economic orthodoxy. In dissenting from this entrenched view, Tyson cites two problems. First, 'only the composition of trade between Japan and the rest of the world will be affected; overall trade balances will not change' under the lash of Japanese mercantilism.[73] Second, and of far greater theoretical importance, Tyson also notes (as List surely would have) that 'standard economic logic assumes that the composition of trade does not matter – a dollar's worth of exports or imports of shoes has the same effect on national economic welfare as a dollar's worth of exports or imports of computers'.[74]

Under the impact of the trade conflicts of the 1980s and in the face of the persistent character of Japan's massive trade surplus, the number of economists and policy-makers who cling to traditional theory has, in Tyson's view, dwindled. In their place has risen a school of moderate free traders who support the free-trade ideal but 'grudgingly concede that it is a long way off and conclude that unilateral measures to serve the national interest may be justified under some circumstances':

> Traditional economic theory provides moderate free traders with three such justifications: the risk of high adjustment costs, potential terms-of-trade losses, and the threat to national security that may result from significant injury to the nation's high-technology producers.[75]

First there are adjustment costs:

Adjustment costs are the costs of writing off or reallocating resources from domestic industries forced to contract as a result of declining markets. When resources are not costlessly mobile – as assuredly they are not in technology-intensive industries with specialized human, capital, and technological assets – adjustment costs can be substantial. Such costs, however, are rarely estimated and even more rarely invoked as a rationale for trade policy.[76]

Then there are losses from deteriorating terms of trade:

If foreigners subsidize their aircraft producers, US exporters of aircraft may have to lower their own prices to match their competition. Likewise if foreigners erect barriers to American computer exports (or if business practices allowable under foreign competition laws are themselves barriers), exports of other American products will have to be increased to maintain the overall level of US exports. To induce these higher sales, US export prices may have to be reduced, either directly or through a drop in the value of the dollar. Or again if foreign trade barriers or structural impediments reduce global competition, the prices of American imports may increase.[77]

A moderate free trader may also be tempted to violate free-trade or free-market principles if foreign trading practices result in over-concentration of suppliers outside the United States:

Foreign market power in a particular high-technology industry can translate into higher prices – a terms-of-trade effect – and restrictions on access to frontier technologies by American consumers and producers – a strategic effect on market competition. These dangers are especially pronounced when foreign suppliers control inputs – for example, semiconductors – that are widely used throughout the economy.[78]

The cautious activist, in moving closer to List and further from Smith, challenges such free-trade thinking on three fronts. First, Tyson contends that

A dollar's worth of shoes may have the same effect on the trade balance as a dollar's worth of computers. But ... the two do not have the same effect on employment, wages, labor skills, productivity, and research – all major determinants of our long-term economic health. In addition, because technology-intensive industries finance a disproportionate share of the nation's R&D

spending, there is a strong presumption ... that they generate positive externalities for the rest of the economy.[79]

Second, consistent with Japanese national experience and policy practice, Tyson concedes that competitive advantage in strategic industries may be created by government. Third, national boundaries matter. High-tech industries are located in a select number of the world's leading industrial powers. Externalities may encourage the flow of the benefits of modern technology across international borders, benefiting rich nations no less than poor ones, but the cautious advocate of managed trade seeks to ensure, like the mercantilist maker of industrial policy, that his nation should play host to a significant share of such advanced industries.

This intellectual position encourages the embrace of managed trade, because, as Tyson observes, 'the choice between self-serving unilateralism and cooperative multilateralism does not exist'.[80] Tyson dresses her revolutionary break with more liberal colleagues in careful bows of positive liberal economic orthodoxy. This inhibits her from making a more resolute challenge to positivist orthodoxy.

Take, for example, the question of government's ability, in alliance with business, to alter a nation's comparative advantage. Traditional free-market theory remains sceptical of such policies on scientific and ideological grounds. For an economist, the test is whether such policies generate observable benefits over costs. These are, as Tyson rightly concedes, 'devilishly difficult to measure with any precision'.[81]

> Any such calculation depends on a number of imponderables, including the exact form of the policy, its effects on other industries, and the reactions of both domestic firms and foreign firms and governments.[82]

But given the scientific and ideological pressures on contemporary economic thinking, it is unlikely that a committed free marketeer will wade through such imponderables to reach the clarity demonstrated by Japan's mercantilist philosophy and business practice. Confronted with uncertainty, the timid economist yields to the magnetic draw of positivism.

In search of additional grounds for caution, Tyson cites the sorry record of American pork-barrel politics and flawed sectoral interventionism. These examples feed doubts about the ability of the US government to intervene in the economy effectively. But here, as elsewhere, it is important to tease out the true facts of policy-making history from the tangles of positivist thought and assumption. The record of policy failure is exaggerated when viewed from the standpoint of positivist law-making. Empirical research is more subtle and more illuminating.

Finally, Tyson appears horrified at the prospect of being labelled a 'protectionist'. Yet, she leaves no doubt that she understands that Japanese policy-makers and businessmen have few qualms about protectionism. She cites the conclusive data on protectionist South Korea's economic rise without hesitation. Protectionism may be the great bogey of contemporary modern liberal theory, but it is not obvious that this spectre has been analysed with the kind of rigour that Japanese success demands. Tyson herself recognizes, in her discussion of trade bilateralism vs. multilateralism, that 'a more complicated vocabulary is necessary to capture a more complicated reality'.[83] Positivism impedes the development of this vocabulary. By seeking to deny Japan's modern achievements, positivism has diminished not just economics, but much of Western social science with it.

ANTI-CLASSICISM

> Genius is not a gift but the way that one invents in desperate cases.
>
> Sartre

Vienna–Cambridge–Oxford

The successive schools of logical atomism, logical positivism and logical empiricism revolutionized the Western understanding of logic and science. The work of Russell, the early Wittgenstein and the Vienna Circle are among the splendours of the twentieth-century mind. But should the fruits of this extraordinary flowering of European philosophy be applied to the social sciences? During the course of the twentieth century, many social scientists, particularly in the English-speaking world, have accepted the general thrust of the logical positivist approach. There has been a broad willingness to observe the gross distinction between empirical statements, 'true or false by virtue of what observation shows to be the case' and formal statements, as one finds in mathematics, which are 'true or false by virtue of the meanings of their constituent terms alone'. Subsequent dilutions of the uncompromising stance of the Viennese school have only eased, not eliminated, its rooted suspicion of evaluative statements, such as moral imperatives or subjective preferences, as inherently 'meaningless'.

It is the view taken here that such dictates stand in the way of progress in the social sciences. Given the achievements of the Vienna Circle and its philosophic allies one would wish to echo Sir Isaiah Berlin's valedictory remarks on the Holy Grail of verification when he concluded that 'after due homage has been paid to its therapeutic influence, it needs to be abandoned or else considerably revised, if it is to be prevented from breeding new fallacies in place of those which it eradicates'.[84] This is the proper stance for those who seek to further the cause of a post-positive social science. Given the critical armoury that still attends Anglo-American writing on political theory, there is, however, an understandable temptation to adopt a harsher, less compromising position, and to embrace a strategy of total 'epistemic break'.

The French philosophical tradition has been shaped by successive sharp reversals in position by those who have sought to demolish the work and influence of their immediate predecessors. Husserl's use of the term 'bracketing' suggests yet another strategy. But what must be made clear is that the proper understanding of Japanese politics and political thought demands a phase of development that is free of the strictures of logical positivism. In the social sciences, positivism, in its most dogmatic guises, has conspired for much of the past century against the advancement of political philosophy in the classical sense. This is no longer acceptable if the goal of a genuine Japanese classicism is to be pursued. Indeed, in the study of the politics of non-Western societies, such anti-classicism has never had a legitimate place.

Anglo-American timidity

The devaluation of political classicism, in Britain and particularly at Oxford, 'which more perhaps than any other place in the English-speaking world is the home of political theory and philosophy', is rooted in epistemological distinctions drawn by logical positivists.[85] None of the shackles imposed on modern social science in the name of Russell and the Vienna Circle has done more harm than these dogmas. But for the strength of the classical tradition at Oxford, this attempt to banish all alternative modes of thought from social scientific discourse might have brought the teaching of classical political philosophy, from Plato to Marx, to its knees.

This failed act of academic patricide was executed in the name of certitude. Because the classical canon of political reflection is ripe with evaluations, advocacy and moral judgements, Anglo-American philosophy has rejected it as qualifying as neither science nor philosophy. The result has been a novel programme for political theory which has broken with the enabling assumptions that have sustained Western political thought from antiquity until the end of the nineteenth century. Today, this logical positivist crusade should be judged to have been a grave error. Certainly the positivist stance is utterly inadequate to the task of grasping the canonic achievements of postwar Japan or Europe's place in a post-European world.

The failure and the inadequacy are part of the price that the twentieth-century mind has paid for its embrace of anti-classicism. In *'Bunmeiron no Gairyaku' o Yomu*, Maruyama Masao chafes at the limitations that historical positivism has imposed on the thoughtful reading of the political classics of Occidental and Oriental tradition. The birth of literary structuralism in France provoked a fierce and famous debate over the status and provocation of the classics. In Chapter 11, Maruyama's musings will be contrasted with the row between Roland Barthes and Raymond Picard over Racine, and both compared with the assertion of the rights of the classic thinker within German academic thought as articulated by Werner Marx of Freiburg University. Here, however, the Anglo-American situation, as summarized in David Miller's article on 'Political theory' in *The Blackwell Encyclopedia of Political Thought*, provides an important sounding of the scale of damage that logical positivist dogma has inflicted on political reflection in the English-speaking world.[86]

How, then, have marginalized political philosophers in Britain and America coped with the crumbs from the tables of logical positivist dogmatists? First, they have fallen back on the concept of political theory as the history of political thought. Under this rubric, political theorists were reduced to textual specialists who sought to establish the authentic meaning of the political classics of an inherited textual canon. At its most sober, this historical and philological strategy sought to recapture the vision of politics that animated Aristotle, Machiavelli or Locke. At its most ambitious, it has sought to outflank the canon with secondary works and the background minutiae of the European intellectual inheritance in an effort to dethrone the works of canonic tradition. But even the more modest effort merely to establish the indisputable facts about a great political thinker in a programme of quiet textual conservation fell foul of positivist strictures. Thus, 'if there really is a logical error involved in moving from empirical or formal statements to evaluative judgments, this error cannot be avoided by pointing out that it has frequently been committed in the past'.[87]

The second danger has been eunuchry.

> An historical approach which seeks to establish the texts' authentic meaning must increasingly pay attention to the precise intellectual context in which they were composed: the audience to which they were addressed, the author's aims in addressing that audience, the language available to him in making his approach, and so forth.[88]

The consequence of a such a narrow focus is that 'it becomes steadily more difficult to use the classic works to illuminate contemporary issues posed in a radically different context'.[89] Maruyama's unhappiness with the Japanese version of such 'historicist' restrictions will be considered in Chapter 11.

The result is a disturbing scientific and cultural imbroglio for which the craven attitude of social scientists towards logical positivist pretension is entirely to blame. Burdened by impressive, if narrow, criteria for assessing the cognitive status of a political idea, logical positivists have subverted progress within the European tradition of political philosophy. This in turn has undermined the effort to teach and transmit the glories of tradition as well. As the promised dawn of scientific certitude has failed to arrive, perhaps it is time to take a tally of the damning costs that social science has paid for logical positivist excess.

At root, the core difficulty has been the intellectual timidity of the social scientific response, especially in the English-speaking world. Political scientists continue to censure students of theory for failing to abide by positivist strictures. At the same time, a dismissive tone is taken with those who 'wish to appropriate the classics for their own purposes with little regard to context'.[90] Fearful of the intellectual legacy of their grandfathers, the modern political theorist, like the textual positivist, instinctively applies the brakes. The contrast with the confident posture of Continental Europeans is striking.

Political scientists must learn to ignore the pretentious claims of logical positivism. Neither too much nor too little should be asked of intellectual historians. Werner Marx's canonic list of readers of Hegel's *Phenomenology of Spirit* includes Karl Marx, Lukács, Kojève, Bloch and Habermas.[91] None is a historian. None of these first-class thinkers lets any academic school curb his efforts to produce what we now regard to be texts of classic or near-classic stature.

Nor should any thinker keen to write a classic response to Japan's post-war achievement.

Some political scientists argue that the strictures of logical positivism reduce political philosophy to the task of clarifying concepts. The polysemic nature of such key words as 'democracy', 'freedom', 'justice' and 'free markets' offers a justification for such semantic house-cleaning. But the ideological predisposition of the house-cleaner tends to intrude on the pursuit of objective-sounding definitions. As Miller notes, 'defending an interpretation of a political concept usually means defending the general ideological stance with which the interpretation is linked'.[92] More significantly, he concedes that those who seek to clarify political concepts are actually engaged in 'the more substantive form of political theory that the classical authors undertook'.[93]

This argument may, however, be reversed. The obvious limitations of 'conception clarification' derive directly from the logical positivist creed. Does this not provide yet another reason to abandon the positivist straitjacket which has encouraged this troubled exercise? A classic exposition on the post-war Japanese miracle must make explicit the meaning of key words such as 'development state', 'corporatism' and 'economic nationalism', and the implications that Japanese practice challenges traditional definitions of 'democracy', 'egalitarianism' and the 'free market'. But this is only a small part of the larger task of which the writing of a major political classic on contemporary Japan forms the centrepiece.

Challenged by logical positivist ideals, still other political scientists, particularly in the United States, have sought to reanimate political philosophy by building formal models. Miller casts aspersions on this school because of its tendency to mix normative prescription with empirical description. Those who would resurrect the classical tradition are perfectly comfortable with such mixing, as were Aristotle and Hegel. The real failing of the model-building approach for the classical-minded student of modern Japan is this school's decisive dependence on neo-liberal economic theory, with its procrustean impulses and anti-Japanese 'individualist' prejudices. In their fundamental assumptions about human nature, the model-builders reject all of post-war Japan's claims to world-historical significance before a single fact of the case has been pursued. Their objections are theoretical; not empirical.

Another substitute for the classical tradition has been sought in transforming traditional political theory into a 'theoretical political science' or 'the more theoretical aspect of the discipline'.[94] This tends to be a broader version of the house-cleaning role developed by concept clarifyers. The problem here is the meaning attached to the term 'theory'. Mesmerized by a bastardized version of Newtonian physics and false claims of logical positivism, such theoreticians have been all too keen then to impose this scientistic agenda on modern social science. This failure is the direct consequence of the way, in Miller's summary, that this school seeks to synthesize 'particular observations and low-level empirical generalizations into a general explanatory framework, rather as theoretical physics provides a systematic explanation of our everyday experience of the physical world'.[95]

This kind of thinking provides the intellectual grounding or substructure for political 'analysis', in some of its most influential manifestations. The blossoming of this approach offers further evidence of the astonishing staying power of positivist methodology long after the success of rebellions in other branches of social science against positivism. But the judgement must stand that this style of theoretical political science has little or nothing to offer the potential author of a classic statement about the post-war Japanese polity. It points the horse in entirely the wrong direction.

At best it may assist the vital task that Fukuzawa Yukichi (1834–1901), in Maruyama's reading, saw for a *giron no kotsu seiri* or a rectification of concepts in the discourse of the public sphere.[96] But the need for mechanisms to curb the temptation of philosophers or political thinkers to fall into the Cartesian fallacy (I think something, therefore it must be true) does not require a scientific methodology which distorts reality more than it clarifies it. One does not have to be Sir Isaac Newton to tell the truth.

Reviewing the whole picture, Miller concludes that the anti-classical movement in post-war political science has run aground on two important problems: embedded normativism and empirical inadequacy. Writing on the normative issue, Miller observes that:

the attempt to construct a political theory free of normative elements seems doomed to fail. The reason, it appears, is that any explanation of political events involves an interpretation of the actions and intentions of the participants, and such an interpretation will draw on the disputable general view of human needs and motives that in turn carries normative implications with it.[97]

In reaching this conclusion, Miller cites the criticism of objectivism contained in Charles Taylor's essay 'Neutrality in political science'.[98] As long as Miller is seeking only to offer a *critique* of political theory as it is practised in America and Britain today, then it is persuasive to cite the work of Taylor. But Taylor is no ally of logical positivism. Any *remedy* for Miller's complaints demands the rejection of logical positivism in favour of alternative approaches, such as Taylor's Hegelianism. This is because Taylor, like Werner Marx, is heir to two centuries of hermeneutic reflection on the difficulties of univocal textual interpretation and the inherent unlikelihood of a theory of 'innocent' or 'objective' readings. Neither Taylor nor Marx would have fallen into the positivist trap in the first place.

Finally, Miller believes that 'the greatest practical difficulty that now faces political theory is simply the immense body of empirical material that modern political science has collected'.[99] He acknowledges the important work of contemporary political philosophers such as Oakeshott, Rawls, Nozick and Dworkin, but concludes that 'none of these combines the philosophic analysis of political principles with an empirical understanding of political processes in a wholly successful way'.[100] This may be so. It nevertheless remains certain that the cure for a fawning dependence on logical positivism will not be found in an uncritical awe of empiricism, which is the other great flaw of the Anglo-American tradition. The limits of empiricism will be addressed in the next chapter.

Nunc Dimittis

Miller's assessment of the reduced state of contemporary political philosophy should be resisted. The empirical data harvested by political scientists is not 'the greatest difficulty', practical or otherwise, facing Western political thought today. Rather the heart of the problem is the application of inappropriate standards to the reading and writing of political philosophy. A vulgarized vision of Newtonian physics does not offer a sound standard for judging the work of the social scientist. Logical positivism is inappropriate to the practical business of the political scientist who is also an empiricist. Indeed most front-line researchers take little or no notice of such positivist pronouncements. At the same time, outside the rigorous tutorial chambers of the professional philosopher, Russell's epigoni have inadvertently helped to foster stupefaction about logical positivism and its truth claims among social scientists with a weakness for woolly scientism.

Empirical research is more tentative and intuitive than the over-tidy version of how physicists work that seems to underwrite the complaints of the contemporary acolytes of positivism. In his study of Genet, Sartre famously observed 'Genius is not a gift but the way that one invents in desperate cases'.[101] For 'desperate', one might substitute 'urgent'. In political philosophy today, our most urgent need is for creative political thought of the first rank. Indeed, the divine intervention of genius may offer the only cure for the havoc wreaked on the study of politics and society in the names of Russell and Carnap.

Confronted with the challenge of producing a political classic worthy of the ancients and of Japan's modern achievement, it should be clear that the greatest obstacle that now faces political philosophy is positivism. This is the root of many of our sorrows and almost all of our discontents.

4 Empiricism

The only method is to be very intelligent.
T. S. Eliot

Positivism and empiricism dominate the methodological horizon of the European social sciences. No Western student of Asian politics has freed himself from fundamental dependence on one or both of these two scientific approaches. Positivism and empiricism determine, to an astonishing and often unexamined degree, what we see when we observe the workings of a non-Western society. These two methods form our most consequential pieces of philosophic baggage. They legitimate our enterprise. Sometimes they confound it.

The difficulty with positivism is that it obscures as much of East Asian reality as it illuminates. The sins of the positivist – his scientistic procrusteanism, his misplaced faith in logical and mathematical methods, his anti-classicism and his surrender to universal economic laws – have been emphasized in the previous chapter. Empiricism overcomes many of these failings. Indeed, empirical methods, as reflected in the work of the past two generations of Western students of Japanese politics, have laid bare some of the central truths about the Japanese experience of government. But any effort to grasp more fully the significance of post-war Japan also demands that the political scientist challenge and, where necessary, transcend the limits of the pure empirical approach.

Such transcendence should begin with the recognition that social scientific empiricism is more than 'analysis', a rubric vital to those political scientists who abhor the kind of empirical 'description' one finds in nineteenth-century legal formalism and constitutional study. Political science began with the singular discovery that the true locus of power in a polity is not necessarily where constitutional nicety would confine it.

Analysis urges the political scientist to probe and pinch social reality. This is its strength. But the analyst often tends to understate the difficulty of mere descriptive accuracy. Analytic suspicion of the unadorned fact also encourages the political scientist to yield to the seductions of scientism, which would have him transmute empiricism into positivism. These two limitations – the slighting of description and the embrace of scientism – may explain the condescension towards political journalism and the neglect of tribal knowledge that scar political science today. The discipline may float on the sea of journalistic fact, yet analysts often overlook the reality-defining or ontological role of political journalism. Journalism reflects an astute reaction to the ontologies of time, and how 'reality' is generated and destroyed over time and through time, in ways that have been neglected by both the historian and the political scientific analyst.

Pace the scientific claims of positivist law-making, area studies fundamentally depends on culturally informed knowledge of an alien society. Such tacit knowledge is garnered not only through disinterested observation but also through subjective experience. The dialectic of the perceiver and what he perceives subverts the claims of those proponents of analysis who seek to marry their style of empiricism with the scientific rigours of positivism. Tribal knowledge is grounded in disciplined observation. As such it shares much with apositivist empiricism, but tribal knowledge is informed by the life experience of the social researcher, where the term 'experience' reflects the interplay of intuition, insight and the impact of the life world (*Lebenswelt*) of his tribe on the researcher. This is not what John Locke meant when he insisted that 'experience' forms the anti-metaphysical foundation of empiricism. Nevertheless, tribal knowledge, like journalism, is a powerful expression of the empirical spirit.

This chapter is divided into two parts: 'Methodological angst' and 'Canonic Japan and empiricism'. In the first, the empirical foundations of the political science of modern Asia are subjected to close scrutiny. In the second, a major thesis is proposed: post-war Japan should be acknowledged as a canonic polity, a political system important enough, in world-historical terms, to demand comparison with Plato's Athens, Machiavelli's Florence or John Rawls' America. I contend that it is no longer defensible, on empirical grounds alone, to write a survey of the history of political philosophy, Western or otherwise, without the inclusion of a chapter on post-war Japan.

METHODOLOGICAL ANGST

Empirical rejection of positivism is not an idle surrender to shifts in philosophic fashion. Confronted with Kant's identification of the two schools of nature which dominate the European sciences, the political scientist appears to crave the best of both approaches. In theory, he endorses the claims of the universalists who insist that reality is the same for the physical and social scientist; but, in practice, the same political scientist refuses to be constrained by universal laws when he does research.

The practical researcher's resistance to positivism is not rooted in a prior commitment to the principal rival schools of anti-positivist reflection and method, such as critical theory or hermeneutics or even philosophic realism. Nor has political scientific resistance or indifference to positivism been inspired by the radical privileging of the human sphere, as opposed to the natural, by Vico and his successors.

Indeed, the successive revolutions that have shaped the philosophy of social science, from the 1840s down to the present, have left Orientalism and area studies of the non-European world largely untouched. There has been no attempt to make sense of the argument that the cultural and natural sciences speak to different ontologies of existence, an insight developed by Wilhelm Dilthey (1833–1911), or that the cultural and natural sciences embody different theoretical values or interests or methodologies, an idea articulated by Heinrich Rickert (1863–1936) and other Southwest German neo-Kantians in response to Mill's arguments in *A System of Logic* (Book VI). Even these inspired attempts to map afresh the sovereign distinction that Kant drew between positivism and empiricism in *The Critique of Pure Reason* are little more than magnificent cavalry charges late in this scientific debate for most methodologically aware students of Japan.

This rubric of 'lateness' is important. Whatever obeisances political scientists have paid to logical positivist dogma or to the inflated claims of the post-Comtean nomological or law-giving sciences, the origins of the political scientist's methods and concerns, assumptions and ambitions, all pre-date not only the rise of logical positivism but the philosophy of social science itself. If political science, sociology and anthropology, as we understand them today, are products of the social scientific revolution of the late nineteenth and early twentieth centuries, then their epistemological and ontological foundations can be traced back to the empiricism of Bacon's era and the crucial concept of the social 'fact'.

The key development was the secularization of politics, a process that subsequently contributed to the growth of what Habermas has called 'the public sphere', anchored in a recognizably post-medieval definition of what is the socially 'real'. A complex horizon of scientific meaning, itself the outcome of centuries of reflection on the nature of reality, stands behind Durkheim's famous declaration in *The Rules of Sociological Method* (1895) that 'social facts must be treated as things'.[1]

One result is that the Western encounter with Japan has been mediated by a definition of social reality which has remained essentially unaltered since the birth of the modern age. When one recalls how art, science and technology have been revolutionized during the past two and a half centuries, how they have been shaken by one 'epistemic break' (Gaston Bachelard) after another, this continuity of the political and social sphere is nothing less than remarkable. The continuities that underwrite political and historical analysis have been so secure that it is only recently that political scientists who study Japan have felt any need for greater methodological clarity. But for their recent struggle with the vexed issue of Japanese public policy and Japan's post-war nationalist achievement, and the conflict that this has sparked with economic positivists, behaviouralists and rational-choice theorists, the demarcation question might never have arisen among Orientalists and area specialists.

The political science of Japan today reflects the dualism that prevails in social science as a whole. In *Zur Logik der Sozialwissenschaften* (1967), Habermas held that such 'dualism' was at work in the divide between the nomological and historical–hermeneutic sciences.[2] In a comparable way, Anglo-American political science sets the empiricist against the positivist. Positivists insist on the unity of *theory*; empiricism demonstrates a duality of *practice*. But the result is exactly as Habermas describes it: social scientists take this duality in practice 'for granted', but shy away from discussions of 'the logic of science'. We must banish such shyness from the study of Asian politics. Our progress tomorrow demands a narrowing of this gap between our theory and our practice today.

Consistent with Hegel's 'sequence of faculties', the empirical discovery of Japan has preceded the need for a fuller, more self-conscious grasp of non-universalistic empirical science, via philosophical and methodological scrutiny. The positivist or nomological sciences, 'whose aim it is to formulate and verify hypotheses concerning the laws governing empirical regularities', have not touched the core concerns of most Asian experts.[3] The student of modern Japanese government thus arrives at the door of philosophy with a set of scientific problems specific to political science and Asian studies. This has invited the pragmatic testing of the various philosophic methods and perspectives that now rule the scientific horizon. The questions posed are supremely practical. Does the proposed method work or not? Does it help or hinder the advance of our special branch of learning?

Hume's havoc

Many front-line researchers in the empirical sciences suffer from methodological angst. When the historian is confronted by claims that sure grasp of objective reality always eludes us, such as one finds in Simon Schama's *Dead Certainties*, ('We are doomed to be forever hailing someone who has just gone around the corner and out of earshot'), or that the best historical research is riddled with errors of logic, as David Hackett Fischer has argued in *Historians' Fallacies*, the political scientist also shudders in the philosophic chill.[4] Methodologists may be a tiny minority among political scientists but they bring to their readings of the work of their colleagues a destructive gleam. They know the rhetorical force of Hume's damning aside: 'When we run over libraries persuaded of these principles what havoc must we make?'[5]

The key word in Hume's flourish is 'principles'. Any student of Asian government who would secure the epistemological foundations of his empiric science must achieve strict clarity about which standards of logic and science apply and which do not. Fischer's list of inappropriate logical constraints is as telling as it is long, and is as pertinent to the labours of the political scientist as to those of the historian:

> The logic of historical thought is not formal logic of deductive inference. It is not a symmetrical structure of Aristotelian syllogisms, or Ramean dialectics, or Boolean equations. Nor is it precisely inductive logic, like that of Mill or Keynes or Carnap. It consists neither in inductive reasoning from the particular to the general, nor in deductive reasoning from the general to the particular. Instead, it is a process of *adductive* reasoning in the simple sense of adducing answers to specific questions, so that a satisfactory explanatory 'fit' is obtained.[6]

Almost all of the methodological wrangles that have divided social scientists turn on what is meant by the term 'satisfactory'. Fischer is clear what he means. Too many social scientists, especially in English-speaking countries, have refused to be content with any satisfactions but those promised by the close-minded and methodologically intolerant positivist. Here is the root of much of the methodological havoc that has threatened the integrity of the social sciences during the twentieth century, particularly since 1945.

In *How Policies Change: The Japanese Government and the Aging Society*, John Creighton Campbell devotes an entire chapter to 'A theory of policy change'.[7] He describes his initial plan of attack as 'an almost purely inductive approach ... to identify the most significant policy changes in the old-age policy area, find out what caused them, and then look for general patterns and variations'.[8] But he was forced to abandon this approach under pressure from the policymakers whom he interviewed. Many scholars who have exploited qualitative techniques, such as the interviewing of expert witnesses, will recognize Campbell's conundrum.

> The questionnaire I drew up for my first interviews [was] full of questions about ... various actors who might be demanding various benefits, and ... mechanisms for systematic research on social problems and policy solutions.
>
> My respondents (mostly middle-level bureaucrats) tried their best to come up with answers to both sets of questions. Many, however, wound up with shrugs and blank looks. I increasingly got the impression that my two pictures of policy change seemed to have little to do with participants' perceptions of what they were doing.[9]

Misconceptions about *what* is at stake in a particular sphere of policy may also reflect false preconceptions about *how* policy is formulated.

> I had similar difficulties in applying the usual sorts of explanations for how policy decisions get made, in general .... It was not so much that my material was rejecting hypotheses from the literature; rather, it seemed not to be operating on the same logic, at least much of the time.[10]

As Campbell explains, the political scientific literature has, after more than a generation of thinking about how the world-views of political actors colour the character of the data gleaned by the interviewer, evolved several strategies for dealing with such difficulties. Campbell began to a search for 'a more open, less deterministic theoretical approach, one that would allow an assessment of whether various cause-and-effect relationships suggested in the literature were working, but would also allow the possibility of different logics altogether, perhaps several logics working simultaneously'.[11] Campbell turned to the work of scholars such as Graham T. Allison's *Essence of Decision: Explaining the Cuban Missile Crisis* (1971) and the inelegantly titled 'garbage-can theory' of organizational choice developed by Michael D. Cohen, James G. March and Johan P. Olsen.[12] The language of this theory is not about 'mobilization and social movements, about issue-broadening and the search stage, about bureaucrats and agency mission, about progressive or conservative ideologies, about leadership, or about anything very specific'.[13] Rather, garbage-can theorists stress 'how opportunities for change appear and disappear, how participants come and go, and how problems and solutions develop and are linked together'.[14] Campbell concedes that policy-making dynamic can be usefully viewed as the product of 'unrelated processes, and they are linked up not by an inherent logic but by "accidents" of the timing and sequence of their arrival on the scene'.[15]

Such considerations threaten methodological orthodoxy. Campbell's approach does not qualify as positivism or even induction. When he evokes the language of early modern mathematics, physics and philosophy with references to billiard balls, vectors, force and energy, these images are, as he admits, mere metaphors.[16] The contrast between the almost Zen-like reticence of Campbell's call for 'clearing the mind of preconceptions' and the procrustean rigour with which the public-choice positivist bludgeons not only research methods but political reality itself could hardly be greater.[17] Campbell is seeking only a satisfactory explanatory 'fit' to answer his specific questions, what Hackett calls 'adduction'.

The garbage-can approach, which Campbell labels 'artifactual', emphasizes the neglected role of the accidental, the quirky and the unintended in the formulation of public policy.[18] He contrasts this approach with three other modes of explaining policy change: the inertial which locates the source of policy change in unbidden social and economic trends, thus reducing the political system to a passive 'black box'; the cognitive approach, which assigns special weight to official actions and ideas, to national goals and administrative learning curves; and finally, political explanations, which suggest that public policy is determined by the outcome of struggles between conflicting classes or other interest groups.[19] Campbell insists that all four approaches should be brought to bear on a problem in the search for a comprehensive model. But what must be avoided is the dogmatic application of one method at the expense of another:

> It is remarkable, for example, how often writers have concluded in effect that decision making in Japan is rational and in the United States is political, after examining quite different sets of factors and using different logics of explanation for the two countries.[20]

It would have been useful to know which writers Campbell has in mind, but his insistence on methodological pluralism is sound. The implicit rejection of positivist claims is unambiguous. *Pace* Popper, who insisted that a theory must be falsifiable to qualify as a theory, Campbell argues that 'none of these [four] interpretations is falsifiable, and thus untrue'.[21] The door on social scientific interpretation does not close when one discovers that future welfare spending by this nation or that can be predicted by reference to just two or three variables. Such inertial explanations should form but a single arrow among many in the quiver of the empiricist. So despite the occasional bow to the quest for prediction, Campbell remains a Weberian: reality is by and large what his Japanese bureaucrats think it is. But, Weberian or not, Campbell is clearly not a positivist. The methodological pluralism and empirical practicality of *How Policies Change* feed the suspicion, therefore, that the aroused positivist would, in Hume's phrase, 'commit it to the flames' as unscientific.

Japan and behaviouralism

One of the most important recent attempts to impose positivist orthodoxy on the study of modern Japanese politics is *The Japanese Voter* (1991).[22] The bulk of the analysis by Scott C. Flanagan, Shinsaku Kohei, Ichiro Miyake, Bradley M. Richardson and Joji Watanuki is 'based on a large nationwide panel survey of Japanese citizens conducted before and after the December 1976 House of Representatives election'.[23] *The Japanese Voter* seeks to apply ideas and quantitative techniques associated with the behaviourist revolution of the 1950s and 1960s to understand Japanese voting patterns. This large study suggests that, even in decline, behaviouralism remains a contentious creed.

To the eyes of the committed behaviouralist, *The Japanese Voter* sweeps away decades of flawed analysis of the Japanese political scene. In his Foreword, Warren E. Miller observes that:

> The accomplishments of the authors of *The Japanese Voter* are the more extraordinary as they bridge a formidable and heretofore virtually unsurmountable cultural gap. They eliminate a language barrier that has long deprived most occidental scholars of more than journalistic accounts of Japanese electoral behavior. Even more crucial to the internationalization of our scholarship, they successfully bring Japanese political research into the intellectual mainstream in a comprehensive treatment commensurate with the established tradition of national election studies in the Atlantic community.[24]

Miller's use of the term 'cultural gap' is perplexing. It is not clear from his praise of *The Japanese Voter* whether he shares the view of many behaviouralists (in contrast to behaviourists) that 'it is unscientific to study mental processes and other phenomena which are not directly observable and measurable'.[25] This matters because classic behaviouralism denies that people and animals have minds. This ontological and epistemological stance underwrites the rejection of the cultural explanation of social phenomena by behaviouralists. It explains their preference for studying activities such as 'pressing buttons, eating, running through mazes, making noises' or marking ballot papers.[26]

Equally troubling is Miller's reference to 'a language barrier', presumably the one between English and Japanese. It is not obvious why this barrier matters when behaviourists, like economic positivists, reject the assumption that differences between the English and Japanese languages can account for any significant contrast between Japanese and American political behaviour. This is one of the central dogmas of scientific universalism.

The real point of this surprising talk of gaps and barriers is quite different. Because Japanese culture may be said, in this scientific sense, not to exist, it is important to Miller and other students of voting behaviour that non-behaviouralist approaches to Japanese politics be labelled as 'cultural' or 'anthropological' in order to deny the claims of the non-behaviouralist to scientific respectability. Thus, in the preface to *The Japanese Voter*, Scott C. Flanagan justifies his behaviouralist project by casting doubt on the soundness of the bulk of the political scientific literature:

> Heretofore most of the readily available English-language books

on Japanese parties, elections, and political behaviour have followed a case-study approach that adopts an anthropological style of analysis. These studies frequently stress cultural categories and explanations, drawing our attention to unique patterns that have no cognates in the West.[27]

It would be helpful to know which English-language books on Japanese politics Flanagan is criticizing because this appears to be an indefensible argument. In what useful sense can the textual labours of Robert Scalapino, Arthur Stockwin, Hans Baerwald, Kent Calder, Gerald L. Curtis and Ronald J. Hrebenar, to cite some of the leading figures in the study of Japanese politics, be described as 'anthropological' or 'cultural' in their methods of research? If the case-study or institutional approach is suspect, then what of Flanagan and Richardson's own work in *Japanese Politics*?[28] If orthodox 1960s behaviouralism is the only methodology that qualifies as science, then *Japanese Politics* will not win the approval of behaviouralism orthodoxy and its singular privileging of certain quantitative research methods at the expense of all others.

Whatever may divide the intellectual orientation of Chalmers Johnson from Richard Samuels or Arthur Stockwin, they are united by their shared scepticism toward Japanese exceptionalism. They do not look with favour on cultural explanations of political behaviour. What Miller means by 'cultural' and Flanagan by 'anthropological' appears to refer to any approach or method that does not conform to the behaviouralist rubric. To dissent from behaviouralism is to depart from political *science*. This is the monist message of Flanagan and his colleagues.

In attempting to produce a Japanese sequel to such celebrated classics as *The American Voter* or *Political Change in Britain*, Flanagan and his colleagues would stamp *nihil obstat* on the universalistic impulse in behaviouralism to denigrate the relevance of linguistic knowledge and cultural frames of reference.[29] The appearance of the names of the three Japanese contributors on the cover of *The Japanese Voter* sends an explicit message to Western behaviouralists: even Japanese scholars endorse the view that Japanese literacy is not essential to the sound interpretation of Japanese political behaviour. The behaviouralist goal is to distil away the Japaneseness of Japanese government in order to make Japanese politics 'both familiar to and interpretable by Western scholars' who, by definition, seek to grasp Japan's political reality without mastering its language or political culture.[30] The analogy with the interpretative strategy of positivist economists who study Japan is as exact as it is telling.

It is Miller, however, who draws the key lesson for any branch of area studies which is caught in the outer darkness of marginality: behaviouralism can 'bring Japanese political research into the intellectual mainstream'. The price for scientific respectability and mainstream stature is total theoretical dependence. Only strict conformity to quantitative methodologies in the Anglo-American mould will suffice.

If Miller's informed judgement accurately reflects the orthodox view of the labours of the expert on Japanese politics, then the battle must be taken to the mainstream. This theoretical revolt should have as one of its principal goals the demonstration that the political scientific empiricism embodied in the most influential postwar scholarship on Japanese party politics, from Scalapino's *The Japanese Communist Movement* and Stockwin's *The Japanese Socialist Party and Neutralism* to Curtis's *The Japanese Way of Politics* and Calder's *Crisis and Compensation*, is nothing of which we need be ashamed or for which apology is required.[31] Such pioneering work qualifies as political science whatever the dogmatic behaviouralist may think or argue.

A passage to India

The god of positivism admits no creed but monist orthodoxy: the belief that all genuine scientific problems have one and only one solution (one God, one truth, one science). But students of non-Western societies tend to observe a flexible form of polytheism. Thus, the political scientist may offer his pinch of incense to the stern god of positivism as often as it is demanded by his more nomologically minded colleagues, but when he is engaged in empirical research he tends to honour less demanding spirits. Nietzsche insisted that in polytheism is to be found a kind of freedom. For the modern practitioner of area studies, this freedom from monism has been an indispensable ingredient to research success.

Most students of modern Japanese politics rejoice in this freedom. But where there is rejection of such freedom, positivist monism is often at work. The resulting stresses and strains are exhibited in *The Japanese Voter*. But the tension between scientific orthodoxy and empirical practicality is effectively exposed, with perhaps unique clarity, in the writings of a political scientific rarity: a student of Asian politics who has also surveyed some of the principal methodological approaches of post-war American political science. Robert L. Hardgrave is the co-author of both *India: Government and Politics in a Developing Nation*, and *Comparative Politics: The Quest for Theory*.[32]

So faithful have Hardgrave and his co-authors been to the contrasting positivist and empiricist approaches to doing social science that these two books demonstrate the fundamental conflict over methodology at issue. *Comparative Politics* carefully describes the pursuit of certitude that drives scientific positivism. *India*, an empirical study of Asia's most populous democracy, denies this positivist impulse. *India* contains hardly a nod to John Stuart Mill's insistence that every science worthy of the name develop universal laws in the Newtonian manner. Reading these two studies in contrast forces the conclusion that the only cure for this methodological contradiction, from the standpoint of the scholar committed to the vitality of area studies, lies in the rejection of the closed political science of the dogmatic positivist in favour of empirical tolerance.

The content of *India* contains few surprises for the student of comparative politics and area studies. There are chapters on recent Indian political history, the constitutional framework, on federalism, party politics, elections, foreign policy and public policy and group politics. The key theme is India's 'current dilemma' understood as a revolution of 'rising frustrations'.[33]

In contrast, *Comparative Politics* offers an overview of some of the main branches of American comparative politics: political development, political culture, group politics, political elites, class politics and 'functionalism and systems analysis'. While area studies presents the researcher with endless opportunities to test a body of scientific theory against the political facts of the case, it also appears to be true that the strictures of positivist science are lightly borne or flatly ignored by the practical empiricist. So does *India* reflect the 'quest for theory' set out in *Comparative Politics*?

In *Comparative Politics*, Bill and Hardgrave set out a programme of five complex stages, linked in the manner of a circle, that should govern 'scientific theory building':

Problemation/Questioning/Issue Determination
Observation/Classification/Description
Generalization/Explanation/Understanding
Confirmation/Testing/Verification
Application/Prediction/Control[34]

These clusters of goals are not independent options. In the positivist schema, they not only represent the necessary phases of an individual research schema, but also summarize the pre-ordained stages of genuine scientific progress. Newtonian physics represents a triumphant unity of all five stages. Any genuine science, as defined by Mill and his scientist heirs (political behaviouralists, for example), must pass through all the stages noted to qualify as a rigorous science. The choice is sharp. If this five-step endeavour defines 'the quest for theory' in modern social science, then none of the research findings offered in *India* merits theoretical laurels.

Take, for example, the first chapter of *India*, which is entitled 'The globalization of the development change'. Hardgrave and Kochanek evoke the theory of 'political development', but the chapter is entirely empirical and descriptive. Chapter 2 provides a historical survey of Indian politics, spiced by occasional references to modernization theory. Chapter 3 ('The framework: institutions of governance') and Chapter 4 ('The challenge of federalism') skilfully blend legal–formalistic description with journalistic analysis. Chapter 5 ('Arenas of conflict: groups in Indian politics') borrows from the language of group theory, one of the least 'rigorous' approaches to comparative politics, but without any references to the school's most influential theorists: Bentley, Truman or Olson. Chapter 6 ('Parties and politics') and Chapter 9 ('Policy and performance: the international context') are wholly dependent on journalistic reporting, as is Chapter 7 ('Elections and political behavior') which contains not the slightest concession to methodological behaviouralism. Chapter 8 ('Policy and performance: the politics of development') is a piece of political analysis. It is the most analytical of the chapters in *India*, but by the standards of public-choice theory or the new classical economics or Easton's functional analysis, it does not qualify as theory.

In terms of methodology, *India* shares more with the historian of Indian politics and the serious journalist who covers India, as it were on the ground, than with the theoreticians discussed in *Comparative Politics*. Strip away the occasional scientific conceit and the discussion of the Indian model, and *India* begins to resemble J. A. A. Stockwin's *Japan: Divided Politics in a Growth Economy*, for example, more than David Easton's *A Framework for Political Analysis*.[35]

A sceptical reader might also argue that if Easton's influential labours capture the scientific high ground, and therefore set the standards for political scientific achievement, then the methods and findings summarized in *Comparative Politics* itself – the chapters on political socialization, group politics, elite theory and class analysis – all fall radically short of the research ideals summarized in the book's five-stage quest for theory. Only an Eastonian positivist should regard this as a failure. The positivist camp alone insists that the pluralist practices of the front-line political scientist and regional specialist should be stamped out in the name of methodological monism and its promise of epistemological certitude. But surely the true cure for methodological angst – the endless laments of distinguished political scientists over the unscientific character of modern political science – is to abandon the quest for theory in the positivist mode.

Most experts on Japanese politics seek neither to contribute to a Newtonian theory of social behaviour nor to apply modernization, socialization, group, elite or class theory to interpreting Japanese political reality. Western political scientists who work on Japan tend to be neither functionalists nor systems analysts. Others may suffer positivist pangs, but not the Japan expert. It is the nightmare of 'wild empiricism' that haunts the Japanese political scientist, not the dangers of positivist procrusteanism.[36]

Take the vexed questions posed by modernization theory. Japan's post-war success challenges the theoretical validity of this approach to Asian studies in one vital way: Japan stands at the cutting edge of developmental change. On several key fronts, it is Western nations that must follow in her wake, not the other way around. This achievement leaps, in a single bound, over the liberal or politically correct scruples of a generation of political scientists who have sought to distinguish 'modernization' from 'Westernization'.

For the student of modernization theory, Japan is the model case study. That the fact of this supremacy is taking decades to recognize and even now is an object of systematic neglect – the existing corpus of theory about Japan remains scanty – may be the single greatest failure of post-war Western political science. The left-wing assault on the Modernization School in the 1970s is largely to blame for this failing within Japanese studies. Modernization theory provided a rubric for grasping Japanese greatness; the moralistic critique that humbled the Modernization School has sought to bury Japan's modern achievement under a hail of liberal and radical censure. In this failure may be found yet another source of the limits of modern social science. Perhaps if Japan were taken more seriously, India itself, and all its enormous potential, would be viewed in a different light.

Tribes and journalists

Every political scientist who is also committed to area studies must have a sure grasp of two other approaches to the factual understanding of modern politics: tribal knowledge and political journalism. Confronted with the complex diversity of Indian politics, the anthropologist or tribal expert would first wish to know in what ways Hindi, for example, influences the modern discourse of Indian political life and whether the impact of this linguistic horizon is adequately reflected in social scientific studies of India by Westerners. The same line of reasoning could be applied to all of India's linguistic communities. This provides an important motive for the tribal expert to probe the religious and cultural foundations of Indian political values, practices and perceptions. Such tribal scrutiny would press home the issue of whether and to what degree India's English-language media provide an adequate empirical and interpretative window to assess the Indian-ness of Indian government and politics. These are not positivist questions. Yet such non-positivist questions touch the heart of the enterprise that would grasp the true character of any non-European polity. Certain dangers must be countered. In his essay 'Understanding and ethnocentricity', Charles Taylor warns that

> the influence of inappropriate, Western and pseudo-universal models over the social science of some non-Western countries – exemplified, I would argue, by the impact of American behaviouralism on Indian political science – is due to more than historic relations of unequal political power.[37]

There must be at least an attempt, in the words of B. Parekh, 'to test the major ideas and categories of Western political theory against the Indian political experience, and to show their ethnocentric bias and limitations'.[38]

This provides still another reason that the tribal expert must know his tribe. For the Western Orientalist this imperative involves the demanding struggle to grasp the values and facts of his tribe through the resistant medium of a difficult Asian language which may map political and social reality in ways different from those of any European tongue. The tribal expert will be a master at transcending the gap between the intellectual horizons of these different communities. Like the social anthropologist, the Orientalist must hone many skills but few are as important as inter-cultural translation.

The enlightened Orientalist, again like the tribal anthropologist, does not seek to change his tribe, but to understand it. This ambition demands a certain effort at acclimatization, of living among his tribe and identifying with its values, customs and goals. This may even require a degree of assimilation, however bracketed, of aliberal or illiberal values and social practices. It may furthermore demand, in an Asian context, a heightened sensitivity to the primacy of 'group' over 'individual' in both the cultural and methodological spheres. In all this, the goal of the tribal expert is to acquire a 'native feel' for his tribe.

To claim as much is not to deny the power of positivist research methods to illuminate patches of the tribal landscape, but it is to assert that the universalistic bias of positivism is fundamentally alien to the needs and ambitions of the tribal expert. It is also radically at odds with understanding Japan as a canonic polity. This points to the failure of non-European political philosophy. As Parekh has argued in 'The poverty of Indian political theory':

> Post-independence India has failed to throw up either a major political theorist or significant theoretical works on such subjects as social justice, the specificity of the Indian state, secularism, legitimacy, political obligation, the nature and structure of political argument, the nature of citizenship in a multi-cultural state, the nature and limits of law, the ideal polity, and the best way to understand and theorize the Indian political reality.[39]

This is the quest for theory that matters. Positivism cannot be allowed to stand in the way of responsible theorizing about the non-European world.

Time's river

Journalism, like tribal knowledge, embodies an approach to the facts of social life that is closely allied to empiricism. The journalist is a meticulous scrutineer of the 'contemporary'. His profession raises methodological problems of a different kind from that of the tribal expert. Thus, if the scholar decides to make himself a student of Japanese trade politics, to take a contentious field, then he is in effect choosing to live in close proximity with a distinct political tribe, over an extended period of time, to master its dynamics and nuances. But the study of this kind of tribe, as in the case of Campbell's welfare bureaucrats, forces one to distinguish the approach of the journalist from that of the tribal expert. This, in turn, necessitates a heightened awareness of the Heraclitean paradox at work in contemporary social science.

In the Preface to *India*, Hardgrave and Kochanek salute the importance of journalistic reality. After setting forth the prehistory of the volume and its major concerns, the text is interrupted by an 'Update', a summary of recent developments 'as we go to press'.[40] This is the scholarly equivalent of a news flash, what the Japanese call a *gogai* or 'extra'. It points, unerringly, at the central ontological truth of front-line empirical research: time creates the social reality that forms the horizon of meaning of the modern social scientist.

The meaning that human beings apply to the stream of events that unfolds in time is what we call history. For the student of contemporary events, this stream is a flood. But each day's events may also contain momentous singularities: one decisive development which may force the researcher to recast the whole thrust of earlier interpretations. A single new fact may shatter the edifice of a confident theory. American political reality significantly alters between the Monday and Wednesday of one week in November every four years. An analysis, however incisive, written on that Monday risks total repudiation by the first gleamings of Wednesday morning. Herein lies the relevance of Hardgrave's *gogai*.

Time is at once a great destroyer and creator of reality. Time consumes his creations. The point may be illustrated by a Japanese example chosen almost at random. In the spring of 1990, the American government made a series of demands on Japan to change its laws governing retail trade. These proposals were part of the so-called Structural Impediments Initiative (SII). Begun in September 1989, the talks were derailed five months later in part because of a dispute over the retail issue. An emergency summit between President Bush and Japanese Prime Minister Toshiki Kaifu in Palm Springs followed in March, and as a result of pressure, Japanese policy-makers decided to reform the legislation in question.

Because the economic interests of thousands of independent retailers were protected by such legislation against competition from large chains (Japanese as well as foreign), this proposed change was a sensitive issue for ruling-party parliamentarians from urban areas with large blocs of conservative-voting small shopkeepers.

On 10 April 1990, an article on the problem appeared in *AERA*, the Japanese news weekly published by Asahi Shinbun. Michio Watanabe, then MITI minister in the Kaifu Cabinet, was quoted as saying that the reform of the Large Retail Store legislation must not endanger the LDP's urban electoral base in Tokyo and other cities. This was a clear signal that, although the government would honour its pledges to the Bush Administration to ease licensing controls on retail outlets, such change would be implemented with the interests of supporters of the then ruling party in mind.

The facts contained in the *AERA* article represent but a tiny fraction of the empirical data generated by the contentious trade relationship between the United States and Japan since the late 1950s. The conflict has produced millions of facts. Just as important, the great bulk of these available facts begin to disappear almost as quickly as they come into being. Much of the relevant information is contained in what psychologists term 'the short-term memory'. On the day of his press statement, Watanabe would have had a precise grasp of where he had travelled that day, to whom he had spoken and what he said and thought. A week later, this confident grasp would have all but disappeared. Five years later, the few memories of that otherwise unexceptional day would be beyond recall but for the existence of records such as the *AERA* article.

The social scientist who wanted to grasp the context and significance of Watanabe's pronouncement on that day would consult the relevant published material and interview those involved with its production. To peruse the *AERA* article is do research of an essential kind, but in fact it is only to sample the crumbs from that day in April 1990 that were recorded because a journalist asked a question. Ideally, the political scientist who wanted a more complete command of the facts would have been at the journalist's elbow. The key difference between the political scientist who studies contemporary Japan and the historian who researches the court of Charles II or the battle of Sekigahara is that the political scientist can be at that elbow.

The Watanabe press conference was a part of a sea of information over which the journalist cast a net of hierarchic ordered need: what he believes to be germane to the issue of the day he translates into 'information' which, through the publishing process, often becomes *the* record of the event to survive. The *AERA* article was one of perhaps hundreds of pieces of analysis of the thousands of facts generated by the wrangle over the SII which scholars, reporters and commentators may now study at their leisure. The value of the *AERA* article rests on three facts: (1) the journalist was there; (2) he netted something of perceived importance from the myriad of facts available; and, (3) his catch, in published form, has semi-permanence as a source of reference.

The stream of data or potential information produced by a postmodern society is a vast unceasing river, into which, as Heraclitus observed, no man can ever step twice. From this flow, journalists, through the investigative and editing process, 'create' a picture or representation of reality. The job of the political scientist who studies Japanese government would be impossible without the highly selective filter imposed on such data streams by the print media. All the facts and information contained in all the Japanese newspapers printed since 1945 represent the tiniest sample of the potential 'database' created by Japanese society during that period. In turn, an introduction to Japanese politics, in a single volume, represents only a minute sampling of this immense journalistic harvest (the product of millions of man hours which no scholarly enterprise could match).[41]

Even five years after the article was written, no one could assume that the author of the article or any of the people he interviewed could reproduce precisely what they said or thought at the time. What is beyond doubt is that the moment when the reporter cast his net into the data stream in 1990 is gone forever. Historians speak of the need for a certain distance from the events in order to gain perspective. But it is at least as important that the passage of time destroys overwhelmingly the larger part of the potential facts. Without such destruction, empirical reality would be unmanageable for the researcher. It would be literally beyond his comprehension. Here, for the social scientist, is the true teaching of Heraclitus' paradox.

The ephemeral but also invaluable quality of such data makes it arguable that even though the political scientist may never quote the *AERA* article, it is more important that he should have read it, and any number like it, on the slight chance that it contained a single decisive fact that might alter his understanding of Japanese reality. Might this exercise be more valuable than spending any number of hours refining his grasp of methodological technique reading, for example, Ernest Nagel's positivist classic, *The Structure of Science*?[42]

The prime obligation of the student of contemporary Japanese politics is to stand in this stream, net in hand. For the political scientist, who is an empiricist rather than a positivist, this unstoppable river of ever-renewing facts *is* reality. In this radical sense, being there – in it – wet up to the chest, is everything. The search for tribal knowledge merely tells one where to stand. The essence of the problem is how time creates and destroys reality. *In tempore, veritas.*

This conception of political or social reality places special weight on the individual journalist and scholar. The quality of the data he harvests, his powers of analysis and skills of expression will, to a large degree, determine which bits of this data stream survive as objects of consciousness. The importance of the individual is radically affirmed by Heraclitus' paradox. The intelligent scrutiny and assessment of such harvests of potential information – the building blocks of political knowledge – is central to a rigorous purchase on contemporary politics.

This suggests that the political science of Japan bears a deeper affinity to print journalism than to the natural sciences. Print journalism is a daily struggle with vast streams of data. It is the art of knowing where to stand in Heraclitus' river of flowing reality. In the reporter's question – how long has your net been in the water? – journalism offers a constant admonishment to the armchair temptations of the scholarly life. Journalism is the science of editing reality. No one understands the dangers of hyperfactualism better than a journalist. His work gives him an intuitive grasp of what the language of information science terms 'total regress', where genuine knowledge of a complex system, such as a human community, demands the impossible: knowledge of 'all that is the case'.

If eighteenth-century chemistry provided Kant with telling illustrations of the positivist impulse to tyrannical clarity, then modern journalism provides a perhaps unrivalled example of the bracing chaos of empirical appetite. One conclusion appears to be irresistible. Despite the positivist's insistence that the chief methodological problem facing the social scientist is the quest for certitude, the most arresting epistemological conundrum challenging the empiricist is: how does time generate and destroy reality? This is the principal, if neglected, ontological question of twentieth-century social science. It points to the wisdom of Derrida's confession: 'It is to Heraclitus that I refer myself in the last analysis'.[43]

CANONIC JAPAN AND EMPIRICISM

The politics of astonishment

Great political systems are so rare that it matters little to posterity whether they issue from sovereign precedent or inspired practicality. Republican Venice embodied such a system. The city proudly called itself the 'La Serenissima' (The Most Serene), and rightly so. Between the creation of its constitutional order in the fourteenth century and the extinction of its liberty by Napoleon in 1797, the city was never conquered from without nor had its political system overturned from within. As foreign conquest and domestic instability were the rule in European politics during this turbulent half-millenium, Venice's achievements were astonishing.

And Europe was astonished. Venice may have ignored the lessons of the polities of the ancients in the design of her constitutional system, but the canonic impulse in early modern European thought and sensibility feed the ripe perception that Venice embodied a community of eminence. Faced with the political triumph that was Republican Venice, Europe reached out for an answering text. It found it in Casparo Contarini's *De Magistratibus et Republica Venetorum* (1543), 'one of the most widely read books on politics of the age'.[44] Eight editions in Latin, seven in Italian and two in French are recorded. In 1599, Contarini's masterpiece was translated into English by Lewes Lewkinor as *The Commonwealth and Government of Venice*. Widely discussed before, during and after the Civil War, Contarini's portrait of Venetian greatness won the endorsement of John Milton as offering an ideal solution to England's miseries. Such was the impact of Contarini's confident conclusion that:

> There have been many commonwealths which have far exceeded Venice as well in empire and in greatness of estate, as in military discipline and glory of the wars: yet have there not been any, that may be paragoned with this of ours, for institutions and laws prudently decreed to establish unto a happy and prosperous felicity.[45]

Something approaching a canonic moment arrived when James Harrington (1611–77), the English political thinker on whom modern reflection would confirm pantheonic status, exploited Contarini's portrait of Venetian governmental excellence in *The Commonwealth of Oceana* (1656). Harrington had observed the workings of the Venetian state at first hand, and in *Oceana* he sought to glean the principles of political stability by exposing what he called the 'political anatomy' of past constitutions.[46] His aim was to find a permanent cure for the convulsions that shook the English state before the Glorious Revolution. Venice was an exemplar of how this might be achieved.

Through an extraordinary process of revolution and restoration, this canonic torch passed from Venice to England. This passage was registered in a pantheonic procession of texts, from Hobbes through Harrington to Locke. Montesquieu's reflections on English greatness in *De l'espirit des lois* (1748) left its mark on the constitution of the American republic. Such works were monuments to the miraculous transformation of English political fortunes from the seventeenth century.

> After the 'Glorious Revolution' of 1688, England entered a period of development which made her the most powerful and most influential nation in Europe. Many observers of the shift of the European centre of political gravity towards a previously negligible island on the western edge of the continent credited the emergence there of a superior system of government with playing a leading role in this remarkable turn of history. By the mid-eighteenth century, England was widely viewed by political commentators, as Venice had been earlier, as a working exemplification of an ideal system of government.[47]

After 1945, the centre of political and economic gravity shifted towards Japan, another previously negligible island on the margins of global affairs. In material and intellectual terms, this movement has been one of the most important developments in Asian history.

Like England's after the Glorious Revolution, Japan's post-war revival was sudden and decisive. The Japanese are the first non-White nation to break the chains of modern underdevelopment and poverty. Japan's arrival at the forefront of the community of nations has signalled the broad renewal of Asian energy and prosperity after three centuries of decline, disorder and despair. This marks the end of the long era of Western domination of world affairs.

As the temptation to deny Japan's canonic importance has been so frequently yielded to, it is time for Westerners to accept that the Japanese have achieved a political brilliance fully comparable to that which earlier centuries assigned to the Venetian republic and England after 1688. Japan's record of successful economic management, as measured by GNP growth, price stability, levels of employment and relative equality in distribution of income, has, when contrasted with the trials of the major Western nations since the First Oil Shock, given this Oriental polity an almost golden patina. Life expectancy, educational attainment, crime control and some success in the provision of health care complement this picture of public policy achievement. Do we think of ancient Sparta, Spinoza's Holland or Bismarck's Germany as having achieved as much?

We must crack the shell of our resistance to the idea of a canonic Japan if we are to savour the kernel of the intellectual counter-reformation that it promises. Admission of Japan into the political pantheon would offer hopeful evidence of a new openness within the mainstream disciplines of the human sciences that have hitherto been closed to non-European ideas and ventures. A healing balm would thus be applied to the abraded racial feelings and sensitivities that have hardened outlooks on our shared planet.

Given all this potential gain, where is the text that would consummate modern Japan's canonic triumph? Where is the classic demonstration that a superior system of government has played a decisive role in this remarkable turn in twentieth-century history? Why have a host of talented empiricists working in the main centres of political scientific research across the Euro-American world grasped this rare opportunity only to drop it? It is not only the Western positivist who has failed Japan.

The appearance of Robert D. Putnam's *Making Democracy Work: Civic Traditions in Modern Italy* (1993) is a reminder of what bold, empirically sound political science may strive for and attain.[48] Putnam's work has been compared with the classic labours of Tocqueville, Pareto and Weber. If Italian politics offers such fertile ground, then this must also be true of modern Japan.

The Western denial of Japanese greatness is a fact. Positivist universalism has no doubt contributed to this denial, but empiricists also bear responsibility. The most troubling barrier is to be found not in the stars of social scientific tradition, but in the stance of the Japan expert and his discipline. Quite simply, the ambitions, skills and intelligence of the individual thinker, writer and scholar count for far more than is conventionally conceded. If Dante enforces on his readers a street-by-street intimacy with thirteenth-century Florence, what anchors the classicism of *The Divine Comedy*: late medieval Florentine society or the fact that Dante was a late medieval Florentine? What ontological weight lies behind the claims on contemporary sensibility of middle-class Jewish women in *fin-de-siècle* Vienna or nineteenth-century French Catholics or East Saxon Junkers or Trobriand Islanders? Is the validity of these claims the result of the special features of these small samples of humanity or the consequence of their selection for special perusal by Freud, Durkheim, Weber or Malinowski? The phenomenon is not enough.

Even more than the masterpieces of these social scientific revolutionaries, the canon of political philosophy disciplines our expectations about what constitutes textual greatness. It sets universal reach across time against the apparent randomness of the classic objects of late-nineteenth century and early twentieth-century social science. To celebrate Japan as a canonic polity is to insist that such greatness is rooted in the political sphere.

Modern Japan offers an unrivalled ground for the recasting, in a revolutionary, Nobel Prize-winning way, the foundations of economic positivism and social science as a whole. Among the great projects that beckon, few are as exciting or as challenging as the struggle to loosen the grip of positivism on the study of human behaviour in the economic sphere. To sail through and beyond positivism's Pillars of Hercules is to begin to map afresh the latitudes and longitudes of our self-awareness as social beings in ways that may reach beyond even the great achievements of the European founding fathers of modern social science.

Early promise

The neglect of Japanese greatness by empiricists surprises because the forces of history have always influenced the Western study of Japanese government. From the end of the American occupation of Japan (1952) until the Second Oil Crisis (1979–81), foreign policy and party politics dominated the scholarly horizon. With the success of the US Occupation of Japan and the mounting tensions of the cold war, national character analysis, which blended 'Orientalist' essentialism with the imperatives of wartime propaganda and policy-making, quickly yielded to the very different needs of cold-war struggle.

The impact of social science on the study of Japan in the English-speaking world distinguishes it from the philological and historical methods that still prevail in European Orientalism. But even more important has been the way that post-war Japan has engaged the political, economic and social concerns, or what Edward Said terms the 'material' interests, of the United States and the White dominions of the British Commonwealth. Although British imperial power has almost entirely been withdrawn from China and South-east Asia, Australia has remained exposed to the renewal of Japanese influence. This Australian exposure has, in turn, decisively shaped British research on Japanese politics and society in ways that distinguish it from Orientalist practice in Germany, France and Italy. The stamp of such 'real-world' concerns has persisted even as the disinterested study of party politics proper expanded within the discipline after the turbulence of the 1950s and early 1960s.

The primacy of electoral and party politics was gradually challenged by the political implications of Japan's rapid economic growth: roughly 10 per cent per annum during the 1960s. Japan's economic take-off was viewed then in a different light. Japan's economic expansion was often regarded as the fruit of Occupation reforms or as an ancillary consequence of the uninterrupted rule by pro-business conservative governments.

American proponents of the Modernization School recognized post-war Japan's economic achievements, but tended to view them against Japan's tradition of underdevelopment. The fruits of the era of high-speed growth were judged within a Third-World frame of reference. Japan's economic trajectory seemed likely to carry it no further than the middle ranks of the OECD. Even after the First Oil Shock of 1973–74, Japan's brief but sharp bout of hyper-inflation again masked her emergence as an industrial power of first rank. Only later did it become clear that Japan, alone among oil-dependent manufacturing nations, had triumphed over the difficulties of a huge increase in world oil prices and the 'stagflation' that followed. But it took the punishing blows of the Second Oil Shock and the 1980–81 recession for the Western world finally to awaken to the full measure of what Japan was achieving as a nation in both the public and private sectors. Political science was not indifferent to this sea change. Arthur Stockwin made the revolution in Japan's international status his point of departure in the first edition of *Japan: Divided Politics in a Growth Economy*, published in 1975.[49] His textbook opened with the powerful recognition that 'No country has achieved such spectacular economic progress since the 1950s as Japan'.[50] In a rare gesture in a political science primer of the times, Stockwin addressed the issue of capital investment from the very first page. This was followed by a balanced assessment of the causes of Japanese economic growth. The role of Japan's formidable Ministry of International Trade and Industry (MITI) was highlighted; the system's dependence on political consensus stressed.

Stockwin remained committed to the prevailing view that party politics remained the core concern of the Japan expert:

> When we turn from economics, however, to the broader field of politics, conflict is often more evident than consensus. Japan is a seriously divided polity, although the divisions have been partially concealed by a long period of conservative government.[51]

Stockwin judges Japan's economic policy-making as no more than a subset, albeit an important one, of the political process as a whole. Although the structure and function of Japan's central government, particularly the higher bureaucracy, are given due recognition in his textbook, there is no doubt that the electoral struggle between the country's various political camps, particularly the ruling Liberal Democratic Party (LDP) and the Japan Socialist Party (JSP), form the heart of his inquiry. Economics can be safely left to the economists.

Seven years and another oil crisis later, the impact of Japan's economic success began to provoke a paradigm shift in the Western study of Japanese government. In 1982, Chalmers Johnson published *MITI and the Japanese Miracle: The Growth of Industrial Policy, 1925–1975*.[52] No work by a Western author did more to elevate the claims of Japanese public policy as the field of the future in political science. Thus, the enterprise set in motion by Campbell's *Contemporary Japanese Budget Politics* (1977) and Johnson's *Japan's Public Policy Companies* (1978) was consolidated and raised to a higher plane.[53] Johnson's MITI study, together with T. J. Pempel's *Policy and Politics in Japan*, which also appeared in 1982, helped to transform a diverting subdiscipline into one of the three main pillars (party politics and foreign policy studies being the other two) of Japanese government research.[54]

It was Johnson's assault on the classic divide between political science and economics that gave his book its long-term importance. The first sentence of *MITI and the Japanese Miracle* was a manifesto: 'Perhaps the oldest and most basic subject in the study of political economy is the relationship between governmental institutions and economic activity.'[55] For a political scientist to launch a programme of major research on this classic issue was to call into doubt the division of labour between politics and economics as autonomous academic disciplines. Johnson dedicated his book to William W. Lockwood, that rarest of scholars, a political scientist turned economist, who, in Johnson's words, 'pioneered this subject'.[56] Johnson's provocative motto ('It is only managers – not nature or laws of economics or governments – that make resources productive') comes from Peter Drucker, the Austrian-born American business thinker, who has repeatedly clashed with positivist economists studying Japan over the contentious issue of the Japanese-ness of Japanese economic behaviour.[57] But the real bite in the motto was provided by Johnson's implicit gloss of Drucker's words: bureaucrats are managers, and Japanese bureaucrats have been successful on a world-beating scale.

For the economist, Johnson's title, *MITI and the Japanese Miracle*, is absurd. It appears to brush aside centuries of positivist reasoning which argues that economic miracles are impossible. I say 'appears' because Johnson never addresses in a specific way the claims of positivist law-making, although no scientific doctrine poses a greater threat to the credibility of his thesis. Nevertheless, the territorial contest between political scientists and economists left its mark on Johnson's thinking. In the middle of a vigorous defence of the government's (particularly MITI's) creative role in Japan's post-war miracle, Johnson confesses that: 'I cannot prove that a particular Japanese industry would not or could not have grown and developed at all without the government's industrial policy'.[58] More is at issue in this concession than the recognition that history permits no experiments. On the contrary, this sentence encapsulates one of the fundamental problems of the study of Japanese industrial policy: the failure of political scientists and economists alike to devise a formal proof, one that John Stuart Mill might have found acceptable, that government policy contributed in a decisive way to the progress of this Oriental economic miracle.

It is no accident that this problem lies precisely on the boundary between political science and economics. Reviewing *MITI and the Japanese Miracle* in 1983, I put the issue this way:

> The difficulties of asking whether bureaucracy via a set of industrial policies might serve as a more effective instrument of economic progress than the merely regulated market are the direct consequences of blind spots in the political economic paradigm. Economists by virtue of their training will not address this question; political scientists by virtue of theirs cannot. Yet the need to know remains.[59]

The more damning insight may be that, given the premises of Smithian economic thought, a formal proof is impossible. The main barrier to a proof of industrial policy success lies not in the misreadings of economic reality by Japanese policy-makers, but rather in the very fabric of economic thought as formulated by the classical school. At this point, what Edmund Husserl called the 'intellectual horizons' of the problem seem to take on a distinctly ideological taint. This would be convenient because ideology is a political flaw with which the political scientist is trained to deal.

If, however, this failure of mind is correctly blamed not on ideology but on science, then the Asian specialist will have to master new tools of thought. How else is the student of Japan to discriminate, with confidence, between the competing claims and relative capacities of economics and political science, as formal disciplines, to characterize Japanese reality? Here we confront a problem of philosophy.

Johnson's effort represented the high point in the campaign within political science to bring specifically Japanese insights to bear on the academic understanding of public policy. During the 1980s, Ezra Vogel and Ronald Dore also urged Westerners 'to take Japan seriously' within the more flexible (anti-positivist) framework provided by sociology.[60] But, as the coda to *MITI and the Japanese Miracle* hinted, the future was pregnant with a different kind of revolution:

> The Japanese [have] built on known strengths: their bureaucracy, their zaibatsu, their banking system, their homogeneous society, and the markets available to them ... the institutions of the Japanese developmental state are products of Japanese innovation and experience.
>
> This suggests that other nations seeking to emulate Japan's achievements might be better advised to fabricate the institutions of their own developmental states from local materials. It might suggest, for example, that what a country like the United States needs is not what Japan has but, rather, less regulation and more incentives by the government for people to save, invest, work and compete internationally.[61]

Johnson's remarks reflect an awareness of a new intellectual and political climate. During the course of the 1980s, the imperatives of disinterested scholarship weakened out of a sense of perceived economic and social necessity. Japanese public policy success made that nation a model for imitation by other nations, especially in the rest of Asia. This threw into doubt the effectiveness of post-war public policy in the United States and much of the West. But rather than 'look East', Westerners fell back on the intellectual foundations of the Enlightenment. The result was the triumph of economic liberalism and social neo-conservativism known as Thatcherism and Reaganomics.[62]

The Second Oil Crisis had put paid to the Keynesian consensus that dominated public policy thinking after the Second World War. Monetarism emerged with almost irresistible force. The erstwhile contradiction between macro- and microeconomic theory (which had provided the theoretical foundations of the so-called 'mixed economy') had been subjected to heavy attack since the early 1970s. Over the course of the 1980s, liberal market doctrine and economic individualism congealed into the ruling orthodoxy. The resulting ideological wars shook many of the key political and scientific assumptions of Western society. The shotgun marriage of free-market liberalism and social conservatism (the contradiction was never resolved) transformed politics and policy-making in America, Britain, Australia and New Zealand, but no advanced democracies were left untouched by this right-wing revolution. Almost everywhere, national debates over the role of the individual, the state and the market acquired a sharper edge.

The impact of free-market theory made Japanese economic institutions and policies more difficult to understand. The new conservative climate cast a distinctive shadow on Daniel I. Okimoto's *Between MITI and the Market: Japanese Industrial Policy for High Technology* (1989).[63] Classical market theory, positively assessed, plays a conspicuous role in Okimoto's thinking about Japan. As with Johnson, no formal proof of the effectiveness of industrial policy is offered. Some might argue that Okimoto was too influenced by free-market theory even to attempt one. Yet, what is striking about his analysis is how much the old question of the Japaneseness of Japanese industrial policy intrudes. The power of positivist economic theory is acknowledged, but its explanatory limits are also noted.

Okimoto echoes the approach of Stockwin and Johnson to the boundary dispute that arises from the differing approaches of political scientists and economists. They all acknowledge the importance of economics, but tend to reject its more excessive claims:

> It is possible to argue, as most economists do, that Japan's postwar success owes more to the soundness of macroeconomic policies than to its industrial policy.... But without entering into the pros and cons of the argument, one can propose a variant hypothesis: sound macroeconomic management greatly facilitates – and may in some senses be a condition of – effective industrial policy.[64]

Equally important is Okimoto's summary of the MITI critique of liberal, that is positivist, economic theory:

> In the eyes of Japanese officials, the 'pure' market is flawed by several shortcomings: imperfect information; narrow, short-term pursuit of instrumental gain; primacy of individual company interests over collective interests; 'free ride' approach to the public good; opportunistic behavior; scant spirit of cooperation; structural change and social dislocations; potential subordination to foreign commercial interests; and inattention to national goals.

Although the market imparts substantial impetus to long-term economic efficiency, it offers no guarantee that broader social. political, or economic security interests will be served. Because collective objectives are important in Japan, a goal-oriented country, MITI officials rely on industrial policy to compensate for the above-mentioned shortcomings in the marketplace.[65]

Three issues of theory, as opposed to empirical research, must be kept in mind when reading the Western literature on Japanese public policy. First, Japanese economic success, however defined, has a political dimension. Second, the study of Japanese public policy, including industrial policy, necessitates constant attention to the epistemological and empirical implications of the boundary between political science and economics. Third, most Western students of Japanese government remain unwilling to concede primacy to liberal economic theory either in Japanese political science as a whole or in public policy studies in particular.

Economics is a positive science in the classic sense: it aims to devise universal laws of human behaviour that meet the most important demands made of any branch of learning which matches the rigour of the natural sciences. But it does not follow that for a political scientist to reject the claims of economics is for him to renounce the only body of theory (in George Homans' sense) that could underwrite a genuine claim by political science to be a genuine science.

Thinking back to Johnson's use of the term 'proof', it should be clear now that the central failing of political scientific analysis of Japan during the 1980s was its lack of confidence in the face of positivist dogma. The lack of so-called 'strong theory' remains the great weakness of the Western student of Japanese government. To be faithful to the quality of the empirical data uncovered by the expert on Japanese public policy, political scientists must generate their own body of rigorous theory. Such a corpus of theory could have revolutionary implications.

Given all that we have learned since the appearance of *MITI and the Japanese Miracle*, it is obvious that if it could be proved that action by government improved Japan's national economic performance in ways that surpassed the theoretical perfections of the free market, then political scientists and economists alike would stand on the shore of what Thomas Kuhn would call a 'scientific revolution'.

Doubting empiricists

Rather than boldly to plunge into this new uncharted sea, in antici-
pation of fresh, paradigm-shattering discoveries, some of the West's
most prolific students of Japanese government have preferred to
camp on the beach in empiric discontent. Under the guise of a
variety of approaches and ideologies, scholars such as Kent Calder,
David Friedman and Richard Samuels have let this precious scientific opportunity slip from their fingers because they hold, on empirical grounds, that Japan is not significant politically. Consciously or
not, these scholars have surrendered to the view that, in terms of
grand theory, Japan is nothing.[66]

Such interpretations lend succour to economic positivists and
other free marketeers who remain anti-statist, anti-bureaucratic
and, in the precise canonic sense, anti-Japanese. The canonic argument underlines the implicit endorsement of Eurocentrism by these
doubting empiricists. Whatever their intentions, their research findings lend factual weight to those who argue that the modern world
is a Western invention. Neither Asian experience nor Asian ideas,
not even those of the Japanese, ontologically matter. The desolate
conclusion is that Japan has achieved nothing of decisive historical
consequence, nothing that might force mankind to rethink how to
make public policy. This is to deny canonic status to the Japanese
polity and, by natural and inevitable extension, to the entire non-
European world.

The charge of 'Orientalism' looms over these empirical labours.
The complex and contentious dialectic between science and 'Orientalism' is so sensitive, so vulnerable to rhetorical excess, that it must
be handled with care. The heart of the matter is intention. Martin
Bernal insists in *Black Athena: The Afroasiatic Roots of Classical
Civilization* that Western scholars have laboured for the past two
centuries to 'fabricate' an intellectual portrait of ancient Greece that
denigrated Egyptian and Levantine influence and achievement in
order to protect the image of pristinely White excellence.[67] But
to argue that this was a consequence of European and American
scholarship on classical Greece is not to demonstrate that this was
the scholarly intention. As science, the research of Calder, Friedman
and Samuels is worthy of the closest inspection.[68] But their denial
of the significance of government and politics, Japanese or otherwise,
troubles the political scientist unmoved by the tendentiousness of
Eurocentric controversy and 'Orientalist' critique. It is odd for a
political scientist to commit himself to the task of proving that his

discipline is irrelevant to the wider public discourse on Japan's importance, but this is what these doubting empiricists have done, because, in their view, the facts allow no other conclusion. Given the stakes in Japan's pantheonic quest, the matter cannot be allowed to rest, as it were, on the beach of this sea of formidable scientific promise.

Atalanta's challenge

The Greek parable of Atalanta and Hippomenes, related by Ovid, teaches that it is the objective, not running the race, that counts. Has this truth been lost sight of among political scientists who study Japan? Of all the ambitions that may entice the Japan expert, none finally matters as much as the goal of intellectual significance. Unlike the study of foreign policy and party politics, Japanese public and industrial policy has offered the discipline an unrivalled opportunity to 'make it new'. This is the point that is lost on Campbell when he remarks in *How Policies Change* that 'There is more to Japan than industrial policy'.[69]

In seeking to test the sinews of Johnson's thesis that the Japanese miracle has political foundations, the discipline has come away with some golden prizes. Previously unexamined facets of Japan's political and economic system have been subjected to close scrutiny. An impressive shelf of full-length monographs has been assembled, and the study of Japanese government and politics has won new respect and stature. But somewhere along the path of would-be innovation that stretches from Johnson's developmental-state theory to the canonic Japan thesis, we appear to have been empirically waylaid. This has the makings of a tragedy because Japan's canonicity may be the closest that our subject ever comes to possessing a thesis that might bear comparison with Durkheim's theory about suicide or Weber's Protestant ethic thesis.

Hardly anyone denies Japan's national importance, but few Western thinkers, philosophers or scholars are willing to concede canonic significance to Japan. Almost none of the books that have been written since the 1970s in response to Japan's economic success recognizes Japan's 'world-historical' significance. This is one reason that the race was, in some important ways, lost during what should be the second great phase in the rise of Japanese public policy studies: the era of high empiricism.

During the first phase of this rise, the era of pioneering discovery, Johnson attacked the assumption that politics had made *no* contribution to the flowering of the Japanese miracle. Johnson's seminal point has often been lost on his critics among political scientists. Indeed, no feature of the subsequent critique of the developmental-state theory set out in *MITI and the Japanese Miracle* has been more astonishing or disappointing than the rush by political scientists to deny the significance of Japanese politics. But then, as Campbell has remarked, there is a strange tendency among students of government to concentrate on policy failure where, in contrast, students of business celebrate corporate success.[70] Calder's paean to the glories of private enterprise in *Strategic Capitalism* and his dismissive stance towards bureaucratic achievement not only mirror the endemic opti-mism of business studies and debunking pessimism of policy analysis, but also point to the persistent temptation of Johnson's critics to downgrade politics into a second-class piece of social reality.[71]

The economic positivist or advocate of free enterprise argues that this is only natural because the market is always superior to government. This perception has decisively influenced how the books of our doubting empiricists, such as David Friedman's *The Misunderstood Miracle*, have been read and interpreted.[72] The great fear must be that the entire import of *Strategic Capitalism*, *The Business of the Japanese State* and *Financial Politics in Contemporary Japan* will be read to confirm the thesis that the market is always right and government intervention always wrong.[73] This perverse interpretation highlights the dangers of ivory-tower research that ignores the fact that the outside world has its own influential agenda of ideas and ideologies which may *determine* the wider impact and meaning of our empirical labours.

Within the academy, Japanese greatness demands more than a modest influence on the study of comparative politics. This raises two issues. If it is arguable that none of Johnson's critics has pub-lished a book of more lasting impact than his, then it might also be fairly observed than none of the volumes spawned by Max Weber's thesis, from R.H. Tawney's *Religion and the Rise of Capitalism* to Robert N. Bellah's *Tokugawa Religion*, has equalled the scientific force and influence of *The Protestant Ethic and the Spirit of Capital-ism*.[74] Or might it be that *MITI and the Japanese Miracle* has pro-vided a sandy and false foundation upon which to erect a social scientific cathedral worthy of Japan's post-war achievement? Is John-son to blame for the misdirected energies of his opponents?

The temptations of business studies (Calder) or rational-choice theory (Ramsmeyer and Rosenbluth) or the ethical defence of small businesspeople (Friedman) have diverted the political science of

Japan from the main objective of demonstrating that the world is more than a Western invention.[75] But the most diverting of all Hippomenes' apples has been Johnson's assertion that the Japanese bureaucracy 'rules' the policy-making process.

The issue of where the true *locus* of power lies within in a polity is a classic political question. But in addressing the issue of bureaucratic domination, political scientists have repeatedly fallen foul of the kind of anti-bureaucratism that it took the genius of Weber to see beyond. Too many scholars appear deaf to Samuels' lament about the theoretical and intellectual dependence of Japan studies upon the Euro-American mainstream: 'One looks in vain for concepts exported from the subfield to the discipline. One looks in vain for studies of Japan driven by original theoretical questions.'[76] What is true of Japanese studies in America is even truer of Europe. As a result, the political science of Japan, like Atalanta, has lost ground in the race towards the principal goal.

The pearl divers

Reflecting on the study of Japanese politics in the 1970s, Samuels concluded that 'Overall, Japanese political studies were marked by a failure to cumulate knowledge and to build upon previous research'.[77] This bleak scholarly landscape provoked Samuels into quoting William Steslicke's often cited remark that 'we have many pearls, but few necklaces'.[78] Twenty years on, students of Japanese government may boast that they have collectively threaded the most impressive necklace that Japanese political studies has yet to produce. Written in response to the impact of Japanese public policy, this lustrous string of substantial books by single authors includes some of the best-known names in the discipline.

Examination of this necklace demands careful scrutiny of the notion of 'microempiricism'. In *Strategic Capitalism*, Calder writes: 'There is no substitute for a micropolitical, economic and social perspective, combined with a detailed sense of the interpersonal networks that integrate the nation as a whole.'[79] This is a sweeping claim. In itself, microempiricism is nothing more than a commitment to a certain 'depth' of research; it is not a method. In pursuing 'depth', scholars have brought a variety of methods to bear on their microempirical labours. But the doctrine of microempiricism assumes that greater depth of research must, in principle at least, always result in enhanced factual grasp of the social domain under investigation. But how would reality have to be organized for microempiricism to be valid? Until the required ontology is set out in a compelling manner, mircoempiricism will remain as vulnerable as social scientific positivism, albeit in another way, to onotological critique.

Empirical research methods illustrate the inherent difficulty. Take, for example, the research interview. This technique was exploited by Campbell in his study of Japanese welfare policy, while Calder speaks of the 'literally hundreds of scholars, government officials, politicians, business people, and especially economic journalists – in Tokyo, and throughout Japan – with whom I have puzzled over the details of Japanese public and private credit allocation, in search of the larger picture'.[80]

Talking with expert witnesses, in a structured or informal manner, may be invaluable to the interpretation of printed primary and secondary sources. In tracing policy or other kinds of networks, discussion with participants in the network may provide unrivalled insights into group dynamics. Vast amounts of data, one is tempted to say 'nearly infinite amounts', may be garnered from such interviews. But such information may be harvested in many different ways because reality is so varied that it calls into question not only the validity of the microempiric quest, but also the reach and authority of claims for microempiric knowledge as knowledge. Such epistemological weaknesses may be illustrated.

Calder, for example, seeks to demonstrate that the 'window guidance' of the Bank of Japan (BOJ) has been ineffective as a tool for implementing public financial goals. He also insists that the Japan Development Bank (JDB) has been effectively thwarted in its efforts to serve as an efficient conduit for public finance. In contrast, Calder argues that the Industrial Bank of Japan (IBJ) has achieved rare success in advancing its financial goals precisely because it is in the private sector.

Whom did Calder interview to acquire the data needed to buttress such claims? It is inconceivable that all the officials at the BOJ, JDB and IBJ uniformly reinforced Calder's thesis with their testimony. On the contrary, a scholar studying public finance using interviews will gradually piece together a picture of how the institutions in question work. In this process, some interviewees will count for more than others.

My research on the British Home Office pivoted on the quest for what I call the '15th man', the network figure with the intelligence, experience and patience to illuminate the whole institutional horizon with insight. The more one tests the truth of the testimony of the

'15th man', the more his evidence will come to outweigh that of numerous other 'insiders'.[81] The success of interviews as a research technique is not, in essence, about interviewing hundreds of people but rather about locating and talking with a handful of the right people. Microempiricism must be as much about quality as quantity.

There is, furthermore, little point in interviewing hundreds of network 'insiders' if the researcher does not listen to what they say. When Campbell presented his original thesis to his welfare bureaucrats he came to the conclusion that his ideas departed from the logic of the network that he was studying. Campbell's first thesis did not, in his view, address institutional realities. Hence the rule of thumb of the wise interviewer: the preconceived thesis of an outsider about an institution will almost always prove to be inaccurate.

In *How Policies Change*, Campbell identifies at least four conflicting ways of picturing the realities of public policy-making. There are others. And this brings us to one of the core limitations of pure empiricism understood as *scientific* research. In the analysis of Comte's rules or guarantees for sound positivist science discussed in the last chapter, it was concluded that the scientific doctrine of intersubjectivity was one of the two rules that applied to both positivist and empirical research.

In the natural sciences, a discovery is not accepted as truth unless it can be reproduced in a different laboratory by a different group of scientists. If the examination of the same body of fact does not yield the same conclusion then the doctrine of intersubjectivity demands that such research findings not be judged as sound because they have not been verified objectively. Truth should not vary with the scientist. This is the point of establishing the intersubjective validity of research findings.

Yet, if Johnson rewrote Friedman's history of the Japanese machine tool industry or Friedman rewrote Johnson's history of MITI, who could guarantee that they would examine precisely the same body of fact? Social reality is so rich, the number of relevant facts so enormous that the social scientist is tempted to slice a complex piece of Japanese data neatly so that it confirms his theory and his alone. And this does not begin to address conflicts between different theses, ideologies and values. What would *MITI and the Japanese Miracle* look like if Calder had written it?

Intersubjectivity poses a significant challenge for the microempiricist. Take, for example, one of the more surprising conclusions that Calder draws in *Strategic Capitalism*: that the Toyo Shinkin scandal was a more or less minor event that the historian of IBJ should set to one side. In this unhappy business, IBJ lent $1.8 billion in unrecoverable loans to Onoue Nui, the infamous Osaka restaurateur who speculated on the stock market with $2.6 billion in loans based on forged certificates of deposit.

In his lengthy analysis of IBJ, Calder mentions Onoue just twice: notably in a paragraph that hails IBJ's 'sophisticated analytical network', its 'uncanny prescience' and its skill in using 'its industrial finance expertise and human network to aid new industrializers in China and other developing countries'.[82] Buried in the middle of this paragraph of high praise, Calder observes that:

> But the IBJ made some spectacularly naive lending decisions during the speculative, easy-money era of the late 1980s, including unrecoverable loans of $1.8 billion to a Kansai restaurant owner, Onoue Nui, that forced the resignation of IBJ chairman Nakamura Kaneo in October 1991.

In the second paragraph, Calder seeks to downgrade the importance of the Toyo Shinkin scandal, which he never mentions by name, by blaming the complications of credit assessment and 'the fluid environment' of the 1980s bubble for 'the bizarre Onoue lending scandal of 1991'.[83]

Bizarre or not, the Toyo Shinkin scandal dealt IBJ's reputation for sobriety and prudence a heavy blow. When the staff of the Nikkei Kinyu Shinbun published their analysis of IBJ's prospects for the 1990s, titled *Kogin no Henshin* (IBJ's Metamorphosis), the impact of the Toyo Shinkin scandal was addressed in the very first sentence of the book's prologue.[84] The Nikkei Kinyu analysis includes an entire chapter on the Toyo Shinkin affair. It would not have been creditable to have done otherwise, given the shock that the Onoue farce delivered to IBJ's many friends and fans among Japan's financial press, to say nothing of IBJ's elite workforce.

According to the notion of microempiricism, more research must, in principle, *always* yield better understanding. But what happens when two authorities conflict? On the Toyo Shinkin scandal, Kent Calder and the reporters on the Nikkei Kinyu Shinbun, one of Japan's most presitigous organs of newspaper news and analysis of the financial sector, cannot both be right. The result is a logical conundrum: if two authorities are not better than one, then, in principle, why should a third (the author of yet another book on IBJ's industrial finance during the 1980s) necessarily be a *decisive* improvement on the first two books? At this point, the methodological sceptic might turn quite sour on the claims of the microempiricist because the central doctrine of microempiricsm – more research is always better – is not true.

The troubles of microempiricism do not end there. Whom is Calder quoting for his judgement of the irrelevance of the Toyo Shinkin affair? Whom did he ask for their opinion? What explains this apparent intention to understate the impact of this fiasco? The quality of microempiric data hangs on the answers to such questions which are not answered in what is a substantial and otherwise excellent study of Japanese industrial finance. But there may be another reason for Calder's interpretation of the Toyo Shinkin scandal: it offered ammunition to those who might disagree with his denigration of public policy-makers in favour of private banks. How much evidence is being suppressed in our pursuit of necklaces rather than individual pearls?

Here, it appears that Calder has tapped into the long Japanese argument between private assertion and public authority, but the line that Calder, as well as Samuels, tends to draw between 'private' and 'public' sectors is much more rigid than that of Japanese commentators treating this issue. Hence, the suspicion that *Strategic Capitalism*, like Friedman's *The Business of the Japanese State*, echoes the long and intense *American* debate over the relative virtues of private freedom vs. public-sector responsibility (what Robert Reich has called the 'two cultures' of modern America)[85] far more than the Japanese discourse about the issue. These are two Americans speaking; they have not reproduced the precise feel of the discussion that the Japanese have conducted among themselves. We must be philosophical about such limitations. As Vico warned long ago, 'whenever men can form no idea of distant and unknown things, they judge them by what is familiar and at hand'.[86] To engage in the science of Orientalism or any branch of area studies is to risk this kind of error every day of one's working life. Political scientists must not pretend that such risks are irrelevant or always avoidable.

To sum up, microempiricism falters on the illusion of depth. The only remedy that the advocate of microempiricism may suggest to ease the IBJ vs. JDB conundrum is to urge 'more research'. If Campbell insists that 'there is more to Japan than industrial policy', then surely there must be more to Japanese public policy than the relentless pursuit of the details of one bank's industrial credit strategy.

More may not be the answer; microempiricism offers no cure. Rather we must take to heart Kant's warning that researchers 'who are especially empirical, are constantly endeavouring to differentiate nature in such manifold fashion as almost to extinguish the hope of ever being able to determine its appearances in accordance with universal principles' or indeed any general thesis whatever.[87] The universe of social fact may not be structured in such a way that greater depth of research always results in more accurate purchase on reality. On ontological grounds alone, as we have seen, microempiricism is vulnerable. When a scholar demonstrates his mastery about this political party or that bureaucratic agency, the discipline recognizes this expertise. But the whole business works to a large degree on trust because the research exercise in question is never likely to be repeated. The question is, therefore, how much 'trust' should be extended to any piece of empirical research, however massive?

The normal scholarly empiricist reads with his fingers crossed; so should the microempiricist. This is because the data at work in empirical research are no doubt facts, but they are ordered around contrivances of argument. Indeed, hyperfactualism fans the suspicion that, like the journalist, the scholarly empiricist's central task is not discovering reality but editing a representation of it. This limits the claims that the social scientist may legitimately make for his work. No monograph, certainly none on a large contemporary topic, is definitive. Microempiricism is not indispensable.

The habits of the ghetto

One achievement of Chalmers Johnson remains unmatched by any of his learned critics. He formulated a thesis that influenced opinion about the how the world works in the mainline disciplines that dominate social science. *MITI and the Japanese Miracle* was the first study of the political science of Japan to break with the cycle of theoretical dependence upon the Euro-American social scientific mainstream. He held up the promise of academic significance for the political science of Japan. Among Western political scientists who publish, only John Zysman, Daniel Okimoto and myself have sought to build on Johnson's declaration of intellectual independence by seeking to win new provinces for our discipline.[88]

Elsewhere there has been a retreat into scientific respectability. Research of a high standard has resulted; but this research has fed the urge to occult the political significance of the Japanese miracle. The principal message of theories such as 'crisis and compensation', 'reciprocal consent' and 'strategic capitalism' is unambiguous: Japan is not significant.

Reading only the three or four books at issue, the mainstream Western scholar may safely conclude that Japan has nothing special to say to him. Japan comfortably conforms to the Euro-American paradigm in which John Maynard Keynes and Fredrich Hayek divide the public policy world between them. This represents a victory for the ghetto mentality that pervades Japan studies on both sides of the Atlantic. Confronted with the choice between intellectual significance and academic respectability, some of our best scholars have embraced the bourgeois option. The result is that where once the mind of Europe celebrated the singular feats of the Venetian Republic and the miraculous surge of English power after the Glorious Revolution, today we greet Japan's record of political achievement with the fog of empirical denial.

Coda

The 1990s have changed the face of global politics, and the alert political scientist has been powerfully stimulated by this transformation. Sometimes the scope of change reached beyond stimulus to destruction. Certainly this was the case with Sovietology. With the demise of the Soviet Union, a historic turning point which was not predicted by Kremlinologists and has yet to be satisfactorily explained by them, Soviet studies may pass into the keeping of the historian.

There is a moral to be drawn from the sorry fate of Sovietology because among all the branches of area studies in the Western university it may have been uniquely blessed with expertise, funding and public interest. The wrangle between Sovietologists over the fallen carcass of the Soviet Union has been vigorous and, on occasion, even brilliant. But this heated debate has often been disturbingly old-fashioned. For some of the old guard, it seems that nothing at all has changed.[89] Much recent argument appears to turn on contradictory claims that 'my empiricism is better than yours', and the reason that mine is better is that my ideological orientation, left or right, is sounder.

The end of the cold war shook Japanese politics. Doubly burdened by the bursting of the Japanese speculative bubble at the end of the 1980s and the costs of the 1995 Kobe earthquake, the Japanese state is now struggling with the most complex and resistant set of challenges it has faced since the end of the Pacific War, if not since the Meiji Restoration of 1868.

The response of Japanese studies to this intellectual change may also be described as vigorous, even brilliant. But I believe that Japanese political studies has been evolving in ways that may allow it to match the high standards espoused by the great Kremlinologists of the past, and perhaps even to surpass them. My confidence has been enhanced by the arrival of what I see as the third great phase in the rise of Japanese public policy studies that has begun to take shape during the 1990s. The first two stages – pioneer theorizing and high empiricism – have been described above. The defining concern of the third phase is methods. In essence, Japanese public policy studies, together with other subfields of the discipline, most notably the analysis of Japanese political parties and electoral behaviour, is caught in what Germans call a *Methodenstreit*: a dispute over methodology.

Reviewing the progress of the past two decades from the vantage point created by the current controversies within Japanese studies, it should be obvious that there has been a remarkable consolidation of academic standards. The appearance of John Campbell's pioneering study, *Contemporary Japanese Budget Politics*, in 1977 helped to slay the inhibitions within the discipline against the writing of a single substantial book by one author on a single research theme within the policy field. This scholarly precedent was taken to heart by the leading Western students of Japanese public policy since the late 1970s.

The heroic phase of Western research on the Japanese bureaucracy flowered during and immediately after the Second Oil Shock. Chalmers Johnson's *MITI and the Japanese Miracle* was one of the most important books published during this first crucial phase of public policy research because it, more than any other volume produced during this rich period, helped to provoke the second phase: the era of high empiricism. Any list of the monographic monuments written during this second phase must include Kent Calder's *Crisis and Compensation* and Richard Samuels' *'Rich Nation, Strong Army'*.[90] John Campbell's *How Policies Change* confirmed the importance of the large book on a single subject by a single author for the political science of Japan. *'Rich Nation, Strong Army'* may embody one of the last expressions of total confidence in the monumental empiricism that dominated the scholarly landscape between 1982 and 1994.

If the attack on Johnson's developmental-state thesis found its most compelling voices in Friedman's *The Misunderstood Miracle*, Samuels' *The Business of the Japanese State* and Calder's *Crisis and Compensation* and *Strategic Capitalism*, then Samuels has come full circle in 'Rich Nation, Strong Army' by confirming the overriding importance of nationalist drive and collective ambition as the governing ethos of those parts of the Japanese public and private sectors which have sustained the post-war economic miracle. Like my own *Japan: Beyond the End of History*, 'Rich Nation, Strong Army' looks as much to the past as it does to the future. The fate of the miraculous web of public and private institutions, as well as the values, attitudes and opportunities that buttressed this high-GNP, low-employment machine may now be caught in decisive transition. My reaction to this possibility has been to argue that the period between 1945 and 1990 marks a specific golden age not only in Japan's long history but also in the history of the political systems that have dominated the reflection of European political philosophers at least since Hobbes and Harrington. The canonic thesis, in my judgement, offers one of the richest veins for work by the political theorist and student of political institutions. But if the debate between Johnson and his critics, particularly Calder, Friedman and Samuels, generated the most sparks during the 1980s, today the struggle is over methodology. The division in *Japan: Beyond the End of History* between 'politics' and 'philosophy' was my bow to this change.

Calder's forceful advocacy of microempiricism has already been assessed. Campbell's musings on research methods strikes me as being as important as any of the empirical chapters in *How Policies Change*. Rosenbluth has now abandoned the cautious empiricism that held sway in *Financial Politics in Contemporary Japan* in favour of rational-choice theory in *Japan's Political Marketplace*, which she co-authored with J. Mark Ramseyer. Maurice Wright's massive study of Japan's Ministry of Finance is keenly awaited not least because of the singular powers of network analysis that the author so forcefully advertised in *The Promotion and Regulation of Industry in Japan*, which he co-edited with Stephen Wilks.[91] Finally, Chalmers Johnson and E. B. Keehn have ignited a sharp controversy over the usefulness of rational-choice methods in understanding Japanese politics and policies in their 1994 article in the *National Interest*.[92]

At every turn in these often intense exchanges, we are arguing as much about methods as about bodies of fact. The dangers are that one increasingly needs only to know the method of the researcher to be able to predict with fair accuracy what his research findings will be. The compensating benefit is that full grasp of the intellectual demands of methodology may now be expected from every serious participant in what is without question the most vital and stimulating front in all Japan political studies today. Methodological naivety and innocence is dead.

In *Japan and the Enemies of Open Political Science*, I seek to show that Japan's canonic potential is confirmed by the capacity of this extraordinary political system to feed a *Methodenstreit* which, with luck, may some day be compared favourably with the major intellectual debates of the past, including the celebrated dispute over positivism (*Der Positivismusstreit*) that galvanized German sociology during the 1960s. If our current efforts can be sustained, then the political science of Japan will match, and perhaps overtake, the intellectual successes achieved under the banner of the Princeton Modernization School between the late 1950s and early 1970s. In so short a time, we have come this far. The Italian poet Carducci was right: 'Tomorrow is holy.'

5 Orientalism

Orientalism [is] the corporate institution for dealing with the Orient
– dealing with it by making statements about it, authorizing views
of it, describing it, by teaching it, settling it, ruling over it: in short,
Orientalism as a Western style for dominating, restructuring, and
having authority over the Orient.

Edward Said

Since Aristotle and Bacon, a cardinal move in the European sciences
has been 'division', the reduction of a problem to smaller, more
manageable units for purposes of scientific scrutiny. Empiricism
reflects this strategy in its commitment to the endless refinement of
the universe of fact. Positivist-style analysis gives chase to an even
larger, if less differentiated, body of data with the butterfly net of
positivist laws. Both methods exemplify the doctrine of 'divide and
conquer'.

There is an opposing school which insists that students of human
society should, in E. M. Forster's words, 'only connect'. In the wake
of Western Marxism's decline, the most influential expression of
this demand that thinkers brood on totalities ('Nothing escapes
Imperialism') at the expense of scientific dissection is post-structuralism and its popular mask of 'politically correct' advocacy.[1] This
embrace of essentialist totalities is at once the greatest strength and
most damning weakness of Edward W. Said's attempt to marry
amoral post-structuralism with a moralistic left-wing critique of the
evils of colonialism.

Said is motivated by an unforgiving ethical vision that seeks to
banish life's sheltering ambiguities in favour of a moral palette
limited to stark blacks and whites. The discourse of anti-colonialism
is a form of post-Christian Manichaeism which dramatizes the

unequal battle between the Western oppressor and his non-European victim. The key motive at work in this critique is what Nietzsche called the 'resentment' of the weak against the strength of the strong. In this struggle between Whites and non-Whites, Said sets the moral rights of the oppressed against the majestic claims to truth of the European empirical and positivist sciences. It is this Manichaean urge that presses Said to see, perhaps too vividly, that classical social science, like European high culture, has played servant to Western power, encouraging the European and Euro-American alike to entertain an exquisite daydream of irresistible Eurocentric superiority. A similar conceit is at work in Jacques Derrida's assertion that metaphysics is nothing more than 'White mythology'. The Western student of Japan and Asia surrenders to this mythology every time he succumbs to what Said terms 'Orientalism'.

WHAT IS ORIENTALISM?

Said and his post-structuralist allies seek to correct the imbalance of power between mainstream Euro-American disciplines and the marginalized specialities that study non-European cultures by making White colonialism the pre-eminent burden and distress of the European spirit. This is a bold intention. The meaning and import of Hitler's massacre of European Jewry, to take a cardinal example, is transformed if we accept, with Césaire and Fanon, that the Nazis 'merely' brought home to Europe the horrors of the slave trade and Conquistador slaughter in the New World.

Said's moral crusade hangs on the successful redefinition of a single word: 'Orientalism'. Unlike the watchdogs of political correctness who want to hound the word 'Oriental', as a racial designation, from popular and academic usage in the United States, Said does not seek to ban the term 'Orientalism'. Rather he would firmly attach negative connotations to this complex word that had, until his intervention, been gradually disappearing from educated usage.

The *Shorter Oxford English Dictionary* defines 'Orientalism' as:

1. Oriental character or style; an oriental trait or idiom.
2. Oriental scholarship; knowledge of Oriental languages.

Both definitions are addressed in Said's critique of the Western understanding of Asian societies and cultures, but to these two definitions, he would add a third:

3. A Western political ideology or discourse about the Orient which has stressed its sensuality, its tendency to despotism, its aberrant mentality, its habits of inaccuracy, its backwardness, as a justification for European, American and Israeli colonization of Asia.[2]

All branches of Orientalism are implicated in modern Western domination of the Orient. Literary Orientalism, as a style or theme in European letters, is condemned for providing an ideological defence of European empire-building in Asia and Africa. The offending writers include Flaubert, Kipling and Conrad. Such 'crimes' are not confined to fiction. The religious learning of great Orientalists, such as Sir Hamilton Gibb and the liberal-minded Louis Massignon, is also censured because it failed to develop a remedy for willful Western misrepresentations of the Orient.

Said paints a harsh picture: 'Formally the Orientalist sees himself as accomplishing the union of Orient and Occident, but mainly by reasserting the technological, political, and cultural supremacy of the West'.[3] The central flaw of the Orientalist is his weakness for 'essentialism': Oriental complexities are reduced to a shorthand of caricature and cliché ('the unchanging East' or 'Islamic medievalism' or 'African darkness' or 'the Yellow Peril'). Such essentialism has survived the retreat of European and American imperialism. Indeed, Said argues in *Covering Islam* (1981) that the worst recent offenders are American journalists who cover Asian and African affairs.[4]

Said rejects the argument that social science has liberated Asian studies from the bane of this kind of racist essentialism. Rather this danger is ever present because research by Westerners on the non-European world cannot elude the impact of the exercise of Western power over the Orient. Disinterested science is a myth. The social scientific revolution of Weber, Durkheim and Marshall has not rendered the 'European or American studying the Orient' immune from the main circumstances of his actuality: that 'he comes up against the Orient as a European or American first, as an individual second', or from the fact that this Westerner belongs not only 'to a power with definite interests in the Orient' but 'to a part of the earth with a definite history of involvement in the Orient almost since the time of Homer'.[5]

The force of such criticism cannot be ignored. But it must be stated plainly that Said's attack is insufficiently rigorous to justify the abandonment of either Western social science or area studies. Indeed, the methods developed by social scientists and Western students of the non-European world during the past century offer a powerful cure for the very left-wing essentialism that compromises both cultural theory, as advocated by Said and radical scholars such as Stuart Hall, and subaltern studies, as proposed by thinkers such as Gayatri Chakravorty Spivak.

Saidian scepticism cannot, however, be dismissed out of hand. The European weakness for right-wing essentialism, be it racist or 'Orientalist', when discoursing on the non-European world is so ingrained that Said's *Orientalism* deserves a conspicuous and permanent place among those corrective texts that serve to keep the Western scholar true to his scientific and disinterested calling. Let us now examine the grounds for this claim.

INTELLECTUAL IMPERIALISM

More than the geology of the earth's surface, it is the accidental boundaries of human geography that determined the grid lines of area studies. The East Asian, Latin American or Middle Eastern expert inherits the age-old Orientalist commitment to the projection of understanding across space. In contrast, positivism is geographically obtuse because it is anchored in the search for universal laws which, by definition, transcend geographic boundaries. The social fact of the positivist is no respecter of human frontiers; positivist methods apply equally everywhere. This approach reflects the hunger for universal knowledge that has driven the European intellect since the late Middle Ages.

The regional specialist must reaffirm the geographic core of his scholarly vocation. Said's meditation on 'culture' is a call to arms in the struggle to liberate the geography of understanding from the constraints of social scientific universalism. Culture, for Said, has a spatial as well as a textual component. As a radical reader of classic texts, Said is an heir of Georg Lukács, the Hungarian critic and the greatest Marxist philosopher since Lenin. But in attacking the geopolitics of imperialism, Said allies himself also with Antonio Gramsci, another Marxist giant. Said stands firmly within the modern intellectual discourse of Continental Europe since Hegel and Vico:

> Lukács belongs to the Hegelian tradition of Marxism, Gramsci to a Vichian, Crocean departure from it. For Lukács the central problematic in his major work *History and Class Consciousness* (1923) is temporality; for Gramsci, as even a cursory examination of his conceptual vocabulary immediately reveals, social history and actuality are grasped in geographical terms.[6]

In his essay 'Some aspects of the Southern [Italian] question' Gramsci 'gave, as his towering counterpart Lukács did not, paramount focus to the territorial, spatial, geographical foundations of social life'.[7] Whatever divides Lukács and Gramsci, Hegel's notion of the 'subject' serves as the prime mover that sets history in motion.

> we assume that the better part of history in colonial territories was a function of the imperial intervention; in the other, there is an equally obstinate assumption that colonial undertakings were marginal and perhaps even eccentric to the central activities of the great metropolitan cultures. Thus, the tendency in anthropology, history, and cultural studies in Europe and the United States is to treat the whole of world history as viewable by a kind of Western super-subject, whose historicizing and disciplinary rigour either takes away or, in the post-colonial period, restores history to people and culture 'without' history.[8]

The imperial theme not only reflects but also sustains a one-sided intercourse between Europe and the Other, between the West and the rest. Because, in Said's phrase, 'Nothing escapes imperialism', a surprising range of disciplines, sciences and texts have been blamed for feeding the hidden complicities at work in the projection of Western power since Vasco da Gama. The remedy is plain. In the name of the intellectually marginalized, the area expert should abandon his habit of obeisance before the dais of mainstream scientific privilege. No one, however worthy, is above criticism if he has helped to fan mainstream indifference to the creative claims of the non-European world.

Said is unsparing. He lays the charge of 'Eurocentrism' even at the feet of Raymond Williams, the Marxist critic and the British father of cultural studies. Said challenges Williams' portrayal of the 1840s, a revolutionary decade for the English and French novelist. In his introduction to *Dombey and Son* (1847–48), Williams characterizes the decade as 'a transforming, liberating and threatening time' but without a single reference to India, Africa, the Middle East and Asia although 'that is where transformed British life expanded to and filled, as Dickens slyly indicates'.[9] Williams' lacuna is fatal, for as Said observes in his discussion of Conrad's *Heart of Darkness*, 'Without empire, I would go so far as saying, there is no European novel as we know it'.[10] What is true of the novel is true of European social science.

Even the demigods of French post-structuralism are judged vulnerable to such censure. Michel Foucault, a supposedly *outré* French thinker, was enthralled with the Eurocentric paradigm. The radical impulse at work in the revisionist labours of Foucault and Williams suffer from self-inflicted limitations because, in Said's words, both thinkers judge 'the imperial experience as quite irrelevant' to their larger enterprises.[11] A similar indictment may be brought against those European sciences that have sought to swaddle Japan's canonic achievements in silence.

Just as geographic imperatives propel Said's assault on all those Western disciplines and discourses that would occult the true power relationship between the West and the non-White world, so the successes and failures of imperialism haunt the labours of the area specialist. White power may have drawn back to the Euro-American heartland during the course of the past century, but European science still mimics, in the sphere of the intellect, the nineteenth-century domination by the European centre over the non-European periphery. Gramsci's word for this cultural condition is 'hegemony'.

Said concludes that

> one has the impression that interpretation of other cultures, texts and peoples – which at bottom is what all interpretation is about – occurs in a timeless vacuum, so forgiving and permissive as to deliver interpretation directly into a universalism free from attachment, inhibition or interest.[12]

Just as the literary critic of imperialism will censure the matter-of-fact Dickensian embrace of the politics of imperial exile (the policy of Australian penal transportation is central to the plot of *Great Expectations*) or flinch at the modesty of Jane Austen's hints that the comfort and elegance of life at Mansfield Park rest firmly on the income of Sir Thomas Bertram's slave plantation in the West Indies, so the proponent of Japanese canonicity will challenge the positivist neglect of Japan's economic rise by the followers of Adam Smith and David Ricardo or the denial of Japan's pantheonic ambitions in political philosophy by the epigone of Auguste Comte and Bertrand Russell.

In other words, 'Orientalism', in the Saidian sense, is not confined to culture or literature. Political science and modern philosophy have not flowered in air-tight isolation from conflicting human interests or scientific blindness. On this point, Said is resolute and wounding. If Jane Austen 'sublimates the agonies of Caribbean existence to a mere half-dozen passing references to Antigua',[13] then John Stuart Mill forthrightly endorses the imperatives of imperialism in the *Principles of Political Economy* (1848):

These [outlying possessions of ours] are hardly to be looked upon as countries... but more properly as outlying agricultural or manufacturing estates belonging to a larger community. Our West Indian colonies, for example, cannot be regarded as countries with a productive capital of their own... [but are rather] the place where England finds it convenient to carry on the production of sugar, coffee and a few other tropical commodities.[14]

Said insists that the traditional Western strategies for dealing with 'cultural experience', broadly defined, must be set to one side. Thus, 'if it has been the practice in the West since Immanuel Kant to isolate cultural and aesthetic realms from the worldly realm, it is now time to rejoin them'.[15] Furthermore, if culture and aesthetics are no longer immune to real-world imperatives, then modern social science, with its worldly commitments, never has been.

This geographic critique may be extended to the philosophic classics that form the foundation of social scientific method. According to the philosopher Harry Bracken, students of Western philosophy still 'conduct their discussions of Locke, Hume, and empiricism without ever taking into account that there is an explicit connection in these classic writers between their "philosophic" doctrines and racial theory, justifications of slavery, or arguments for colonial exploitation'.[16]

Almost nothing, it appears, eludes the reach of 'Orientalism'. This includes the body of nineteenth-century social and political theory that anchors twentieth-century political science, including the study of Japanese government and politics. Both Mill and Hegel have accounts to settle with the non-European world. The reader of Alexis de Tocqueville must set his remarkable penetration of the racial dilemmas of American life against his defence of the French conquest of North Africa. Whatever their disinterested achievements, as positivists and empiricists, the classic thinkers of modern social science were all, in their different ways, deeply involved in European self-definition *vis-à-vis* the non-European 'Other'.

This includes Max Weber. With Durkheim, this great German sociologist may be the most admired of all social science's founding fathers. Maruyama Masao once observed that Weber occupies the middle ground between English empiricism and Hegelian historicism.[17] But Weber's career as a thinker about the non-European world leaves him uneasily poised between the armchair positivism of Comte, Spencer and John Stuart Mill, with their hierarchic schemas of the civilized and the savage, and the twentieth-century revolution in field-research methods.

One difficulty is that Weber's scholarship on Oriental societies – India, ancient Israel and China – is as dependent on the same kind of evidence, the reports of missionaries, travellers and explorers, as the labours of Comte and Spencer. This calls into doubt the soundness of Weber's conclusions about the non-European world (Chinese scholars have long expressed dissatisfaction with the way that Weber interpreted Confucianism and Taoism in *The Religion of China*).[18] It also invites scrutiny of Weber's effort to re-centre European civilization in the face of Nietzsche's grim prophecies and the disturbing role of human reason and rationalization in the 'disenchantment of the world' (Schiller).

Said highlights Weber's link with Orientalism and the intellectual defence of Western domination over the Orient:

> Weber's studies of Protestantism, Judaism, and Buddhism blew him (perhaps unwittingly) into the very territory originally charted and claimed by the Orientalists. There he found encouragement amongst all those nineteenth-century thinkers who believed that there was a sort of ontological difference between Eastern and Western economic (as well as religious) 'mentalities.'[19]

But the difference, ontological or otherwise, is not one between civilized equals. Western superiority is the latent assumption in Weber's vast programme of reflection. His meditation on contrasting civilizations shares more with the hierarchic concerns of nineteenth-century positivism and Orientalism than with the non-evaluative and relativist posture that has increasingly governed Western anthropology since Weber's death in 1920.

Said judges Weber's impact on Islamic studies to be particularly pernicious:

> Although he never thoroughly studied Islam, Weber nevertheless influenced the field considerably because his notions of type were simply an 'outside' confirmation of many of the canonical theses held by Orientalists, whose economic ideas never extended beyond asserting the Oriental's fundamental incapacity for trade, commerce, and economic rationality.[20]

Weber's celebrated notion of 'ideal type' has, as it were, retractable claws. Mindful of such 'tigeritude', Said calls into doubt the ruling assumption of post-war area studies: that the social scientific revolution of Durkheim, Marshall and Weber has liberated the area specialist not only from the limitations of nineteenth-century philology, in which 'texts matter more than people', but also from the affliction of 'Orientalism' itself.[21] Has, therefore, the social scientific revolution failed Japanese studies?

JAPAN AND ORIENTALISM

Said teaches that science is a poor match for prejudice. The social scientist's 'proclivity to divide, subdivide, and redivide the subject matter' of the Oriental sciences has left untouched, in Said's view, the central Orientalist myth: the Orient is 'always the same, unchanging, uniform and radically peculiar subject'.[22] Has Japanese studies fallen foul of anti-Asian prejudice? Many social scientists would concede that the study of Japan in the West has surrendered to the rigours of specialization. But in the wake of the scholarly revolt against national character analysis after 1945, the dogma that the Japanese are, in essence, an unchanging race benefits from little support today, certainly among social scientists who are area specialists.

To rebel against a brand of cultural explanation is not enough. Positivism, empiricism and Orientalism continue to conspire against the recognition of the canonic status of modern Japan. In the name of scientific universalism, the Western positivist ignores Japan and the achievements of the non-European world. Hyperfactualism threatens the empiricist with an anarchy of scholarly endeavours, ideological commitments and private compulsions at the expense of proper recognition of the historically significant. The ever-shifting frontier between Orientalism and 'Orientalism' (studying the Orient versus dominating the Orient) encourages the sly to cloak Eurocentrism in pseudo-scientific respectability. On methodological grounds alone, it is worth asking why it has taken the labours of a specialist in English and French literature to demonstrate the ways that 'Orientalist' mythology continues to haunt the science of the modern area specialist. Said's *oeuvre* offers further evidence of the unacceptable price that Western social science has paid for its uncritical homage to Newton, Mill, Russell and Carnap.

If physics does not provide the sole legitimate model for the study of society, and if the social scientific revolution of Weber, Pareto and Durkheim remains incomplete, then how deeply should the regional expert yield to the Saidian critique? The answer turns on Said's understanding of science. In his assault on Orientalism, as a field of knowledge, Said concentrates his fire on Middle Eastern or

Islamic studies which, he argues at length, have been among the more methodologically retarded of the Oriental sciences. But this attack is curiously qualified in a nod to objectivity:

> Today there are many individuals working in such fields as Islamic history, religion, civilization, sociology, and anthropology whose production is deeply valuable as scholarship. The trouble sets in when the guild tradition of Orientalism takes over the scholar who is not vigilant, whose individual consciousness as a scholar is not on guard against *idées reçues* all too easily handed down in the profession.[23]

The research success of Japanese studies, at its most vigorous, is undeniable, but have we been sufficiently vigilant? There is much to be vigilant about because such *idées reçues* flicker to life whenever there is geo-political confrontation between the Orient and the Occident. Michael Crichton's *Rising Sun* and Karl van Wolferen's *The Enigma of Japanese Power* may not be racist tracts, but both works pander to 'Orientalist' prejudice. More than two thousand years of Western fear of and contempt for 'the East' stand behind the publishing success of such attacks on Japan. This phenomenon lends ammunition to Said's claim that 'Orientalism . . . puts the Westerner in a whole series of possible relationships with the Orient without ever losing him the relative upper hand'.[24]

With this proposition in mind, the devil's advocate might narrate the obscured history of such *idées reçues* in the public discourse on modern Japanese politics. Take, for example, the evolution of post-war American images of Japan discussed by Richard J. Samuels in his essay 'Japanese political studies and the myth of the independent intellectual'.[25]

The immediate post-war period was dominated by the perception that the Japanese were 'culturally predisposed' to aggression.[26] This view slowly yielded to the position that the Japanese could be democratized. From the late 1950s, the Modernization School developed the thesis that the astonishing expansion of the Japanese economy showed that Japan was successfully making its way up the path already pioneered by the West. This provoked a left-wing critique of the Modernization School which held that the modernizers were 'too favorable' and 'too optimistic' about Japanese prospects.[27] From the early 1970s, ecologists also hammered on this point. After the briefest flowering of the 'learn-from-Japan' boom in the wake of the Second Oil Shock, proponents of Japanese success were shouted down by the same left-wing critics who had routed the Modernization School. In the late 1980s, anti-Japanese revisionists sought, once again, to demonize Japan. After the Japanese economic bubble burst, American opinion appears to have settled on one of two views: that the Japanese may safely be dismissed or that Japan should be forced to be 'free'. At the same time, a feminist and minority-rights critique was nurtured in academe and elsewhere which censured the male-dominated, majoritarian character of Japanese society.

Amid the shifting battle of American argument about Japan, only one feature has held constant. For almost the entire post-war period, a thoughtful American has been able to weigh the merits of the Japanese case with complete confidence that political virtue, cultural superiority and economic prowess were *always* on his side. Post-war 'Orientalism' appears to have fulfilled its duty to ensure that the Westerner has indeed been placed in a great variety of relationships with Japan 'without ever losing the upper hand'.

This sour conclusion may be resisted on three fronts. First, the Western view of Japan has altered out of all recognition since the middle of the nineteenth century despite the constant temptations to stereotype the Orient and the Oriental. In his 1970 T.S. Eliot Memorial lecture, titled *In Bluebeard's Castle*, George Steiner observed:

> Never again, I imagine, will a white statesman write as did Palmerston in 1863, at the occasion of a punitive action in far places, 'I am inclined to think that our relations with Japan are going through the usual and unavoidable stages of the Intercourse of strong and Civilised nations with weaker and less civilized ones'.[28]

The subsequent century has witnessed a revolution in European and Euro-American sensibility, and as a result 'A ubiquitous anthropology, relativistic, non-evaluative in its study of differing races and cultures, now pervades our image of "self" and "others" '.[29] Behind the field-research labours of Malinowski, Evans-Pritchard and Franz Boas stands a radical revaluation of Western civilization. This has been a genuine, if neglected, source of progress in Japanese studies.

Second, the vigour of the attack on the paradigm of Orientalism has led some critics to misinterpret recent developments in the Western study of Japan. Take the contrast that Said cites between the backwardness of Middle East studies and the 'revolution led by The Committee of Concerned Asia Scholars [CCAS] in East Asian studies'.[30] The CCAS movement was not, as Said implies, an uprising against Orientalist philology. In political terms, it was a left-wing critique of Japanese nationalism which left Westerners firmly in possession of the moral high ground *vis-à-vis* Japan. The CCAS was dismissive about Japan's drive to modernize and overtake the West. In methodological terms, the CCAS campaign was a counter-revolution against the social scientific approach of the Modernization School. The CCAS critique led to a more empirically varied picture of Japan, but in methodological terms, it was often reactionary. It abandoned the scientific gains achieved by the Modernization School; and it struck an almost fatal blow at the Western discovery of Japanese canonicity. When Samuels asks how it was possible that Chalmers Johnson's *MITI and the Japanese Miracle* did not appear until twelve years after Herman Kahn's *The Emerging Japanese Superstate* (1970), part of the responsibility for this lost decade lies with those who sought to destroy the Modernization School.[31]

Said also neglects the seminal achievements of the Orientalists, who have made Japan their concern. It is the wordsmiths of Orientalist studies, the philologists and not the social scientists, who have written the most important twentieth-century texts on Japan. The summit of these labours is almost certainly the two translations of *The Tale of Genji* by Arthur Waley and Edward G. Seidensticker.[32] This impression of literary success is reinforced by the wide impact of translations into English, French, Russian and other Western languages of the work of Mishima, Tanizaki and Kawabata.

The arts and religion have not exhausted this achievement. Indeed, what is striking about discussions of Asian political thought in standard Western works of reference is that it is the Orientalist, not the political scientist, who has had the greater impact. In dictionaries and encyclopedias on which modern Japan casts hardly a shadow, the force of pre-modern Japanese thought, like its Islamic, Chinese and Indian counterparts, has been judged worthy of Western respect and study.[33] The contrasting poverty of impact of the 'modernist' or anti-philological approach points to one of the singular failures of social scientific area studies in the American mould, which has been so anxious to free itself of textual study and philology. The social scientific revolution has yet to live up to its promise to advance Japanese studies.[34]

This should be a reminder of how we moderns still stand in the shadows of the ancients. During the fullest flowering of nineteenth-century technology, Marx brooded on the apparent inability of Western modernity, unrivalled in so many fields of human endeavour, to eclipse the cultural standards of the classical Greeks. At the end of

A Contribution to the Critique of Political Economy, Marx famously concluded that 'The difficulty we are confronted with is not, however, that of understanding how Greek art and epic poetry are associated with certain forms of social development', that is the social scientific problem.[35] But rather, 'the difficulty is that [Greek forms] still give us aesthetic pleasure and are in certain aspects regarded as a standard and unattainable ideal'.[36]

If the textual excellence of Greek and Latin literature served as the supreme justification for its dominant place in European education from the Renaissance to the First World War, then Orientalism's commitment to the tireless study and dissemination of the finest religious and literary texts of pre-modern Asia reflects a parallel vulnerability to artistic monuments and their powers to communicate across the centuries. These powers may explain why American philosophers, such as Robert Nozick, have learned to take Indian philosophy so seriously or why Arthur C. Danto is willing to compare the impact of the Columbia University lectures of D. T. Suzuki on Zen in the 1950s with the celebrated seminars of Alexandre Kojève on Hegel in Paris during the 1930s.[37]

Marx's assessment of the status of the fine arts and epic poetry offers almost casual evidence of the astonishing intellectual breadth of this 'founding father of social science'. The unsurpassed mastery demonstrated by the ancients calls into question the social scientist's banishment of the poets and artists from the ambit of his concerns. Orientalism has its monuments. Where are ours?

Third, it is precisely such pressures and the temptations of *idées reçues*, the racial and cultural stereotypes that have scarred Orientalism in the past, that explain why the objective-minded social scientist and area expert have been determined to defend what Said would dismiss as pretence: the claims of 'pure' or disinterested knowledge. Indeed, the greatest failing of Said's critique of Orientalism is his rejection of science.

At the beginning of this chapter, the proposition was put forward that the 'embrace of essentialist totalities is at once the greatest strength and most damning weakness' of Said's attack on Orientalism. The strengths are genuine. After *Orientalism* and *Culture and Imperialism*, one rereads F. R. Leavis's high assessment of Jane Austen and Alan Ryan's generous study of John Stuart Mill with greater intensity and awareness.[38] But Said's critique has encouraged unwarranted scepticism towards science among his followers. Caught up in a web of 'only-connect' totalities, Said's acolytes in subaltern studies, for example, appear unable to square up, honestly and clearly, to an obvious truth: it *is* possible for a White man or woman to study Asia in an objective and disinterested manner. A rigorous science of the Orient is not only conceivable, it has been achieved. Against the failings of Silvestre de Sacy, Edward William Lane and Ernest Renan, the leading spirits of nineteenth-century European Orientalism, one may set the contemporary achievements of Japanese studies and of most branches of area studies.

This does not allow us to ignore the problems posed by some forms of positivism and empiricism. The imperviousness of the mainstream disciplines of European reflection on human society, and not just economics and philosophy, to Asian insights or ideas represents a persistent stain on Western reflection on Asia. Positivist economics is applied to non-Western societies; Asian experience has not informed the science of economics. One need not subscribe to Said's critique of 'Orientalism' to ask how long can the hour of scientific reckoning be delayed?

BEYOND ORIENTALISM

There have been three key moments in the unfolding of the post-war critique of Eurocentrism. First, there was the appearance in 1961 of Frantz Fanon's *The Wretched of the Earth*.[39] This was followed by Lévi-Strauss's famous attack, in the final chapter of *La Pensée sauvage* (1962), on Sartre's meditation on Hegel's monist concept of History in the *Critique de la Raison Dialectique* of 1960.[40] Then, in 1978, Said exploited the speculative critique of power and knowledge developed by Michel Foucault to challenge the foundations of the cultural sciences and area studies in *Orientalism*. More recently, Said has sought to address the barbed issue of textual classicism and European power in *Culture and Imperialism* (1993), which should be read as a coda to *Orientalism*.

My call for us to move 'beyond Orientalism' is an attempt not only to answer Said's *Orientalism*, but also to digest the insights of this provisional canon so that area studies may move beyond it. The word 'beyond' is used here in a Hegelian sense: the problem posed by this chain of argument, which stretches from Fanon and Lévi-Strauss to Foucault and Said, must first be recognized, then criticized, and finally transcended. Here, Fanon's legacy has been reassessed in Chapters 2 and 9. *Pace* Lévi-Strauss's misconceived assault on Sartre, the French philosopher's true failing was not to have been Hegelian enough, and this issue is addressed in Chapter 8. Finally, a fresh approach to the Orientalist and social scientific inheritance of the contemporary area expert is proposed in Chapter 12. In all of this, the goal is mastery and fruitful synthesis. This may require subversion of the would-be canonic chain of anti-European texts that has taken shape since Fanon. But then canonic betrayal is another cardinal move of what Eliot once called 'the mind of Europe'.

Such betrayal is motivated by the belief that the intellectual and scientific solution for Said's lament lies in the recognition that the Japanese have generated a canonic piece of scientific reality which merits a place in the European pantheon. As Said would be the first to recognize, it is Asian power and success, not literary criticism, which offers the most potent cure for European neglect of the non-European mind.

Words

6 Languages

No two of us learn our language alike, nor, in a sense, does any
finish learning it while he lives.

> V. O. Quine

Human beings do not live in the objective world alone, nor alone
in the world of social activity as ordinarily understood, but are
very much at the mercy of the particular language which has become
the medium of expression for their society.

> Edward Sapir

Political science, like poetry, is made of words. The human substance
of the social sciences is as verbal in character as Stephane Mallarmé
claimed was true of verse. All our perceptions, representations and
interpretations of factual reality are manifested through the medium
of language. We think with words. To the degree that the student of
politics and society suffers from what Louis Massignon, the great
French Orientalist, once called *soif ontologique* (ontological thirst),
the social scientist should drink in language. This is a thirst that
anti-language cults, such as pure mathematics or symbolic logic,
literally cannot satisfy. Language alone answers our need for a
confident, indeed resolute, *human* sense of self-possession and grasp,
not only of the objects that we seek to understand, but also of the
enabling truths of 'self' and the 'other' which we nurture in
the course of our intellectual vocation.

To this linguistic need, the Orientalist brings two issues of consequence, what Althusser called 'problematics'. The first arises from
the fact that mankind speaks more than ten thousand different
languages. In this post-Babel condition, the axiomatic assumption
of Oriental studies is that the linguistic horizon of meaning which
provides the Orientalist with his subject of study is normally encoded
in a language radically different from his own. That two political

communities, which share as much as England and France do, might speak different languages is an occasion for wonder. That social reality may be explored and ordered through the lenses of such contrasting visions of reality as we find at work in the modern English and Japanese languages, to say nothing of their ancient and medieval ancestors, is nothing short of astonishing.

The second linguistic conundrum of the Oriental sciences is equally important. Printed objects – the review essay, the scholarly article, the probing monograph, the full-length book, the definitive *Gesamtwerk* – are the executive means of the political and social sciences. The labours of the social scientist are caught up in the web of words that is the ontology of the page.

The Orientalist brings special pressure to bear on this ontology. As Edward Said has noted of the writings of perhaps the twentieth-century's most influential British student of Muslim society, Sir Hamilton Gibb's 'oeuvre purports to be Islam':

> There is no dislocation, no felt discontinuity between Gibb's page and the phenomenon it describes, for each according to Gibb himself, is ultimately reducible to the other. As such, 'Islam' and Gibb's description of it have a calm, discursive plainness whose common element is the English scholar's orderly page.[1]

Other branches of Asian studies may muster their own canonic examples of the orderly and ordering page to answer Orientalism's dazzling list of printed objects. This list includes the exotic exuberance of 'd'Herbelot's alphabetic encyclopedia, the gigantic leaves of the *Description de l'Égypte*, Renan's laboratory-museum notebook, the ellipses and short episodes of Lane's *Modern Egyptians*, Sacy's anthological excerpts, and so forth'.[2] Although the modern reader of Western texts on Japan might regret having so few occasions to meditate on the interplay of text and image, as Barthes has famously done on the great pictorial plates of Diderot's *Encyclopédie*, the issue transcends the exotic and the antiquarian.

All European and American texts on Japanese politics and society are quests for the linear prose authority of discursive analysis which we find in the books and articles of Massignon and Gibb. Said concludes that the semantic totality ascribed to 'Islam', as we find them in Gibb's *Modern Trends in Islam* or Massignon's *L'Occident devant l'Orient*, has been a special bane to the progress of Middle Eastern studies. But Johnson's *MITI and the Japanese Miracle* and Samuels' *The Business of the Japanese State* are, to paraphrase Said, no less representations of some Japan communicated by the Japan specialist to the reader.

J. A. A. Stockwin's *Japan: Divided Politics in a Growth Economy* and Gerald L. Curtis's *The Japanese Way of Politics*, to cite two of the most important introductory texts on Japanese government written during the 1980s, are unambiguously 'printed objects'.[3] Such books are inevitably reductive in the edited 'presentations' of the Japanese political facts that they describe. Neither author is a prisoner of the metaphysical perception that his text is reality, but there is little doubt that these texts could compete effectively for the attention of an initiate Westerner even if he were sitting in the main chambers of the Japanese Diet, where all that would be necessary for him to 'see' political reality would be for him to look up from his page.

Pace empiricism and textual positivism, social science is quintessentially about mediating phenomena with texts. The texts and the phenomena are very nearly two sides to the same coin of ordered sight. For most readers of Stockwin and Curtis, their books are portable substitutes for a reality that they will never personally examine. For such readers, this printed object, this textual 'presentation' of the Orient, is an unchallenged re-presentation of reality, a reality made, of course, from facts, but also of words.

AFTER BABEL: LANGUAGES AND POLITICAL REALITY

Together with the relevant chapters from Herodotus and Aristotle's *Constitution of Athens*, Chapters 10 and 11 of the Book of Genesis, where the folly of the Tower of Babel is narrated, form the *loci antiqui* of what today we call the study of geographic areas and comparative government. Genesis offers a marvellous myth to explain the mystery of the polyglot nature of the human condition. Retrospectively, both the Orientalist and area expert draw, across the millennia, on such canonic precedent. It is around ideas such as these that the Western mind has sought to organize its understanding of the *esprit humain* and the social world that inhabits the regions and continents that lie beyond the pale of Europe. The sciences that have resulted are grounded in linguistic understanding.

As area study, in its modern social scientific guise, has become more professional in its standards, the notion of a student of Arab society or Japanese politics who is unable to speak or to read Arabic or Japanese has become increasingly unpersuasive. But what more does a speaker of Japanese know about Japanese government, for example, than someone who does not speak and read Japanese? This question has an obvious pedagogic dimension. Among the growing army of Western students with an interest in Japanese civilization, few are steeped in the Japanese language. If there is a linguistic gap between Japanese and English, a breach with significance for the sound understanding of Japanese political life, scholars are obliged to bridge it for those they teach.

Linguistic nominalism

The arguments developed thus far in this chapter defy some of the central tenets of modern linguistics and the philosophy of social science. Language has not escaped the reach of the positivist who insists that the linguistic chasm between societies is either trivial or does not exist. This view is grounded in the doctrine of linguistic nominalism.

In *An Introduction to Modern Political Theory,* Norman P. Barry defines nominalism as:

> The theory of language that accounts for the meaning of general words not in terms of some universal entity they represent, but as labels to attach to things that share a common property. Nominalism is the approach to language adopted by the empirical sciences.[4]

This definition is crucial. Barry rejects the claims of two rival schools of thought. One is Platonism and its insistence that 'universal entities', such as the 'State' as an ideal form or prototype more real than any example of it, truly exist. The other camp is composed of linguistic relativists who contend that words and languages actually exist and are not, therefore, mere 'labels'. Whatever the weaknesses of Platonism, it is unlikely that one can be a linguistic nominalist, as Barry is, and also an effective student of non-European societies.

The issue merits careful statement because political science is overwhelmingly a language act. The political scientist spends much the larger part of his working life in reading and working with words rather than in the field observing a special slice of reality. In Barry's language, such scholars expend more energy on the transcription or translation of 'labels' than looking at what he calls 'things' (the objectified facts of the case).

This is but one way of looking at what the social scientist does. Barry must not be allowed to confound us with his nominalist doctrine. Indeed, it is essential to see that to the degree that the area specialist understands political and social science, not only as a science of observation but also of translation, it will be necessary for him to repudiate linguistic nominalism.

NOMINALISM AND JAPANESE STUDIES

Let us recapitulate the argument to this point. Nominalism is the ruling doctrine of language within Western positivist science, particularly in English-speaking countries. Proponents of this doctrine deny that languages 'exist'. Languages are viewed as a set of labels, not as a set of facts forming part of social reality. The motive behind this doctrine is the scientistic imperative to deny any theory that resists the claims of scientific universalism and the systems of positivist laws that serve such universalism.

This is not a satisfactory method for confronting cross-cultural differences. Fortunately, there are at least two other different approaches to the relationship between empirical reality and language that may appeal to the student of non-European politics and society. In addition to (1) nominalism, there are also (2) languages as world-views or linguistic relativism, and (3) the convergence model of social reality (e.g. modernization or Westernization).

Barry has provided us with a concise statement of the nominalist viewpoint. Confronted by significant difficulties in translation between languages, the nominalist would urge us not to take such difficulties seriously because they may endanger social science's claims to be a genuine positivist science. The nominalist insists that one learns Japanese to understand Japanese politics because the Japanese just happen to speak Japanese and not English. He would be appalled by the suggestion that there might be an entire dimension of Japanese political life, arising from the fact that the Japanese speak Japanese, and not English, that would be lost on the English speaker merely because he speaks English, and not Japanese. The anti-nominalist compounds nominalist umbrage when he contends also that the handicaps of the English-speaking student of Japanese politics are interestingly multiplied if the English speaker in question is also monolingual.

For the nominalist, the Japanese language is not a part of objective reality that must be explained by the student of Japanese society. It is merely a set of arbitrary or accidental labels. A significant gap between Japanese-grounded modes of political thought and behaviour and those of English-speaking societies must, by definition, not exist. The social scientific nominalist must believe, to be consistent, that the language barrier between Japan and the West is illusory. The fact that the Japanese call democracy *minshushugi* is merely a consequence of arbitrary variation in labelling. Since what is being described is theoretically the same (the Japanese also speak of 'American *minshushugi*'), the gap between English-language labels and their Japanese equivalents is nothing more than variations in nomenclature. The nominalist would dismiss the subtleties of nuance at work in the Japanese use of the imported word *demokurashi* as in the terms *Taisho demokurashi* or *Amerika ni Okeru Demokurashi*, as the title of Tocqueville's classic is rendered.

TRANSLATION AND LINGUISTIC RELATIVISM

Is language merely nomenclature, a varying set of names for an unvarying set of objects? Does the gap between Japanese and English fall under the rubric of the Saussurean notion of the essential arbitrary nature of the *signifiant* or signifier? But if languages are not just nomenclatures, what are they? The area specialist must have answers to such questions if only to protect himself from the uncompromising arguments that whirl about the problem of language.

This is because linguistic nominalism has uncompromising critics. Rather than expend fresh energy on the ancient but still inconclusive debate over how to define the essence of language, the linguistic relativist, speaking for our second school of thought about languages, seizes on the differences between languages that come to the fore in translation. Given the complex and very different political experience of Japan and the English-speaking peoples, the linguistic relativist would challenge the view that 'democracy' is an adequate rendering of *minshushugi*.

'Translation' is the key word because if languages embody only differences in nomenclatures for 'identical' things or facts, then problems of translation should never arise. Indeed so sharp are the gaps between languages that are demonstrated in translation that some linguistic relativists insist that languages better resemble closed linguistic systems, almost as singular in essence as the monads of Leibnitz. The more languages may be shown to resist translation, the more nominalist claims are reduced to the status of scientistic fictions intended to console the positivist-minded universalist.

Relativism appropriately houses various shades of opinion. The relaxed relativist may shy away from monadic extremism, but he still insists that different languages map the world in strikingly different ways that make exact translation between languages impossible, and all but the most general communication between speakers of two languages difficult. Linguistic relativism today, moderate or otherwise, is often a response to the theories of Edward Sapir (1881–1939) and Benjamin Whorf (1897–1941), two of the best-known linguistic relativists, who argued that the thoughts and world-view or *Weltanschauung* of speakers of a particular tongue are informed, even determined, by the way that different languages shape our view of reality. Sapir firmly rebuffs nominalism:

> The fact of the matter is that the 'real world' is to a large extent unconsciously built up on the language habits of the group. No two languages are even sufficiently similar to be considered as representing the same social reality. The worlds in which different societies live are distinct worlds, not merely the same world with different labels attached.[5]

Whorf is also a representative of a tradition of reflection that dates back at least to Leibnitz and Herder. He was a student of Amerindian languages. In the 1930s, he elaborated what he called 'an American Indian model of the universe' about which he cogently concluded that the ways that the Hopi language mapped temporality and space gave it easier purchase on the physics of wave processes and vibrations than, for example, modern English.[6]

Whorfian relativism poses powerful questions, particularly for the student of societies other than his own. To think in English is not to think in Arabic or Japanese or Latin:

> And every language is a vast pattern-system, different from others, in which are culturally ordained the forms and categories by which the personality not only communicates, but also analyses nature, notices or neglects types of relationship and phenomena, channels his reasoning, and builds the house of his consciousness.[7]

Translation provides the key test. Whorf observes that:

> In translating into English, the Hopi will say that these entities in process of causation 'will come' or that they – the Hopi – 'will come to' them, but in their own language, there are no verbs corresponding to our 'come' and 'go' that mean simple and abstract motion, our purely kinematic concept.[8]

Any bilingual person will be able to cite similar examples. Japanese has no specific set of future tenses. Verb endings alternate not only between present and the past, but also with the relative social status of the person speaking, the person to whom he is speaking or the person being spoken about.

Paraphrase falls short of satisfactory translation. The ability to translate a key idea will fade or strengthen in different contexts. Thus, there are numerous occasions in Japan's dialogue with and about the English-speaking world where *minshushugi* is a more or less accurate rendering of 'democracy'; but historical context, cultural inheritance and social circumstance may confound this apparent ease of translation.

Take, for example, the early post-war debate in Japan over the nature of *minshushugi* as it unfolded in the writings of Maruyama Masao, Shimizu Ikutaro and Yoshimoto Takaaki. The particular tonalities assigned to *minshushugi* defy even strained paraphrase in English. It is almost inconceivable that the essence of this complicated argument could be recast in English in an effective way: that is, in a manner that would allow it to influence the values and intellectual concerns of a non-native speaker of Japanese with the kind of impact that it once had on the Japanese intelligentsia. So great is the mental, cultural and linguistic gap that the force of this post-war Japanese discourse would be almost entirely lost on the monolingual speaker of English.

One way to demonstrate to a Westerner who lacks an Asian language what is at issue here is to point, as George Steiner has done, to the difficulties of 'translating' within the same language. In *After Babel*, Steiner cites four examples from English literature, chosen, as he says, almost at random which resist effective paraphrase in contemporary English: the monologue of Posthumus in Act II of *Cymbeline*, two paragraphs on the psychology of Elinor Dashwood from Austen's *Sense and Sensibility*, a poem by Dante Gabriel Rossetti and a well-known passage from Noel Coward's *Private Lives*.[9] In all these examples, however recent, Steiner is able to demonstrate that 'Our current feelings move in another key'.[10] If such 'feelings' can alter so dramatically over time, then they can differ between cultures and across geographic space.

As every polylingual area specialist knows, English does not exhaust the complexities of inter-lingual and intra-lingual mappings. Take, for instance, the successive interpretations of the term 'mercantilism' in Japanese. Post-war Japanese trade policies have been frequently described by the Western business press, usually in negative terms, as 'mercantilistic'. In the writings of Otsuka Hisao, the economic historian, 'mercantilism' (*jushoshugi*) stands in vital tension with 'national economics' (*kokumin keizai*).

During the 1930s and early 1940s, a period which for many was the summit of Japan's mercantile orientation (much of the legislation that underwrote post-war Japanese protectionism was passed during Japan's struggle with China and then with Britain and America), Japanese militants repeatedly denounced 'mercantilism' as a disloyal ideology because it was seen to place stress on business interests before those of the nation. This misplaced criticism was partly the consequence of the way that 'mercantilism' was rendered into Japanese from English and German during the late nineteenth century. It was translated as *jushoshugi*, where the *ju* meant 'weighted towards' or 'priority given to', *sho* was the Chinese character for commerce or business or wealth, and *shugi* was the conventional rendering of 'ism'. In other words, the Chinese characters were being read literally, and therefore incorrectly, by native (if poorly educated) speakers of Japanese.

A closer rendering in English of what mercantilism really means in Japanese is contained in the title of Richard J. Samuels' study of Japan's energy industry, *The Business of the Japanese State*.[11] Yet, as Samuels would be among the first to admit, the nuances of the word 'business' and 'state' in English do not reproduce the precise feel of either the Japanese term or the ideology that it states in capsule form.

A satisfactory translation or paraphrase of *jushoshugi* from Japanese back into English demands a confident grasp of the semantics of Japanese policy practice and rhetoric before, during and after the Pacific War. Under this rubric also would fall not only the Japanese native tradition of mercantilist thought, but also how such ideas fared under the impact of foreign thinkers such as Friedrich List. But the problem of understanding does not end here. Indeed, it may be all but inexhaustible.

Total purchase on what is meant by *minshushugi* and *jushoshugi* is finally elusive. If 'no aspect of Elizabethan and European culture is formally irrelevant to the complete context of a Shakespearean passage', then, in theory, no political text is irrelevant to the evolving discourse of Japanese policy and philosophy.[12] Any exercise in 'total reading' is potentially unending. It is what Wittgenstein famously called 'all that is the case'. A native speaker's vulnerability to the whole history of his mother tongue distinguishes him from someone who may claim only non-native purchase. It a question of personal ontology: how has my history of my language influenced what I feel and think to be naturally 'real'?

Convergence theory seeks not to resolve the unresolvable conflict between relativism and universalism, but to finesse it. The convergence theorist points to the ways that patterns of life in advanced industrial countries are drawing closer. As the previous differences between Japanese and Western life ease, reality is increasingly the same; and thus descriptions of it converge, significantly easing, at least in theory, the problems of translation and inter-cultural translation.

Examples of convergence theory applied to Japan include Marxism (before the Frankfurt School), the Modernization or Princeton School, and the free-market convergence model today. Convergence theory has comparatively little impact on the political science of Japan but in *Parties and Politics in Contemporary Japan* by Robert A. Scalapino and Junnosuke Masumi (1962), the authors do describe the 'increasing universalization of basic values' as probably 'the most significant single development of the 20th century'.[13] The values being universalized are West European and American. They include 'progress, industrialization, science and democracy'.[14]

If the facts change, then the nominalist will cheerfully concede that semantic 'labels' must follow suit. Similarly, if the linguistically coded horizon alters, the relativist will accept that the balanced equation of language and reality also will be transformed. But the very flexibility of convergence ensures that it offers no definitive grounds for choosing between nominalism and relativism.

LANGUAGE AND NATIONAL CHARACTER

Such linguistic difficulties challenge not only the assertions of the linguistic nominalist, but also the curt rejection of cultural explanations by post-war students of Japanese society. Among the explanations of Japan's economic miracle, the 'national character' school holds, according to Chalmers Johnson, that 'the economic miracle occurred because the Japanese possess a unique, culturally derived capacity to cooperate with each other'.[15] Culture thus underwrites the successful Japanese pursuit of consensus. It also explains not only Japan's relatively low crime rates, but also 'the subordination of the individual to the group; intense group loyalties and patriotism; and, but not least, economic performance'.[16]

If, however, post-war Japanese society has displayed 'virtual agreement among government, the ruling political party, leaders of industry, and people on the primacy of economic objectives for the society as a whole – and on the means to obtain those objectives', then it is obvious also that such consensus has been achieved and maintained through a linguistic medium: the language of Japanese nationalism and post-war social consensus.[17] Johnson's summary of the 'national character' school of economic miracle research may be 'a persuasive definition' (a definition that aims, in this case, to convey information but also disapproval of what is being defined). But one may share his recoil against the cultural assessment of the Japanese miracle and still perceive that the issue of language must be addressed by anyone who seeks a sound understanding of the causes of Japanese economic growth.[18]

The German school of *Sprachphilosophie*, under Herder's impact, argued that national character is imprinted on language and reciprocally bears the stamp of language. In summarizing Herder's thoughts on the subject, Steiner observes that the German thinker

> was convinced of the irreducible spiritual individuality of each language, and particularly of German, whose antique expressive strengths had lain dormant but were now [1772] fully armed for the light of a new age and for the creation of a literature of world rank.[19]

There is much in Herder's speculations that we would today dismiss as fanciful, but to deny that economic nationalism has played a cardinal role in Japan's post-war rise to superpower status is to fall foul of the 'anything-but-language' approach to the Japanese miracle or any other kind of political research. Yet even someone as alive to the quiddities of different languages as George Steiner, a man who is natively trilingual in English, French and German, acknowledges the power of the universalist case against linguistic relativism.

This case may be argued on four fronts: the physiological, the phonological, the grammatical and the semantic. The strongest of these is the first, for all human beings manifestly possess 'the same neurophysiological equipment with which to emit and receive sound'.[20] Claims for phonological universals, in Steiner's view, are less convincing. Like grammatical universals, phonological generalizations can be overturned by a single contrary example, of which real languages and dialects abound. Semantics has also been a graveyard of universalist ambitions. Witness the fate of Chomsky's bold effort.

Whatever its weaknesses, universalism has its powers. In Barry's definition of nominalism, as an outcropping of linguistic universalism, language is described as a set of 'labels to attach to things that share a common property'. For the empirical nominalist, the most important of such 'things' are social facts.

Now if facts exist prior to and independently of our description of them (as many facts do), then the claims of linguistic relativism will be circumscribed. The language relativist may contend that the selection of facts and their interpretation is shot through with linguistic considerations, but this leaves the extra-linguistic nature of empirical reality largely uncontested. This kind of probing highlights the circularity of reasoning in linguistic relativism:

> Seeing a dripping spring, an Apache will describe it as 'whiteness moving downward'. The verbal formulation is clearly different from that in current English. But what direct insight does it afford into Apache *thinking*? It is tautological to argue that a native speaker perceives experience differently from us because he talks about it differently, and then to infer differences of cognition from those of speech. Behind such inference lies a rudimentary, untested scheme of mental action.[21]

The key word in Steiner's summary is 'untested'. Because linguistic science is dominated by universalism, the prime compulsion among linguists is to prove the correctness of the universalistic case and to deny the validity of alternative approaches. A forceful monism is at work in linguistics, just as it is at work in economic positivism. The area student has learned from hard experience not to accept at face value supposed violations of logic's laws because such arguments have repeatedly been abused to prevent scientific examination of uncomfortable slices of empirical reality.

Colour discrimination has offered an important test of the supposed limits of linguistic formulations. The universalist concludes that the human eye can distinguish between a great variety of hues of browns, to cite the famous example of the language of Argentine gauchos, although the non-gaucho being tested may lack words to identify with precision the shades of brown presented to him.

Japanese has a rich vocabulary of colour terms, but in ordinary usage the word for blue is *aoi* and for green is *midori*. Yet, confronted with a number of objects that an English speaker would describe as 'green', many Japanese speakers will identify the relevant colour as *aoi*. This is even more emphatically the case when the object in question is 'orange', which many Japanese will describe as *akai* (red) rather than use the term *dai-dai iro* (the colour of an orange). The issue is not one of optic discrimination alone, but also of efficiency of expression and world-view. The larger the accumulations of subtle distinctions of nuance and mapping, the more difficult communication between linguistic communities becomes. One can speak and think against the grain of one's language but only with great effort. Step back from the world of immediately identifiable objects, and the genus begins to erode into species.

Against E. H. Lenneberg's argument that 'There is no cogent reason to assume that the grammarian's articulation of the stream of speech is coterminous with an articulation of knowledge or the intellect', one may set Steiner's own view that 'No metaphysic is speechless, none escapes from its own vernacular into some realm of pure material evidence'.[22] In other words, between the black and white extremes of linguistic nominalism and Whorfian relativism, reality posits a vast stretch of grey which resists the extravagant claims of scientific monism. In the realm of language, as in other spheres of life, empirical reality is so complex and polysemous that only pluralism and intellectual tolerance will do. About this need, Kant was correct.

SAUSSUREAN THEORY AND JAPANESE REALITY

Imperiousness and intellectual intolerance appear to be built into the very psychology of positivist science. The area expert, like other victims of positivist occultation, should be grateful to Noam Chomsky for the defeat that he inflicted on the reductive pretensions of linguistic behaviourism in 1959.[23] But the Orientalist and regional specialist must remain guarded about Chomsky's programme of linguistic universalism. Such scepticism must also be extended to Ferdinard de Saussure (1857–1913), the father of modern linguistics, precisely because of his impact on Japan studies.

The Saussurean notion of the arbitrariness of the sign (and the signifier, in particular) is active in Roy Andrew Miller's *Nihongo: In Defence of Japanese,* Peter Dale's *The Myth of Japanese Uniqueness* and J. Marshall Unger's *The Fifth Generation Fallacy.*[24] All three scholars dissent from the traditionalist defence of the use of Chinese characters or *kanji* in writing Japanese.

Very briefly, Saussurean linguists hold that all writing systems are arbitrary. Jonathan Culler illustrates Saussure's point:

There is no natural or inevitable link between the signifier and the signified. Since I speak English I may use the signifier represented by *dog* to talk about an animal of a particular species, but this sequence of sounds is not better suited to that purpose than another sequence. Lod, tet, or bloop would serve equally as well if they were accepted by members of my speech community. There is no intrinsic reason why one of these signifiers rather than another should be linked with the concept of 'dog'.[25]

Furthermore, notes Culler,

If one says that the concept 'dog' is rendered or expressed by dog in English, *chien* in French and *Hund* in German, one implies that each language has an arbitrary name for the concept which exists prior to and independently of any language.[26]

In Japanese, this four-legged concept is called an *inu*.

If Saussure is correct, then there is no sound linguistic reason that Japanese has to be written in *kanji*. Romanization or the hiragana syllabary would, in theory, do just as nicely because these writing systems are equally arbitrary but much easier to learn (but less agreeable to read once one has learned *kanji*). Claims that *kanji* are ideograms or ideographs that directly represent a concept or thing, rather than just serving as a complicated label for it, are implicitly overthrown. Critics such as Miller and Unger argue that the Japanese cling to their laborious writing system because they hold a false notion of linguistic hierarchy which places writing above speech. In this, the Japanese, so their Saussurean critics insist, are being irrational.

Given the nonsense that has been inflicted on Japanese society by nationalist ideologues, the claims of universal reason have been defended by Westerners with untiring vigour. But the area expert and student of Asian societies must keep this Saussurean critique in perspective. Languages are arbitrary in theory, not in practice. It may be true that 'cat' or 'bat' are arbitrary labels, but I dare the Saussurean linguist to test such arbitrariness in a pet shop. In practice, languages are anything but arbitrary. Let the area student pretend, even for a moment, that English or French usage governs how Japanese or Arabic is spoken, and he will depart immediately and decisively from Japanese or Egyptian speech and social reality. Such departures violate the basic principles and entire purpose of area studies.

The Saussurean critique of *kanji* is the exception that proves the rule. It is not language but languages – in their concrete, historical and unarbitrary spoken and written manifestations, as reality – that dominate the labours of the Orientalist and every area specialist who studies a society other than his own. As Culler correctly concedes, it is a linguistic community that determines what linguistic practices merit the attention and care of the regional expert. The importance of arbitrariness, as a linguistic doctrine, must not be overstated.

The area expert has always to be wary of the sweeping and often destructive aspirations of universalism. Universal science has not been designed with the meticulous student of other societies in mind. Universal science is a formidable achievement of the European intellect, but it is anti-empirical and unsympathetic to concrete particulars. In *Aspects of the Theory of Syntax,* Chomsky declares that:

> The main task of linguistic theory must be to develop an account of linguistic universals that, on the one hand, will not be falsified by the actual diversity of languages and, on the other, will be sufficiently rich and explicit to account for the rapidity and uniformity of language learning, and the remarkable complexity and range of the generative grammars that are the product of language learning.[27]

This is a grand programme. Chomsky offers one of the key manifestos of twentieth-century universalism in the positivist mode. But its relevance to area studies is distinctly limited. This is because so few linguistic universalists are willing to take seriously 'the actual diversity of languages'. Note the word is 'languages', not 'language'.

7 Criticism

> The most corrupting of comforts is intellectual comfort.
> Lacan

It is a measure of the reduced state of the contemporary public discourse on the relations of the West with Japan that some of the most strident participants would have us believe that calling the Japanese names actually does hurt them. Or, more to the point, that the failure of scholars and commentators to write ill of Japan suggests disloyalty or the subversion of Western political and strategic interests. The only virtue in such otherwise arid pyrotechnics is that they encourage us to clarify what the term 'criticism' means within the Western tradition of writing about the non-Western world.

THE CRITICAL ACT

For political criticism to succeed, it must embody our most powerful reading of reality. To criticize something is to seek to change it. The success or failure of this endeavour provides the only valid criterion for assessing the quality of a critical act. Mere censure is ubiquitous. Criticism that alters reality is far less common. Mere 'nay-saying' – the uttering of disagreeable truths or opinions about a political regime in public – does not qualify as political criticism. Nor is political criticism a merely corrective empiricism, the scientific perusal of a neglected political institution that has previously been regarded as too sensitive for scholarly probing. Nor, for that matter, is political criticism mere politics, the defence of this or that interest or ideology in the marketplace of ideas and public judgement.

The true political critic seeks to understand the object of his censure in order to destroy it, so that new life may take root. Even reform demands destruction. Because social institutions may be stubbornly resilient, and the political critic's only weapon is words, the near-mortal wound sometimes must suffice. Even so, history tells us that the resulting damage may be conclusive. The French Roman Church, like the French monarchy, never recovered from the eighteenth-century assault on its place in French thought and society. Under the weight of a century and a half of intellectual and moral dissection, slavery, it is safe to conclude, will never again return to the Americas. One may even assert with conviction that in 'classless Britain' (John Major), the aristocracy will never again rule. The undermining of the pre-Meiji feudal regime by its political critics, after Ogyu Sorai and Yamazaki Ansai, ensured, to the degree that words and ideas can guarantee anything, that the Tokugawas never again ruled Japan.

In these examples, the operative word is 'never'. This encapsulates the supreme goal of effective political criticism.

TEXT AND CONTEXT

The tradition of Europe stands at the heart of any Western enterprise that would assess the quality of modern Japanese political life. To pretend otherwise is jejune or dishonest. Effective criticism never unfolds in an intellectual vacuum. Values always nibble at the edifice of the most scientific of critical acts. The first ambition of the critic must, therefore, be self-knowledge. This task brings us back to Gramsci's remark in his *Prison Notebooks*: 'The starting-point of critical elaboration is the consciousness of what one really is, and it is "knowing thyself" as a product of the historical process to date, which has deposited in you an infinity of traces, without leaving an inventory.'[1]

More often than not, Gramscian inventories are formed from texts. We are what we read. Our identities are formed not from what Japanese have written or thought but from what Europeans (and Euro-Americans) have written and thought. To compile such an inventory requires that the Western student of Japan attain natural purchase on the values and sciences of European civilization. This imperative explains my frequent citation of the classics of European tradition as they bear on any critical scrutiny of modern Japanese government. This means breaking down the false categories of Western scholarship which would place Oriental studies in one corner and European tradition in another. Criticism must destroy, but it must also be self-aware.

The European Enlightenment remains the touchstone of Western criticism in the political sphere precisely because of the pre-eminence of the thinkers who animated the eighteenth-century mind: Kant, Locke, Hume, Smith, Burke and, in their vital role as arch disseminators, Voltaire, Diderot and Gibbon. But more than its creative largesse, it is the decisive critical legacy of the Enlightenment, its sheer destructive impact on the values and institutions of the *ancien régime*, that make us its heirs and disciples. It is under the press of its unforgiving genius that we judge the achievement of twentieth-century political critics. How else is one to explain that, while in the light of the demise of the Soviet Union, it is just conceivable that the Romanovs may one day again rule Russia, it is inconceivable that the Bourbons will ever again do so in France. The suggestion is that, as political critics, Marx and Lenin failed where Voltaire and Diderot succeeded. It is the political influence of such Enlightenment thinkers and their texts that provides the irresistible answer to Kant's question: 'What is Enlightenment?'

Kant's credo can be recast in the unambiguous language of the contemporary West: common humanity is not inevitably a slave of its passions. Men and women are intrinsically capable of mature, rational and adult conduct and self-government. All that is required is a political order that allows the full development of these natural virtues. Effective political and religious criticism is the indispensable vehicle for reaching that desired state.

The Enlightenment forms the cornerstone of any serious Western assessment of the successes and failures of the modern Japanese polity. This revolutionary tradition not only encourages us to broach the issue of the quality of political life in contemporary Japan, but it also allows us to achieve an unrivalled economy and penetration in any conclusions that we might draw about that nation. This economy and penetration may be illustrated by reference to a contentious body of Western writings about the failings of Japanese political and intellectual life. The heritage of the Enlightenment lends an otherwise unattainable edge and ballast to works such as Peter Dale's *The Myth of Japanese Uniqueness*, J. Marshall Unger's *The Fifth Generation Fallacy: Why Japan is Betting Its Future on Artificial Intelligence*, Roy Andrew Miller's *Nihongo: In Defence of Japanese*, Benjamin Duke's *The Japanese School: Lessons for Industrial America* and Karl van Wolferen's *The Enigma of Japanese Power: People and Politics in a Stateless Nation*.[2]

The European Enlightenment secures the radical framework and the moral dispensation for our probes of the 'darker side' of the

Japanese political system as a distinctively *Western* project. It is the Enlightenment that encourages us, by merely leaping an ocean, to ask at what point, in America's recent 'liberal hour', did the reformist impulse behind MacArthur's Japanese Occupation policies co-mingle with the in-gathering of Kantian moral scruple that animates John Rawls' *A Theory of Justice*? It is the European Enlightenment that provides the most rigorous grounds for asking whether the Meiji state, and its reincarnation after 1926, represents the most intriguing realization of the vision of the polity contained in Hegel's *Philosophy of Right*. It is the European Enlightenment that forces us to ask: is it possible to conceive of the scope and direction of post-war Japanese social policy – the issue of the position of women in society, for example – without reference to Locke and John Stuart Mill? Or, to extend the argument to the field of economics, is it credible to dissect the continuing liberalization of Japan's foreign trade regime without reference to the insights of Smith, Ricardo and, again, Mill?

It is the classicist view that allows us to argue that Mill, rather than Marx, was the Enlightenment's most fruitful nineteenth-century heir, because his reading of reality has proved finally, as recent events in Central Europe and elsewhere show, to be critically the more efficacious. In their insistence on privileging Marx over Mill, the left-wing Japanese ideologues have written their epitaph of critical failure.

To repeat: for political criticism to succeed it must embody our most powerful *reading* of reality. The word 'reading' is meant in two senses here. First, the term is used as a metaphor. To speak of 'reading reality' means to grasp mentally the world that stands outside our subjective awareness. The goal of such an act is to achieve a certainty of purchase on the social–material world, where 'certainty' refers not to pure philosophical or scientific understanding alone but also to our collective human ability to manipulate and change social reality. This means to engage, even obliquely, the problem of how a discourse or text relates to reality, in this case modern Japan. But, in a century that has repeatedly attacked the so-called 'transcription theory of reality', which has at numerous points surrendered to Nietzsche's assertion that 'there are no facts; only interpretations', one must respond that the first step towards relinquishing our ability to improve on social reality is to cease believing in such a reality. Reflecting on the Japanese experience of government, it is possible to argue that it is the decay of our belief in reality, our agnosticism towards the historical sphere, that defines the current crisis of Western society and politics.

Here the word 'reading' is also meant literally. The Enlightenment remains 'a past that is a present' not only because it forms an essential part of our system of values and beliefs, our common sense, but because it exists all around us as texts.

We may concede that all such texts are of a major stature, and still acknowledge that they vary in their capacity to blunt the intellectual defences of an existing political, economic and social order. The political impact of classic literature is a potent example. In attempting to delineate 'the very fabric of suppression which defines Russian history as a whole', George Steiner has observed that 'The cases of Tolstoy, of Pasternak, of Solzhenitsyn show that the balance of power between the state and the writer's single voice (between context and text) is, at some level, very nearly equal'.[3] This may be the case in fiction, but in the world of politics it is possible to argue that at numerous points in the Western experience of government since Socrates and the birth of Christianity, it is the text that has overwhelmed the political context, the state. Yet it is the failure of any Western text to overturn the foundations of the Japanese state that invisibly fans the frustrations of Japan's many critics in the West.

Whatever its impact on Japan, the Western political tradition defines our past. It should encourage us to see the Enlightenment as a sustained act of reason, of political criticism, and therefore as an exercise in textual creativity of the first order. It is such creativity that laid the foundations for the destruction of the French monarchy. I do not believe that George III and his ministers would have regarded Thomas Paine's *Common Sense*, that revolutionary best-seller, as a merely bookish phenomenon. Two hundred years later, it is Edmund Burke (dead for almost as long) who has had the last say on the French Revolution of 1789.

It is the classic text of political thought that provides the most convincing, because most complete, gloss on Mallarmé's proposition that the aim of the universe is the creation of *le Livre*: 'the "text of texts" so integral, so comprehensive of truth and ontological form, that it subsumes, negates all "context" '.[4] For our purposes here, we may modulate Mallarmé's claim, and simply say not only that 'the world exists to become a text' but that great texts exist to become the world. In the modern West since the Enlightenment, those texts have more often than not been political ones. The Enlightenment, as a body of texts, literally underwrites the Western assessment of the quality of political life in modern Japan. If a European text capable of breaching Japan's nativist walls is to be had, it will be found here.

For purposes of economy, the Enlightenment will be defined here not as a revolution in scientific and philosophic method, but as, first, a benchmark for any definition of effective political criticism, and second, a set of values, the most important being individualism, which have furnished much of what is attractive in the political commitment of the Western intelligentsia during the past two centuries. These constitute the two swords of the European Enlightenment. Thus, politically minded individualism, after the Enlightenment, may be seen not only to give moral substance and weight to the identity and sensibility of the educated Westerner, but also to equip the European mind with an extraordinary exemplar of efficacious, because destructive, political criticism.

The Enlightenment's legacy of effective political criticism has an important lesson to offer critics at work in the field of the political science of Japan. Their critical discourse has focused on two different but related themes. First, there is the perceived irrationality in the formation and implementation of Japanese public policies. Second, and more important, there has been umbrage at the systematic neglect of the interests of the individual – and by natural extension, civil society as a whole – in the design of the Japanese polity. Such concerns combine political and cultural criticism so as to hammer at the institutional design of the Japanese polity and at the value system that animates that political system. Of particular importance is the Western argument that the failings of the Japanese state, in all its guises – ancient, medieval and modern – is the consequence of the Japanese failure to embrace Western-style individualism.

But has individualism had decisive impact on any non-Western state or society? If not, the impotence of the discourse of Western individualism, in a trans-cultural context, may explain the confusion that scars the critique of Japanese government and politics by Westerners today.

THE DARK SIDE

A significant settling of accounts is taking place among Western political scientists who study Japan. Difficult issues are being raised. Among the more contentious is the New Left's old question: have Western political scientists neglected the 'darker side' of Japanese politics? Another challenge to the Asian studies establishment has been given angry form by economic nationalists who charge that Western academics, by praising, indeed coddling, Japan in print, have been betraying not only their professional calling but also their countries. The accusation of 'neglect' accelerates the pulse precisely because of the climate of nationalist irritation that has come to characterize the West's relationship with Japan since the late 1980s. Furthermore, because scholars of East Asia were among the principal victims of the MacCarthyite purges in America during the 1950s, the subject is not easily dismissed as journalistic froth.

It is to his credit that Richard Samuels of MIT (it is he who has once again raised the 'neglect' question) has insisted on giving the dispute an intellectual cast, rather than a partisan or ideological one.[5] The result is that it is the critique of a fellow mandarin that has put the question into sharper focus. Samuels holds up the ideal of 'the independent free-floating intellectual'. This is of course Karl Mannheim's formulation, but it harks back to Julien Benda's 1927 classic, *La Trahison des clercs*. There Benda grimly observes: 'Our age is the age of the intellectual organization of political hatreds. It will be one of its chief claims to notice in the moral history of humanity.'[6] It is the contemporary weight of this charge that should make *La Trahison des clercs* essential reading for any defender of anti-Japanese revisionism.

Samuels insists that the political scientific community in the West suffers from a double disability: poor eyesight and a weakness for intellectual conformity. He blames academic blindness for the failure of political scientists to grasp the revolutionary importance of Japan's economic miracle. Such obtuseness is painfully matched, in Samuels' view, by the scholarly equivalent of the herd instinct. The Japanese development state has been transformed into an all-consuming industry. This bout of academic trendiness has encouraged scholars to neglect their other duties, including, by implication, their responsibilities to examine the 'dark side' of Japanese politics and to hold up the mirror of liberal or radical virtue to the unhappy face of the Japanese polity.

The roots of the 'neglect question' are recent and shallow. The attack on the pursuit of value-free neutrality and objectivity in Asian studies was a phenomenon of the late 1960s and 1970s, and is usually understood as a revolt against the achievements and ideology of the Modernization School, so influential in American scholarship on Japan during the late 1950s and 1960s. Marius Jansen, a key figure in the modernization movement, has summarized the views of the anti-modernists in this way:

Younger scholars, led by those who took leading roles in the Concerned Scholars of Asian Studies (CSAS) held that 'modernization' had contributed to a view of modern Japan that was too favorable and too optimistic and that it had neglected the darker side of Japan's economic growth and regional expansion.[7]

Echoing Jansen's phrase about the darker side, Samuels has written dismissively about recent American political science on Japan:

> Studies of Japanese politics between 1960–1985 tended to avoid focusing on authoritarianism, gender, corruption, discrimination, and coercion as factors in Japanese political life .... There was, in short, little beyond the anti-war movement that rocked the scholarly boat and that held up this underside of Japan to close scrutiny – and even with all this criticism, there was little critical *scholarship*.[8]

Samuels' critique, however, may be seen to be miscast. Let us borrow an idea from Freud's *The Interpretation of Dreams* (1900) to illustrate the point. Freud suggested that there are two ways to enter Rome: 'as Winckelmann, the Vice-Principal, or Hannibal, the Commander-in-Chief'.[9] Here, Freud's Rome will stand for Japan. The suggestion would be that the social scientist, as a scientist, will seek to imitate Winckelmann in his quiet reverence and empathy for his subject of study and in the exquisite care he must exercise if his empiricism is to serve him and posterity well. Hannibal the would-be conqueror of the Eternal City is aiming for a wholly different goal: he seeks the surrender of his foe. This is the task and calling of the true political critic. But vulnerable ground divides these two very different approaches. Dangers lurk in this no-man's-land for the political scientist of Japan. They may be illustrated by reference to three recent examples of 'political criticism': Gavan McCormack and Yoshio Sugimoto (eds), *Democracy in Contemporary Japan*; Susan J. Pharr, *Losing Face: Status Politics in Japan*; and Karl van Wolferen, *The Enigma of Japanese Power: People and Politics in a Stateless Nation*.[10]

Here it will be argued that as scholarship or analysis all three books have considerable merit. But as criticism of the Japanese political system, *Democracy in Contemporary Japan* often verges on critical nullity, mere nay-saying; that *Losing Face* is a suggestive example of Western corrective empiricism but one that flirts with the vulnerable ideologies of the 1960s; and that *The Enigma of Japanese Power* trembles uneasily between pulp non-fiction and 'the intellectual organization of political hatred'. None of these books, however, aspires to the status of political thought, in the grand European manner, and none qualifies as 'political criticism', as defined by the only standard of such criticism worthy of discussion, that of the European Enlightenment. All three books may add to our understanding of Japanese social reality; none will change it. And that, as Marx observed, is indeed the point when we speak of genuine political criticism.

UNDER WESTERN EYES

'No issue has been as central to twentieth-century democracies as that of equality.' With this powerful assertion, Harvard's Susan Pharr begins *Losing Face: Status Politics in Japan*. The jarring untimeliness of this sentence is like a symphonic blast from Prokofiev or Shostakovich in the ear of someone who would rather have dozed through a Delius rhapsody. No notion has aroused greater conservative ire during recent decades than that of politically enforced 'equality'. Political conservatives therefore find Pharr's ideological stance deliciously provocative. It asks us not only to ignore the past two decades of conservative political and intellectual dominance in Britain and America, but also to pretend that Friedrich Hayek's *The Road to Serfdom* (1944) and *The Fatal Conceit: The Errors of Socialism* (1988), and, for that matter, Milton Friedman's classic *Monetary History of the United States, 1857–1960* (1963), had never been written.

How does one explain either this extraterritoriality towards the main political developments of the past two decades or the studied neglect of 'the best that has been thought and written' in our time? The problem is not confined to Pharr. The data brought into play in *Democracy in Contemporary Japan* and *The Enigma of Japanese Power* are fresh and abundant, but the mind-sets at work in these books, the values that galvanize these studies, reflect an indifference to crucial chapters in post-war Western political thought and experience. Indeed all three books give the unintended impression that the Western world stopped thinking and theorizing about politics sometime in the autumn of 1969.

This impression is part of a larger problem: the ghetto status of Japanese studies within the academic paradigm of Western political and social science. Glen Hook has rightly pointed to the 'protected' or 'closed' character of many, perhaps most, branches of Japanese research.[11] Samuels' frustration with what he sees as the manifestly inferior status of Western scholarship about Japanese politics is a reaction against the intellectual insularity of a comfortable ghetto.

Samuels insists that such scholarly ghettos have unwelcome consequences. Writing of a dry season in recent American political scientific scholarship on Japan, he concludes:

> The 1970s saw the production of scholars (and of scholarship) but little cumulation, virtually no comparison of Japan with other industrial states, and too little direct communication between the field and the discipline. To the extent there was such communication, it took the form of wholesale importation of then current analytical conventions in the discipline.[12]

Western studies of Japan have suffered because of a neglect of Western and Japanese political theory, both ancient and modern. Despite the impact of Hayek, Popper and Friedman, none of these modern masters has cast an important shadow on the Western study of Japan. Is this their failing or ours?

In response, one must insist that Pharr's book resists the charge of neglect. First, by tackling three examples of status politics – the inter-generational struggle within the Liberal Democratic Party that resulted in the birth of the New Liberal Club in 1976, the legal battle begun in 1974 by some Hyogo high-school students to win formal acceptance of a *burakumin*-problem study group by school authorities, and a 'tea ladies' revolt' among female civil servants in the Kyoto city bureaucracy – Pharr has shown that political scientists in America's elite centres of Japanese studies are willing to deal with the less flattering, because darker, side of Japanese politics.

Pharr's openness to the suggestion that Japanese policy practice challenges some of our most rooted intellectual assumptions makes *Losing Face* a late, though effective, exploitation of the brief opening in the Western mind, achieved through the writings of Ronald Dore, Ezra Vogel and, most importantly, Chalmers Johnson between 1979 and the late 1980s, which revolutionized the scientific paradigm in Japanese government studies.

The result is a subtle compromise: Pharr argues for learning positive lessons from the Japanese but in an essentially negative context, that of the elite muffling of pluralist dissent from below in the still remarkably hierarchic Japan of the 1970s. By virtue of her choice of topic and angle of attack Pharr can be seen to be probing the 'darker side' of the Japanese polity, but she quite rightly does not press the point. She rejects compromise with the fashion of Japan-bashing among American intellectuals and in the mass media. As every serious scholar knows, blasting Japan today is no bold expression of academic freedom. Rather it is a surrender to the prevailing climate of chauvinist opinion which would have won the approval of neither Mannheim nor Benda.

This distinction is crucial for the spirit of Mannheim does inform Pharr's study and contributes to her book's success. Thus, *Losing Face* is neither mere 'nay-saying', nor mere politics (although a quiet advocacy of egalitarianism, particularly as a feminist quest, forms a conspicuous thread of her book), nor political criticism in the grand eighteenth-century manner of Voltaire, Burke or Gibbon. Rather it should be regarded as a thoughtful form of 'corrective empiricism'. But, *pace* Samuels, this corrective empiricism is aimed not at Japanese ideas and perceptions, but at *Western* ones.

Political criticism is almost never effective across cultural barriers, indeed hardly ever potent across national frontiers even within the same linguistic community. Has, for example, the unrelenting British assault on industrialism, materialism and conspicuous consumption (one of the pillars of English anti-Americanism, and indeed a pivotal assumption of British sensibility from Dickens and Matthew Arnold to the advent of Thatcherism) had any impact whatever on American thought and values? It is such national barriers that force us to ask whether any Western text, however critical of the Japanese state or society, has provoked significant change in Japanese thought or social practice. Ideas arriving on the tips of bayonets (MacArthur's democratic reforms, for example) are an entirely different matter. But the larger issue must be this: effective political criticism is almost always a domestic affair; outsiders who engage in it are wasting their time if their purpose is to alter a foreign society.

If this is true, then criticism of Japan in a Western language is, almost by definition, doomed to fail. This proposition calls into question the entire body of Western critical writing about Japanese politics (and Japanese criticism of Western politics as well) because it denies its main premise: that the non-Japanese critic not only should but *can* force social change on Japan and the Japanese. This problem of the nullity of trans-cultural political criticism is well illustrated in *Democracy in Contemporary Japan*, edited by Gavan McCormack and Yoshio Sugimoto.

In their introduction, McCormack and Sugimoto observe that:

> Over 50 years ago one Japanese scholar used the phrase 'cool fascism' to describe the kind of state control he perceived being born in 1930s Japan. Others have used formulas like 'friendly

fascism' (to describe tendencies in the United States) or, more recently, 'democratic fascism' of Japan in the 1970s. . . .The fact that some outstanding scholars can see elements of a model for emulation in Japan's development of the 'control society,' while others describe it as a form of fascism underlines the importance of focusing the most careful attention on studying what is going on.[13]

If the United States and Japan are fascist regimes, then does any government in the developing world qualify as anything else? Indeed is any existing regime not fascist? Is Japan or the United States – or Australia, for that matter – to be condemned for failing to meet a set of standards that no polity has ever met? The suggestion reduces the research contained in *Democracy in Contemporary Japan* to a melancholic politics of utopian advocacy. Is it possible nowadays to evoke the notion of 'fascism' without conjuring up the meaning given to it during the 1960s student revolt: 'Fascism: anything with which one intensely disagrees'? Furthermore, to cite the voluminous writing by Japanese scholars on fascism is a two-edged weapon. Whatever its claims to a role in the twilight struggle between left and right in post-war Japanese politics, this most overworked of left-wing clichés is ready for retirement. To flaunt this slogan today is to suggest a double failure: having failed to win the battle for the hearts and minds, as well as the votes, of the Japanese electorate, the old left of the Japanese intelligentsia continues to roll out the tired slogans of a half-century ago. This has militated against the development of fresh ideas and perspectives within left-wing criticism and Japanese social science, which has generated, in Freud's analogy, many Winckelmanns but no Hannibals. This is the intellectual and political desolation that cowers between the pages of *Democracy in Contemporary Japan*.

Beverly Smith's article, 'Democracy derailed: citizens' movements in historical perspective', in *Democracy in Contemporary Japan*, focuses on the infamous Matsukawa train derailment case.[14] Early in her article, she quotes from John G. Roberts' *Mitsui: Three Centuries of Japanese Business*, where he asserts that during the American Occupation of Japan, US intelligence agencies and their Japanese agents 'infiltrated virtually every politically significant [Japanese] organization after 1945'.[15] Smith goes on to cite this passage from Roberts:

> taken as a whole, this joint operation to suppress the left wing was perhaps the most massive and certainly the most sophisticated

machine for political sabotage ever set into motion, and whatever its net effect may have been, it was fervently welcomed by its beneficiaries – zakai potentates and their right wing political establishment.[16]

Smith glosses this quotation by observing that: 'The enemy they were mobilized against was not the right, reaction or fascism, but the left, and the struggle for grassroots democracy'.[17] But was it? Roberts himself notes, two paragraphs before the one quoted by Smith, that the goal of placing what he calls 'ideological missionaries' and 'Japanese agents' was 'to identify left-wing radicalism and isolate it from the relatively unperturbed mainstream of Japanese life'.[18] Smith does not explain why grassroots sentiment was not more keenly supportive of 'the struggle for grassroots democracy'. She also appears to neglect Roberts' claim for the success of such ideological penetration. Roberts suggests that some of these 'Japanese agents'

> remaining at their posts over periods of many years, had become high officials of their respective groups, and few have been dislodged even to this day by retirement or death. This curious and little-known phenomenon may account for some of the unpredictable, erratic, and idiotic if not suicidal policies adopted by Japanese left-wing organizations with depressing regularity.[19]

But for Roberts' footnote to this paragraph, we might have the crust of an arresting empirical exercise: to discover what impact those leaders of left-wing groups who joined these organizations during the later Occupation (and perhaps at GHQ behest) have had on the political orientation and policies of such bodies. Unfortunately for such a project, Roberts' footnote reads: 'Since the author has learned from reliable sources that most left-wing organizations have been infiltrated by intelligence agencies, it is not unreasonable to suppose that political sabotage is involved.'[20] The notion of 'reliable sources' is important in journalism, but suspect in scholarship because the facts in question cannot be checked. This puts intolerable pressure on Roberts' logical inference. As scholarship, his claims are highly vulnerable. Despite Roberts' diverting speculations, an empirical project could be salvaged from these difficulties, and Smith uses the balance of her article to address, in some detail, the miscarriage of Japanese justice in the Matsukawa case. Nowhere does she demonstrate, however, that the Occupation was a conspiracy against grassroots democracy. Rather the author gives the impression that she wants her readers to accept an unproven moral imperative diluted by private political belief. The truth of her thesis is assumed. It comes close to the preaching of left-wing common sense to the converted. The result is a vessel of sand (*suna no utsuwa*): criticism that does not destroy; scholarship that does not build.

Such trials by moral conviction may generate a vast number of worthy facts, but the end product is not science but rather a moral discourse which is incapable of responding to Karl Popper's insight that: 'A theory "proves its mettle" by withstanding our determined efforts to refute it. It is falsifiability, the capacity for being falsified, that distinguishes science from nonscience, including metaphysics.'[21] The rhetoric that gives *Democracy in Contemporary Japan* its bite dissolves under such scrutiny, and here Popper is the unambiguous heir to the Enlightenment's discourse of reason.

In the same vein, late nineteenth-century founders of European sociology have influenced all subsequent social science by their insistence on a strict separation between 'facts' and 'values' in the name of objective or value-free science. This distinction poses a problem for the potential political critic to which he should not simply surrender, nor simply pretend does not exist, nor assume that it presents no problem for his labours. This is a simplified statement of the problem of fact and values, from the point of view of the political critic. Let us take the issue of feminism and the political scientist, as it occurs in Pharr's *Losing Face* or in the article 'Women in the new Japanese state', by Sandra Buckley and Vera Mackie, in *Democracy in Contemporary Japan*.

One might begin with the question of the quality of life of Japanese women today. In logic, 'quality' is the characteristic of a proposition that makes it affirmative or negative. In criticism, quality refers to the relative 'goodness' or 'badness' of a social condition. A judgement of quality is a value judgement. Given a distinct set of values, one could fashion (that is the assumption) a standard for comparison, a set of attributes – scaled, for example, from one to ten – that would reflect a society redesigned to satisfy a 'politically correct' feminist. An empirical exercise might then be undertaken to determine how well or poorly Japan met the suggested standard. Having conducted such empirical research, one might then proceed to restructure Japan's political and social system so as to make it conform better with such a standard.

An empiricist, especially one working in the shadow of the twenti-eth-century positivist tradition, would have some very rude things to say about such an exercise. First, only the empirical part of the exercise would qualify as science. Reforming Japan is not an act of scholarship. A rigorous empiricist might therefore reject such politicking as having no place in the university. In the name of the distinction between 'facts' and 'values', he might challenge the very notions of 'feminist scholarship' or 'gay political science' or 'black studies' as contradictions in terms. Such a line of attack would lead to questions about the nature of the proposed standard. The construction of such a standard, from an articulated set of values, is by definition not an empirical exercise. If one adopts a strictly empiricist definition of science, then such model construction, so different by nature from the kinds of models used in physics experiments, would not count as science. A logical positivist would term the resulting structure 'non-sense'. Might, therefore, our standard be a philosophical construct, a principle, a definition? Would then our 'standard' be an analytic or synthetic statement, a truth or an empirical finding? 'John is tall.' Compared to whom? 'Japanese society is anti-feminist.' Compared to what other society?

Ideas such as Popper's are not to be sidestepped but are to be exploited to put political criticism on more solid intellectual foundations. This is surely the message of the philosophically rigorous but also feminist *oeuvre* of Simone de Beauvoir or Julia Kristeva. But, it must be observed also that philosophers of social science would set the bar of critical achievement higher than most critics can reach. Such philosophers would also dismiss the notion of 'critical scholarship' as a non-starter. If such scepticism encourages the committed feminist academic and any other advocate of 'political correctness' to test their theory's mettle by engaging in a sustained scientific effort to refute it, then the whole discipline will benefit. The charge of 'non-science' should keep us all on our toes. Such philosophic and methodological discipline should be cultivated by all political scientists regardless of their political outlook.

In their statement of values, McCormack and Sugimoto endorse 'civil rights and civil liberties, public subsidy for organized competitive political groups, egalitarian distributional measures, public control of investment, workplace democracy, equal opportunity, and a foreign policy informed by the principles of democratic legitimacy that underlie the domestic system'.[22] As an honest statement of personal values this will, of course, stand. It could equally do credit to the party platform of a broad left grouping anywhere in the Western world. But such a platform is neither political thought nor scholarship nor genuine political criticism. One can fall between three stools as well as two.

The battle during the 1970s and 1980s between utilitarian political philosophers and rights-based Kant theorists casts no shadow on the authors of the McCormack–Sugimoto volume. Nor does the recent growth of interest in Aristotelian communitarianism among political philosophers. All three schools demonstrate the rigour of genuine intellectual probing and disciplined reasoning that can enhance political criticism.

If the Western study of Japanese government is to be effective, then it is essential to make a strict distinction between science and criticism. Any political moralism must be informed by what is most vital and incisive in the development of contemporary Western political thought. We must not surrender to the flattering illusion that the mere targeting of a foreign power makes the politics of the parish into an international force. Finally, we must recognize that that by far the greater part of Western political criticism of Japan is an exercise in intellectual nullity because it changes nothing *in Japan*. Such criticism makes no effective claim on the work of the Western scholar of Japanese politics.

Critiqued in this way, is *Democracy in Contemporary Japan* therefore worthless? French theory would say not. The articulation of 'the Other' for any national community is a powerful act. True, most French theorists would regard much of the analysis in this book as distinctly old-fashioned: modern rather than postmodern. But the concerns expressed in *Democracy in Contemporary Japan* reflect a humane vision of political life; the utopian hopes of Marx of the *Economic and Political Manuscripts of 1844* blossom at numerous points in the McCormack–Sugimoto discussion. As an articulation of 'the Other' (in this case Japan and to a lesser degree America) in the discourse of Australian identity, it is encouragingly free of right-wing chauvinism.

Behind the sharp-phrased attack on Japanese political practice, there is an undeniable gloom. It is the gloom that one finds in all broad left or radical groups that have refused to compromise with the promised dynamism of market socialism. It pervades the writings of the Second International, of the Frankfurt School and Theodor Adorno's 'melancholy science', of Jean-Paul Sartre and even more obviously of Simone de Beauvoir. It is the gloom of defeat, of believing your values to be right, but knowing that society is never likely to adopt them. McCormack and his colleagues may at least be seen to be humanists, and in their dejection, to be in good company. There are high decencies at work in their hopes, and these should be recognized.

The writings of anti-Japanese revisionists such as Karl van Wolferen present rather different problems. *The Enigma of Japanese Power* is a polemic. All of this work's strengths and weaknesses are rooted in this fact. There is no question that its slashing attack on Japan and the Japanese has sparked considerable interest among certain Western readers, but as an accurate description of Japanese society, *The Enigma of Japanese Power* has distinct limitations. Wolferen claims, for example, that there is no place in Japanese society where one may assert with confidence that 'the buck stops here'. Lacking a political centre, in this sense, post-war Japan becomes, in the author's dismissive idiom, 'a headless chicken' or 'truncated pyramid' with which trade negotiations are pointless because Japanese negotiators cannot deliver on the promises that they appear to make.

But a flawed premise is artfully hidden in Wolferen's inflated expectations of the Japanese state. His thesis is vulnerable because he condemns the Japanese political system for an improbable failing: its incapacity to execute structural economic change quickly enough to suit the convenience of Japan's principal trading partners. Harry Truman's 'buck-passing' rhetoric aside, where or when has such a state ever existed? No absolutist state, however focused or aggressive, has ever met Wolferen's definition of 'centered-ness'. Neither the court of Louis XIV, nor the brutal Dutch regime in colonial Indonesia, nor the Kremlin of Joseph Stalin, nor Hitler's Germany was able to deliver this kind of structural change, as it were, on demand. The required levers of power were not available. In this sense, post-war Japan is no exception.

Behind Wolferen's rather eccentric understanding of the state's function in the modern world, two improbable assumptions seem to be at work. One is that Japan and, by definition, any modern state, possesses a secret chamber where all social and economic problems can be solved instantly by an act of political will or magic. No such room exists, in Japan or elsewhere. If it did, Margaret Thatcher or Mikhail Gorbachev or Deng Xiaoping, the great revolutionaries of the 1980s, would have quickly discovered this secret chamber and transformed their respective societies. Before she was overthrown in a palace coup, the Iron Lady seemed, to her critics, to be little short of an elected dictator. Yet even she was unable to manipulate at will her country's trade balance or the composition of its imports, let alone revolutionize British manufacturing. In the larger scheme of things, it mattered very little that everyone in Britain knew that the 'buck stopped' at Number 10 Downing Street.

Even more improbably, Wolferen is keen to blame Japan because she lacks another secret chamber of state which houses yet another button which, if pressed, would transform the Japanese economy to suit the requirements of, for example, the United States or the European Community. These two magic rooms are what Wolferen means by the 'state'. Lacking either of these magic chambers, Japan, in Wolferen's view, is a nation without a state. The more sober conclusion should be that the author's definition of the state is hopelessly implausible, and that his central argument is unpersuasive.

As a work of criticism, *The Enigma of Japanese Power* also suffers severe limitations because of the way that the author handles evidence. Wolferen's attack on *The Japan Times*, one of Japan's four English-language dailies, is a particularly useful example in the present context because it is one of the rare Japanese institutions scrutinized by the author in which the key documents are both a matter of public record and in English.

In *The Enigma of Japanese Power*, the author concludes his assault on Japanese opinion leaders in a chapter titled 'The system as religion':

> When in the late 1980s foreign criticism of Japanese economic practices and intransigence on international issues began to be supplemented by more analytical probes into 'nationalistic' Japanese behaviour, a new indignant tone began to creep into the commentary of some of Japan's scholars, editors and other spokesmen. The critical foreigners allegedly aim to weaken the foundations upon which Japanese society is based.[23]

After quoting at length from a translation of an article by Sawa Takamitsu that appeared in *The Japan Times* in February 1988, Wolferen turns on the newspaper itself:

> Foreign scrutiny of the Japanese System and the ideology and notions that help sustain it regularly invites vehement Japanese responses, which seems inevitable. It is, after all, tantamount to analysis of an ineffable divinity – which is destructive to any kind of religion. Thus Japan's unofficial but, to all intents and purposes, most prominent mouthpiece in the world, *The Japan Times*, editorialized – apropos of an exchange in an intellectual magazine

between a foreign author and a Japanese professor propounding Japanist views – as follows:

> any foreigner who lashes out in an angry and inaccurate fashion at this country's identity, its mythology if you will, encourages Japanese deafness to foreign criticism. The claims to guilt-free national identity are now firmly on the human agenda. But such claims are not the stuff of smooth global relations. Hence the need for patience, for understanding, for tolerance, for good manners.[24]

The brunt of the Wolferen critique of *The Japan Times* falls both on the intentions as well as the actions of the Japanese media. The statements and gestures of *The Japan Times* are taken to reflect a pernicious nationalist ideology. But what can we know with certainty about how someone else's mind works? Philosophers have long brooded on the problem of 'other minds'. As for the matter of intentions, we must concede that we will never know for certain what Nakasone Yasuhiro, for example, really thinks about the intelligence levels of American Blacks or Puerto Ricans.

Confronted with this conundrum, Wolferen cites documentary evidence to indict the behaviour and ideology of Japanese institutions such as *The Japan Times*. So what did the newspaper intend in the editorial that so upset Wolferen?

In journalism, timing is all. In the darkening climate of the late 1980s, especially in relations between the United States and Japan, this editorial, which carried the title 'Intellectuals on the warpath', was an attempt to reason with both sides to the dispute. When an issue is hotly debated, civilized manners – patience, mutual understanding, intellectual tolerance, decent restraint and all the rest – become even more necessary. The editorial sought to remind both sides that the younger generation in Japan was bound to feel less constrained by memories of the Pacific War than their parents. This is inevitable. Their historical experience differs sharply from that of the wartime generation. Indeed, among young people on both sides of the Pacific, national confidence is increasingly pronounced. An assertive jingoism has begun to infect public opinion in both countries.

With the passing of time, younger Japanese are less likely to feel either as concerned or as guilty as their parents or grandparents about Japanese war crimes in China, the Philippines or on the Burma railroad. History does not stand still. This is not to suggest that a self-serving amnesia should be encouraged in the young. This charge has repeatedly been made against the Japanese Ministry of Education for its censorship of the facts of Japanese military conduct during the Pacific War. *The Japan Times* has been consistent in its recent criticism of the ministry's stance.

Wolferen's attack on *The Japan Times* is disingenuous not only in the evidence he cites, but also in the evidence he suppresses. When former German Chancellor Willy Brandt died in October 1992, *The Japan Times* observed in an editorial titled 'When even words fail' that 'Throughout his long career as a German politician, [Brandt] sought to redeem his small continent from the moral burdens of a blood-drenched century. This exemplary life offers a lesson for Japan and the Pacific.'[25] On this occasion, the paper refused to surrender to the 'sweet nothings' of contemporary internationalist rhetoric:

> With this man came the supreme gesture. In 1971, Mr. Brandt's tireless pursuit of an opening to communist Eastern Europe (Ostpolitik), first as foreign minister and then as chancellor, took him to the monument which memorializes the slaughtered thousands of Poland's Warsaw Ghetto. There, in an unprecedented act of atonement, Mr. Brandt sank to his knees. This high moral gesture transfixed Germany, its neighbors and the world. Years later, in his memoirs, he confessed that, at that moment in Warsaw, he 'looked into the depths of German history, and, under the weight of the millions of those who were murdered, I simply did what men do when words fail.'
>
> A well-deserved Nobel Peace Prize followed. For this and his later work for The Brandt Commission on the global problems of the North–South divide, Mr. Brandt was much admired in this country. But in death, he should be more than admired here.
>
> Looking back now over the whole of the postwar period, it is obvious, or should be, that Japan's relations with its Asian neighbors as well as with its old English-speaking foes across the Pacific have suffered because no Japanese statesman has ever made the kind of moral journey that Mr. Brandt made to Warsaw.
>
> Japanese diplomacy has been uniquely hobbled not from a lack of good intentions or sincerity, but from a deep-rooted inhibition against making the kind of moral gesture required. Fortunately, it is not too late even now to follow in the footsteps of Germany's 'peace chancellor.' Skill with words has not been a traditional strength of Japanese political life, but there are things one can do when even words fail.[26]

Earlier, on the day that the late Emperor Hirohito was buried,

7 February 1989, *The Japan Times* published an editorial titled 'A time for sadness – and amends':

> The Showa Era must not close without the Japanese people, particularly its leaders, acknowledging the sins of the 1930s and 1940s. Evasion will no longer do. We must collectively as a people state, without protective and self-serving ambiguity, that the pain and suffering inflicted on our wartime enemies was wrong and should never be repeated.
>
> In altered circumstances, and for different historical reasons, the German people, our wartime allies, have done the same. Whatever the differences between the wartime conduct of Japan and Nazi Germany, we have our own ample reasons for conceding that what we did – as a belligerent and as a colonial power – was wrong.[27]

The editorial on this sensitive imperial occasion concluded:

> It appears that all too many of this country's present generation of leaders have mastered the art of self-righteous double-talk in the face of the indefensible. Those Japanese who refuse to address this task will only succeed in spoiling the fresh promise of the Heisei Era with the fifty-year-old ghosts of another time. Let, therefore, the Showa Era come to its just and fitting conclusion.[28]

It must be left to the reader to judge whether this is the voice of a self-deceiving Japanese chauvinism or what Wolferen calls 'the System as religion'.

The handling of evidence is the decisive issue here. If Wolferen stumbles over English-language materials, it is fair to question his understanding of Japanese institutions when almost all the key documents in question are in the Japanese language, which he apparently neither reads nor speaks. Even Masao Miyoshi, who offers fulsome praise of Wolferen's research, observes that:

> [Wolferen] did not learn the [Japanese] language, which seems to have severely isolated him from his environment. His work [*The Enigma*] is a nostalgic, homesick, colonialist book, which no doubt has powerful appeal to a great many Americans who know nothing about Japan and do not wish to think seriously about the United States or Europe.[29]

Ronald Dore has suggested that the pro or anti stance adopted by Western writers may be less well explained by how much money they receive from Japanese sources than by 'the extent to which their Japanese is fluent enough for them to have warm and relaxed friendships with non-English-speaking Japanese'.[30]

The undisguised hostility towards so many aspects of Japanese society, the inaccurate picture painted of institutions, either out of ignorance or rhetorical intent, and the contentious conspiracy theory which gives the book its narrative drive have encouraged most Japanese either to ignore it or to classify it as mere *yomi-mono*, yet another example of 'chewing gum for the eyes' by a foreigner. Whatever its impact on Western readers, Wolferen's critique changes nothing in Japan.

Confronted with such a literary phenomenon, the French theorist will not ask about the work's status as science or politics, but about its nature as a text. To what genre does *The Enigma of Japanese Power* belong? If the McCormack–Sugimoto book may be said to house a series of thrusting morality plays, then Wolferen has written a political thriller. The premise of the McCormack–Sugimoto book is that all societies are imperfect; Wolferen's is that imperfection is confined to Japan.

Jacques Lacan has observed that 'the most corrupting of comforts is intellectual comfort'.[31] The grimmest lessons of our grim century suggest that there is no intellectual comfort more corrupting than the smug assumption of moral superiority. This forms the core of Orientalism at its most abhorrent and the thinking Westerner is obliged to resist its call.

A FAILURE OF MIND

It has been argued in this chapter that the Hannibals of the West – to refer again to Freud's suggestive contrast between Hannibal and Winckelmann – have not fared well against the Japanese Rome. Nor do Japanese critics of the modern Japanese political system have much cause to erect triumphal arches. Take the most important motif in all post-war Japanese political criticism: the left-wing argument for the slippery slope, the claim that any weakening of the immediate post-war institutional restraints on Japanese military activity, as embodied in Article 9 of the MacArthur Constitution, will invite a prompt return to the kind of imperialist adventurism abroad and military oppression at home that Japan suffered in the 1930s. This anxiety continues to mesmerize the Japanese left, but, however worried, the Japanese critic with progressive ideological credentials has not succeeded as a political critic: he has not administered anything like a mortal wound to those Japanese conservatives who would turn back the clock to the Japan of the pre-1945 era. Granted, such slippery-slope fears did help to blunt pressures for Japanese involvement, however pacific, in the Gulf War, but the Japanese critic still cannot say 'never' about the the possibility of a return of Japanese militarism. Such Japanese critics, as critics, have failed. This reflects a failure of words, arguments and ideas: that is, of mind.

This underscores the sheer difficulty of the task of genuine, because effective, political criticism. The European Enlightenment provides the crucial test. Asked why he was seeking to arouse the whole of Europe over the judicial torture of one man, Voltaire answered, in March 1762, '*c'est que je suis homme*'. There is little doubt that Voltaire's three-year-long campaign to establish the innocence of a Protestant father executed on charges of murdering his son to prevent the boy from becoming a Catholic, in the *Affaire Calas*, helped to encourage the abandonment of judicial torture as a legitimate form of public justice. Nevertheless, if Voltaire had been asked during the height of his crusade on behalf of human rights whether he foresaw a more rapid end to torture as an instrument of government or to slavery as a social institution, it is almost certain that this French Hannibal would have judged torture to be the easier target.

Political torture is still with us; slavery is not. In this sense, William Wilberforce achieved more with his campaign than the French philosopher won with his. Nevertheless, neither Wilberforce nor Voltaire may be said to have mistaken his target. Political criticism, as an act destructive of values and institutions, forces the recasting of Marx's dictum: the point is not to interpret or understand the world but to find a target that one can strike with the weapons of the mind. The Enlightenment's warning to the contemporary Japanese critic is clear. Feudal Japan is dead; the spectre of Japanese revanchism is not. Edo and early Meiji political critics may therefore be judged to be in a class above their twentieth-century successors.

It is all the more damning that Japanese socialists have been blind to the political (rather than the economic) potential of the policy proposals put forward by American trade negotiators during 1989–90 under the aegis of the Structural Impediments Initiative (SII). The SII proposals, if realized, would have contributed to the radical restructuring of the Japanese economy in favour of market forces. This would not only cut off Japanese ultra-nationalism at its roots, but it would also undermine the tripartite conservative alliance of the Japanese ruling party, the elite bureaucracy and big business more decisively than any scenario of change then being debated in Japan.

This emphasizes the importance of critical clarity. The effective political critic must know where he wants to go and where history is likely to take him. It has been observed that the American Catholic bishops at the Second Vatican Council, called by Pope John XXIII (1958–63), had much to teach their Spanish colleagues, because, although the Spanish Church was much older, the Americans already had an ample experience of religious pluralism, a condition that the Spanish hierarchy had yet to taste, but which was clearly on the future agenda of Spanish Catholicism. Religious and secular pluralism was not inevitable in Spain; just likely. But the American experience gave US bishops a kind of critical clarity which the engaged political critic will only envy.

In a similar vein, Susan Pharr's social liberalism and commitment to egalitarianism provided her with an indispensable dose of critical clarity when writing *Losing Face*. Indeed this clarity of belief may have helped her to deliver a subversive blow in the cause of equality in Japan by her repeated use of the term 'majority culture' or 'majority Japanese'. Just as to argue in the 1960s that America was more than White America was to invite the explosive radicalization of US ethnic politics, so to suggest that there is more than one type of Japanese, that *burakumin* Japanese are Japanese too, and that women are not 'incomplete Japanese' but a different kind of Japanese, has the potential to echo powerfully within the English-language discussion of the Japanese polity. Whether it can be effectively translated into Japanese and retain the rhetorical force that it has in American English is another matter. Still it seems doubtful whether a reformist liberal can or should speak about Japan's evolution with the same kind of confidence with which those American bishops could analyze the future evolution of Franco's Spain a full twelve years before the death of the Spanish dictator. Critical clarity should therefore be seen to turn on two issues: lucidity of purpose and malleability of object, the target of one's criticism.

Throughout this chapter, political criticism has been viewed preeminently as an act of mind. Slavery will never return to the American South, not because of the presence of Union bayonets, but because something momentous has occurred in the minds of millions of Black Americans – and not only in Black minds. In like manner, the future of Japanese values and practices, of Japanese nativist conservatism and cosmopolitan liberalism, is entirely in Japanese hands – or, more accurately, in the keeping of Japanese minds – not ours.

In her introduction to *Russian Thinkers* by Sir Isaiah Berlin, Aileen Kelly observed in 1978 that 'The Russian Revolution and its aftermath have done much to strengthen the belief, deeply entrenched in the Anglo-Saxon outlook, that a passionate interest in ideas is a symptom of mental and moral disorder'.[32] The Socratic view would be that the truest civilization is one at home with fully examined ideas, in which it is intuitively recognized that philosophic and political ideas are the true motors of life fully realized. Certainly the effective political critic must live, think and argue as if this were so.

Three conclusions seem to follow: first, there must be recognition that, in the words of Kelly,

> Enthusiasm for ideas is not a failing or a vice; that on the contrary, the evils of narrow and despotic visions of the world can be effectively resisted only through an unswerving moral and intellectual clarity of vision that can penetrate to expose the hidden implications and extreme consequences of social and political ideals.[33]

Second, the notion of 'critical scholarship' cannot be accepted on faith. Given that critical explorations of the 'dark side' of Japanese politics tend to be mere politics, or mere nay-saying or, even when effective as criticism, entirely parochial in character, we must conclude that the claim that scholars have some obligation to engage in such explorations is unpersuasive. On this issue I think Samuels is wrong. Political thought exists; political criticism exists; but critical scholarship is a misnomer, a *non sequitur*. If the idea has any validity at all, then it will not be found in the ruminations of an intellectually exhausted New Left nor in the angry chauvinism of the New Right, but rather in the work of the political scientific revolutionaries who have laboured to recast the discipline's academic paradigm in ways that have made Western ideas, not Japanese ones, the target.

Third, political criticism should be recognized for the supremely difficult task that it is. Unless one captures a political system, as it were, on the hip – the suggestion has been made that both Voltaire and Václav Havel had easy targets in absolutist France and communist Czechoslovakia – then truly efficacious criticism of any human institution tends to be as difficult as it is rare.

The would-be critic of Japan should ponder afresh the scorch marks that David Hume's critique left on the foundations of Western metaphysics or John Locke's defence of the right of revolution. Such examples may explain why today's best critic is more often than not a man of the Enlightenment. Confucius may have been the patron saint of the Enlightenment, but Adam Smith is the patron saint of our era, for he still works feats of mind.

As a good citizen, as an intellectual, as a patriot in time of war, a Westerner may harbour other thoughts; but the European scholar of Japanese government should feel no compulsion to engage in the 'critical act' – rigorously defined – unless he also feels, like Wittgenstein, 'the duty of genius'.

8 Readers

A book has always been for me a particular way of living.
Flaubert

Our age threatens one day to appear in the history of human culture
as marked by the most dramatic and difficult trial of all, the discovery
of and training in the meaning of the 'simplest' acts of existence:
seeing, listening, speaking, reading – the acts which relate men to
their works, and to those works thrown in their faces, their 'absences
of works'.
Althusser

Among Althusser's simplest acts, reading has a special meaning for
the social scientist. But this simple act has been neglected by those
who have given modern social science its classic form and outlook.
A one-sided epistemology is often at work in such neglect.
Defenders of this unbalanced theory of knowledge insist that all
languages are freshly scrubbed windows, made of uniform glass,
through which an unresisting reality may be discovered merely by
looking. The systematic denial that languages – Japanese and English, for example – differ significantly conspires with naive or
common-sense empiricism, which would have us believe that reality
is composed entirely of 'things' and 'observers of things'. Both
doctrines – nominalism and classic empiricism – understate the opacity of linguistic codes and the difficulties involved in their decipher-
ment. Where languages are judged irrelevant, reading, too, will be
undervalued.

The positivist and empiricist both denigrate reading in all but
its instrumental forms. Political science has been hobbled by this
denigration. The student of Asian politics has not eluded the hazards

and insecurities that have resulted. Indeed, the kind of textual classicism that demands close reading, what the poet and essayist Charles Péguy (1873–1914) once called '*une lecture bien lue*', is almost entirely absent from the goals of the political scientist who studies Japan, the absence of great texts ensuring the absence of excellent readers.[1]

Such denigration is perplexing because 'reading', in all its complexity, has been one of the most fertile themes in all twentieth-century reflection. The dense interplay of author, reader and text have seeded, like the teeth of Cadmus's dragon, a battlefield of rich controversy. The combatants have included Saussure and Mallarmé, the Russian and Czech formalists, the Anglo-American New Critics, after Eliot and Richardson, the Constance school of reception theory and the textual hermeneutics of Heidegger and Gadamer, and more recently, textual deconstruction and Said's critique of Orientalism.

Crouching behind the 'mirror' theory of reality and the positivist insistence that every text, however great, is little more than a tossed salad of external causes, many social scientists and political philosophers have turned a blind eye towards the problematic of readers and reading. Such short-sightedness suggests that it is not only the Japan expert who has sought to shelter in an intellectual ghetto.

Our ghetto walls, however thick, offer inadequate protection against one of the most consequential cultural metamorphoses of postmodern sensibility: the decay of high literacy. The erosion of the authority of reading in European and Japanese civilization reflects drastic changes in the climate of educated sensibility. To interpret such modulations as 'crises' is to take the German philosopher Edmund Husserl as our prophet.

As the Nazi nightmare descended on Central Europe, Husserl addressed, in two famous lectures – the first in the form of a letter written in 1934 and the second given by the philosopher in Vienna in 1936 – what he called 'the crisis of the European sciences' (*Die Krisis der europäischen Wissenschaften*).[2] He sought to locate the roots of this European catastrophe in the practised disdain for the life-world (*Lebenswelt*) promoted by the positivist science of Galileo and Newton. As Germany's greatest living philosopher, but also as a Jewish-born Christian barred, perhaps by Heidegger's order, from his own faculty library at Freiburg University in 1933, Husserl knew that the life of the spirit, in that darkening climate, was under siege from forces both outside and inside the university.

Today the crisis of reading that threatens what S. E. Finer once called the 'bookish' character of the modern university involves no storm troopers marching down the rue Descartes or across Prague's Charles Bridge. But social scientific literacy is not immune to this dissolution of educated norms nor the blight now withering those delicate inner forms that European excellence has woven over the past two and a half millennia. This contemporary reincarnation of Husserl's 'crisis' demands that each scholar, scientist and intellectual probe the textual foundations of his subject and ask whether his discipline stokes or dampens the fires of this cultural emergency.

READING AND THE CRISIS OF A EUROPEAN SCIENCE

If we are serious

The world is a terrible place. This is the European view. Given the horrors of the twentieth century, who would fault the pessimism of those who were most threatened by barbarism's modern face? The urgent language of social emergency and cultural tumult has, nevertheless, tended to be dismissed as excessive by English sensibility. As Henry James observed in discussing Pierre Loti's fiction,

> the English reader is rather apt to see in any demonstrative view of difficulty or danger, any tendency to insist that a storm is bad or a mountain steep – a nervous exaggeration, the emotion of one who is not as Englishmen are.[3]

Is the evocation of Husserl's term 'crisis', in a discussion of reading, merely another example of European excitability?

We must weigh English calm and confidence against our doubts about the state of British and European high culture today. Nothing in our contemporary condition encourages complacency about the most vulnerable element in James's summation of the Anglo-Saxon outlook: 'the English reader'. Since the 1970s, a certain anxiousness has set the tone.

> If we are serious about our business, *we shall have to teach reading.* We shall have to teach it from the humblest level of rectitude, the parsing of a sentence, the grammatical diagnosis of a proposition, the scanning of a line of verse, through its many layers of performative means and referential assumption, all the way to that ideal of complete collaboration between writer and reader as set out by Péguy.[4]

Few educators are convinced that student literacy, in England or elsewhere, has improved since Steiner published this desolate conclusion in 1976. Slowing growth in newspaper readerships has fanned worries about young adults who are literate but for whom reading is not a habit. Television news provides a litmus test.

As newspaper readerships have contracted or aged or both, as in the United States, the influence of televised news has grown. A potent cocktail of forceful images, enforced concision and undemanding technology has contributed to television's blossoming at the expense of the quality or serious newspaper. Both media will report on election results, policy decisions and responses of the relevant interest groups or outside experts, but what television gains from its ability to tell its story with pictures and sound, it loses with the severe reduction in the amount of information and analytic depth that it can communicate. The text that the television presenter reads over a thirty-minute bulletin is much shorter than that digested by all but the most casual and selective of newspaper readers during a similar period.

Powerful technologies may be used as well as abused, but since the 1980s, a set of cultural changes – call them 'postmodernism' – has put unwelcome pressure on the content of television news. Institutions, such as the BBC or Japan's NHK, somewhat more secure with public funding, have resisted what elsewhere has become an apparently irresistible trend: a new stress on local news, sport, glamour and media gossip at the expense of the previous commitment of television news desks to serious print journalism. Thus, in a survey of television viewer preferences in Britain conducted after the Japanese Lower House elections of July 1993, reporting of the election, the most important in thirty-eight years, was judged germane and relevant by only a tiny fraction of the mainstream television audience. Among a list of twenty news items, the Japanese election came last. If such opinions are acted on, Japanese politics could slip from sight of those who glean their picture of the world solely from television news, a trend that twenty-four-hour news channels, such as CNN and the BBC world service, have helped to combat.

The metamorphosis of news analysis during the last two decades of the twentieth century appears to confirm three trends: less serious reading, less serious news reporting on mainstream television, and diminished marketability of the kind of genres previously judged indispensable to the nourishing of informed democratic electorates. For political science, with its commitments to reading, writing and a specific slice of serious knowledge, this change in popular perception of the importance of raw news poses a significant challenge.

Our students arrive in the lecture hall and the seminar room less committed to serious analysis (by virtue of lack of exposure), less informed by television, and certainly less well read than their predecessors.

The social phenomenologist puts the nature of the culture of reading under a revealing light. Among social scientists, the intellectual heirs of Husserl – most notably Alfred Schutz, Thomas Luckmann and Peter Berger – have articulated the view that human beings, collectively, construct a significant dimension of social reality. Like the philosophic idealist, the social phenomenologist has often been criticized for cultivating a weakness for ideas. The phenomenologist does not pretend, in Marx's famous quip, that the idea of 'oxygen' will save the drowning man. Nor does the phenomenologist deny that each individual is everywhere born in the chains of material scarcity and social constraint, what Sartre termed the 'practico inert'. Rather this school insists that a significant part of the *Lebenswelt* is composed of the meanings that human beings assign to their cosmos. These meanings, their efficacy as ideas and values, can be maintained only by intellectual labour.

The culture of the serious reader is such a construct. The modern assumption that society is sustained by a culture of mass readers – literate believers in mass religions, educated voters, well-read workers and managers – did not apply in medieval Europe. Mass literacy has its European roots in the Protestant Reformation and the slow nurturing of Catholic mass literacy under the pressure of Protestant and secular challenge. The modern newspaper, the linchpin genre of political science, only came into being in the late seventeenth century. George Steiner has concluded that 'Our style of reading, the unforced currency of our business with books is not easy to document before, say, Montesquieu'.[5] Universal literacy as an object of state policy is a nineteenth-century phenomenon. Nothing guarantees that this condition will last.

If society's commitment to mass literacy erodes, political science as it is known today will change beyond recognition. Already, and this has been apparent in the graduate or post-graduate seminar for some time, the cult of deep reading by students of primary and secondary school age, which flourished from the time of Montaigne until the childhood of Sir Isaiah Berlin, is in retreat.

Will a generation of Europeans ever again produce the kind of unself-conscious ingestion of high culture that allowed the House of Commons to stand and complete a Latin quotation that Pitt the Younger had temporarily forgotten or made it unsurprising that

Harold Macmillan, severely wounded in the First World War tren-
ches, was discovered prostrate on the battlefield reading Aeschylus'
Prometheus in Greek? Such cultures of reading are made, not born.
The cultural excellence so carefully nursed by our ancestors will
dissolve if neglected. We must not ask too much of the dedicated
news channel.

This is not only a classroom phenomenon. In the battle for adver-
tising revenue, network managers have often sought to ease evening
news programmes from their traditional evening slots. The civic
importance of a minority of news programme viewers has been
consciously devalued by labelling them as 'news junkies'. To the
degree that this mocking dismissiveness of the serious television
viewer is more fact than label, it suggests a significant erosion of
the ideal of the informed citizen. Many, perhaps all, of the best
students of undergraduate and post-graduate programmes in political science will be 'news junkies'. When this valued elite of television
viewers makes its way to university, they may have to be taught to
read.

Declining voter turnouts, the deepening crisis in the newspaper
industry, and falling audiences for even the Pablum that increasingly
defines television news point to the arrival of high-tech medievalism.
The decline in the quality press in the United States, much the
largest market for all genres of political writing in the English
language, could sweep away the pillars upon which twentieth-
century political science has been built.

For the student of politics no less than the committed democrat,
reading is a way of organizing, ordering and valuing the world, of
giving our time on the planet weight and meaning. If we wish this
'way of life', to borrow Eliot's expression, to survive, we shall have
to fight for it or rethink our discipline. Reading stands at the heart
of this new *Kulturkampf.*

READING JAPAN TO THE LETTER

If language is in crisis and reading under threat, political science
faces a choice. One option would be to abandon the production of
printed objects in favour of pictorial presentation. Exploiting the
potentialities of computer graphics and the technologies of virtual
reality would accelerate the decline of the established curriculum
and redefine teacher expertise while revolutionizing the function of
the modern university.

The second choice would seek to reanimate traditional practices by a bold effort to construct and maintain a social reality that may be read, while embracing strong models of reading grounded in an uncompromising political classicism. Here, the potential of this second option will be examined.

In his essay 'Text and context', George Steiner identified a rich yield of texts on texts, which clarify 'the instrumentality of reading' and 'the relations of the act of reading to the possibilities of culture and society'.[6] Steiner lists:

> the early sections of Charles Péguy's *Dialogue de l'histoire et de l'âme païenne* of 1909; Heidegger's articles on Hölderlin composed, mainly, during the 1940s and two essays on Nietzsche's 'Death of God' and on a saying by Anaximander, published in *Holzwege* in 1950; Philip Rieff's *Fellow Teachers*, which first appeared in 1972; and the consideration on the role of the classics in American education and society which Donald Carne-Ross enunciated in *Arion* in 1973.[7]

A student of Japan might reply with his own list: Maruyama Masao reading Ogyu Sorai and Fukuzawa Yukichi; Hiromatsu Wataru reading Marx and Engels; and Otsuka Hisao reading Defoe, Franklin, List and Weber. If such masterpieces of creative reinterpretation, of close reading, are 'to concern us, astonish us, fulfill us' (Barthes), they must be grounded in still stronger, more ambitious models of reading.[8] Mature statements of such models may be found in Althusser's essay 'From *Capital* to Marx's philosophy' and in the third part of Sartre's monumental reading of Flaubert, *The Family Idiot*.[9]

Marx as reader

Most acts of reading fall under the rubric of the 'ephemeral, the utilitarian, the mechanical, and the nearly somnambular'.[10] But where the religious reader is ingesting his text or the serious student of contemporary affairs is digesting his newspaper (what Hegel called the 'morning prayer of modern man'), such censure does not apply. Nor does it apply to the best newspaper writers (the class of professional readers with which the political scientist shares so much) who aim for more than immediate consumption. In political analysis, the most incisive journalist will match the work of the professional political scientist. But even the best journalism is surpassed by a more resolute school of reading: those who generate and interpret classic political texts.

Among these generators and interpreters, Marxists are the only secular readers of our times who match the sovereign disciplines and compulsions that thrive in the most acute communities of Christian, Jewish and Muslim readers. Like the religious textualist, 'the primary reflex in Marxist feeling and political–social application is that of citation, of re-reading':[11]

> Marxism–Leninism and the ideological idiom professed in communist societies are 'bookish' to the root. The scheme of origins, authority and continuum in force in the Marxist world derives its sense of identity and its daily practices of validation or exclusion from a canon of texts. It is the reading of these texts – exegetic, Talmudic, disputative to an almost pathological degree of semantic scruple and interpretative nicety – which constitutes the presiding dynamic in Marxist education and in the attempts to 'move forward' from sacred texts, to make of Marxism an unfolding, predicative reality principle. The critique, 'textual' in the deepest sense, of the ancient empiricists, of Hegel and of Feuerbach, impels Marx's own writings. The critique of alternative texts – Proudhon, Dühring, Ernst Mach, Bogdanov – is the fundamental occasion and performative genre of the great body of theoretical writing from Marx and Engels down to Lenin's *Empirio-Criticism* and the *Philosophical Notebooks*.[12]

It is a rare Western scholar of non-Western societies – the name Joseph Needham springs to mind – who brings a comparable force, confidence and need to his labours as a reader. Is it possible that these dead Marxists may still be the object of some curious reader long after all the works produced by European and American scholars about Japan during the twentieth century have been forgotten? This question stands even in the face of the disappearance of the very object that anchored, as hope or reality, the twentieth-century chapter of this Marxist discourse: the Soviet Union itself. How would Japanese studies fare if the fantasy of Komatsu Sakyo was realized, and Japan sank beneath the Pacific?

The deep textualist – this phantom absence in the Western meditation on Japan since Meiji – finds his vocation anticipated in 'the myth of the Scriptures, in which the body of truth, dressed in its words, is the Book: the Bible'.[13] According to Althusser, 'a certain idea of *reading* which makes a written discourse the immediate transparency of the true, and the real discourse of the voice' is alive in Galileo's 'Great Book of the World' and Hegel's *Phenomenology* no less than in scripture.[14] For the early Marx, to know the essence of things, the essence of the historical human world, of its economic, political, aesthetic and religious productions, was simply to read (*lesen, herauslesen*) in black and white the presence of the 'abstract' essence in the transparency of its 'concrete' existence.[15]

For the mature Marx, this is not enough. It is Althusser's conviction that the author of *Das Kapital* broke with the young man who wrote the *1844 Manuscripts* by abandoning the religious myth of reading under the impact of Spinoza, the first man 'to have posed the problem of reading' and 'a philosophy of the opacity of the immediate'.[16]

The mature Marx first reads and then re-reads Adam Smith, Ricardo and the other classical political economists. In the first reading, Marx reads Smith's discourse through his own discourse. At this stage, Marx asserts that Smith falls victim to oversights or *bévues*: Smith does not see what was staring him in the face.[17] 'What Smith did not see, through weakness of vision, Marx sees: what Smith did not see was perfectly visible, and it was because it was visible that Smith could fail to see it while Marx could see it.'[18]

This emphasis on correct vision is grist to the mill of any empiricist. It is the prime motivation behind the pursuit of empirical depth, the search for a 'deeper' truth that inspires, for example, Kent Calder's study of the politics of Japanese public finance or David Friedman's examination of the machine tools industry or Richard Samuels' research on the energy industry.

But Althusser would have us reject the mirror myth of knowledge where everything is, in principle, perfectly transparent, thus reducing Marx's first reading to 'Smith minus myopia'. Rather Althusser argues that the mature Marx executed a second 'quite different' reading. Thus, in a key analysis of Smith's 'price of labour', Marx unveils what Althusser calls 'a protocol of Marx's reading of classical economics'.[19] This is how Marx read Smith to the letter.

> The original question as the classical economic text formulated it was: what is the value of labour? Reduced to the content that can be rigorously defended in the text where classical economics produced it, the answer should be written as follows: '*The value of labour (   ) is equal to the value of the subsistence goods necessary for the maintenance and reproduction of labour (   ).* There are two blanks, two absences in the text of the answer. Thus Marx makes us see blanks in the text of classical economics' answer.[20]

Where are the 'blanks' in the political science of Japan? The young Marx's protocol of reading highlights the problem of myopia: the failure to see what is clearly visible. But focused empiricism may leave 'blanks' that only a stronger protocol of reading may effectively address. This is what is at issue in Chalmers Johnson's attack on occultation: the refusal of social scientists to acknowledge the possibility of a *political* explanation of the Japanese miracle. Discovering such absences comes closer to the protocol of reading that Althusser believes drove the mature Marx's dissection of the texts of the classic political economists.

> Why is political economy necessarily blind to what it produces and to its work of production? Because its eyes are still fixed on *the old question*, and it continues to relate its new answer to the old question; because it is still concentrating on the old '*horizon*' (*Capital*, T.II, p. 210) within which the new problem 'is not visible'.[21]

This mode of textual scrutiny is all too rare in the social sciences. This shortfall should encourage us to ask in what ways has positivism, both as philosophic outlook and scientific method, littered the discourse of the empirical student of Japan with 'absences' which only a strong model of reading may reveal?

Rigorous protocols of reading link organically with textual classicism. Althusser insists that a handful of texts provides the contemporary reader with unrivalled purchase on the world.

> Contrary to all today's reigning appearances, we do not owe these staggering knowledges [of seeing, listening, speaking and reading] to psychology, which is built on the absence of a concept of them, but to a few men: Marx, Nietzsche and Freud. Only since Freud have we begun to suspect what listening, and hence what speaking (and keeping silent) means (*veut dire*); that this 'meaning' (*vouloir dire*) of speaking and listening reveals beneath the innocence of speech and hearing the culpable depth of a second, quite different discourse, the discourse of the unconscious. I dare maintain that only since Marx have we had to begin to suspect what, in theory at least, reading and hence writing means (*veut dire*).[22]

Both of the protocols of reading that Althusser assigns to Marx, that marvellous Talmudic reader, assume that Smith and Ricardo were worth reading: closely, intensely, totally. For Althusser, reality is glimpsed through two lenses. We read Marx to read Smith in order to grasp the truth. In the richest disciplines, those with the securest foundations in reading, this double reading is irresistible. But what does it say of disciplines that lack an Adam Smith to set the project in motion?

Sartre and Japan

Mathematics and music, metaphysics and image-making all promise privileged access to reality. So does reading. Kant's dispensation – the world and our ability to understand it are, of necessity, grounded together – demands it. Humean scepticism may not otherwise be banished. But Kant's dispensation must be earned. This the major thinker – Sartre's examples include Baudelaire, Genet, Tintoretto, Verdi and Flaubert – achieves by mastering himself and the world.

The young Marx read not only to understand but also to criticize the British and French tradition of capitalist economics. But crucially he read Smith and Ricardo in order 'to situate himself with respect to the acknowledged masters of political economy'.[23] As a master reader who becomes a master writer (the two activities are dialectically linked), Marx hopes to achieve an exact balance between object and subject, between the weight of the external world and the truth of internal perception. To perceive, Sartre writes in *The Idiot of the Family*, 'is to situate oneself'.[24] But when Hegel or Smith, Marx or Flaubert, Sartre or Althusser situates himself, he may situate us as well by virtue of his status as a master reader/writer.

All this has special meaning if one is working and thinking within the Hegelian framework. In the *Phenomenology of Spirit*, Hegel elaborates the idea of History having both an object and a subject. The object is not an inert body of data, but rather the process of consciousness unfolding in time. This is the Objective Spirit or what later Hegelians, such as Sartre, would term the 'Totality'. The subject of History, where the term 'subject' is understood as 'self' or 'mind', is the prime mover of this conscious unfolding. But the process is not the same as the understanding of the process or what Hegel calls, in the *Phenomenology*, 'science'. The subject of History must undergo the process but also stand outside it in order to 'totalize' it. This dynamic confers a unique importance on the master reader/ writer, which, in the case of the *Phenomenology*, is Hegel himself.

The status of oracle that Sartre assigns to Flaubert, but also the cardinal role that Sartre allocates to himself as the greatest reader of Flaubert, may be traced back to this Hegelian ontology. This ontology explains why Sartre refuses to renounce, even in defeat, what is for him the supreme vocation: the urge to become a master reader/writer.

In the third part of *L'Idiot de la famille: Gustav Flaubert de 1821 à 1857* (henceforth referred to as *IF 3*), Sartre argues that if human beings are to enter into the flow of History, 'individuals have to transcend their local situation by interiorizing, through reading, elements of class culture or even world culture'.[25] Here, once again, Sartre insists that reading offers unique purchase on social reality.

Sartre's insistence on transcendence through reading provides another way of understanding the retreat sounded in his abandonment of the search for the intelligibility of History, in the second volume of *The Critique of Dialectical Reason*, in favour of the oracular reader, that is the Flaubert of *The Idiot of the Family*.

For the student of modern Japan, the key term here is 'world culture'. This must refer to those privileged spheres that drive History, not to the sum total of the facts or detail of human culture on our planet. History is understood as progress, broadly defined to include but reach beyond the technological to include everything assigned by Hegel to the Objective Spirit. Many of the commanding heights of world culture today are occupied by the Japanese, not (*pace* Sartre) as individuals but collectively.

Hegelian History radically privileges certain spheres and certain actors because they make History: their contribution decisively outweighs the significance of alternative forces, collective actors or individuals. This is the central axiom of Hegel's *Lectures on World History* where he sets out his vision of History developing from its Persian roots, through Greek liberty, down to the French Revolution. Thus, for an adequate understanding of who and what are significant to the unfolding of History in twentieth-century 'world culture', attention must be paid to the post-war Japanese economic miracle, both the phenomenon itself and the understanding of the phenomenon by a thinking subject, a master reader/writer.

The Japanese miracle is a 'phenomenon' in search of a 'text'. The dual character of the 'subject' must be stressed. Over-emphasize the role of the subject as Historical agent and the textual need, the 'science', is endangered; over-emphasize the subject as textualist and an essential passive picture of the Historical agency results. Peter Caws argues that 'The trick is to find an agent or class of agents who understand *fully* what they are doing at the time in the light of a cumulative and all-inclusive historical totalization'.[26] The Japanese example offers a different view: the trick is rather to find an agent or class of agents who have changed History (that ability alone is sufficient as practical 'understanding') and then to nourish a master reader/writer who understands *fully* what has been achieved. Change, that is significance, comes first; totalizing understanding comes after.

All this must be kept in mind when assessing Sartre's insistence that there is 'such a thing as world culture apart from its distributive objectification in the practico-inert', the material conditions that the past imposes on the present.[27] Conscious that man's potential to make History is limited, Sartre is seeking to develop a theory of History-making which avoids Engels's surrender to 'natural laws', while deflecting Merleau-Ponty's complaint that heroic individualism is powerless before the juggernaut of Historical change. Retrospectively, Sartre may be seen also to offer us a bulwark against post-Historical nihilism.

Sartre insists that the Objective Spirit acts only through 'the activity of men and, more precisely, that of individuals, each of whom, in his study, in the classroom, in the library, totalizes his own reading in his own way'.[28] This would appear to bestow a concrete task on the student of the Japanese miracle that differs from that imposed on those who have already left their mark on History. Alerted by Sartre's radical privileging of the writer and writing, the student of modern Japanese government should seek to produce a text to match the ontological weight of the Japanese miracle.

Sartre's Hegelian instincts served him even in the apparent defeat contained in *IF 3* where he concludes that 'despite this apparent atomization, the conjunction ceaselessly realizes an exhaustive totalization but without a totalizer'.[29] As the *Critique of Dialectical Reason* was judged by Sartre, and his critics, to have ended in an impasse of totalization without a totalizer, it is important to see that in *IF 3*, 'Sartre still feels the need of a determining drive for History'.[30]

Viewed in the light of the Historical significance of the Japanese miracle, and freed from some of the philosophic constraints that Sartre imposes on his project in the two *Critiques* and the *Flaubert* study, the Hegelian instinct behind this 'need' may be worthy of defence. Certainly any student of the Japanese miracle would affirm the truth of Sartre's conclusion in *What is Literature?*: 'the world and man reveal themselves by *undertakings*. And all such undertakings we might speak of reduce themselves to a single one, that of *making* History.'[31]

Because of his commitment to the concept of Totality, the chief philosophical constraint at work in *IF 3*, Sartre is, however, eventually forced to acknowledge that:

As the ensemble of works published every day far transcends the individual possibility of totalizing written culture, this perpetual addition of fresh material has the effect of preventing the totalization from closing on itself and turning into a calm totality: this is what will be called the life of the objective Spirit, a material detotalization that interiorizes itself in the demand to be totalized and that contradicts this dream in stone....The objective Spirit of an epoch is at once the sum total of the works published at the time in question and the multiplicity of totalizations effected by the contemporary readers.[32]

For the social scientist wary of the perpetual dangers of hyperfactualism or total regress implicit in the empiricist's ontology, Sartre's privileging of the ontological function of published texts is persuasive. Language and, more narrowly, the corpus of printed texts, serves as an indispensable informational filter. All the works published in the French language in 1980, the year of Sartre's death, capture but a fraction of the potential facts available to these French authors/readers. The threat of hyperfactualism makes such a mediating filter essential if the understanding of History, or even history, is to be intelligible. But a tighter filter is necessarily in operation when History itself is being made.

The weight that Sartre assigns to the concept of Totality must be lightened. Hegelian significance as the work of Reason in History, no less than the example of the Japanese miracle itself, should encourage us to see that the Objective Spirit is not captured by all the published texts of an era. All the texts of Hegel's critics and rivals of 1806/7, to say nothing of the detritus published in German during the Napoleonic era, do not define the Objective Spirit for Hegel's time in Jena. The text that counts is the *Phenomenology of Spirit*.

This assumption is pivotal to Althusser's perusal of *Das Kapital* and Sartre's penetration of Flaubert's *oeuvre*: these are not close readings of anything or everything. Few works merit the kind of close reading that Althusser applies to Marx or Sartre to Flaubert. But Sartre seems to conclude that he has failed as a writer/reader because he could not read all the printed works published in the French language during his lifetime.

This brings us again to that key lacuna in Sartre's remark that 'individuals... transcend their local situation by interiorizing, through reading, elements of class culture or even world culture'. The heart of Sartre's dilemma is that for the whole of his life as a thinker, the Objective Spirit was, in certain crucial ways, ceasing to speak French. But for much of the same period, certainly from the 1930s onwards, it was learning to speak Japanese. This is one change of History's path that may explain the gap between Sartre and Flaubert. An oracular writer, this singular universal, may indeed embody his age: Sartre insists that Flaubert embodied his age. But did Sartre embody his own?

Three issues are involved in the answer to this question. First, the Japanese miracle constitutes what Sartre calls 'an undertaking' that has made History. Second, there is the contrast in the Historical/historical circumstance between Flaubert and Sartre as 'oracular readers'. Third, there is the role of the proletariat in Sartre's schema, both as an historical actor who may have successors and as a Hegelian concept. In the wake of Marx and Lukács, Sartre's concept of the proletariat is so philosophically pristine that it defies comparison with other Historical agencies.

Such agencies include the workers of the Japanese miracle. During Sartre's maturity, Japan displayed an ever surer grasp of how to make History in the economic sphere. Books in French about Japan's rise were essentially reflective. Through them, Sartre might have learned about the birth of the first non-European economic power since the seventeenth century. But it is essential to observe that at no time between the publication of *Esquisse d'une théorie des émotions* in 1939 and Sartre's death in 1980 did the phenomenon of the Japanese miracle attract an oracular reader. This failure confirms the resistant nature of Historical significance. It makes the suggestion that Sartre himself might have lived and worked in Japan during the 1930s all the more tantalizing.

Second, there is the Flaubert–Sartre problematic. Peter Caws has seized on the Sartrean concession contained in the phrase 'multiplicity of totalizations', calling it the 'mature image of history' that he finds in *IF 3*, in contrast to the Marxist immaturity of the *Critique of Dialectical Reason*.[33]

In his study of *The Family Idiot*, Sartre attempts to establish 'an almost mystical parallel between Flaubert and the July Monarchy' and later with the Second Empire.[34] Sartre would make Flaubert a 'universal singular', an individual human actor who bears, as it were, on his person the full burdens of an entire era of human history or, failing that, the history of an epoch of national life. Flaubert's life as a master reader/writer is 'oracular' for it demonstrates that 'the finitude of an individual or micro-organic temporalization can embody the finitude of a macroscopic temporalization, that is the finitude of a historical period'.[35]

This sets Sartre against Lukács. As a writer, Flaubert stands near the end of what we would now call the grand liberating narrative or *récit* of the heroic bourgeoisie. This turning point figures famously in the literary criticism of Lukács.[36] He contrasts the achievement of Balzac with the failure of Flaubert (and Zola) in the light of the retreat of bourgeois heroism after 1848 under the systematic demands of industrial capitalism. For Lukács, Flaubert is caught in the fissure between the rise of working-class power and the retreat of bourgeois revolution. But committed to the philosophical rigour of the Hegelian system, Sartre will not accept that History moves through ruptures and breaks.

> The truth is, in fact, that History, this ongoing totalization detotalizes itself unceasingly in and by the very movement of totalization, because even if one were to assign it a single subject for centuries (the bourgeoisie since Etienne Marcel, the proletariat since the Commune, etc.), this subject would itself be broken.[37]

Resigning himself to a view of History as a set of 'broken off sequences', Sartre abandons History in favour of mere history, the 'finitude of a historical period' that Flaubert embodies.[38] Rather than a broken-off sequence, History may be better understood as a sequence of relay races, where the baton is passed from hand to hand, from liberating/transforming *récit* to *récit*: from bourgeoisie to proletariat, from the European to the non-European. This suggests the aptness of the Japanese miracle metaphor: the succession of leaders that sustains a flight of geese, one bird replacing another as its moment of leadership comes and goes.

By the time of Sartre's death, the French working class was thoroughly entrenched in the bosom of the welfare state or what John Kenneth Galbraith has ironically termed 'the culture of contentment'. The goals of the Third International had largely been achieved. In the place of the working-class question, History is asserting new demands: the role of women, racial minorities within White societies, homosexual liberation, and, most important in this context, the shift of the nub of economic and technological dynamism from the Atlantic to the Pacific.

Sartre's despair results almost entirely from his commitment to philosophic stringency and its demand for a seamless History ending in 'a calm totality'. Sartrean doubts offer the student of Japan more evidence that philosophy always makes the wrong turn. But Sartre, like Balzac, is so faithful to the truths of his age that his framework helps to bring fresh realities to light. After the failure of the project of the two *Critiques*, Sartre, together with Beauvoir, helped to recast these 'new demands' within grand narratives by giving them classical expression, but at the price of abandoning the formal philosophic imperatives with which Marx and Lukács, most influentially in *History and Class Consciousness* (1923), burdened the concept of the proletariat as a Historical agency.[39]

Sartre was true to his age, but it was changing in ways that undermined his principal goal. As with Hegel at Jena, Sartre's example should force us to see that Marx's insistence on changing History, rather than understanding it, can be misunderstood. History must be watched with an owl-eyed gaze worthy of Athena. That is the lesson of the Japanese miracle conceived in Hegelian terms. Every decisive shift in History's course demands a text worthy of the closest reading. This is the Sartrean teaching for the student of the Japanese miracle.

Thought

9 Philosophies

Life is elsewhere.
Milan Kundera

It is my ambition to know *India* better than any other European
ever knew it.
William Jones in a letter to Lord Althorp (1787)

STRANGERS TO OURSELVES

Cultures differ. The positivist denial of this fact of human life is
unpersuasive. But the raw instinct at work in such denials should
not be ignored. The murderous history of our species demonstrates
that we are poorly equipped either for crossing cultural frontiers or
for accepting the consequences of cultural difference. It may be no
accident, therefore, that it took a bi-cultural thinker such as Adam
Ferguson (1723–1816) to set the project of modern anthropology in
motion. In the informed and brilliant society that was Enlightenment
Scotland, Ferguson was 'an alien':

> He was a Highlander whose origins were in Perthshire, on the
> marches of two cultures, one animated by honour, marital virtue
> and tribal bonds, the other by commerce, speculation and ortho-
> dox learning. Marginality is no disadvantage to the sociologist.
> Being an alien, familiar with, yet estranged from, two cultures is
> an undoubted gain.[1]

The bi-cultural state embodies the ideal and highest ambition of the
area expert or Orientalist. We seek after this Holy Grail not only
for scientific reasons, but also for personal and practical ones. The
anthropological approach to the human sciences requires that the
researcher hone certain skills that are at once psychological and

analytical, but mainly human. Without such skills, the pursuit of the bi-cultural condition is illusional.

In advance of his voyage, the explorer of other cultures must draw up an accurate inventory of his abilities. Does he listen well? Is he adept at acquiring tacit knowledge? Can he see as well as look? Given the great weight assigned by empirical tradition to accurate vision, the particular irony here is that very few scientists, social or otherwise, are genuinely gifted in judging the *precise* meaning of an isolated fact. Finally, is he able to put enough of his identity at risk to make his 'tribe' slightly more real for him than a representative member of his own society? For a Westerner to study a non-European society successfully is to perfect these skills.

For the adventurous, an alien milieu provides unimagined opportunities for personal transformation. When we pursue cultural estrangement, we become, in Julia Kristeva's pregnant phrase, 'strangers to ourselves'.[2] There is a price to be paid for such alienation, but to submit to it is to become a more complete, more perfect human being. The stakes at risk in this adventure include one's sense of self as a thinking person. Language holds the key.

In addressing things Japanese, only extraordinary intelligence can compete with a thinking relationship with the Japanese tongue. The virtues of bilingualism, the natural cognate of bi-culturalism, are compelling. In contrast, monolingualism is a near fatal handicap. Inter-linguistic travel is a voyage of the spirit which speaks, literally, to a person's *vie intérieure*, no less than to external truths. To set up house in a foreign language makes us what we are because it puts our essence at risk. This is also part of the Orientalist's gain and gamble.

At some level of intellectual compulsion we must acknowledge that the struggle for genuine intercultural communication between Japan and the Western world is more effectively engaged by the literary labours, in Japanese, of Hideo Levi, the American novelist and denizen of Tokyo's Shinjuku district, than the conventional definition of the Japan expert either admits or encourages. Bi-culturalism stretches the human psyche with language-drenched experience. Positivism, with its armature of philosophic certitude, stands mute before it.

As the history of Orientalism shows, this Western adventure, in which our *cahiers de voyage* become our books on Asia, is peppered with failure. This is perhaps inevitable because genuine bi-culturalism, as exhibited in the life of Ferguson, is an unattainable ideal which the Western student of Asian cultures must strive for even though he knows, from the outset, that he will never achieve it. Full native grasp of the target culture *finally* eludes the non-native. The native speaker is born, not made.

The signal weakness of Edward Said's critique of Orientalism, for all its virtues, is his failure to recognize the objective truth of this ontological divide. Being native to both Arab and Western societies, Said pays insufficient heed to the horizon of difficulty. Because the Western student of Islam and Arab civilization has failed to perceive what is obvious to Said, as a Palestinian and native speaker of Arabic, he insists on treating the problem as a moral contest in which the Western Orientalist always trips over the ideological and religious fault-lines of European and American politics.

At root, the conundrum is not a moral but a scientific, almost technical, snare. Once again, it is language that illuminates the core difficulty:

> Certain experts in the field of simultaneous translation declare that a native bilingual speaker does not make for an outstanding interpreter. The best man will be one who has consciously gained fluency in his second tongue. The bilingual person does not 'see the difficulties', the frontier between the two languages is not sharp enough in his mind.[3]

Nor is it in Said's mind. Invincible ignorance forms the secret heart of the Orientalist's programme of learning. The ambition of Sir William Jones (1746–94) to 'know *India* better than any other European' is nonsense without the European qualification because millions of Indians knew their country, its languages and institutions, better than any eighteenth-century European could have.[4] Not even the formidable Jones, perhaps the most remarkable student of the Orient that Oxford has yet produced, could close the gap of knowledge that separated him from the Indian native speaker and his society. This is the true meaning of Lord Curzon's remark that 'the East is a University in which the scholar never takes his degree'.[5]

This cultural fissure has challenged every European student of Asia that Said censures, from Schlegel and Renan to Robertson Smith and T. E. Lawrence. Whatever the egotistical obsessions of writers such as Chateaubriand and Flaubert or the racial stereotypes entertained by Orientalists such as Ernest Renan (1823–92), the great renovator of nineteenth-century philology, and William Lane (1801–76), author of the *Manners and Customs of the Modern Egyptians* and translator of *The Thousand and One Nights*, the final bar to genuine understanding has nothing to do with intention, culpable or otherwise.

This is true also of the second barrier to Orientalist success: the one that arises not from the fact that he sails for a destination that he will never reach, but rather that he travels *from* a culture as well as towards another.

ROMAN WALLS

Cultures imprison. They teach us to see and value certain ideas and practices, and not others. In *Sertorius* (Act III), when Corneille has Pompey declare that 'Rome is to me more than a close of walls', he declares that the spirit of the imperial city is not confined to a strategic site on the Tiber.[6] But the fact that his gods travel with him does not mean that he is any less their creature. Home truths are not built with stone. Rather they are formed from gross mixtures of unexamined prejudices and the fine weave of national philosophic assumption. When the European travels somewhere, he almost always remains, philosophically and scientifically, at home.

As social science has been credited with liberating Asian studies from the trammels of 'Orientalist' bias and philological methods, we must reflect afresh on the impact of national schools of European thought and learning on the human sciences. Whatever its strengths, social science has not begun to overturn the philosophic world-views that glue together such national ideologies and methodologies. Indeed without its foundation in national philosophies, social science is unthinkable.

The challenge posed by mono-cultural prisons to the ideal of bi-culturalism affirms the importance for the Western student of Asian societies of Kant's call for methodological tolerance in *The Critique of Pure Reason*. The weaknesses of positivism and empiricism provide ample reason why the regional expert or Orientalist should reject the notion of 'philosophy' in favour of 'philosophies'. The example of Ferguson underlines the importance of such pluralism.

While all cultures imprison, Europe offers easier access to such methodological pluralism than perhaps any other great civilization. Where an intellectual and cultural tradition is rich and diverse, as is manifestly the case with Europe, then our civilized mansion may come with many rooms. A certain freedom lies in wait in this elaborate cultural prison. The area expert and the Orientalist are obliged to make something of these freedoms, and the contrasting intellectual options that they guarantee.

The two great wings of the edifice of European civilization are formed from an argument sustained since antiquity between Athens and Jerusalem. This ancient quarrel stands behind the distinction that Matthew Arnold drew in *Culture and Anarchy* (1869) between 'Hebraism' and 'Hellenism'. For Arnold, to set Jerusalem against Athens was to weigh the virtues of religion against those of science and objectivity. In the Christian or post-Christian West today, the grand narratives of racial and sexual liberation, no less than the rhetorical small change of political correctness, echo the Hebraic demand for justice. Hebraism espouses solidarity. In contrast, the Hellenist makes a cardinal virtue of scepticism, not of solidarity.

Japan studies has been deeply influenced by the contest between Hellenes and Hebraists. The post-war history of the discipline has been of the struggle between assertions of science, objectivity and scepticism towards the Western tradition (the critique of national character analysis, the Modernization School, and the defence of the Japanese model) and the claims of liberal Western culture with its roots in Jewish and Christian moralism (the wartime crusade against Japan, the critique of the Modernization School, and the attacks on Japanese imperialism, economism, male dominance and majoritarianism).

As Hebraism has defined the emotional thrust of most Western reflection on Japan (science being a minority taste), more attention needs to be paid to Hellenism which is also a broader church. In his introduction to *The English Philosophers from Bacon to Mill*, Edwin A. Burtt sets out the two large philosophic questions that have dominated the national traditions of the European mind since the Renaissance:

> Is philosophic understanding coextensive with the whole of man's life and experience, and is it the supreme accomplishment of which life at its best and fullest is capable? Or does life essentially transcend knowledge, being a larger and more significant whole in relation to whose ends our philosophic apprehensions should be viewed as subordinate though still very valuable means?[7]

Although he is careful to qualify so broad a generalization, Burtt identifies the ancient Greek and modern German approach to philosophy with the first question; the Roman and British tradition with the second. The empirical and positivist schools of social science have, in the main, adopted the Anglo-Roman outlook, although the influence of Hegel on Continental European reflection suggests that the contest has not been one-sided. Indeed, Hegel and John Stuart

Mill have between them laid down much of the methodological foundations of the human and social sciences.

No Orientalist or Asian specialist can afford to ignore the epistemological foundations of what he does. Nor should he assume that his research can proceed without scientific guarantees. At every stage of research, the scholar is drawing epistemological distinctions, whether he is aware of it or not. All social scientific research must proceed from an *idea* of what constitutes proper science, and such propriety will nurture a conscious relationship with philosophy. This is true regardless of whether we accept Peter Winch's famous formulation of the problem or reject it.[8]

The assault on 'objectivism' (the belief that external reality does exist) sustained by Richard Rorty in *Philosophy and the Mirror of Nature*, like the doubts raised about 'naive empiricism' by deconstructionalists, make it urgent for the regional specialist to secure his position in the methodological debate now swirling around him and his field.[9] If Japan studies remains 'foundationalist' despite recent pressures on the notion of the 'real world', which has been central to traditional Anglo-American empiricism and positivism, then it is obvious also that some of the liveliest minds now working in the philosophic mainstream believe that this creed is untenable. If the Japan expert still seeks to wrap himself in the legitimating mantle of 'social science', then the reasons need to be stated in a manner capable of responding to the new philosophic and scientific climate.

This is all the more important because intensive study of East Asian reality has not resulted in a European embrace of Buddhist or Confucian cosmologies or scientific methods. If Asian studies have an epistemological or ontological foundation, it is not a Japanese or Chinese groundwork, but a Western one. European epistemologies remain so obviously above challenge that when the student of pre-modern or modern Asia seeks to gain his methodological bearings, he must orient himself by struggling with the kind of large questions that Burtt believes anchor the Western philosophic tradition. For the Asian expert, Rome is much more than 'a close of walls'.

NATIONAL SCHOOLS

The reach, authority and utility of national schools of social reflection are best illustrated *in extremis*. In the *oeuvres* of Frantz Fanon (1925–61) and V. S. Naipaul (b. 1932), the intellectual exile brings the pressures of life at their most expansive, creative and highly charged to bear on French and British orthodoxies. Confronted by the challenge of mastering the colonial and post-colonial condition from the point of view of the colonized, Fanon and Naipaul learned to exploit the very grain of French and English thinking.

If writers from the British West Indies, such as Naipaul, have 'gravitated naturally towards the novel as a means of conveying the particularities of racial confrontation in all their subtlety, variance and ambiguity', Fanon yielded to the French temptations of forceful philosophizing, in which a powerful rhetoric, at once abstract and didactic, allowed him to cut 'through the myriad confusion of surface detail'.[10] The French and English models impose a particular rhythm and structure on the liberating labours of the colonized. V. S. Naipaul fashioned *A House for Mr Biswas* (1961) in a manner consistent with the empiricism of British fiction: 'the hero we first encounter is a person called Mr. Biswas; only gradually, hesitantly, ambiguously, do we learn about Mr. Biswas' colour, job, status and attitudes'.[11] Published the same year as *A House for Mr Biswas*, Fanon's *Les Damnés de la terre* exploits essentialist stereotype: 'the black', 'the white', 'the colonizer', 'the peasant', 'the bourgeois'. There is an abundance of fact cited in Fanon's writings, but his thought 'moves with impatience from the individual man into Hegelian categories'.[12]

Colonialism made Fanon a post-Marxist French *philosophe*, while it forged Naipaul into an English empiricist and follower of Defoe and Conrad. Both writers exhibit what Sartre might have called the 'genius of desperate cases'. Their biographies and family histories narrate the kind of involuntary dislocation and cultural transformation that stands beyond the experience, perhaps even the imagination, of many Western students of the non-European world. But their voyages and achievements of mind, as Ferguson would have affirmed, define the fullest measure of what an outsider may make of the high places of another culture. No Western student has probed Japan as deeply.

THE INDIVIDUAL VOICE

Nothing may be as subversive of a native national philosophy as formal education in another equally elaborate but different school of thought. Exposure to Descartes and Sartre in a California high school or to Russell and Wittgenstein in a French *lycée* may produce a set of tensions between traditions that allow the student to master his national school without being mastered by it. Similar advantages may be won by a Westerner educated in Japan, where the study of things Japanese can neither be marginalized nor isolated within the curriculum, or by a Japanese educated in Europe, where Japanese centrality may be relentlessly marginalized and subverted. A unique cast of mind may result from these tensions.

Such opportunities are rare. More frequently, even the great scholar is trapped within the confines of the native intellectual tradition which he has breathed in as a child. Weighing the achievements of H. A. R. Gibb and Louis Massignon, two of the twentieth century's most influential Orientalists, Said has concluded that they sadly 'fulfilled all the expectations created for them by their national traditions, by the politics of their nations, by the internal history of their national "schools" of Orientalism'.[13]

Such expectations are moulded by the facts of the real world. Just as Henry James contended that the French novelist Pierre Loti wrote endlessly about the sea because of the dearth of French overseas possessions, the French Orientalist Sylvain Lévi has stressed the impact of the possession or lack of empire to explain the contrast between French and British Orientalism.[14] The British ruled the East; the French were fascinated by it.

> The political interest that ties England to India holds British work to a sustained contact with concrete realities, and maintains the cohesion between representations of the past and the spectacle of the present. Nourished by classical traditions, France seeks out the human mind as it manifests itself in India in the same way that it is interested in China.[15]

What makes this inter-war contrast interesting now is that the study of East Asia in Britain no longer benefits from this imperial stimulus. American domination of the political science of Japan as well as the conspicuous role of Australians in Japan studies reflect the influence of political and economic interests in the Pacific which are felt less strongly in Europe. This may explain why Orientalist philology continues to prevail in Germany despite the efforts of Viennese-trained social anthropologists and historians. But it also highlights the powers of the French approach which has traditionally viewed the East as a kingdom of the imagination and Asia as a rich embodiment of *l'esprit humain*. Only a Frenchman could have written *L'Empire des signes*.

What is perhaps more striking is how the inter-war polarity around which Said organizes his understanding of Anglo-French Orientalism, in which English learning is 'sober, efficient, and concrete', while French scholarship is 'universalistic, speculative and brilliant', has survived the end of empire.[16] What secures these traditions in the face of the reality of decolonization are contrasting scientific doctrines or philosophies.

Thus, Gibb perceived 'two registers' in the writings of Massignon, one consistent with the demands of ordinary scholarship and the other an exuberant expression of a kind of French-ness in which 'objective data and understanding were absorbed and transformed by an individual intuition of spiritual dimensions'.[17] Said, however, observes that the very blindness inflicted on Gibb by his fitful empiricism prevented him from seeing how often he fell into the metaphysical trap of Orientalist essentialism.[18]

Albert Hourani regarded Gibb as an institutional figure, who moved up the ladder of professional academism, at London and Oxford, before becoming director of Harvard's Center for Middle East Studies.[19] If Massignon was the supreme outsider, then Gibb was the classic insider. Said believes that Gibb paid a high price for such intellectual domesticity. Gibb knew many Muslims, but like Lane, they appear to 'have been useful friendships, not determining ones':[20]

> The Orient for Gibb was not a place one encountered directly; it was something one read about, studied, wrote about within the confines of learned societies, the university and the scholarly conference.[21]

These were Anglo-American institutions where a commitment to dilute empiricism and textual positivism prevailed. It was less social science than a congenial blend of academic history and political journalism. But the traditional British aversion to the examination of ideas and first principles also probably ensured that Gibb, like his teacher Duncan Black Macdonald, never addressed 'the epistemological and methodological difficulties of "Islam" as an object (about which very large, extremely general statements could be made)'.[22] The main cause of such difficulties may be traced to the rooted hostility toward methodological rigour and theoretical 'reflexivity' that is characteristic of the orthodox British approach to the study of Asia.

The joy of Massignon's strategy can be found in its verve, brilliance and methodological confidence. Here is a set of techniques, values and ambitions that could sharpen the blade of Anglo-American methods. First, there is Massignon's determination, *as an Orientalist*, to learn, without fawning acquiescence, from some of the most stimulating thinkers and artists of his time: Bergson, Durkheim, Mauss, Maritain and Paul Claudel. Later, Massignon would cheerfully exploit the latest scientific innovations, from psychoanalysis to structural linguistics. Such mental adventurousness, coupled with an astonishing mastery of 'the entire corpus of Islamic literature',[23] gave Massignon a catholic cultural range which, Said insists, even Gibb, his closest rival, could not match.[24]

Second, there was the Frenchman's vital relationship with the French language: 'There is no austerity in Massignon's work, which is formulated in one of the great styles of the century.'[25] Massignon may have written with 'the flair of an artist',[26] but his literary artistry 'gives his scholarly work an appearance of capricious, overly cosmopolitan, and often private speculation'.[27] Said rejects this impression as inadequate to Massignon's gifts and ambitions:

> Everywhere his attempt is to include as much of the context of a text or problem as possible, to animate it, to *surprise* his reader, almost, with the glancing insights available to anyone who, like Massignon, is willing to cross disciplinary boundaries in order to penetrate to the human heart of any text.[28]

Third, Massignon demonstrates with rare force both the burdens and opportunities that Europe's diverse intellectual heritage presents to the student of Asian politics and culture. In the essay on Islam in Africa that Massignon contributed to Gibb's *Whither Islam?* (1932), the French Orientalist displays a firm statistical grasp of the Islamic forces in French Africa, coupled with a detailed investigation of the factions and publications that expressed Islamic feeling during the final stable phase of French rule in North Africa.[29] But he moves with ease from practical politics to a consideration of the question of 'What are the governing ideas of Western Islam?'[30] The most remarkable aspect of his essay is the opening flourish where he warns of the precariousness of 'European establishments in Islamic lands'. His analysis of how Islamic opinion takes shape, from the 'inward call' of conscience which trembles within an apparent calm, to its sudden manifestation in a mobilizing summons, is pure Massignon.[31]

Massignon's analytic skill, in which 'no reference is too extravagant so long as it is governed by an eccentric interpretative gift', contrasts with Gibb's guileless empiricism.[32] If Gibb's writings are animated by Protestant confidence that words can register the external world of Lockean fact, Massignon places his faith in Catholic *esprit* and the mental powers of Cartesian introspection. Massignon trusts his own mind because he is not afraid to explore it. His reading of Islamic culture is, like Descartes' *cogito*, 'wholly responsive to the dazzling gifts' that he brought to it and which 'in a sense made it up as a subject'.[33] Massignon teaches the student of Asia that along with the voyage, as goal and test, there is also the voyager, with all his rights, privileges and needs.

BEGINNINGS

The plurality that should be attached to the notion of philosophy by the student of Japan reflects not only the need to navigate between different methods, styles and world-views which possess a living force, but also the impact of past choices that his discipline has made. During the twentieth century, the most significant of such decisions has been the abandonment of the philological study of Oriental languages in favour of some form of social science. This is part of a wider revolution. The study of literature is no longer dominated by the methods and ideas of the classical philologist.[34] Oriental philology, with its ancient roots and formidable achievements, was not abandoned easily. In his influential study, *Area Studies Reconsidered* (1964), Gibb warily welcomed the new trend when he proposed that the traditional Orientalist work with 'a good social scientist'.[35] This synthesis remains unconsummated.

An obscure history stands behind the rejection of Orientalist philology, the key intellectual event in the evolution of modern Japan studies. In this decision, a variety of internal factors, both political and academic, have been accelerated by revolutions in the intellectual climate of Europe strong enough to shatter the scientific legitimacy of classical Orientalism. The birth of logical positivism was one of the these revolutions. The battle over philology between Nietzsche and Ulrich von Wilamowitz-Moellendorff (1848-1931) sparked by the appearance of *The Birth of Tragedy* in 1872 launched the other revolt.[36]

As we have seen, the logical positivist revolution continues to exert a terrible influence on Anglo-American social science. The victory of Nietzsche's children, secured by the triumph of literary modernism, opened the way for the rise of French theory and the contemporary transformation of the study of literature even in Japan, where the strategy of 'inversion' (*tento*) pursued, for example, in *Nihon Kindai Bungaku no Kigen* by Karatani Kojin is all but unthinkable outside the shadow of the Nietzschean critique of nineteenth-century philology.[37]

This double revolution is rife with choices between 'philosophies' parading as 'philosophy'. Neither a new Orientalism nor a genuine social science of Japan can afford to ignore these revolutions. The effects of the successful revolt of Russell and Carnap have been examined. Now we must turn to Hegel and his formidable epigone.

10 Thinkers

In 1759, Anquetil finished his translation of the *Avesta* at Surat; in
1786 that of the *Upanishads* in Paris – he had dug a channel
between the hemispheres of human genius, correcting and expanding
the old humanism of the Mediterranean basin. . . .
In our schools, up to that time limited to the narrow Greco-Latin
heritage of the Renaissance, he injected a vision of innumerable
civilizations from ages past, of an infinity of literatures.

Raymond Schwab

Japan is nothing.
Takeuchi Yoshimi

INTRODUCTION

In his famous *Introduction to a Reading of Hegel*, Alexandre Kojève
concluded that 'It may be that the future of the world, and thus the
sense of the present and the significance of the past, will depend in
the last analysis on contemporary interpretations of Hegel's works'.[1]
It will be argued in this chapter that none of these contemporary
interpretations may matter more than the effort to grasp modern
Japan's significance in Hegelian terms.

Because Japan experts have been insulated behind the ghetto
walls of our hitherto marginal discipline for so long, the intellectual
world outside now beckons us with a myriad of opportunities for
creative renaissance. As a result, the student of Asian societies is
confronted with a classical occasion to 'make it new' in a manner
undreamt since the time of the great philological investigations of
ancient Hebrew and Sanskrit. This making, in its first phase, centres
on the need for methodological self-mastery.

For better or worse, the entire methodological inheritance of the

Western student of Asia is European. I have argued that Hegel and John Stuart Mill dominate the methodological horizon of Europe. The strengths and limitations of the great British programme of positivism and empiricism that Mill helped to shape have been scrutinized. Now the challenges posed by German and French thought since Hegel must be addressed.

The vigour and intelligence of European definitions of what does and what does not count as 'thought' house the most important of the 'challenges' raised by post-Hegelian reflection. In *Glas*, Jacques Derrida weaves a parallel reading of texts by Hegel and Genet, while writings by Plato and Mallarmé are similarly wedded in Derrida's essay ' The double session'.[2] Such Derridean precedents should encourage the Japanese expert to see what he may glean from his own parallel set of texts which might place, for example, the notorious double-suicide scene from *Yukoku* by Mishima Yukio across the page from a 'relevant' passage from *Gendai Seiji no Shiso to Kodo* by Maruyama Masao.[3] Marvellous as it is, Anglo-American social science does not encourage such unsettling brilliance.

Given the rooted prejudices against French theory that persist among the children of Mill, a social scientific reading of Roland Barthes' *Empire of Signs* is proposed in this chapter. The self-referring character of Anglo-American social science all but ensures that few hardened social scientists will be moved by this interpretation, but my hope is that Barthes' example will encourage the Western student of Asia to exploit fully the double methodological patrimony, both Anglo-American and Franco-German, to which he is naturally heir.

Such open-mindedness is vital because there is a strong current of intolerance and obscurantism in the Continental European camp, particularly on the left, among post-structuralists. Like the Anglo-American positivist, many followers of Lévi-Strauss, Foucault, Derrida, Cixous and Spivak refuse to recognize non-European achievement in either the material or spiritual spheres. The post-structuralist campaign to 'decolonize' the mind of Europe has resulted in an ideology that consciously ignores and unconsciously denigrates the Historical significance of the Japanese miracle and East Asia's modern economic rise. The post-structuralist is united with the positivist in his determination to offer no quarter to Japan's classic need or its canonic potential.

EUROPEANS

European civilization is a meditation about the world that has made the world. This is what Hegel meant when he spoke of 'World History'. But this European book of the world comes with at least two Asian chapters. It was the ancient Persians who, as Hegel insists, launched the project of History. It is post-war Japanese success that has now brought to a close the long European domination of this project. As we have seen, few Western thinkers are willing to endorse what this pair of Hegelian arguments affirms: the fact of Asian importance. This denial leaves the field to the European tradition.

Eurocentrism demands that the Westerner who commits his life to the study of non-European societies resigns himself, before he walks an Asian street or learns an Oriental language, to a suspect vocation: the mastery of what is ontologically marginal to the intellectual world that has given him birth. Why might one seek such mastery?

Edward Said believes that the object of discourses such as Orientalism, which he understands as a poisonous mix of racial ideology and practical knowledge, is to enable the West to dominate the rest of the world. Orientalism, it is claimed, not only legitimates this domination in ways that befuddle the liberal conscience, but it also saps the urge of the dominated to resist Western domination. Epistemological colonialism sustains the intellectual hegemony of Europe over the non-European world even now.

This hegemony has persisted despite the recession of the political and economic power of Britain and France. Indeed, Said himself remains mesmerized by European high culture because he thinks that it exhibits a peerless brilliance. Such unrivalled excellence matters. European intellectual hegemony today demonstrates the force of ideas *bereft* of power. The competent exploration of this theme demands that we dismiss Foucault's insistence that knowledge and power are two sides of the same coin. The hold of European thought, including Foucault's, on the contemporary world does not benefit from bayonets. It is entirely dependent on the quality of European ideas as ideas. The sheer energy of European civilization, despite the Nazi slaughter and the vapid levelling of postmodernity, offers a study in contrast with Japan's intellectual invisibility and the scientific dependency of the Japan expert. Both Japanese cases exhibit a failure, not of the will to power, but of the will to thought.

REVISIONISTS

The Western school of Japanese Revisionism (*shuseishugi*) provides a test case for this perceived failure of mind. The Revisionist reinterpretation of the nature and significance of Japanese politics was the work of Western intellectuals, academics and journalists, beginning in the late 1970s. The term 'Revisionism', as applied to Japan, was coined by the editors of *Business Week* in response to the growth of anti-Japanese criticism in the American mass media during the late 1980s.[4] In the public sphere, this adverse reaction to Japan's new influence was perhaps predictable given the almost organic process of national rise and fall. The relative decline of the United States *vis-à-vis* Japan since 1945 ensured that American policymakers would eventually have to rethink the axioms of post-war US foreign policy in the Pacific. The weakness of the Japanese economy in the early 1990s undercut the impact of Revisionism, but if Japan continues to close the economic gap between it and the United States, then anti-Japanese Revisionism will almost certainly revive.

The recasting of American attitudes and perceptions of Japan was a complex and influential process. As a media phenomenon, it successfully encouraged negative public sentiment towards the Japanese. There were important parallels to this development in Europe and Australia. But academic Revisionism has been consistently chary of stoking anti-Japanese passions. Rather, Revisionists in the Western university have sought to sweep aside the ideological occultations that the cold war inflicted on the Western understanding of government and politics in Japan, South Korea and Taiwan. Such occultation often reduced these three countries to the status of flattering Asian versions of the American dream. Ivory-tower Revisionism may have been Revisionism *avant la lettre*, but it was often more rigorous than its journalistic successor and rarely anti-Japanese.

For the political scientist, the key text of academic Revisionism was Chalmers Johnson's *MITI and the Japanese Miracle* (1982). This book helped to transform the paradigm of the political science of Japan. And this text's influence outside academe was confirmed when anti-Japanese journalists and policy intellectuals exploited Johnson's thesis to argue that Japan's political system differed dangerously from that of America and Britain. Yet *MITI and the Japanese Miracle* was not an anti-Japanese book. Indeed it was only later that some of the most widely read of the media Revisionists discovered what was genuinely important about Johnson's book: its modest questioning of the soundness of liberal economic theory.

However different, both versions of Revisionism helped to recast Western perceptions of Japan. In what sense, therefore, does Revisionism count as thought and the Revisionists as thinkers? An answer may be found in the evolution of words and language. Under the heading of 'revisionism', *Webster's Encyclopedic Unabridged Dictionary of the English Language* (1983) lists the following definitions:

> 1. advocacy or approval of revision. 2. (among Marxists) any departure from a Marxist doctrine, theory or practice held by the one making judgment to be authoritative. 3. a departure from any authoritative or generally accepted doctrine, theory, practice, etc.

The *New Collins Concise English Dictionary* (1982) offers more detail:

> Revisionism 1. (sometimes cap.) a. a moderate, nonrevolutionary version of Marxism developed in Germany around 1900; b. (in Marxist-Leninist ideology) any dangerous departure from the true interpretation of Marx's teachings. (2) the advocacy of revision of some political theory, etc.

The enormous impact of Marxist thought and communist ideology on the modern world justifies such dictionary entries. Two landmark events made 'revisionism' a key term in twentieth-century thought and politics: the publication in 1899 of Eduard Bernstein's *Die Voraussetzungen des Sozialismus und die Aufgaben der Sozialdemokratie*, which appeared in English as *Evolutionary Socialism*, in 1909, and the Twentieth Congress of the Soviet Communist Party in 1956. Khrushchev's speech at the 1956 Congress, which provoked the charge of 'revisionism' from his foes across the communist world, was, together with the 1962 Cuban Missile Crisis, one of the two most important events in his controversial career as Soviet leader.

In the case of Bernstein, *Evolutionary Socialism* secured for him a place of significance in the intellectual history of the twentieth century, as demonstrated, for example, by the long entry about him in works such as *The Fontana Dictionary of Modern Thinkers.*[5] The collapse of European communism and the decline of socialism as a viable option for liberal democratic societies in the West call into question both of these definitions of revisionism as well as Bernstein's historical importance. From being an active force in the lives of men, Marxist or Communist Revisionism is slipping into the keeping of the historian and the antiquarian of *passé* ideas. But at least the Marxist revisionist had his hour in the sun.

Will Japanese Revisionism be as fortunate? Will it leave any trace on dictionaries and other standard reference books? If not, why not? Perhaps Marxist Revisionism was too obviously a real force in human affairs to provide a standard for assessing the significance of Japanese Revisionism. The fate of Sovietology illustrates the limitations of ideas that fail to metamorphose into thought. As a branch of area studies, Sovietology benefited from more public interest, more resources and more manpower than has ever been true of the post-war study of Japan. The demands of the cold war did produce a crop of theoreticians and analysts who have been judged to qualify as 'thinkers', but they were mainly experts in strategic studies, including the most famous of the RAND analysts: Bernard Brodie, Thomas Schelling and Albert Wohlstetter. A rank below, there is Herman Kahn, one of the very few 'thinkers' of the twentieth century to have written a full-length study of Japan's political system.

Sovietology never attracted this kind of talent. More damning, Sovietology defaulted in its main task: understanding the politics and policies of the Soviet leadership. As a result, Sovietologists were unable to predict the disappearance of the main object of their research, the Soviet Union itself. The opportunity of the Russian or Soviet expert to leave his mark on the intellectual life of his times may now have passed, perhaps forever.

The final decades of the twentieth century gave the Japan expert his chance to shine. But if the Marxist entry under the term 'Revisionism' is now doomed to disappear, it is not obvious that the *Collins Concise Dictionary* will someday soon replace it with: 'Revisionism 1. (sometimes cap.) a. critique of the ruling assumptions of postwar Western policy towards Japan that began in the late 1980s. b. a reordering of social scientific thinking to reflect the importance of the postwar Japanese economic miracle.' As things now stand, Khrushchev's fame may absurdly outlast that of Prime Minister Ikeda Hayato (1960–64), one of the key architects of the Japanese miracle.

KNOWLEDGE AND POWER

The reputation of Japanese Revisionism, as a potential school of thought, rises and falls with the success of the economies of East Asia. Japanese power makes knowledge about Japan important. Only success is rewarded. The disappearance of the Soviet Union has reduced Soviet studies to an agreeable pastime for historians. Sovietology exemplified a body of fact and theory that was wholly dependent for its influence on Soviet might.

Ideas, however, can take on a life and force of their own. There are intellectual discourses which demonstrate that knowledge may flourish in the absence of state power. Four examples of such discourses – Orientalism before the consolidation of Western rule over Asia, the long tyranny of ancient Greece over modern Western thought, the flowering of Russian literature despite Stalinist persecution, and the impact of French thought since the second World War despite the relative decline of French geo-political influence and economic power – illustrate the enormous range of historic possibilities.

During its first phase, Orientalism in the West may have been deeply prejudiced against Islamic civilization, but Orientalism was not an ideology for ruling over the Orient because, between the seventh century after Christ and the last siege of Vienna (1683), European civilization was under almost constant pressure from Arab or Turkish power. Yet it was during this long era of European vulnerability to Asian power that images and stereotypes that would decisively colour the ideology of European ascendency took shape.

If Orientalism, as a field of study, reflected European weakness, then the impact of classical Greek thought on Europe is the prime example of the power of ideas as ideas. As Horace was one of the first to acknowledge, it was the sheer textual and artistic force of Greek ideas and art that negated the triumph of Roman arms over the Greek communities that had survived the decay of Greek military prowess. Two thousand years on, the European mind has yet to free itself from intellectual bondage to the dead Athenian past.

Greek classicism did not exhaust the unique energy of ideas. The astonishing excellence of modern Russian letters since the Bolshevik Revolution – the poetry of Mandelstam, Akhmatova and Brodsky; the novels of Pasternak, Solzhenitsyn and Grossman – gives contemporary demonstration to the redeeming powers of thought and the imagination in the face of state oppression. The greatest texts provoked by Soviet communism were not books of strategic analysis or political economy, but *samizdat* literature. Now, with the Soviet Union dead and buried, which book has a greater claim not only on contemporary need and feeling but also on future centuries: Nadezhda Mandelstam's unforgiving masterpiece *Hope Abandoned* or Robert Conquest's once influential *Power and Policy in the USSR*?

Ideas that do not work and do not last do not merit our highest labours. This is the lesson that the fate of Soviet studies teaches. Sovietology no longer offers compelling reasons for learning Russian, but Osip Mandelstam's poem 'Tristia' and Joseph Brodsky's 'The end of a beautiful era' will for centuries hence.

By such standards of intellectual impact, the first blossoming of virgin or 'green' (*aokusai*) Japanese Revisionism may have been too much a creation of fashionable journalism to sustain itself as a system of ideas. How, therefore, should that Japanese Revisionist proceed? A beginning can be made by asking what the Revisionist notion of 'containing Japan' meant in intellectual and scientific terms. In essence, such containment required fighting Japanese mercantilist policies with American mercantilist measures. But in the sustained wrangle during the Bush and Clinton administrations over how to redress the American trade deficit with Japan, the trade nationalists never decisively defeated the proponents of positivist free-trade theory (in Japan, of course, the opposite situation prevailed). Because of the influence of such positivist logic, US mercantilist policies were often stillborn. The point is not only that the American deficit with Japan persisted deep into the 1990s, but that macroeconomic reasoning may be a powerful and complex way of misconceiving marketplace realities.

In the realm of ideas, the implications for this debate on how economics, as a science and a framework for making policy, is understood have ramifications that reach far beyond the US–Japan struggle over markets. This is the argument set out in *Japan: Beyond the End of History*. Alone among my critics, Carol Gluck seized on the central point:

> Chalmers Johnson has called for the Clinton administration to get tough with Japan and levy a 10 per cent import surcharge on Japanese goods. Williams urges Western social scientists to get tough with themselves and change their thinking about the politics of the economy on the basis of the Japanese experience.[6]

In short, mature Japanese Revisionism, properly understood as a revolution of ideas, may still leave its stamp on the world if it can develop a profound critique of positivist economics. Mercantilism is the idea that counts. It stands at the heart of one of the key intellectual struggles of our times: the battle to rethink economic positivism in the light of Japanese and East Asian economic success. This, in turn, demands fresh attention to the writings of German economist Friedrich List, particularly the concept of 'national economy' or what Otsuka Hisao and other Japanese mercantilist thinkers call *kokumin keizai*.[7] The challenge of List's great project offers an unrivalled opportunity for the mature Revisionist 'to make it new'.

PARISIANS

Despite well-advertised fears of an approaching dark age in high culture, let us assume that political science and area studies will survive because of their power to instruct. But will they flourish if they fail, in Barthes' phrase, to 'concern us, astonish us, fulfill us'?[8] This is the quest that French theorists should be seen to press on the political scientist who studies Japan. The logical positivist demands a rigorous answer to the questions: is the political science of Japan genuine knowledge? Is it more than linguistically mediated *bricolage*? But French theory poses an entirely different query: Is the political science of Japan, as practised in the West, old-fashioned, a hidebound discipline, a modern science in a postmodern world? The implication would be that Japanese public policy studies, barely a decade or so old, is already out of date, not in terms of current events but in terms of its methods, science and philosophy.

Just as empirical political science derives its epistemological foundations from Locke, Berkeley and Hume, the French School is heir to Continental philosophy after Rousseau, Kant, Hegel, Marx, Nietzsche and Dilthey. The keynote of the French School, as a response to German thought, is found in Nietzsche's observation that 'there are no facts, merely interpretations'.[9] This view reflects a larger revolution in perception. Joachim Pissarro has remarked that in aesthetics Monet's cathedrals can be seen as 'an example of the emergence of a new vision of reality, inherent in modernism, and which Baudelaire had already identified as "ephemeral, fugitive, contingent upon the occasion" '.[10] In retrospect it should be clear that modernism, as Baudelaire and Nietzsche understood it, is Romanticism's final revenge on industrialism, on statistical order, on politics and its iron laws.

In response to this new view of reality, the French School has unfolded in generational waves since the appearance of Claude Lévi-Strauss's *Les Structures élémentaires de la parente* in 1949. Structuralism, post-structuralism and deconstruction have had considerable impact on the methodological approaches and concerns of a wide range of disciplines. Indeed the influence of this series of anti-foundational revolts on French intellectual life has been momentous;

it allows one to speak with sober conviction about 'the defenestration of Paris'.

Early in her literary and philosophic career, Simone de Beauvoir confessed that she made the best of Paris that she was able. How might the Japan expert do the same? A beginning may be made by asking in what ways the French School calls into doubt what the empiricist means by 'reality'. Let us consider the only major text generated by the French School that bears exclusively on Japan: Roland Barthes' *Empire of Signs* (1982).

This text is a provocation. The Japanese reality that engages the exhausting labours of the specialist casts, or would appear to cast, hardly a shadow on *Empire of Signs*.

> Twenty-six long fragments reflecting on some aspect of this culture
> – food, theatre, faces, elaborate packages with nothing of conse-
> quence inside, haiku, slot machines – sketch Barthes's utopia,
> where artifice reigns, forms are emptied of meaning, and all is
> surface. The capitalist Japan of economic miracles and technologi-
> cal supremacy makes no appearance.[11]

As Barthes himself notes in the first essay of *Empire of Signs*, titled 'Faraway':

> If I want to imagine a fictive nation, I can give it an invented
> name, treat it declaratively as a novelistic object, create a new
> Garabagne, so as to compromise no real country by my fantasy
> (though it is then that fantasy itself I compromise by the signs of
> literature). I can also – though in no way claiming to represent
> or to analyze reality itself (these being the major gesture of
> Western discourse) – isolate somewhere in the world (*faraway*) a
> certain number of features (a term employed in linguistics), and
> out of these features deliberately form a system. It is this system
> which I shall call: Japan.[12]

Thus Barthes' Japan project is characterized by a negative clarity of purpose:

> Hence Orient and Occident cannot be taken here as 'realities' to
> be compared and contrasted historically, philosophically, cul-
> turally, politically. I am not lovingly gazing toward an Oriental
> essence – to me the Orient is a matter of indifference, merely
> providing a reserve of features whose manipulation – whose
> invented interplay – allows me to 'entertain' the idea of an

unheard-of symbolic system, one altogether detached from our own.[13]

If *Empire of Signs* is an empirical exercise, it is a wholly anti-social scientific one. What matters in Barthes' treatment of Japanese facts is the way that he refuses to submit, not to the claims of 'observable' social reality, but to the previous conquests or preoccupations of Japan by other Western scholars in the empirical or any other tradition. This Barthian 'refusal' is a predictable consequence of the working assumption, shared by almost all the members of the French School, that classical empiricism has been overthrown by a 'crisis of representation'. It is not that empirical reality has ceased to exist, but rather it no longer speaks to us in the old confident voice. If our confidence in empirical facts is dissolving, then Barthes or anyone else committed to reanimating the Western discourse of mind about what we call 'Japan' is not only free but also compelled 'to make it new'.

At the heart of this paradox of freedom and compulsion is a perceived crisis in how external reality should be contemplated or 'represented to consciousness'. This crisis throws into doubt the conventional practice of empiricism, particularly in Anglo-American social science. According to Frederic Jameson, the Marxist theoretician, the notion of a 'crisis' in twentieth-century empiricism reflects a breakdown of epistemological realism which would have us understand representation as 'the reproduction, for subjectivity, of an objectivity that lies outside it'.[14]

This has important implications for the empiricist's mirror theory of knowledge and art, which depends on such fundamental evaluative categories as 'adequacy, accuracy and Truth itself'.[15] But for the social scientist, the true sting is to be found in the fundamental rethinking of the nature of science by natural scientists: 'the cognitive vocation of science would however seem even more disastrously impaired by the analogous shift from a representational to a nonrepresentational practice' in the natural sciences, the North Star of positivist assumptions about what kind of science the social sciences are.[16] Viewed in this light, French theory is not anti-scientific. On the contrary, thinkers such as Barthes appear to be more alert to shifts in the paradigms of natural science than many social scientists.

Confronted by either the challenge of a scientific crisis or the weight of scientific orthodoxy, the French theorist displays none of the passivity that characterizes his positivist or empiricist colleagues. Thus, in Jameson's view, Lyotard cleverly saves:

the coherence of scientific research and experiment by recasting its now seemingly non- or postreferential 'epistemology' in terms of linguistics, and in particular of theories of the performative (J. L. Austin), for which the justification of scientific work is not to produce an adequate model or replication of some outside reality, but rather simply to produce *more* work, to generate new and fresh scientific *enouces* or statements, to make you have 'new ideas' (P. B. Medawar), or, best of all (and returning to the more familiar aesthetic doctrine of high modernism), 'to make it new.'[17]

This is the social scientific version of 'the shock of the new'. In this spirit, Lyotard urges us to voyage '*Au fond de l'Inconnu pour trouver du nouveau!*'[18] This quest furnishes a perfect gloss on the assumptions at work in *Empire of Signs*. The crisis of representation has sparked a realignment of interdisciplinary boundaries and orientations in natural science, aesthetics and social science. This reflects a fundamental change of paradigm. What should the political scientist make, if anything, of Barthes' Japan project?

First, if Barthes is even partially correct about recent changes in philosophic and scientific thought, then his enterprise, as it touches on Japan or any other social phenomenon, is defendable. Indeed *Empire of Signs* may be seen to reflect a much more active grasp of recent changes in Western philosophy and science than any rival text on Japanese society by a Western social scientist. It is Barthes who is the vigilant Orientalist, for he is the one who is methodologically self-aware.

Taken on its own assumptions, *Empire of Signs* will stand regardless of its obvious flaws. Lyotard's critique of Newtonian science, as interpreted by Jameson, should make it clear that however impressive John Searle's dissection of Derrida's reading of J. L. Austin or J. G. Merquior's drubbing of Foucault's interpretation of the early modern history of European ideas and beliefs, the positivist and empiricist critic may simply be missing the point.[19] Barthes' philosophic and scientific awareness, together with his sensitivity to recent changes in Japan culture (decadence and postmodernism), makes it unwise for the political scientist of Japan to do what otherwise he would almost certainly be tempted to do: dismiss *Empire of Signs* out of hand.

HEGELIANS

Faced with the orphan status of Japan in the intellectual discourse of the contemporary West, Continental European thought suggests three remedies. All three strategies are reactions to Hegel. One is to accept, as Takeuchi Yoshimi did in the wake of Japan's defeat in the last war, that Japan is nothing (and the West ubiquitous).[20] If the History of the world is European history, the non-European is reduced to the status of an epiphenomenon that exists merely naturally or empirically. This is what Hegel meant when he observed that 'Africa has no history'.[21]

By setting the bar of civilized achievement so high, Hegel's standard for what qualifies as 'making History' has angered left-wing Hegelians and their truculent post-structuralist off-spring. When Derrida declares that metaphysics is a 'White mythology', he is not arguing that African or Asian metaphysics is genuine while Europe's is not, but rather that a valid metaphysics exists nowhere.[22] Caught in the web of post-Hegelian reflection, Derrida concedes that the West is History's only true centre, the sole privileged sphere where History is made, and the only way to shatter this superiority is to 'decentre' the West: to pervert its methods, deflate its science and dethrone its philosophy.

This left-wing Hegelian cure for History, the second of our remedies for Japan's marginality, is an attempt to make the world disappear by closing one's eyes. Post-structuralists seek to deny the existence of Hegel's concept of History and the privileged place that he assigns to the West in making modern History. If you cannot become an actor on the central stage of History, what Shakespeare called the world, then burn down the theatre or pretend it never existed. The cure proposed for Eurocentrism is to marginalize everyone and every pursuit, the non-European world being already marginalized.

This overreaction to Hegel merely confirms his importance. But the unsuccessful revolt of French theory against Hegelian History, which begins with Lévi-Strauss's attack on Sartre in *The Savage Mind* (1962), forms a vital chapter in the prehistory of Said's critique of the European sciences in *Orientalism*.[23] But, in fleeing History, Said is left with only utopian remedies for the inescapable demands and terrors, the striving and triumphs of the human condition.

But Hegelianism offers a third remedy for Japan's marginality which is, in essence, a reformed version of right-wing Hegelianism. If the non-European society, confronted with European intellectual superiority, feels itself to be deprived of its own subjectivity, then a more satisfying cure may lie in becoming an actor on the stage of the world by learning how, in Hegel's sense, 'to make History'. This is what Japan has accomplished with its post-war economic miracle.

Japan's achievement demands Western recognition. We have not garnered even the first methodological, scientific and philosophic fruits of the Japanese miracle. Because the West is today falling behind on so many fronts, what is needed now is to recognize what the Japanese have achieved. Just recognition must proceed from correct perception. Japan's example should encourage the shock troops of the European sciences to see how erroneous Marx's censure (the source of Lyotard's attack, for example, on Hegelian contemplation in criticizing Habermas) was in 'Eleventh thesis on Feuerbach', where he condemned philosophers for merely interpreting the world rather than changing it.[24] The Japanese achievement is fact. What the mainstream disciplines of the West are refusing to do is to 'see' it. Today the Japanese miracle requires, above all else, what Henry James called 'the deep breathing fixity of total regard'. If this is contemplation, so be it.

DIALOGUES

Nothing demonstrates the greatness of European Orientalism more than its imaginative conquest of space and time. Mindful of the material impact of the dredging of the Suez Canal, Raymond Schwab argued that Abraham-Hyacinthe Anquetil-Duperron (1731–1805), the French Orientalist who translated the *Zend-avesta* into French and a Persian version of the *Upanishads* into Latin, 'dug a channel between the hemispheres of human genius'.[25] It is only with the writings of Anquetil that the Orient was, according to Said, finally revealed to European sensibility in the full 'materiality of its texts, languages and civilizations'.[26]

It is the textual labours, heroic in scale and ambition, of scholars such as Anquetil and William Jones that have underwritten much of the extraordinary density and intelligence of the long European meditation on the Orient. Social scientists have, for the past half-century, sought to surpass the achievements of the great French and British schools of Oriental science and literature. In this new effort to excavate a fresh channel between the spheres of the intellect that are the mind of Europe and the civilizations of Asia, the systematic study of Japan looms large.

Despite much progress, the social scientist has to rival the achievements of the Orientalist who continues to cast much the larger shadow on Western thinking and feeling about East Asia. This reveals a double Japanese lacuna. There has been the manifest inability of Japanese reflection to match the force of practical Japanese attainments. One must also accept that the art and thought of pre-modern East Asia still tower over the work of the moderns. Both of these factors have constrained the imaginative and theoretical reach of Western thought about East Asia. The greatest era in Japanese history has not generated the finest text written in Japanese. That remains the *Genji*. Heian Japan retains its superiority over the present precisely because it gave birth to Lady Murasaki's masterpiece. In a golden age, the social scientist has been content to mine silver.

Nevertheless, an unprecedented density has been achieved in the dialogue between Japan and the West during the last half of the twentieth century. America has provided the central laboratory and forcing house of this dialogue. Through the brutal experience of three wars since 1941, a blood-soaked field of shared trial and tragedy has been nourished with hundreds of thousands of lives on both sides of the Pacific. In war and peace, media coverage, popular literature and the film have transmitted a sea of images between the societies with the greatest stakes in this trans-cultural dialogue. The Pacific is now the centre of global economic, commercial and technological exchange. Only the supreme contest of high culture remains unaddressed. Here, thinkers have a key role to play.

11 Classics

Entropy is the world's natural direction, its slow collapse, its physical
and spiritual unwinding. The function of genius is to contradict for
a moment this inevitable sinking, to take pains amidst the universal
carelessness.

Edmund White

At the same time Francis Bacon was going all out for
monumentality. The gamble was for high stakes in the old
European tradition, and the pictures were to deserve either the
National Gallery or the dustbin, with nothing in between.

John Russell

IMMORTALITY

Do political scientists die? The question should not suggest that
scholars may have discovered the elixir of eternal life. Rather the
intention is to probe what is for the student of politics a more
disturbing mystery. Why do political scientists write as if they were
immortal? Why does the expert on politics think, live and teach as
if there were no tomorrow? If textual longevity is measured in the
number of years, sometimes months, after publication that a piece
of analysis or research continues to be cited in the political scientific
literature, then the truth of the matter appears to be that the 'shelf-
life' of the social scientist's book, monograph or article is remarkably
short.

Indeed, modern textual lives are all too brief. On this point,
scholarly bibliographies exhibit a pronounced consistency. One has
to know only the date of publication of an academic work to be
able to predict, with fair accuracy, that the vast bulk of the secondary
research cited will have been written in the decade immediately

preceding the book's appearance. Even political scientific books that have a historical character, such as Chalmers Johnson's *MITI and the Japanese Miracle*, published in 1982, a study of 'transwar history', adheres to this pattern of citation.[1] Thus, Johnson writes about the successive changes in Japanese industrial policy between 1925 and 1975, but only a few examples of English-language research are cited from the 1960s, fewer still from the 1950s, and just two from the 1940s. Of all the English-language scholarly books and articles written about Japan before 1940, only a single unpublished doctoral thesis is mentioned in Johnson's bibliography.

Bibliographies follow this pattern for sound reasons, but this only reinforces the truth that if a political scientist desires to retain his place in the scientific literature – and surely that is the point of the arduous business of scholarly writing – then he must publish, as it were, forever. Cease writing and your name will disappear, quickly and decisively, from the cited literature. This is to die as an author.

Scholars are not immortal. Why do political scientists write works that contain the seeds of rapid decay and disintegration? Their meaning and significance, as texts, will have all but disappeared long before the paper on which they are printed begins to rot. In such cases, even dusty libraries offer no salvation.

Many factors are at work in this tireless pursuit of almost instant obsolescence, but none may be more germane than how the political scientist defines reality. If one of the meanings of the word 'history' is 'past events, especially when considered as an aggregate', then the study of current government pivots on the assessment of a flood-tide of data about political events.[2] This flood is renewed each day.

The impact of this process of 'updating' on previous writing is conclusive. It ensures the rapid evaporation of the significance of almost all texts devoted wholly to excavating the importance of 'yesterday'. Journalism reflects the process with precision. With each passing day, the claims that a piece of political reporting or commentary may exert on tomorrow come to depend, almost entirely, on its chance relevance to the historian. Barring this comforting exception, the reach and scope of 'instant' analysis is governed not by positivist ideas, such as 'covering laws', but by a very different iron law: old news is no news. Here the key model for the labours of the social scientist is to be found not in physics or biology but in journalism.

Authors outlive their books today. This is true of almost every branch of serious reflection about politics. Only in the corpus of classic texts, from Plato to Marx, do we find a body of work that is incontestably worth printing on acid-free paper. Indeed these master-texts are all but immortal. The canon of political thought challenges the political scientist's obsession with 'now'. One can assert with confidence that in a hundred years, Plato, Machiavelli and Hobbes will still be read. Even James Harrington (1611–77) and Adam Ferguson (1723–1816) may remain objects of sustained study long after every piece of political science written during this century in a Western language about Japan will have been forgotten by everyone but the antiquarian.

The political scientist should be troubled by this phenomenon. Why does the paper on which more than four thousand books, monographs and articles published on the philosophy of Martin Heidegger yellow less quickly than that of even the best political scientific monograph written a decade ago? Heidegger's claim on immortality keeps the paper of those who write about him slightly fresher. Hence the suggestion that an insight into *Being and Time* hammered out in 1930 may have a better chance of being read in the year 2050 than even the most incisive analysis of the historic Japanese parliamentary election of 1993.

Understanding political phenomena of transient interest is without question one of the principal responsibilities of the social scientist. Who else is going to sift through the contemporary ramifications of the politics of typhoon relief in Shimane or the rise and fall of Uno Sosuke or the complications of the Large-scale Retail Store Law if not the political scientist of Japan? So to question the amount of attention devoted by political science to the bric-à-brac of contemporary political life is to ask only whether the political scientist should commit *all* his energies to perusing today's headline news. According to Roland Barthes, 'only writing can give meaning to the insignificant'.[3] But writing, in and of itself, cannot confer durability. Compared to the intellectual reach of Plato's *Republic* or Aristotle's *Politics* across the centuries, the ten years or so of active significance that limits all but the best examples of political scientific writing today constitute a scholarly reworking of Andy Warhol's dictum that 'In the future everybody will be famous for fifteen minutes'.

Long before Warhol and the cult of the transient, Baudelaire defined the modern condition as 'ephemeral, fugitive, contingent upon the occasion'.[4] Baudelaire's powers as an observer of social change allowed him to gauge, as early as 1848, the momentous shift in values that was beginning to threaten not only Renaissance aesthetics but also the contours of European life as it is lived outside books and the academy.

Baudelaire's classicism reflects a high consensus. Whatever may divide them as schools of organized perception, Classicism, Romanticism and Modernism are united in their pursuit of immortal fame. Postmodernism is a rebellion against this classic quest. The bewitching 'now-ism' that characterizes the postmodern outlook has its parallel in the instant obsolescence of much social scientific research. But there is a price to be paid for this singular emphasis on the immanent. Sex has been described as the dirty little secret of the Victorians; the subverting little secret of postmodernism is death.

As a key guardian of science and civilization, the social scientist should be less anxious to drink the waters of oblivion. We must be on guard whenever we encounter contemporary dismissals of canonic excellence because 'the news that stays news', in Ezra Pound's adage, finds its true being and epiphany in classicism.

In *In Bluebeard's Castle*, George Steiner articulates a formidable defence of the classic impulse in European civilization. He begins, as every social scientist should, with Eliot's insistence that 'culture is not merely the sum of several activities, but a *way* of life'.[5] The scientist, writer and artist endeavour to 'outmaneuver the banal democracy of death' which gives this way of life its logic and central motion of the spirit: the quest for 'an active afterlife' in and through intellectual and artistic creativity.[6]

> The thrust of will which engenders art and disinterested thought, the engaged response which alone can ensure its transmission to other human beings, to the future, are rooted in a gamble on transcendence. The writer or thinker means the words of the poem, the sinews of the argument, the personae of the drama, to outlast his own life, to take on the mystery of autonomous presence and presentness. The sculptor commits to the stone the vitalities against and across time which will soon drain from his own living hand. Art and mind address those who are not yet, even at the risk, deliberately incurred, of being unnoticed by the living.[7]

Steiner's rejection of the fashionable doctrine of 'now-ness' (*genzai-chushin*) is radical because complete. The 'trope of immortality' inspired Thucydides' claim that he wrote his chronicle of the Peloponnesian War 'to last for ever'. The Chinese have nursed their own canonic equivalent to this proud Western ambition. In European letters, this urge to transcendence energizes the texts of the great political masters, from Aristotle to Rousseau. It conjures up a vision of a political and social science which lasts, which triumphs over individual death and communal extinction.

CLASSICISM DEFENDED

In a way true of no other twentieth-century polity but the United States of America, Japan's pantheonic greatness, its canonicity, offers an unrivalled occasion for the political scientist to test his mental resources to the fullest in the pursuit of a transcendent classicism. Here, as nowhere else, will be found the intellectual glory that, in Pindar's phrase, 'would rise higher hereafter'.[8] This moment must be seized.

Confronted by a god-sent opportunity to escape the grip of the merely immanent, the political scientist has been tempted to let this privileged hour elude him. The reasons for our neglect of death and creative transcendence include the modern suspicion that intellectual excellence, in the Pindarian mould, demands either an aristocratic surrender to 'romantic bathos' or a repellent genuflection before 'elitist idols'.[9] Steiner concludes that 'The notion, axiomatic in classic art and thought, of sacrificing present life, to the marginal chance of future literary or intellectual renown, grates on modern nerves'.[10]

The obstacles to a Japanese apotheosis are not confined to the cultural sphere. There are deep sources of scientific hesitation. Among the more important are textual positivism and historicism. No less than positivist philosophy and science, the positivist approach to the reading and generation of political texts of classical stature conspires also against extending recognition to post-war Japan. Japanese greatness demands a classic text. But, at its core, textual positivism is profoundly anti-classical.

This would matter less if textual positivism were not so influential. Unfortunately it has exerted a damaging impact on how political texts are read and understood by those who think and write about politics. In the name of historicism, the textual positivist would deny the political classic a place in our future.

Dialogues

Such resistance is not limited to Europe. In *'Bunmeiron no Gairaku' o Yomu* (Reading 'An Outline of Civilization'), his three-volume study of the 1875 masterpiece by Fukuzawa Yukichi, Maruyama Masao acknowledges the reasons that historians dissent from classical projects.[11] Maruyama cannot ignore such criticism because he is an intellectual historian, though one who brings to his task rare powers as a thinker. In defence of his heretical proclivities, Maruyama cites the approach of his own teacher, Nanbara Shigeru.

Nanbara insisted that his students enter into a 'direct dialogue' (*chokusetsu no taiwa*) with the thinkers of the past, with Plato and Aristotle, Locke and Bentham.[12] Modern historians, as Maruyama accepts, will have none of this. They insist that the proper under-standing of any major thinker of the past demands an intimacy with the historical conditions that attended the birth of his ideas. Such knowledge is judged not only as indispensable to the sound interpre-tation of a political classic, but also it is often trumpeted as the only valid way to read the classics.

Maruyama chafes at such limitations. In resisting such positivist scruples, he invokes the sovereign examples of the millennial dia-logue that Europeans have nurtured with the ancient texts of Plato, and East Asians have sustained with the Confucian canon (Confucius appears to have been a special favourite of Nanbara). Maruyama's huge Fukuzawa project pivots on the assumption that *Bunmeiron no Gairaku* can illuminate Japan's present no less than its past. But it must also be conceded that Maruyama cautiously yields to the positivist demand that the 'historical conditions' that influenced Fukuzawa's work should be understood by the contem-porary reader, in part because of the uninformed prejudice that encourages the neglect of Fukuzawa's classic in Japan today.[13]

Maruyama may be one of Japan's deepest readers not only of Fukuzawa but also of Ogyu Sorai (1666–1728), perhaps the finest of all Japanese thinkers about politics. The decisive rubric here is intellectual 'greatness'. Neither Sorai nor Fukuzawa may in any useful sense be described as 'positivists', but Maruyama has reflected on the work of these two thinkers for a lifetime. For him, the best of their writings display those qualities of interpretational richness and inexhaustibility which all texts that would win pantheonic per-manence must demonstrate.

Oxford

The classics of political philosophy, as a genre, have fallen from favour among political scientists during the twentieth century. Logi-cal positivism and Newtonian scientism have had a devastating impact on the longevity of political writing. The resulting irony is that the classic texts of Bertrand Russell and Ludwig Wittgenstein, even the works of Sir Freddie Ayer, may retain their vitality and relevance long into the twenty-first century, while their persistent influence conspires against any political scientist writing a text that will survive as long.

Nowhere has the corrosive impact of this positivist rebellion against tradition been felt more strongly than at Oxford, intellectual home to many of the rebels. In his essay 'Does political theory still exist?', Isaiah Berlin, who embodies for many the spirit of classical humane letters in political thought, observed in 1961 that 'writers about politics today would rather talk to each other than commune with the past'.[14] The stature of the history of political philosophy may have radically altered since the early 1960s, but this stricture remains largely accurate. Many scholars still seek to enforce a strict ban on what Nanbara called 'direct dialogue'. This narrowness of outlook is consistent with the immanent focus of contemporary reading and research habits as reflected in many political scientific bibliographies.

One result has been the astonishing neglect in Britain of Berlin's effort to explain how 'the optimistic, progressive spirit gave way to the two dark and dangerous centuries that followed'.[15] Writing on Berlin's *The Magus of the North: J. G. Hamann and the Origins of Irrationalism*, Mark Lilla has observed that:

> It is astonishing that a historian of Berlin's stature, engaged in such an ambitious enterprise, should have received so little attention in his adopted country, where his challenging theses about the character of modernity have been passed over in silence by his fellow historians of ideas.[16]

This lack of regard for Berlin's *oeuvre* may be traced to a particular school of textual historicism within the study of political philosophy which 'has been so intent on reducing the historical and geographical scope within which ideas may be discussed that it simply cannot make out what Berlin is after'.[17] This is an intolerable failure, but one that it may be impossible for historians to put right.

The problem has coloured the academic revival that began to take shape in the late 1960s after the history of political ideas had been declared all but dead. According to Iain Hampsher-Monk, this revolution has sought 'to focus attention on a wider range of texts . . . than hitherto in our attempt to understand the past environment and movement of political ideas'.[18] In practice, this has meant that the serious study of sources has shifted to 'the more manageable area of an episode or particular controversy in which the minor texts, and context, can be brought into focus'.[19] Historians have sought to displace the great political texts from their privileged places in the pantheon of tradition.

This is not the stuff of a direct dialogue with the past. If the main consequence of the vigorous offensive by intellectual historians during the past several decades has been to make Berlin's labours as incomprehensible as the large canonic projects of human history, then perhaps it is time for political scientists to wage their own offensive to address the canonic needs of Japan and our times.

The political classics are more than 'sources'; they are tools to think with. The history of the idea of a 'social contract' illustrates the point. The 'golden age' of social contract theory in the West is conventionally judged to have begun with Hobbes' *Leviathan* (1651) and concluded with Kant's *Metaphysical Elements of Justice* (1796).[20] This forms the key chapter in a genealogy stretching from the idea of *bona voluntas*, as developed by Cicero and Seneca, to the contractarian ideas of Locke and Rousseau. The insistence that people are voluntary agents and that there is no such thing as 'natural' political authority forms one of the fundamental beliefs of the Euro-American civilization that helps to set it apart from other cultures. Our canon tells us what we are because of the powerful way that it organizes our thoughts.

St Augustine's recasting of the pagan ideal of *bona voluntas* did not depend on a pedantic mastery of Roman civil thought, but on his ability to think in an original way about a suggestive idea inherited from tradition. This is as true of the subtle reworking of political voluntarism found in *Tractatus de legibus ac Deo legislatore* by Francisco Suarez, the great Catholic counter-reformation thinker, as it is of John Rawls' exploitation of the modern concept of a social contract in *A Theory of Justice*.[21] *Pace* textual historicism, it is of secondary concern that Suarez misconstrues his Augustine or that Rawls departs at significant points from Kant or Rousseau. What matters is that a body of inherited ideas provides a classic occasion for thinking of the first rank about politics within our tradition.

THE FRENCH REVOLUTION

Positivism offers a strategy for reading classical texts that draws its strength from strict definitions of the ideas of 'truth', 'reality' and 'science'. But positivism's evident powers do not qualify it as the sole legitimate method for perusing classical texts. The chief defect of the positivist approach to canonic texts is its implicit anti-classical spirit, the assumption that the creative re-interpretation of a classic – Marx re-reading Hegel, for example – is not allowed.

This denial of the possibility of fresh textual creation tends to mystify the processes of textual production. The right of Heidegger or Rawls to rethink a master text by Kant must be affirmed by the academy. Both *Being and Time* and *A Theory of Justice* should be seen as triumphs over positivism and its monist dogma.

The attack on positivist interpretation of the classics that took place in France in the wake of the decline of the Sartrean school and the revolt against the 'three Hs' (Hegel, Heidegger and Husserl), challenged textual positivism from a different direction. The first blood in the great quarrels that sparked this French revolution in literary values was drawn in the 1963–64 literary controversy which set Roland Barthes against Raymond Picard in a wide-ranging debate over the sound textual interpretation of the plays of Racine.

The distinction between *la critique universitaire*, with its positivist credentials, and *la nouvelle critique*, with its contrasting stress on interpretative and reinterpretative freedom, highlights the damage inflicted on European culture by both textual positivism and vulgar post-structuralism. Literary forms of structuralism only appear to share with textual positivism a distinct uneasiness before the classic canon. The post-structuralist's assault on the privileges and authority of the author silently assumes the pre-existence of a body of classical writing by Racine, Rousseau and Balzac. It is only post-structuralist rhetoric that denies the possibility of producing fresh canonic nominations for the pantheon. Derrida's students, particularly in America, have been embarrassed and perplexed by an obvious truth: Barthes was a master of French prose with canonic claims.

Unlike many of his followers, Barthes was a serious Romantic for whom the dissolution of canonic form issues, finally, in a revitalization of canonic excellence. But for this canonic turn, post-structuralism would have fallen victim to its supreme weakness: creative impotence. This, too, enfeebles the project of writing a modern classic on Japan. But structuralism's assault on textual positivism does dramatize the anti-creative instincts so alive in textual positivism. This is its value to the student of Japanese canonic greatness.

Barthes targeted the objectivist pretensions of the textual positivist. Armed with a scientific outlook which pretends to transcend all ideologies, the positivist reader is allowed to shirk his responsibilities to spell out his own ideological position, as it touches on the content of the text.

> Without theoretical argument [textual positivism] claims to know the essential nature of literature, and it eclectically accepts or rejects, in the name of common sense, everything offered by ideologically committed criticism. It will reject Freudian or Marxist interpretations as exaggerated or far-fetched (instinctively, Barthes says, it applies the brakes), without granting that this rejection implies an alternative psychology or theory of society that ought to be formulated.[22]

From the standpoint of the classicist, this surrender to common sense smothers all the instincts to answer a classical text with another of rival force and authority. In the name of 'sound' reading, historicism may prove to be the enemy of classical excellence.

In *Critique et vérité*, Barthes set out the canonic creed in a manner consistent with his own Romantic ambitions and classical achievements. As Barthes knew but was reluctant to say lest he scandalize the faithful, it is not the critic but the thinker who provides the executive means for a nation to 'take up periodically the objects of its past and describe them anew, to discover *what it can make of them*'.[23] Such 'making' is what positivism opposes.

Reading Hegel

The alert scholar knows this. In his brief but incisive study, *Hegel's Phenomenology of Spirit: Its Point and Purpose – A Commentary on the Preface and Introduction*, Werner Marx addresses this vexed question with rare clarity.[24] He identifies two approaches to thinking about texts: the 'immanent' and the 'assimilative'. The immanent approach, with which he identifies, seeks to interpret Hegel's *Phenomenology* 'without grinding any philosophical axes'.[25] By contrast, practitioners of the assimilative approach endeavour 'to interpret *The Phenomenology of the Spirit* – or usually only part of it – from a phenomenological, ontological, Marxist, existentialist, or history-of-Being viewpoint'.[26]

Mindful of the impact of the hermeneutic school of textual interpretation on the Continental European approach to classical texts, Werner Marx feels compelled to censure the positivist view, which he describes as 'naive': positivism assumes that it is possible to interpret the text 'as it stands'.[27] Rejecting this approach, Marx insists that every reading or interpretative re-creation of a classic text is inevitably influenced by prejudices and presuppositions which the reader brings to the text that he reads. These prejudices are to be confronted, not ignored.

Werner Marx distinguishes between two types of assimilative readings. The first type involves an effort to equal or surpass the classic stature of the original. This type of assimilative reading demands that the most brilliant of readers metamorphoses into the most forceful kind of writer. Such writers are driven by a hunger for immortality as an author and thinker. They may also seek to change society. In the case of readers of Hegel, the majority of these assimilations 'are born of the needs of the time, and seek to effect a fundamental transformation of man and reality'.[28] The only response to a classic text that is truly privileged is the one that attempts to match the scope, depth and impact of the original. The classic readers of the *Phenomenology* include Marx, Lukács, Kojève, Bloch and Habermas.

In the first type of assimilative reading, the author himself takes up the challenge of interpreting the text of the *Phenomenology* in the 'light of his own general philosophical enterprise'.[29] Marx cites Heidegger's attempt to recast Hegel's masterpiece in the language of 'the history of Being' as a recent example of this approach.[30]

The second type of assimilation is more academic and less original. The researcher 'foregoes either interpreting the text on his own account or adopting any attitude to problems immanent in the work'.[31] Rather he mines 'the textual exposition or views about the composition of the *Phenomenology* which have been worked out by a whole particular school of Hegelian scholars (e.g., those of Rosenkranz, Haym or Haering)'.[32]

While insisting on the legitimacy of academic assimilation, Werner Marx is unequivocal about the stature of the interpretative enterprise of Marx and Lukács, Heidegger and Habermas: 'The first type of assimilation, in which the *Phenomenology* is interpreted "productively" – by changing it – is certainly the most important philosophically.'[33] This concession to the philosophical greatness of Marx and Heidegger is what distinguishes the classicism of Continental textual scholarship from the anti-classicism of the Anglo-American positivist approach, both philosophical and historical, to political philosophy.

Lumps and texts

The imperative of canonic revision spares neither the philosopher nor the social scientist. In his provocative essay 'Lumps and texts', the American philosopher Richard Rorty observes that:

> In the future we shall have to redo our narratives of how scientific theories or paintings or poems or literary essays fit together just as often as somebody does something original and striking that won't fit into the stories we have been accustomed to tell.[34]

The grand narrative of the modern West, as mediated by philosophy and the social sciences, is a story that we have accustomed not only ourselves but the world to tell. But modern Japan has accomplished something 'original' and 'striking' that calls in question the West's self-mastery. In our relationship to Japan, Rorty's 'future' has already arrived.

Poised between the ever-renewing databases of scientific technology and the often brittle truths of common sense, textual canons encompass our most rooted, best-examined truths about ourselves. Literary canons and canonic analogues are, in powerful and demonstrative ways, what we are. Scientific canons should help us to narrow the gap between our ideals and the real world in ways that encourage resistance to the obscurantism of folk myth and the totems of common sense. What Milton might have called the 'loosely disally'd' quality of Western life since the 1970s – the economic turbulence, the dispiriting rise in crime, the decline of educational standards, our tormented domesticity – point to a deep cleavage between our 'speech signals' and the confident grasp of our social circumstances.

Among all the motivations active in the West's still modest campaign to understand Japan, the most neglected remains the need to renovate and perfect the Western canon. Success in this endeavour requires either fresh creation or unprecedented borrowing from other civilizations. Failing that, we may have to re-examine old texts now banished from the canon, and where necessary, resurrect our textual dead.

CODA

The proper understanding of the Japanese miracle may require such acts of rebirth as part of the Westerner's search for a master text. Chalmers Johnson has pointed to the failure of industrial policy intellectuals to produce a body of *loci classici* about the Japanese industrial miracle.[35] The absence of a Japanese answer to Adam Smith or V. I. Lenin should encourage us to return to the German Historical School and the *oeuvre* of Friedrich List. Indeed, List's *The National System of Political Economy* (1841) may qualify as the kind of proto-canonic text with which we might set our project in motion from within the European tradition.[36] The impact of mercantilist thought on the orchestrators of Japan's modern economic ascent makes it reasonable to ask whether List qualifies as the intellectual godfather of the Japanese miracle.

In the larger context of any perusal of the European response to the modern Japanese experience of government, the issue is important because List may be seen as perhaps the prime example of a Western thinker who grasped the essential principles at work in Japan's modernization programme nearly a century before Japan effectively embraced heavy industrialization during the 1930s. List allows us to entertain the comforting notion that at least one European thinker offers a unique vantage from which to understand Japan's modern achievement.

What should be kept firmly in mind from the outset is that List did not repeat Marx's error of surrendering to positivist economic reasoning. Whatever his limitations, and they are many, List's clarity about the limitations of the nineteenth-century theory of political economy sets him apart from the positivist tradition which has sought to monopolize the teaching of economics for the past two centuries. On this point alone, List's scepticism may be seen as liberating. For any Westerner who seeks to understand Japanese economic policy-making in *Japanese* terms, *The National System of Political Economy* is an indispensable text. Its classical claims may redeem us yet.

Part III

On classic ground

If only people were free enough to let *everything* in, something extraordinary might come of it.

Francis Bacon

12 Japan and the end of political scientific marginality: the argument restated

Each time I work I am ready without a moment's hesitation to undo all that I did the day before because each day I have the impression that I see further.

Giacometti

Rome n'est plus dans Rome, elle est toute où je suis.

Corneille

A JAPAN-SHAPED HOLE

Is European social science immune to the impact of the sharp, relative decline in civilized power that the West has experienced since the catastrophe of 1914–18? Is the Western scholar of Asia meeting his obligations to help to prepare his fellow Westerners psychologically and intellectually to live in a world in which the two largest economies may be China and India? Is Japan's post-war miracle the stuff of which social scientific revolutions are made? The academic response, outside Asian studies, to the competitive challenge being mounted by East Asians today does not inspire confident answers to these questions. Indeed, the implied failure casts doubt on the powers of Western political and social sciences, *as sciences*, to capture reality.

In *Japan and the Enemies of Open Political Science*, I have sought to do nothing more than send up a flare to illuminate the whole horizon of epistemological and ontological difficulty facing those who animate the disciplined study of Japanese and East Asian politics in Europe, North America and Australia today. I have concentrated my critical fire on the ways that the methodologies and paradigms that prevail in textual classicism, positivism, empiricism,

Orientalism, linguistic theory and post-structuralism all *appear*, from the vantage of political science and Japanese studies, to deny the canonic achievements of modern East Asians. Nowhere have I sought to deliver a decisive blow. Rather the intention has been only to stimulate awareness of the *Grundprobleme* or foundational problems that the contemporary revival of East Asian energies and ambitions poses for Western social science as it is practised by front-line researchers.

Even the bare formulation of such questions runs the risk of error and distortion. Umbrella concepts such as 'Western social science' or 'East Asian ambition' are at best ripe generalizations. At worst, they may invite imprecision and fan prejudice. Everywhere in such an enterprise, the imperatives of theoretical boldness and empirical caution must be balanced. Mindful of the minefield of theory on which I have proposed to tread, I remain convinced that the gamble must be taken.

Inspiration for this project has come from two of the most conse-quential *oeuvres* in modern European writing on East Asia: Joseph Needham's monumental *Science and Civilization in China* and Ronald Dore's sustained meditation on Japanese society. Both of these scholarly endeavours have succeeded magnificently on their own terms and within the limits of their particular fields. But despite such success, scholars and thinkers in the core disciplines of the Euro-American curriculum remain obdurate in the face of Need-ham's insistence that the intellectual map of mankind should be redrawn in ways that favour the scientific and cultural achievements of Chinese civilization at the expense of those of post-Renaissance Europe. Similarly, the turn or *Kehre* that I believe divides *British Factory–Japanese Factory* and *Shinohata* from Dore's later work reflects his recognition that the academic mainstream in Europe and America continues to refuse 'to take Japan seriously'.[1]

Reflecting only on such labours, it is possible to conclude that painstaking empirical research sustained over a lifetime is not enough. If Needham and Dore had received the kind of recognition that their research merited, there would be less need to pursue the two-volume endeavour housed between the covers of *Japan: Beyond the End of History* and *Japan and the Enemies of Open Political Science*.[2] This battle must now be taken to the Euro-American mainstream.

This is essential if we are to relieve the unnecessary marginality of political science within the Western curriculum. Here, I have proposed a strategy for waging this battle. This is the goal that I sought to identify in *Japan: Beyond the End of History*, where I attempted to elucidate what I called 'the Japan-shaped hole' in the discourse of Western social science.[3] Here, I have argued for pressing social science to its limits in the name of academic tolerance, intellectual pluralism and scientific openness.

JAPAN AND THE END OF POLITICAL SCIENTIFIC MARGINALITY

The march of the glaciers

This book is a meditation about the methods and philosophy of social scientific research as they apply to the understanding of the politics of Japan, Asia and the non-European world. It is an attempt to subvert the conceit, so powerfully alive in much American political science, that the term 'methods' must, where rigorous, apply to certain quantitative tools alone. Modern mathematics is one of great inventions of the human mind, and Europe has made an enormous contribution to the persuasive elegance of mathematical reasoning, both pure and applied. But the success of mathematical approaches (as opposed to statistical ones) has attracted an excessive prestige, particularly in economics, which conspires against the fuller understanding of human reality, be it in Asia or elsewhere. Here I have urged a break with the monist dogmatism that positivism has spawned.

In calling for a revolt against one of the twentieth century's most fruitful intellectual endeavours, I entertain no illusions about the growing impact of mathematical methods in alliance with the new technologies. The influence of mathematics since Newton and Leibniz has been so great in Europe that, in taking this opportunity to insist on the power of words, I identify with the vulnerabilities of Poles and Lithuanians who, having just emerged from the frozen grip of Russian domination, know that some day the ice age may return. In a similar manner, the liberating pluralism of method defended here may some day soon be nipped by the icy winds of scientistic dogma. In exploiting the current retreat from epistemological concerns in philosophy, I have drawn comfort from the fact that the evolution of the European sciences has displayed repeated swings not only towards positivism but also away from it since the late Middle Ages. Today's temporary relaxation of the vice of positivism has provided me with an opportune moment to insist that many scientific problems may have more than one solution, and still qualify as genuine problems.

To be a Western student of Japanese government and politics is to be twice marginalized. First, Japan clearly stands outside the privileged vantage of the Euro-American civilization that has dominated global history for the past half-millennium. Japan's marginal place in the Western academic curriculum, despite that Oriental nation's meteoric rise to the forefront of global leadership during the course of the twentieth century, is one of the most vulnerable legacies of that long era of European supremacy. Indeed, one might today conclude that, short of military conquest of the United States, it is not obvious what more the Japanese could do to win recognition in the West for their post-war achievements.

Second, the specialist in Japanese politics is handicapped by the marginal status of political science itself within the Western curriculum. His discipline has yet to break the chains of theoretical dependence on political science's more 'scientific' neighbours, particularly positivist economics and behavioural psychology. There is hardly a sub-branch of political science, certainly not area studies or political theory or political economy, that has confidently transcended such limitations.

The nature and source of this intellectual and scientific dependence are amply demonstrated in the articles collected in *Perspectives on Positive Political Economy* edited by James E. Alt and Kenneth A. Shepsle.[4] The book is loud with proud claims and scientific hubris. Both the claims and the confidence are grounded in positivist assumptions about the nature of reality and truth. But nowhere in this provocative text is a persuasive ontology for positivism developed. Rather, any positivist claim to scientific validity is assumed to stand beyond question.

Such claims spell the death of open political science. It may be true that rational-choice theories, for example, do represent a way of addressing economic and political institutions in a manner that eluded the singular focus on the individual economic actor which was the ruling doctrine of classical political economy. But such reformed positivism offers only one solution for political scientific marginality: the total absorption of political science by economics. When Mancur Olson reaffirms the positivist conviction, which harks back to Comte and John Stuart Mill, that 'Scientific progress normally leads to scientific consensus', he means that empirical political scientists will learn to comply with the positivist consensus.[5] Peter C. Ordeshook concludes that:

the rational choice paradigm may not yet be the dominant paradigm of political science, it is the most prominent. It serves today as the successor to the behaviouralist revolution of the 1950s and 1960s, and so it is only reasonable to anticipate that the study of politics and economics can once again become wholly integrated.[6]

Even Ordeshook does not see this academic *Anschluss* as imminent. But the reasons he gives for this otherwise inexplicable delay go a long way towards explaining the patronizing tone often adopted by positivists when discussing the benighted labours of the political scientific practitioner of pure empiricism, the unsophisticated seeker after new facts:

> This is not to say, of course, that we can anticipate the imminent demise of disciplinary boundaries at universities. Bureaucratic inertia is a heavy burden, and political scientists and economists do not always share substantive concerns. Nevertheless, the time has long since passed when practitioners of one discipline can ignore the theoretical advances and problems of the other.[7]

The message here is unambiguous. Political scientists are obliged to give way before the 'theoretical advances' of economics because there is only one sound way to do social science: the positivist way. It is equally clear that many political scientists, especially those working in area studies, do not subscribe to the doctrines of a unified science. To positivists, such renegades appear to be the victims of what in Roman Catholicism is termed 'invincible ignorance' because they refuse to comply with a vision of a unified social science. The scientific utopia that Olson sets out in his article in *Perspectives on Positive Political Economy* titled 'Towards a unified view of economics and the other social sciences' compares closely with the project envisioned by the supporters of 'the international encyclopedia of the unified sciences' initiated by such luminaries of the Vienna school of logical positivism as Otto Neurath and Rudolf Carnap. In the crusade for unified science, the whole caravan of twentieth-century scientistic monism is on parade.

Social science has had enough of such scientistic pretence. The illusion must not be entertained that economics, even in reformed guise, has matched the scientific achievements of Newtonian or Einsteinian physics. More often than not, the temptation felt by economists to wrap themselves in the mantle of Newtonian success is mere dressed-up incapacity. When Alexander Rosenberg demands to know 'If economics isn't science, what is it?', many economists will be pained by feelings of exacerbation, even vulnerability, in the face of even this sympathetic scepticism.[8]

The question is, however, does rational-choice theory justify such sweeping claims? Does positivist political economy represent a penetration of reality more powerful than that put forward, for example, in Kant's *Critique of Pure Reason*? Foundational social science must concede, in a way untrue of non-foundationalist or anti-foundationalist science, that the *genus* or reality is logically one. Confronted with the manifest diversity of reality, the universalist (what Kant called those who 'are always on the watch for the unity of the *genus*') endorses the ordering power of positivist laws; the defender of species or diversity seeks rather to exploit that very manifoldness that is the defining characteristic of those who are, in Kant's telling phrase, 'especially empirical'.[9]

Japan stands firmly in the way of this positivist juggernaut. Perusal of the political scientific literature on Japanese government and policy practice makes it very clear that the claims of rational-choice theorists are at best inflated and at worst bogus. More important still, Japanese economic, political and business practice, properly conceived, calls into question some of the fundamental axioms of positivist economics itself. Finally, and of most consequence to the philosophy of social science which secures the very foundations of social science as a whole, the example of Japan provides ample ammunition to lay siege to the very citadel of twentieth-century scientism: logical positivism. If the scientific exploration of *genera* has not abolished *species*, that is the diversity of the human universe, then the logical, scientific and philosophical grounds for abandoning empiricism are insufficient. Here, it appears, Japan has saved Western social science from the worst methodological excesses of the monist fallacy.

Positivist science is powerful. But its natural and respected place among the methods of the social sciences cannot be assured unless positivists embrace scientific tolerance. Pure empiricism has its rights for which no apology is required. On the contrary, no quarter should be given to those positivists who, having failed to win the argument, now appear intent on enforcing a positivist 'consensus' on the practitioners of other methods and approaches, that is by purging empiricists from academic positions or blocking funding for their research. In all of this, the doctrine of intellectual freedom and the highest scientific standards must be uncompromisingly affirmed; the unproven assertions of scientistic positivism on display in works such as

Perspectives on Positive Political Economy, and the dogmatic aggression that they supposedly legitimate, have no place in the free and open university.

To claim that one social scientific method is better than another is a perfectly acceptable, if vulnerable, academic exercise. To insist that one method is the best of all methods is bold in the extreme, but the idea should not be dismissed out of hand without careful assessment of the scientific evidence in question. But to declare that one method alone is to be *permitted* verges on social scientific nonsense and medieval darkness. Clarity about such first principles in the present climate is the most precious philosophic teaching to be gleaned from the close examination of the Japanese experience of government. Here, too, is to be found the remedy for the marginal status of political science as a scholarly discipline.

LOST HORIZONS

During the course of writing this book, it has been dispiriting to discover that to seek to think clearly about such matters is to labour against the grain of much post-war social science. It has been painful to uncover the parochialism and anti-empirical blindness that social scientific positivism has sometimes inflicted on the study of Asia in the contemporary West. Such discoveries encouraged me to turn to the controversial prehistory of modern Asian studies that travels under the name 'Orientalism'.

Whatever his failings, the twentieth-century Orientalist, as thinker and scholar, has often been more alive than the social scientist to the epistemological consequences of the shift of power and influence away from Euro-American civilization and towards the non-European world. Surveying the writings of the most influential British and French students of Islamic culture during the 1920s and 1930s, Edward W. Said has concluded that the Orient was laying down a challenge to Eurocentrist science even before the Second World War.[10] This was because the West was already undergoing a cultural crisis which in part was a direct consequence, in Said's view, of 'the diminishment of Western suzerainty over the rest of the world'.[11] So has Western social science escaped the lacerations wreaked by this crisis?

Keynes astutely argued that the impact of ideas on human affairs is vastly greater than popularly recognized, but the reverse is also true. Events shape ideas. In the wake of the débâcle for civilization that was the Great War, European sense and sensibility sought to register the slaughter of Flanders, Tannenberg and Verdun not only in *The Waste Land* but also in logical positivism, which Leszek Kolakowski has called 'a response to an endangered civilization'.[12] Mature European consciousness could hardly have done otherwise and still have been called 'alert'.

Perhaps nowhere in twentieth-century thought have the burdens of a civilized response to a real-world revolution been more forcefully displayed than in *The Crisis of the European Sciences* (1934–37) by Edmund Husserl.[13] Appalled by the threat posed to the West and European high culture by Nazi and Fascist barbarism, Husserl insisted that we see the crisis of modern Europe as grounded in a particular understanding of philosophy and science. He sought, brilliantly, to elucidate the madness in our methods.

Husserl gave to the term 'intellectual horizon' its modern weight and purchase. Every perception, in Husserl's view, is shadowed by a horizon of meaning and assumption that floats between semi-conscious and full conscious grasp. Horizons of meaning help to order both our perceptions of the objective world of things 'out there' as well as our internal subjective consciousness. Horizons can, notoriously, converge; they can also be lost.

Husserl's critique should encourage us to ask whether the horizon of scientific relevance and meaning, as it influences the Western student of modern Asia, is confined to social science alone. Four alternative horizons have been dissected in *Japan and the Enemies of Open Political Science*: political philosophy, logical and social scientific positivism, and, more contentiously, Orientalism and the higher journalism. It has been insisted here that the thoughtful student of Asian politics and society must seek to negotiate a separate peace with each. These horizons of orientation and commitment may be charted in both diachronic and synchronic fashion (see Figure 1).

Historically, the European pursuit of scientific understanding has been governed by either Eurocentric interests or the Greco-European need to pursue universal truths. Whether Western Europeans regarded themselves as members of Christendom before the modern age or identified themselves with the ideals of European civilization later (Francis Bacon was one of the first to speak of 'we Europeans'),[13] the claims of other geographies and histories tended to be confined to Mediterranean cultures: ancient Judea, Greece and Rome. The demands placed on European identity and intellectual self-awareness by biblical or classical studies were central in

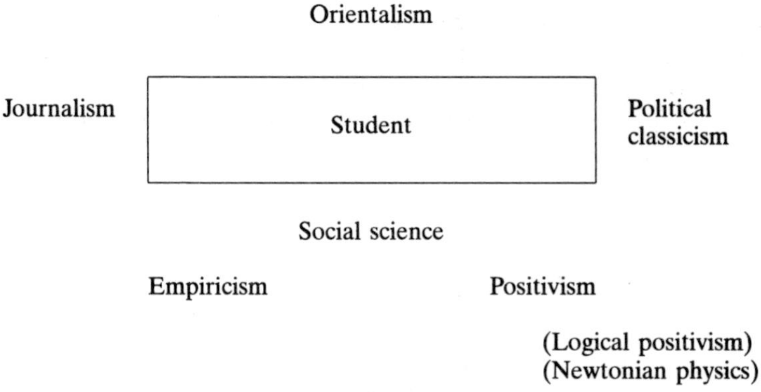

Orientalism

Journalism	**Student**	Political classicism

Social science

Empiricism   Positivism

(Logical positivism)
(Newtonian physics)

Figure 1 The student of Asian politics and his scientific horizon today

the way that reflection on the Oriental world outside Palestine or Attic Greece were not.

This discrimination between Christian and non-Christian, European and non-European imposed a strict hierarchy on scientific understanding. Disciplined study of the Bible, the Church fathers and the pagan classics congealed into the core of the university curriculum. In contrast, the study of Arabic, Sanskrit and Chinese was characterized by an unmistakable marginality. Just as important, the relative freedom to deal with what were for Europeans the non-canonic texts of Islamic and Indic civilizations appears to have been overwhelmed by importation of the methods and approaches of the central sciences. Here are to be found the roots of the methodological dependence that characterize not only the study of Oriental cultures and literatures, but also social scientific research on modern Asian societies. Area studies reflects this marginal condition. We import methods; we do not export insights or generate paradigm revolutions, which remain the work of canonic centre.

This hierarchy of task has strongly influenced the shape of modern social science. Along with biblical and classical studies, the philosophy of the natural sciences, after Galileo and Newton, acquired its canonic place, providing a strict paradigm of achievement against which all later branches of the human sciences have been judged. Similarly, the canonic privileging of Plato, Aristotle and Cicero, as political philosophers, created a pantheon of achievement against which modern European thinkers on politics, from Machiavelli to Rousseau, could be compared and apotheosized. But this quarrel of the ancients and the moderns also generated a set of classical standards against which the less impressive textual labours of non-

European political thinkers could be measured and normally dismissed. But for the student of twentieth-century Japanese politics, particularly public policy, it is the elevation of economics, in the wake of the pioneering labours of Smith and Ricardo, which has conspired decisively against the generous empirical grasp of non-Western societies, particularly post-war Japan (see Figure 2)

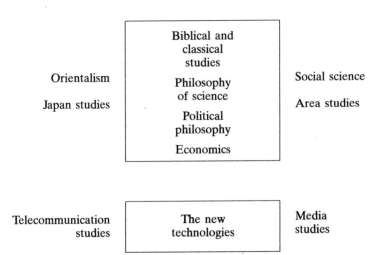

Figure 2 The European sciences: centre and periphery

The resulting domination of the scholarly margins by the canonic centre has given intellectual and scientific Eurocentrism a sovereign authority which transcends callous impulses to unthinking hubris and prejudice. However wary, Said's high regard for European high culture is no accident.

Here, as in *Japan: Beyond the End of History*, I have sought in good Hegelian fashion to pierce the claims of this canonic centre, both to renew it and to make Japan's achievement a part of it. In the face of the growing impact of the new technologies, I have affirmed the view that the traditional canon remains the preferred target because I suspect that telecommunication and media studies remain fundamentally dependent on technical innovation carried out elsewhere. East Asian practice cannot transform the paradigm of the new technologies from outside (Japan's impact on the new technologies from within is another matter). But Japan's modern achievement does provide ample ammunition to question the greatness of European tradition.

Orientalism renewed

The Western student of modern Asia is heir not to one but to two great traditions. Social science, a multi-branched system of knowledge with roots deep in Western thought, is one tradition. But the other pillar is Orientalism, the philological study of Asian texts and traditions. Orientalism, like social science, is the product of a long gestation within the womb of European civilization. Both approaches assign a dominant role to empiricism. Both owe their origins to the shattering of the ontology of late medieval Europe.

The Enlightenment left a profound mark on both traditions, bestowing positivism on social science, and a revolutionary advance in philological methods on Orientalism. More recently, the Western study of Asian societies has been transformed by the social scientific revolution driven by the labours of Weber, Durkheim, Michels, Pareto, Freud, Wundt, Malinowski, Jevons, Walras and Marshall between 1870 and 1930.

Orientalism has been shaken by this revolution. During the course of the twentieth century, philology has been repeatedly attacked on methodological grounds. In *Orientalism* and other writings, Said has developed the charge that Oriental scholarship tends to be fatally compromised by its function as an imperialist ideology.[15] But the Oriental inheritance of area studies makes it essential that Orientalism's positive role not be denied. We must distinguish between Orientalism as scholarship and 'Orientalism' as propaganda or self-deception, just as the art historian distinguishes between *japonisme* and *japonaiserie*.[16]

Orientalism's contributions to the science of area studies flow from its commitment to cultural geography as an ordering motif in human learning. Orientalism insists on rigorous linguistic knowledge of the Asian communities being studied. But perhaps even more surprisingly, Orientalism's involvement with 'Orientalism' also gives it an unrivalled purchase on conflicts between civilizations, including the vexed issue of Eurocentrism, the claims of national and communal identity, and the politics of race. The link between Orientalism and 'Orientalism' should serve to alert the area specialist to the all-too-human temptations and failings that social science has been keen to banish from serious consideration.

But Orientalism's contribution reaches beyond even these vital issues. The textual commitments of Orientalism should teach the modern area student the singular importance of the art and discipline of close reading (one of social science's blind spots). Furthermore, Orientalism has displayed a vigorous commitment to classicism: writing and thinking that lasts.

One epistemological consequence is that Orientalism offers grounds for reasserting the claims of literature, art and philosophy on the ordering intelligence that the area student must bring to bear on his subject. This calls into radical question the massive wall that has been erected during the twentieth century between the humanities and the social sciences. For the area student, philosophy and literature matter more than physics or higher mathematics, although it is the latter that have served, for far too long, as the dominant epistemological model for so-called rigorous social science. Orientalist precedent should encourage the regional specialist to say 'goodbye' to someone that he never knew very well but whose legacy has been allowed to exert a baleful influence on the human sciences: Sir Isaac Newton.

It is essential, in my view, that the area specialist have a precise idea, at once generalized but exact, of what kind of social science a thinker and heir of Newton and Galileo, such as Ernst Nagel or Carl G. Hempel, would have him pursue. But having achieved a certain clarity about the kind of positivist monism at work in the paradigm of Nagel or Hempel, the Japan specialist must be clear enough about his vocation to conclude that, finally, he requires a certain purchase on issues raised by the question of postmodernism and the contemporary discourse on the 'text', a meditation that has its roots in the literary.

AMBITION

Tearing down the wall

In an age of great scientific discoveries and technological inventions, it is the 'works and days' of the scientist and technologist that provoke wonder and excitement. But here, I have sought to argue the contrary case: that area studies has its own special reasons for demanding that the ban which positivists and certain schools of empiricism have sought to impose on the works of the great writers, artists and indeed the humanities as a whole must be overturned.

The conceits alive in this demand, no less than the kinds of argument developed throughout *Japan and the Enemies of Open Political Science*, may be illustrated, with force and precision, by turning to the lives of the great artists. The creative examples of Rodin, Cézanne and Gauguin offer parables of creative struggle which have unique heuristic value for the Western student of Asia. Their almost talismanic careers offer another reminder that the wall that many have been so keen to erect between the social sciences and the arts is an intolerable violation of the unity of the human sciences.

One of these parables might be called 'Rodin and the virtues of marginality'. One of the accidents of Rodin's education and training as a sculptor was that he never studied at the Ecole des Beaux-Arts in Paris. His failure condemned him to an apprenticeship at a less prestigious school which turned out craftsmen, not artists. Yet, Rodin's biographer makes clear that Rodin transcended the marginality of this education to force a revolution in the values and ambitions that governed the artistic mainstream of late nineteenth-century Europe.[17] Few scientific lives, however illustrious, document with equal conviction that marginality need not be a set of chains. This is Rodin's lesson to those who have inadvertently chosen to pursue the life of the mind in the manifestly marginal fields of Oriental and Asia study.

Cézanne teaches the necessity of creative silence. Throughout his early career, Cézanne shunned argument about painting because 'to have engaged in such disputes was to risk defeat'.[18] Cézanne's instincts warned him against exposing his ideas before they had congealed. He carefully husbanded his still vulnerable insights. Cézanne's silence teaches that those who seek paradigmatic revolution from a position of marginal weakness must bide their time.

To maintain a resolute silence is not to refuse to see. In these pages, positivism has been alternately praised, denounced and pitied. All these responses are valid because they form natural stages in a meditated recoil not only against positivism's manifest achievements but also its dogmatism and blindness.

Japanese public policy studies in the West would never have consolidated its present position if it had submitted its early findings and theories to the full blast of criticism from economic positivists. The child does not challenge the Greco-Roman Olympian to a sandbox struggle. But neither should the Olympian deny that the child that offers no contest today may become tomorrow's champion or that Greco-Roman wrestling, to take the example at issue, precludes the very possibility of judo or sumo. As always the world is more complex and diverse than the monist allows.

It is not only the artist but also the social scientist who must learn to trust the sometimes fitful unfolding of his own powers. This is never more true than when radical innovation is the goal. Here, some of the styles, techniques and concerns of the literary textualist have been gingerly exploited to argue for a place for modern Japan in the Western canon of political philosophy. To the eyes of the trained literary critic, the treatment of the creative contest between Neo-classicism and Romanticism by Maruyama Masao in '*Bunmei-ron no Gairyaku' o Yomu* may seem to be thin and unconvincing. But the often hailed discovery of the 'political' by literary critics such as Terry Eagleton and Edward Said leaves the political scientist and professional politician equally unimpressed.[19]

The point is that different disciplines, discourses and professions encounter the problem of texts or politics at different phases in their evolution. Cézanne's strategy does not call for the avoidance of criticism. Rather the French artist would urge us not to submit to such destructive engagements until we are ready. It takes time for the child to become a master.

Finally, Gauguin's life exhibits the revolutionary potential of monumentalism. After his early experiments with primitive marginality in his painting of peasant life in Brittany and at Arles, Gauguin translated the arresting silences of Tahitian life into the idiom of the monumental tradition of post-Renaissance art. A great leap is made when Gauguin recasts and fulfils this tradition by producing a brown-skinned 'Madonna and child' in a manner that captures the solemnities of Christianity transmuted in a South Pacific setting. Behind the ambition set out in *Japan and the Enemies of Open Political Science* to 'deposit something resistant and Oriental beneath the skin of the Western tradition of political philosophy' stands the example of Gauguin.

Diaghilev's command

It is the potential for canonic innovation, for winning new places in the pantheon for fresh deeds, names and texts, even non-European ones, that ensures that the classicist today has the right and obligation to feel the future in his bones. We must believe, with the scientist and Carducci, that tomorrow is holy. But to work out what Pindar boldly called 'the divinity that is busy within my mind' is to surrender to the full weight of human ambition.[20]

To strive after originality is to risk the charge of pretentiousness. Francis Ford Coppola has touched on the perils of pretending in discussing his film *Apocalypse Now*. Whatever its flaws, this film should be seen as a provocative contribution in America's strivings to give its meditation on the Orient something of the force and depth that has long characterized European reflection, with all its proud density, on Near Eastern and Asian civilizations and societies.

In discussing *Apocalypse Now*, Coppola has been philosophical about his aspirations.[21] If the artist is ambitious in the grand manner, but fails, he is subsequently pummelled with charges of pretentiousness, that is, exaggerating his talents. But genuine creativity, as we find it in the work of the film director or the social scientist, requires that we take such gambles. Without such risk-taking one may always fall short of excellence. Trapped in the marginality of his intellectual condition, the regional expert or Asian specialist, no less than the political scientist himself, must strive to respond, in a manner worthy of European tradition and Japan's modern greatness, to obey Sergei Diaghilev's famous command: 'Astonish me!'

Notes

PREFACE

1 Richard Rorty, 'Science as solidarity', *Objectivity, Relativism, and Truth: Philosophical Papers, Volume 1*, Cambridge, Cambridge University Press, 1991, p. 35.
2 See Chalmers Johnson and E. B. Keehn, 'A disaster in the making: rational choice and Asian studies', *National Interest*, no. 36, Summer 1994, pp. 14–22, and the exchange of letters in the *National Interest*, no. 37, Fall 1994, pp. 99–104.
3 Daniel Bell, 'Weber, Karl Emil Maximillian (Max)', in Alan Bullock and R. B. Woodings (eds), *The Fontana Dictionary of Modern Thinkers*, London, Fontana, 1983, p. 806.
4 George Steiner, 'The Archives of Eden', *Salmagundi*, Fall 1980–Winter 1981, p. 71.

CHAPTER 1

1 Edward W. Said, *Culture and Imperialism*, London, Chatto & Windus, 1993, p. 58.
2 Sakai Naoki, 'Nihon Shakai Kagaku Hoho Josetsu' (Methods in Japanese social science: an introduction), *Iwanami Koza Shakai Kagaku no Hoho, III, Nihon Shakai Kagaku no Shiso*, (Iwanami Course on Methods in Social Science, Volume III, Japanese Social Science as Thought) Tokyo, Iwanami Shoten, 1993, pp. 12–14.
3 K. Anthony Appiah, 'African-American philosophy?', *The Philosophical Forum*, vol. XXIV, nos 1–3, Fall–Spring 1992–1993, p. 11.
4 Ibid., p. 27.
5 Ibid.
6 Iain Hampsher-Monk, *A History of Modern Political Thought: Major Political Thinkers from Hobbes to Marx*, Oxford, Blackwell, 1992, p. ix.
7 While it is clear that Rousseau and Rawls (or Locke, for that matter) exploit the notion of a social contract in different ways, the suggested continuity of Western tradition is not a fiction. Indeed, it is strikingly obvious when viewed from outside the European heritage.
8 Sir Isaiah Berlin, 'Nationalism: past neglect and present power', *Against*

the Current: Essays in the History of Ideas, Oxford, Clarendon Press, 1989, p. 350.

9 Ibid.

10 Hampsher-Monk, op. cit., p. xii. Hobbes greatly preferred royal prerogatives to ecclesiastical ones, but his support for the monarchy was qualified despite his dread of the anarchy which he believed prevailed in a state of nature.

11 John Rawls, *A Theory of Justice*, Oxford, Clarendon Press, 1972.

12 Cicero, *De finibus bonorum et malorum*, Book V, with a translation by H. Rackman, William Heinemann, 1971, p. 449.

13 Quoted in George Steiner, 'Dante and the gossip of eternity', *On Difficulty and Other Essays*, Oxford, Oxford University Press, 1978, p. 166.

14 Quoted in Frances FitzGerald, *Fire in the Lake: The Vietnamese and the Americans in Vietnam*, Boston, Little, Brown, 1972, p. 12.

15 George Steiner, *After Babel: Aspects of Language and Translation*, Oxford, Oxford University Press, 1975, p. 7.

16 Maruyama Masao, *Thought and Behaviour in Modern Japanese Politics*, London, Oxford University Press, 1963.

17 Anthony Grafton, *New Worlds, Ancient Texts: The Power of Tradition and the Shock of Discovery*, Cambridge, Mass., The Belknap Press of Harvard University Press, 1992.

18 Ibid., p. 42.

19 Ibid., p. 75.

20 Ibid.

21 Ibid., p. 84.

22 Ibid., p. 79.

23 E. H. Gombrich, *Meditations on a Hobby Horse and Other Essays on the Theory of Art*, London, Phaidon, 1963, p. 126. Gombrich's remarks are taken from his essay on prints titled 'Imagery and art in the Romantic period', in which he seeks to deflate the 'Romantic myth' of the genius who 'creates new forms out of nothing'.

24 Anthony Grafton, op. cit., p. 117. My paraphrase of Grafton's statement of the challenge.

CHAPTER 2

1 George Steiner, 'The Archives of Eden', *Salmagundi*, Fall 1980–Winter 1981, p. 80.

2 Leszek Kolakowski, *Main Currents of Marxism: Its Rise, Growth and Dissolution, Volume I: The Founders*, trans. P. S. Falla, Oxford, Clarendon Press, 1978, p. 1.

3 Peter Conrad, *Imagining America*, London and Henley, Routledge & Kegan Paul, 1980, p. 3.

4 Ibid.

5 This is John Russell's description in his *Francis Bacon*, revised edn, London, Thames & Hudson, 1993, p. 30.

6 Immanuel Kant, *Critique of Pure Reason*, trans. Norman Kemp Smith London, Macmillan, 1929 (second impression with corrections 1933), p. 540.

7 Ibid.

8 Maruyama Masao, *Thought and Behaviour in Modern Japanese Politics*, ed. Ivan Morris, London, Oxford University Press, 1963, p. xiv.

9 Ibid., pp. xiv-xv.

10 My response to claims for 'strong thought' is to ask whether it is indeed 'strong'. It is also worth querying whether such strength is relevant even if it is conceded. For a different approach see the elaboration of the notion of 'weak thought' in *The End of Modernity* (1988) and *The Adventures of Difference* (1993) by Gianni Vattimo (an anthology called *Weak Thought*, edited Gianni Vattimo and Pier Aldo Rovatti, is also keenly anticipated). All these works are published in America by the Johns Hopkins University Press. In Britain, *The End of Modernity* appeared in 1988 (paperback 1991) and *The Adventures of Difference* in 1993, both from the Polity Press.
In the name of Nietzsche, Vattimo is attempting to transcend both English empiricism and Hegelianism by contesting the nature of reality itself. If one tried to translate the essence of 'weak thought' into the empirical or positivist idiom, one might conclude that the characteristic feature of postmodern society is that 'reality' itself has 'weakened'. A notion of 'weak reality' is consistent with the reading of Barthes' *Empire of Signs* offered in Chapter 10, below.

11 Yamamura Kozo and Yasuba Yasukichi (eds), *The Political Economy of Japan, Volume 1: The Domestic Transformation*, Stanford, Calif., Stanford University Press, 1987; Inoguchi Takashi and Daniel I. Okimoto (eds), *The Political Economy of Japan, Volume 2 The Changing International Context*, Stanford, Calif., Stanford University Press, 1988; Kumon Shumpei and Henry Rosovsky (eds), *The Political Economy of Japan, Volume 3: Cultural and Social Dynamics*, Stanford, Calif., Stanford University Press, 1992.

12 *Collins English Dictionary*, 3rd edn, Glasgow, HarperCollins, 1991, p. 1204.

13 Quoted in Malcolm Bowie, *Lacan*, London, Fontana, 1991, p. 5.

14 Quoted in Howard Gardner, *The Quest for Mind: Piaget, Lévi-Strauss and the Structuralist Movement*, N.Y., Vintage, 1974, p. 34.

15 Quoted in Mary Douglas, *Evans-Pritchard*, London, Fontana, 1980, p. 41.

16 See, for example, Robert P. Newman, *Owen Lattimore and the 'Loss' of China*, Berkeley, University of Calif. Press, 1992, p. 8.

17 Ibid., p. 503.

18 Both remarks quoted in Howard Gardner, op. cit., p. 21.

19 See Quentin Lauer's gloss on the Husserlian term *epoche* in his translation of *Philosophy as a Rigorous Science* and *Philosophy and the Crisis of European Man* titled *Phenomenology and the Crisis of Philosophy*, N.Y., Harper Torchbooks, 1966, p. 168, n. 32

20. Quoted in Edward W. Said, *Orientalism*, Harmondsworth, Penguin, 1985, p. 25.

21 I have in mind the 50-volume series, *Nihon no Meicho*, and the 81-volume series, *Seikai no Meicho*, published by Chuo Koron-sha during the early 1970s.

22 In other words, does Japanese writing in *Kanbun* represent the kind of renovation of Chinese that Roman letters underwent with the writing

of St Augustine's *De Civitate Dei*, St Thomas Aquinas' *Summa Theologiae* and even Hobbes' *De cive*?

23 Chalmers Johnson, *MITI and the Japanese Miracle: The Growth of Industrial Policy, 1925–1975*, Stanford, Calif., Stanford University Press, 1982, p. 32.

24 Karl Marx, *The 18th Brumaire of Louis Bonaparte*, New York, International Publishers, 1969, p. 124.

25 Both terms are my own, perhaps coined in ignorance of earlier claims to the terms. The concept of 'thinking nationalism' serves as the leitmotif of my *Japan: Beyond the End of History*, London, Routledge, 1994, and I first discussed the idea of 'motivated bureaucracy' in my review of Tetsuo Najita's *Japan: The Intellectual Foundations of Modern Japanese Politics*, Chicago and London, University of Chicago Press, 1974, which appeared in *The Japan Times* (Tokyo) in 1981.

26 Kojève's remarks are contained in what may be the most famous footnote in all Western writings on Japan. See Alexandre Kojève, *Introduction to a Reading of Hegel: Lectures on the Phenomenology of Spirit*, assembled by Raymond Queneau, ed. Allan Bloom, trans. James H. Nichols, Jr., Ithaca and London, Cornell University Press, 1969, footnote on pp. 161–2.

In his essay, 'One spirit, two nineteenth centuries', Karatani concludes that

The Japanese nineteenth century is distinguished, then, by the fact that, as it begins, the deconstruction of *ri* [the Chinese concept for reason, which Karatani renders as 'meaning'] is already accomplished. It is therefore impossible to consider the nineteenth century simply as a pre-modern era. What stubbornly resisted the modernization of Japanese thought and literature in the twentieth century was not simply a pre-modern sensibility but a mode of thought which in some senses had already transcended the modern. This naturally took the form of a citation of the anti-Western elements of Western thought. Its grand finale was the wartime ideology of 'overcoming the modern.' A similar situation prevails in the Japan of the 1980s.

Quotation from translation by Alan Wolf contained in Masao Miyoshi and H. D. Harootunian (eds), *Postmodernism and Japan*, Durham and London, Duke University Press, 1989, pp. 259–72. The quotation is on p. 271.

27 Maruyama Masao, 'Koten kara do manabu ka', '*Bunmeiron no Gairyaku' o Yomu* (Reading 'An Outline of Civilization'), *jo*, Tokyo, Iwanami Shoten, 1986, pp. 1–23.

28 Maruyama Masao, *Nihon Seiji Shiso-shi Kenkyu*, Tokyo, Tokyo Daigaku Shuppan-kai, 1952. Translated by Mikiso Hane as *Studies in the Intellectual History of Tokugawa Japan*, Tokyo, University of Tokyo Press, 1974.

29 See the notes and commentary on *Taiheisaku* by Maruyama Masao in Yoshikawa Kojiro, Maruyama Masao, Nishida Taichiro and Tsuji Tatsuya (eds), *Ogyu Sorai, Nihon Shiso Taikei, Dai-36 kan*, Tokyo, Iwanami Shoten, 1973, pp. 447–86, 787–829.

30 Maruyama Masao, '*Bunmeiron no Gairyaku' o Yomu*, op. cit.

31 Ibid., *jo*, p. 4.

32 Here I have taken a European rather than a Japanese view of Japan's difficulty with the imperatives of high culture. For Maruyama's own perspective, see ibid., p. 4.

33 Ibid.

34 Ibid.

35 Ibid., pp. 4–5.

36 Ibid.

37 Ibid., p. 5.

38 Ibid.

39 Ibid.

40 Ibid.

41 Karatani Kojin, '*Rekishi to Tasha*' (History and the Other), in *Shuen o Megutte* (Concerning Endings), Tokyo, Fukutake Shoten, 1990, p. 207.

42 In arguing for the canonicity of this list of thinkers, I am insisting that, on balance, intellectual excellence has triumphed over nationalist obscurantism in their works. I nevertheless remain attentive to those historians of ideas who insist that these thinkers remain marginal within the Sinitic canon.

43 Karl Marx and Friedrich Engels, *Die Deutsche Ideologie, 1. Band, 1. Abschnitt*, edited and translated, with commentary by Hiromatsu Wataru, Tokyo, Kawade Shobo, 1974. Karatani Kojin's criticism appears in '*Kindai no Chokoku ni Tsuite*' (Concerning the overcoming of modernity), in Karatani Kojin, *Shuen o Megutte* (Concerning Endings), Tokyo, Fukutake Shoten, 1990, pp. 233–40. For Karatani's stimulating critique of Marxism, including a controversial reading of Natsume Soseki, see *Marukusu: Sono Konosei no Chushin*, Tokyo, Kodansha, 1990.

   For purposes of comparison, it may be worth asking to what degree John Dewey's largely successful attempt to purge American thought of the influence of Plato, Descartes and Kant falls under the rubric of '*Oshu seishin o kiyosaru*'.

44 Karatani Kojin, '*Rekishi to Tasha*', op. cit., p. 207.

45 Asada Akira, '*Rekishi no Owari*' to *Seiki-matsu no Sekai* ('The End of History' and a *Fin de Siècle* World), Tokyo, Shogakkan, 1994, p. 211. Despite such criticism, I remain a deep admirer of Asada's work, and believe that he has made a significant contribution to the contemporary Japanese intellectual scene.

46 Quoted in David Caute, *Fanon*, London, Fontana, 1970, p. 25.

47 Ibid. This is Caute's reading of Fanon's reaction to the poem, pp. 25–7.

48 A profound and organic commitment to classicism is a talisman and badge of identity among two of Europe's most oppressed minorities: Jews and homosexuals.

49 Jasper Griffin, *Virgil*, Oxford, Oxford University Press, 1986, p. 7.

50 Ibid., pp. 7–8.

51 Derek Walcott, *Omeros*, London, Faber & Faber, 1990.

52 V. S. Naipaul, *The Enigma of Arrival*, Harmondsworth, Penguin, 1987.

53 Frantz Fanon, *The Wretched of the Earth*, trans. Constance Farrington, London, Penguin, 1990; *Black Skin, White Masks*, trans. Charles Lam Markman, New York, Grove Press, 1969; *Studies in a Dying Colonialism*, trans. Haakon Chevalier, London, Earthscan, 1989.

54 V. S. Naipaul, *In a Free State*, Harmondsworth, Penguin, 1973, p. 187.
55 Frank Kermode, *The Classic*, London, Faber & Faber, 1975.
56 George Steiner, *In Bluebeard's Castle: Some Notes Towards the Redefinition of Culture*, New Haven, Conn., Yale University Press, 1971, pp. 64–5.
57 Aoki Tamotsu, *'Bunka no Hiteisei'* (Culture as negation), *Chuo Koron*, Tokyo, Chuo Koron-sha, 1987, pp. 104–25.
58 Quoted in Caute, op. cit., p. 28. Fanon, *Black Skins, White Masks*, op. cit. Caute cites British edition, London, MacGibbon & Kee, 1968, p. 203.
59 Candidates proposed for this honour include Otsuka Hisao, the economic historian, and the late Murakami Yasusuke, author of *Hankoten no Seiji Keizaigaku* (Anti-classical Political Economy), Tokyo, Chuo Koron-sha, 1992.
60 *The Collected Works of John Maynard Keynes, Volume II: The Economic Consequences of the Peace*, London and Cambridge, Macmillan/Cambridge University Press, 1971, p. 14.
61 The argument that American high culture is best reflected by the natural sciences and mathematics, as opposed to literature, must be handled with care. The contribution of the flood of European talent that Hitler sent fleeing across the Atlantic should not be understated. It remains to be demonstrated that classicism is an American *métier*, although I agree with Steiner's assessment that 'There is, in a good deal of American intellectual, artistic production (recent painting may be the challenging exception) a characteristic near-greatness, a strength just below the best' (*In Bluebeard's Castle*, p. 111). Steiner has since revised his hopes for America's contribution to painting (see 'The Archives of Eden', op. cit.).
62 Steiner, 'The Archives of Eden', op. cit, p. 62.

CHAPTER 3

1 Paul Edwards (ed. in Chief), *The Encyclopedia of Philosophy*, New York, Macmillan and The Free Press, 1967.
2 Herman Kahn, *The Emerging Japanese Superstate: Challenge and Response*, Englewood Cliffs, N.J., Prentice-Hall, 1970; 'Consider Japan', *The Economist*, 1 September and 8 September 1962.
3 See the Preface to the 4th edition of George H. Sabine and Thomas L. Thorson, *A History of Political Theory*, Fort Worth, Texas, Dryden Press, 1973.
4 Leo Strauss and Joseph Cropsey (eds), *History of Political Philosophy*, Chicago, University of Chicago Press, 1987.
5 William G. Ouchi, *Theory Z: How American Business Can Meet the Japanese Challenge*, Reading, Mass., Addison Wesley, 1981; Ezra F. Vogel, *Japan as No. One: Lessons for America*, Cambridge, Mass., Harvard University Press, 1979; Chalmers Johnson, *MITI and the Japanese Miracle: The Growth of Industrial Policy, 1925–1975*, Stanford, Calif., Stanford University Press, 1982.
6 Wm. Theodore de Bary, *East Asian Civilizations: A Dialogue in Five Stages*, Cambridge, Mass., Harvard University Press, 1988, and *The*

Trouble with Confucianism, Cambridge, Mass., Harvard University Press, 1991.

7 Tetsuo Najita, *Japan: The Intellectual Foundations of Modern Japanese Politics*, Chicago and London, University of Chicago Press, 1974.

8 Richard Schacht's remark on Allan Bloom's *The Closing of the American Mind* (New York, Simon & Schuster, 1987) is quoted by Steven Taubeneck, in his 'Afterword' to Ernst Behler, *Confrontations: Derrida/Heidegger/Nietzsche*, trans. Steven Taubeneck, Stanford, Calif., Stanford University Press, 1991, p. 174.

9 Giovanna Borradori, *Conversazioni americane con W. O. Quine, D. Davidson, H. Putnam, R. Nozick, A.C. Danto, R. Rorty, S. Cavell, A. MacIntyre, Th. S. Kuhn*, Milan, Guis. Laterza & Figli, 1991. *The American Philosopher: Conversations with Quine, Davidson, Putnam, Nozick, Danto, Rorty, Cavell, MacIntyre, and Kuhn*, trans. Rosanna Crocitto, Chicago, University of Chicago Press, 1994.

10 David Miller, Janet Coleman, William Connolly and Alan Ryan (eds), *The Blackwell Encyclopedia of Political Thought*, Oxford, Basil Blackwell, 1987.

11 Scott Gordon, *The History and Philosophy of Social Science*, London, Routledge, 1993, p. 684.

12 *The Routledge Dictionary of Twentieth Century Political Thinkers*, London, Routledge, 1992.

13 See, for example, Otsuka Hisao, *Otsuka Hisao Chosaku-shu, Dai-roku-kan, Kokumin Keizai* (The Collected Works of Otsuka Hisao, Volume 6, National Economics), Tokyo, Iwanami Shoten, 1969.

14 Paul Samuelson, *Economics*, 9th (international) edn, Tokyo, McGraw-Hill Kogakusha, 1973, p. 771.

15 David Begg, Stanley Fischer and Rudiger Dornbusch, *Economics*, London, McGraw-Hill, 1991.

16 Such references reflect Japan's new importance in the world economy, but Japanese practices leave the theoretical framework of Begg, Fischer and Dornbusch entirely untouched.

17 George H. Sabine and Thomas L. Thorson, op. cit. Quote from Preface to the fourth edition.

18 Leo Strauss, *Natural Right and History*, Chicago, University of Chicago Press, 1953, p. 9.

19 Martin Bernal, *Black Athena: The Afroasiatic Roots of Classical Civilization, Volume I: The Fabrication of Ancient Greece 1785–1985*, London, Free Association Books, 1987.

20 Norman P. Barry, *An Introduction to Modern Political Theory*, London, Macmillan, 1981, xvi.

21 John Stuart Mill, *Auguste Comte and Positivism*, Ann Arbor, Michigan, University of Michigan Press, 1961, p. 6.

22 Despite the ingrained opposition to methodological sophistication among front-line social scientific researchers, philosophers of social science have managed to persuade many social scientists that 'facts' or 'brute data' do not exist. In practice, however, this has tended to mean that the term 'fact' is either avoided or 'bracketed' when used. This verbal taboo should not disguise the fact that social scientists continue

Notes 281

to carry out research as if the ontological assumptions behind the term 'fact' are beyond challenge.

23 Mill, op. cit. p. 42.

24 Ibid.

25 Ibid., pp. 42–3.

26 This brings to mind the writings of the late Maurice Pinguet, the University of Tokyo professor of French literature to whom Roland Barthes dedicated *L'Empire des signes*. Pinguet's *Le Texte japon* was translated by Tachiura Nobuo, Tamura Takeshi and Kudo Yoko as *Tekusuto Toshite no Nihon*, Tokyo, Chikuma Shobo, 1987. The personal and intellectual importance of Pinguet is confirmed at a number of places in David Macey, *The Lives of Michel Foucault*, London, Verso, 1994.

27 Quoted in Theodor W. Adorno, Hans Albert, Ralf Dahrendorf, Jürgen Habermas, Harald Pilot and Karl R. Popper, *The Positivist Dispute in German Sociology*, trans. Glyn Adey and David Frisby, London, Heinemann, 1976, p. xi.

28 Ibid., p. xii.

29 Andrew Sayer, *Method in Social Science: A Realist Approach*, 2nd edn, London, Routledge, 1992, p. 19.

30 Leszek Kolakowski, *Bergson*, Oxford, Oxford University Press, 1985, p. 6.

31 Ibid., p. 5.

32 Leszek Kolakowski, *Positivist Philosophy: From Hume to the Vienna Circle*, trans. Norbert Guterman, Harmondsworth, Penguin, 1972. Chapter 8 is titled 'Logical Empiricism: A Scientistic Defence of Threatened Civilization'.

33 Howard Gardner, *The Quest for Mind: Piaget, Lévi-Strauss, and the Structuralist Movement*, N.Y., Vintage, 1974, p. 32.

34 Ibid., p. 34.

35 Ibid., p. 41.

36 George Steiner, *Heidegger*, London, Fontana, 1978, p. 34. Steiner makes this point in a discussion of Heidegger's use of the term *'ent-sprechen'*.

37 See David Williams, *Japan: Beyond the End of History*, London, Routledge, 1994.

38 Quoted in Richard J. Bernstein, *The Restructuring of Social and Political Theory*, London, Methuen, 1979, p. 12.

39 Ibid.

40 Ibid., p. 13.

41 Ibid.

42 Emile Durkheim, *Suicide: A Study in Sociology*, trans. John A. Spaulding and George Simpson, London, Routledge, 1989, p. 157.

43 E. Sydney Crawcour, 'Industrialization and technological change, 1885–1920', in Peter Duus (ed.), *The Cambridge History of Japan, Volume 6: The Twentieth Century*, Cambridge, Cambridge University Press, 1988, p. 447.

44 Ibid.

45 Ibid., p. 446.

46 Ibid.

47 Robert Wade, *Governing the Market: Economic Theory and the Role of*

Government in East Asian Industrialization, Princeton, N.J., Princeton University Press, 1991.

48 Ibid., p. 30.
49 Ibid., p. 19.
50 Ibid., p. 72.
51 Ibid.
52 Ibid., p. 86.
53 Ibid.
54 Ibid., p. 20.
55 Hugh Patrick, 'The future of the Japanese Economy: output and labor productivity', *Journal of Japanese Studies*, vol. 3, no. 2, Summer 1973, p. 239. Quoted in Wade, op. cit.
56 Wade, op. cit., p. 22.
57 Ibid., pp. 22–3.
58 Quoted in ibid., p. 23.
59 Quoted in ibid., p. 23.
60 Ibid., p. 24.
61 Quoted in ibid., p. 24.
62 Ibid., p. 25.
63 Ibid., p. 25.
64 Ibid., p. 26.
65 Ibid., pp. 26–7.
66 Ibid., p. 27.
67 Ibid., pp. 27–8.
68 Ibid., p. 29.
69 Laura d'Andrea Tyson, *Who's Bashing Whom: Trade Conflict in High-Technology Industries*, Washington, D.C., Institute for International Economics, 1992.
70 Ibid., p. 3.
71 Ibid., p. 3.
72 Ibid., p. 10.
73 Ibid., p. 12.
74 Ibid., p. 10.
75 Ibid.
76 Ibid.
77 Ibid, pp. 10–11.
78 Ibid., p. 11.
79 Ibid., p. 12.
80 Ibid.
81 Ibid.
82 Ibid.
83 Ibid., p. 255.
84 Sir Isaiah Berlin, 'Verification', *Concepts and Categories: Philosophical Essays*, Oxford, Oxford University Press, 1980, p. 12.
85 John Plamenatz, 'The use of political theory', in Anthony Quinton (ed.), *Political Philosophy*, Oxford, Oxford University Press, 1967, p. 19.
86 David Miller, 'Political theory', in David Miller, Janet Coleman, William Connolly and Alan Ryan (eds), *The Blackwell Encyclopedia of Political Thought*, Oxford, Basil Blackwell, 1991, pp. 383–5.
87 Ibid., p. 385.

88 Ibid., p. 384.

89 Ibid.

90 Ibid.

91 Werner Marx, *Hegel's Phenomenology of Spirit: Its Point and Purpose – A Commentary on the Preface and Introduction*, trans. Peter Heath, New York, Harper & Row, 1975, pp. xii–xiii.

92 Miller, op. cit., p. 384.

93 Ibid.

94 Ibid., p. 385.

95 Ibid.

96 Maruyama Masao, *'Bunmeiron no Gairyaku' o Yomu* (Reading 'An Outline of Civilization'), *jo*, Tokyo, Iwanami Shoten, 1986, pp. 63–72, but the idea of the traffic management of public discussion, which carries the nuance of a choked condition in public debate to be remedied, is a defining idea throughout the whole of Maruyama's chapter titled *'Nan no tame ni Ronzuru no ka'* (What is the point of argument), pp. 57–92.

97 Miller, op. cit., p. 385.

98 Ibid.; Charles Taylor, 'Neutrality in political science', in P. Laslett and W. G. Runciman (eds), *Politics and Society*, 3rd series, Oxford, Basil Blackwell, 1967.

99 Miller, op. cit., p. 385.

100 Ibid.

101 Sartre, *St Genet: Actor and Martyr*, trans. Bernard Frechtman, London, Heinemann, 1988.

CHAPTER 4

1 Emile Durkheim, *The Rules of Sociological Method and Selected Texts on Sociology and Its Method*, trans. W. D. Halls, London, Macmillan, 1982, p. 35.

2 This first appeared in German in a special supplementary volume of the journal *Rundschau* (February 1967), and was published as a book in 1970 by Suhrkamp Verlag (Frankfurt am Main). Published in Britain as *On the Logic of the Social Sciences*, trans. Shierry Weber Nicholsen and Jerry A. Stark, Cambridge, Polity Press, 1990.

3 Ibid., p. 10.

4 Simon Schama, *Dead Certainties (Unwarranted Speculations)*, London, Granta Books, 1991, p. 320; David Hackett Fischer, *Historians' Fallacies: Toward a Logic of Historical Thought*, N.Y., Harper & Row, 1970, p. xv.

5 Quoted from the *Enquiry Concerning Human Understanding* in A.J. Ayer, *Hume*, Oxford, Oxford University Press, 1980, p. 96.

6 Fischer, op. cit., p. xv.

7 John Creighton Campbell, *How Policies Change: The Japanese Government and the Aging Society*, Princeton, N.J., Princeton University Press, 1992, pp. 25–51.

8 Ibid., p. 8.

9 Ibid., p. 25.

10 Ibid.

11 Ibid.
12 Graham T. Allison, *Essence of Decision: Explaining the Cuban Missile Crisis*, Boston, Little, Brown, 1971; Michael D. Cohen, James G. March and Johan P. Olsen, 'A garbage can model of organizational choice', *Administrative Science Quarterly*, vol. 17, no. 1, March 1972.
13 Campbell, *How Policies Change*, p. 26.
14 Ibid., p. 26.
15 Ibid.
16 Ibid.
17 This sentiment is repeated on p. 24 where Campbell concludes that 'starting from a null hypothesis that whatever occurred might have happened by accident is the best way to keep an open mind about what actually caused what'.
18 Ibid., pp. 31–3
19 Ibid., p. 34.
20 Ibid., p. 379.
21 Ibid., p. 378.
22 Scott C. Flanagan, Kohei Shinsaku, Miyake Ichiro, Bradley M. Richardson, Joji Watanuki, *The Japanese Voter*, New Haven, Conn., Yale University Press, 1991.
23 Ibid., p. 7.
24 Ibid., p. xiii.
25 Aaron Solman, 'Behavioural sciences', in Alan Bullock and Oliver Stallybrass (eds), *The Fontana Dictionary of Modern Thought*, London, Fontana/Collins, 1977, p. 57.'
26 Ibid.
27 'Preface' in Flanagan *et al.*, op. cit., p. xiv.
28 Scott C. Flanagan and Bradley M. Richardson, *Japanese Politics*, Boston, Little, Brown, 1984.
29 Angus Campbell, *The American Voter*, N.Y., Wiley, 1960; David Butler and Donald Stokes, *Political Change in Britain: Forces Shaping Electoral Choice*, revised edn, N.Y., St Martin's. 1976.
30 Flanagan and Bradley, op. cit., p. xv.
31 Robert A. Scalapino, *The Japanese Communist Movement, 1920–1966*, Berkeley and Los Angeles, University of California Press, 1967; J. A. A. Stockwin, *The Japanese Socialist Party and its Foreign Policy*, Carlton, Victoria, Melbourne University Press, 1968; Gerald L. Curtis, *The Japanese Way of Politics*, N.Y., Columbia University Press, 1988; Kent E. Calder, *Crisis and Compensation: Public Policy and Political Stability in Japan, 1949–1986*, Princeton, N.J., Princeton University Press, 1988.
32 Robert L. Hardgrave, Jr. and Stanley A. Kochanek, *India: Government and Politics in a Developing Nation*, 4th edn, San Diego, Harcourt Brace Jovanovich, 1986; James A. Bill and Robert L. Hardgrave, Jr., *Comparative Politics: The Quest for Theory*, Washington D.C., University Press of America, 1981.

   The exception that proves the rule may be Ronald P. Dore, 'Function and cause', in Michael Martin and Lee C. McIntyre (eds), *Readings in the Philosophy of Social Science*, Cambridge, Mass., MIT Press, 1994, pp. 377–89.

33 Hardgrave and Kochanek, op. cit., pp. 22–3.
34 Bill and Hardgrave, op. cit., p. 38.
35 J. A. A. Stockwin, *Japan: Divided Politics in a Growth Economy*, 2nd edn, N.Y., W.W. Norton, 1982; David Easton, *A Framework for Political Analysis*, Englewood Cliffs, N.J., Prentice-Hall, 1965.
36 See David Williams, *Japan: Beyond the End of History*, London, Routledge, 1994, pp. 193–9.
37 Charles Taylor, 'Understanding and ethnocentricity', *Philosophy and the Human Sciences, Philosophical Papers 2*, Cambridge, Cambridge University Press, 1985, pp. 132–3.
38 B. Parekh, 'The poverty of Indian political theory', *History of Political Thought*, vol. XIII, no. 3, Autumn 1992, p. 545.
39 Ibid.
40 Hardgrave and Kochanek, op. cit., pp. vi–viii.
41 This points to the strange limitations of television, as opposed to print media, as a tool for political scientific analysis. The filter of television is at once too narrow, too thin and too resistant to allow cheap and efficient storage or retrieval, although recent technological advances may ease such problems.
42 Ernest Nagel, *The Structure of Science: Problems in the Logic of Scientific Explanation*, N.Y., Harcourt Brace and World, 1961.
43 The remark by Jacques Derrida is quoted by David Wood in his 'Introduction' to David Wood and Robert Bernasconi (eds), *Derrida and Différance*, Evanston, Ill., Northwestern University Press, 1988, p. ix.
44 Scott Gordon, *The History and Philosophy of Social Science*, London, Routledge, 1993, p. 66. I have relied on Gordon's account of Europe's response to Contarini's work.
45 Ibid., p. 67.
46 Quoted in James Cotton, 'James Harrington', in David Miller, Janet Coleman, William Connolly and Alan Ryan (eds), *The Blackwell Encyclopedia of Political Thought*, Oxford, Basil Blackwell, 1991, p. 193.
47 Gordon, op. cit., p. 82.
48 Robert D. Putnam, *Making Democracy Work: Civic Traditions in Modern Italy*, Princeton, N.J., Princeton University Press, 1993.
49 J. A. A. Stockwin, *Japan: Divided Politics in a Growth Economy*, op. cit.
50 Ibid., p. 1.
51 Ibid., pp. 4–5.
52 Chalmers Johnson, *MITI and the Japanese Miracle: The Growth of Industrial Policy, 1925–1975*, Stanford, Calif., Stanford University Press, 1982.
53 John Creighton Campbell, *Contemporary Japanese Budget Politics*, Berkeley, Calif., University of California Press, 1977, and Chalmers Johnson, *Japan's Public Policy Companies*, Washington, D.C. and Stanford, Calif., AEI–Hoover Policy Studies, 1978.
54 T. J. Pempel, *Policy and Politics in Japan: Creative Conservatism*, Philadelphia, Penn., Temple University Press, 1982.
55 Johnson, *MITI and the Japanese Miracle*, p. vii.
56 Ibid., p. v.
57 Ibid., p. ii.
58 Ibid., p. 31.
59 David Williams, 'Beyond political economy: a critique of issues raised

in Chalmers Johnson's *MITI and the Japanese Miracle*', *Social and Economic Research on Modern Japan*, Occasional Paper No. 35, Berlin, East Asian Institute, Free University of Berlin, 1983, pp. 9–10.

60 Ezra F. Vogel, *Comeback*, Tokyo, Charles E. Tuttle, 1985; Ronald Dore, *Flexible Rigidities: Industrial Policy and Structural Adjustment in the Japanese Economy, 1970–1980*, London, Athlone Press, 1986, and *Taking Japan Seriously: A Confucian Perspective on Leading Economic Issues*, London, Athlone Press, 1987.

61 Johnson, *MITI and the Japanese Miracle* p. 323.

62 In Britain, the term 'liberal' is applied to what would be called in the United States libertarian beliefs as well as to the defence of 'free' (that is liberal) markets, but less frequently to social democratic reformism, by which the term 'liberal' is generally understood in America. Also in Britain, the term 'conservative' may mean the ideological commitment to the conservation of free markets or capitalism, as it usually does in the United States. But the British frequently used the word 'conservative' to identify those on the political right or centre-right who oppose the kind of changes that the free markets may inflict.

63 Daniel I. Okimoto, *Between MITI and the Market: Japanese Industrial Policy for High Technology*, Stanford, Calif., Stanford University Press, 1989.

64 Ibid., p. 20.

65 Ibid., p. 12.

66 The term 'grand theory' refers here to political grand theory. See David Williams, *Japan: Beyond the End of History*, pp. 186–93.

David Friedman, *The Misunderstood Miracle: Industrial Development and Political Change in Japan*, Ithaca, N.Y., Cornell University Press, 1988, offers a spirited critique of the convergence thesis in industrial theory. He seeks to defend the importance of what Franklin D. Roosevelt might have called 'the little man' in Japan's post-war success. But his rather novel definition of the 'political' and his utopian moralism make it difficult to re-integrate his conclusions into the main currents of the political scientific literature on Japan. In this particular case, I do not believe that the political scientific literature demands radical reform.

67 Martin Bernal, *Black Athena: The Afroasiatic Roots of Classical Civilization, Volume 1: The Fabrication of Ancient Greece 1785–1985*, London, Free Association Books, 1987.

68 I am thinking in particular of Kent E. Calder, *Crisis and Compensation*, and *Strategic Capitalism: Private Business and Public Purpose in Japanese Industrial Finance*, Princeton, N.J., Princeton University Press, 1993; David Friedman, op. cit.; and Richard J. Samuels, *The Business of the Japanese State: Energy Markets in Comparative and Historical Perspective*, Ithaca and London, Cornell University Press, 1987.

69 Campbell, *How Policies Change*, p. 4.

70 Ibid., p. 393, note 62.

71 The contrast between business studies and public policy research on Japan is nicely captured by the titles of Thomas J. Peters and Robert H. Waterman, Jr., *In Search of Excellence: Lessons from America's Best-Run Companies*, New York, Harper & Row, 1982, and Robert C. Angel,

Explaining Economic Policy Failure: Japan in the 1969–1971 International Monetary Crisis, N.Y., Columbia University Press, 1991.

72 I have discussed the case of Friedman in *Japan: Beyond the End of History*, pp. 196–7.

73 Frances McCall Rosenbluth, *Financial Politics in Contemporary Japan*, Ithaca, N.Y., Cornell University Press, 1989.

74 Max Weber, *The Protestant Ethic and the Spirit of Capitalism*, trans. Talcott Parsons, London, Unwin, 1930; R. H. Tawney, *Religion and the Rise of Capitalism*, Harmondsworth, Penguin, 1938; Robert N. Bellah, *Tokugawa Religion: The Values of Pre–Industrial Japan*, N.Y., The Free Press, 1957.

75 This is the ruling impulse in Calder's impressive *oeuvre*, from *The East-asia Edge*, N.Y., Basic Books, 1982, which he wrote with Roy Hofheinz, Jr., to *Strategic Capitalism*. J. Mark Ramseyer and Frances McCall Rosenbluth, *Japan's Political Marketplace*, Cambridge, Mass., Harvard University Press, 1993. David Friedman, op. cit.

76 Richard J. Samuels, 'Japanese political studies and the myth of the independent intellectual', in Richard J. Samuels and Myron Weiner (eds), *The Political Culture of Foreign Area Studies: Essays in Honor of Lucian W. Pye*, Washington, D.C., Pergammon-Brassey's, 1992, p. 30.

77 Ibid.

78 Ibid., Steslicke is quoted on p. 30.

79 Calder, *Strategic Capitalism*, p. xviii.

80 Ibid., p. xix.

81 My research on the British Home Office and the organization of police training is contained in David Williams, *Provincial Police Training in Britain: Continuity and Reform 1947–1985*, Oxford D.Phil. dissertation.

82 Calder, *Strategic Capitalism*, p. 163.

83 Ibid., p. 168

84 Nikkei Kinyu Shinbun, *Kogin no Henshin: Sangyo Kinyu no Yu wa Yomigaeru ka* (IBJ's Metamorphosis: Can the Hero of Industrial Finance Make a Comeback?), Tokyo, Nihon Keizai Shinbun-sha, 1994.

85 Robert B. Reich, *The Next American Frontier*, N.Y, New York Times Books, 1983, pp. 3–22.

86 Quoted in B.A. Haddock, *An Introduction to Historical Thought*, London, Edward Arnold, 1980, p. 66.

87 Immanuel Kant, *Critique of Pure Reason*, trans. Norman Kemp Smith, 1930 printing with corrections, London, Macmillan, 1929 (second impression with corrections 1933), p. 540.

88 In Chalmers Johnson, Laura d'Andrea Tyson and John Zysman (eds), *Politics and Productivity: How Japan's Development Strategy Works*, N.Y., Harperbusiness, 1989; Daniel I. Okimoto, op. cit.; David Williams, *Japan: Beyond the End of History*.

89 Autopsies on the Soviet Union have appeared in almost every journal of general intellectual opinion in Japan, Western Europe and North America, and perhaps inevitably this row has revived two old debates: the link between Western and Japanese intellectuals and Soviet communism, and what the editors of the *National Interest* described as the 'sins of the scholars'. See, to take the example in question, the special issue of

the *National Interest* titled 'The strange death of Soviet communism', no. 31, Spring 1993.

90 Richard J. Samuels, *'Rich Nation, Strong Army': National Security and the Technological Transformation of Japan*, Ithaca and London, Cornell University Press, 1994.

91 Stephen Wilks and Maurice Wright (eds), *The Promotion and Regulation of Industry in Japan*, London, Macmillan, 1992. I have discussed the methodology of the Wilks–Wright project at length in *Japan: Beyond the End of History*, pp. 195–9.

92 Chalmers Johnson and E. B. Keehn, 'A disaster in the making: rational choice and Asian studies', *National Interest*, no. 36, Summer 1994, pp. 14–22.

CHAPTER 5

1 For a bracing summary of this school of argument, see Robert Young, *White Mythologies: Writing History and the West*, London, Routledge, 1990.

2 I have formulated this definition from the position that Said sets out in *Orientalism*, Harmondsworth, Penguin, 1985, pp. 204–5, and in *The Question of Palestine*, London, Vintage, 1992, *passim*.

3 Said, *Orientalism*, p. 246.

4 Edward W. Said, *Covering Islam: How the Media and the Experts Determine How We See the Rest of the World*, London, Routledge & Kegan Paul, 1981.

5 Said, *Orientalism*, p. 11.

6 Edward W. Said, *Culture and Imperialism*, London, Chatto & Windus, 1993, p. 57.

7 Ibid., pp. 56–7.

8 Ibid., p. 40.

9 Ibid., p. 14.

10 Ibid., p. 82.

11 Ibid., p. 47.

12 Ibid., p. 66.

13 Ibid., pp. 69–70.

14 Ibid., p. 69.

15 Ibid., p. 68.

16 Said, *Orientalism*, p. 13.

17 Maruyama Masao, *Thought and Behaviour in Modern Japanese Politics*, ed. Ivan Morris, London, Oxford University Press, 1963, p. xvi.

18 Max Weber, *The Religion of China: Confucianism and Taoism*, trans. Hans H. Gerth, N.Y., The Free Press, 1951. C. K. Yang sets out some of these qualifications in his introduction to the translation.

19 Said, *Orientalism*, p. 259.

20 Ibid.

21 Ibid., pp. 305, 93.

22 Ibid., p. 98.

23 Ibid., p. 326.

24 Ibid., p. 7.

25 Richard J. Samuels, 'Japanese political studies and the myth of the independent intellectual', in Richard J. Samuels and Myron Weiner (eds), *The Political Culture of Foreign Area Studies: Essays in Honor of Lucian W. Pye*, Washington, D.C., Pergammon-Brassey's, 1992, pp. 17–56.
26 Ibid. The remark is quoted on p. 20.
27 Ibid. Marius Jansen's remarks are quoted on p. 28.
28 George Steiner, *In Bluebeard's Castle: Some Notes Towards the Redefinition of Culture*, New Haven, Conn., Yale University Press, 1971, p. 82.
29 Ibid.
30 Said, *Orientalism*, p. 301.
31 Samuels, op. cit., p. 31.
32 Murasaki Shikibu, *The Tale of Genji*, was translated by Arthur Waley between 1925 and 1933, and published in 1935. Edward Seidensticker published his version in 1976.
33 This issue is discussed in greater detail in Chapter 2.
34 Such concerns highlight the importance of *A History of Japan* by George Sansom, the six volumes of the Princeton Modernization Series, *Asia's New Giant: How the Japanese Economy Works*, edited by Hugh Patrick and Henry Rosovsky (Washington, D.C., The Brookings Institution, 1976), and the three-volume *Political Economy of Japan*.
35 Karl Marx, *A Contribution to the Critique of Political Economy*, trans. S. W. Ryazanskaya, Moscow, Progress Publishers, 1970, p. 217.
36 Ibid.
37 See Giovanna Borradori, *The American Philosopher: Conversations with Quine, Davidson, Putnam, Nozick, Danto, Rorty, Cavell, MacIntyre, and Kuhn*, trans. Rosanna Crocitto, Chicago, The University of Chicago Press, 1994, pp. 78–9 and 98.
38 I have in mind the canonic stature assigned to Austen by F. R. Leavis in, for example, *The Great Tradition*, Harmondsworth, Penguin, 1972. For a positive assessment of Mill's achievements, see Alan Ryan, *J.S. Mill*, London, Routledge & Kegan Paul, 1974.
39 Frantz Fanon, *The Wretched of the Earth*, trans. Constance Farrington, London, Penguin, 1990.
40 Jean-Paul Sartre, *Critique de la Raison Dialectique I*, Paris, Gallimard, 1960. *Critique de la Raison Dialectique II* was only published in 1985, again by Gallimard. Claude Lévi-Strauss's attack was in response to the use that Sartre had made in the first *Critique* of Lévi-Strauss's *The Elementary Structures of Kinship*, which had appeared in 1949. For a recent summary of the 1962–68 dispute, see Robert Young, op. cit., pp. 42–7.

CHAPTER 6

1 Edward W. Said, *Orientalism*, Harmondsworth, Penguin, 1985, p. 283.
2 Ibid.
3 J. A. A. Stockwin, *Japan: Divided Politics in a Growth Economy*, 2nd edn, New York, W. W. Norton, 1982, and Gerald L. Curtis, *The Japanese Way of Politics*, N.Y., Columbia University Press, 1988.

4 Norman P. Barry, *An Introduction to Modern Political Theory*, London, Macmillan, 1981, p. xv.
5 Quoted in George Steiner, *After Babel: Aspects of Language and Translation*, 2nd edn, Oxford, Oxford University Press, 1992, p. 91.
6 Ibid., p. 93.
7 Benjamin Lee Whorf, *Language, Thought and Reality: Selected Writings of Benjamin Lee Whorf*, ed. John B. Carroll, Cambridge, Mass., MIT Press, 1991, p. 252.
8 Ibid., p. 60.
9 Steiner, *After Babel* 2nd edn, pp. 1–17.
10 Ibid., p. 17.
11 Richard J. Samuels, *The Business of the Japanese State: Energy Markets in Comparative and Historical Perspective*, Ithaca and London, Cornell University Press, 1987.
12 Steiner, *After Babel*, 2nd edn, p. 8.
13 Robert A. Scalapino and Junnosuke Masumi, *Parties and Politics in Contemporary Japan*, Berkeley, Los Angeles and London, University of Calif. Press, 1962, p. vii.
14 Ibid.
15 Chalmers Johnson, *MITI and the Japanese Miracle: The Growth of Industrial Policy, 1925–1975*, Stanford, Calif., Stanford University Press, 1982, p. 8.
16 Ibid.
17 Ibid.
18 Ibid., p. 7.
19 Steiner, *After Babel*, 1st edn, 1975, p. 78.
20 Steiner, *After Babel*, 2nd edn, p. 99.
21 Ibid., p. 97.
22 Ibid. The quote from Lenneberg is on p. 97. Steiner's quote is from 'The language animal', *Extraterritorial: Papers on Literature and the Language Revolution*, London, Faber & Faber, 1972, p. 82.
23 Noam Chomsky, 'A Review of B. F. Skinner's *Verbal Behaviour*', *Language*, Volume 35 (1959), No.1, pp. 26–58.
24 Roy Andrew Miller, *Nihongo: In Defence of Japanese*, London, Athlone Press, 1986; Peter Dale, *The Myth of Japanese Uniqueness*, London and Oxford, Croom Helm and Nissan Institute of Japanese Studies, 1986; and J. Marshall Unger, *The Fifth Generation Fallacy: Why Japan is Betting Its Future on Artificial Intelligence*, N.Y., Oxford University Press, 1987.
25 Jonathan Culler, *Saussure*, London, Fontana/Collins, 1976, pp. 19–20.
26 Ibid., p. 21.
27 Quoted in Steiner, *After Babel*, 2nd edn, pp. 98–9.

CHAPTER 7

1 Quotation from Gramsci's *Prison Notebooks* occurs in Edward W. Said, *Orientalism*, Harmondsworth, Penguin, 1985, p. 25.
2 Peter Dale, *The Myth of Japanese Uniqueness*, London and Oxford, Croom Helm and Nissan Institute of Japanese Studies, 1986; J. Marshall

Unger, *The Fifth Generation Fallacy: Why Japan is Betting Its Future on Artifical Intelligence*, N.Y., Oxford University Press, 1987; Roy Andrew Miller, *Nihongo: In Defence of Japanese*, London, Athlone Press, 1986; Benjamin Duke, *The Japanese School: Lessons for Industrial America*, N.Y., Praeger, 1986; and Karl van Wolferen, *The Enigma of Japanese Power: People and Politics in a Stateless Nation*, London, Macmillan, 1989.

3 George Steiner, 'Text and context', *On Difficulty and Other Essays*, Oxford, Oxford University Press, 1978, pp. 6–7.

4 Ibid., p. 8.

5 Richard J. Samuels, 'Japanese political studies and the myth of the independent intellectual', in Richard J. Samuels and Myron Weiner (eds), *The Political Culture of Foreign Area Studies: Essays in Honor of Lucian W. Pye*, Washington, D.C., Pergammon-Brassey's, 1992.

6 Julien Benda, *The Treason of the Intellectuals* (*La Trahison des clercs*, 1927), trans. Richard Addington, N.Y., W. W. Norton, 1969, p. 27.

7 Marius Jansen, 'History of Japanese studies in the United States', in M. B. Jansen (ed.), *Japanese Studies in the United States, Part I: History and Present Condition*, Ann Arbor, Mich., Association of Asian Studies, 1988, p. 66. Cited in Richard J. Samuels, 'Japanese political studies and the myth of the independent intellectual', p. 28.

8 Samuels, ibid., p. 28.

9 Sigmund Freud, 'The intepretation of dreams' (1900), in *The Penguin Freud Library*, Harmondsworth, Penguin, 1976, vol 4, p. 285.

10 Gavan McCormack and Yoshio Sugimoto (eds), *Democracy in Contemporary Japan*, Armonk, N.Y., M. E. Sharpe, 1986; Susan J. Pharr, *Losing Face: Status Politics in Japan*, Berkeley and Los Angeles, University of Calif. Press, 1990; Karl van Wolferen, op. cit.

11 Private communication.

12 Samuels, 'Japanese political studies and the myth of the independent intellectual', p. 29.

13 Gavan McCormack and Yoshio Sugimoto, 'Introduction', in McCormack and Sugimoto (eds), op. cit., p. 17.

14 Beverly Smith, 'Democracy derailed: citizens' movements in historical perspective', in McCormack and Sugimoto (eds), op. cit., pp. 157–72.

15 Smith is quoting from John G. Roberts, *Mitsui: Three Centuries of Japanese Business*, Tokyo, Weatherhill, 1973, p. 459.

16 Smith, op. cit.; Roberts, ibid.

17 Smith, ibid.

18 Roberts, op. cit., p. 459.

19 Ibid.

20 Ibid., p. 529.

21 Anthony, Lord Quinton, 'Popper', in Alan Bullock and R.B. Reading (eds), *Fontana Biographical Companion to Modern Thought*, London, Collins, 1983, p. 609.

22 Gavan McCormack and Yoshio Sugimoto, 'Introduction', in McCormack and Sugimoto (eds), op. cit., p. 10.

23 Karl van Wolferen, op. cit., p. 293.

24 Ibid.

25 'When even words fail', *Japan Times*, October 1992, p. 20.

26 Ibid.
27 *Japan Times*, 24 February 1989. The text is reproduced in David Williams, 'Reporting the death of the Showa Emperor', *Nissan Occasional Paper Series*, University of Oxford, no. 14, 1990, pp. 16–19.
28 Ibid.
29 Miyoshi Masoa, *Off Center: Power and Culture Relations between Japan and the United States*, Cambridge, Mass., Harvard University Press, 1991, p. 86.
30 Ronald Dore, 'An outsider's view', in Kozo Yamamura (ed.), *Japan's Economic Structure: Should It be Changed?*, Seattle, Society for Japanese Studies, 1990, p. 359.
31 Quoted in Malcolm Bowie, *Lacan*, London, Fontana, 1991, p. 3.
32 Aileen Kelly, 'Introduction' in Sir Isaiah Berlin, *Russian Thinkers*, London, Hogarth, 1978, pp. xiii-xiv.
33 Ibid., p. xxiv.

CHAPTER 8

1 Quoted in George Steiner, 'Text and context', *On Difficulty and Other Essays*, Oxford, Oxford University Press, 1978, p. 12.
2 See Edmund Husserl, *The Crisis of European Sciences and Transcendental Phenomenology*, trans. David Carr, Evanston, Ill., Northwestern University Press, 1970.
3 Henry James, 'Pierre Loti', in Henry James, *Literary Criticism: French Writers, Other European Writers, The Prefaces to the New York Editions*, N.Y., The Library of America, 1984, pp. 491–2.
4 Steiner, 'Text and context', p. 16.
5 George Steiner, 'After the book?', *On Difficulty and Other Essays*, Oxford University Press, 1978, p. 188.
6 George Steiner, 'Text and context', p. 11.
7 Ibid.
8 Roland Barthes, 'Chateaubriand: *Life of Rancé*', *New Critical Essays*, trans. Richard Howard, Berkeley and Los Angeles, University of California Press, 1990, p. 41.
9 Louis Althusser, 'From *Capital* to Marx's philosophy', in Louis Althusser and Etienne Balibar, *Reading Capital* (*Lire Capital*), trans. Ben Brewster, London, Verso, 1979; Jean-Paul Sartre, *L'Idiot de la famille: Gustave Flaubert de 1821 à 1857*, Paris, Gallimard, 1971.
10 George Steiner, 'Text and context', p. 3.
11 Ibid., p. 6.
12 Ibid., pp. 5–6.
13 Althusser, op. cit., p. 16.
14 Ibid.
15 Ibid.
16 Ibid.
17 Ibid., p. 19.
18 Ibid.
19 Ibid., p. 21.
20 Ibid., p. 22.

21 Ibid., p. 24.
22 Ibid., p. 16.
23 Ibid., p. 18.
24 Jean-Paul Sartre, *L'Idiot de famille*, part 3, p. 12. Quoted in Peter Caws, 'Sartre's last philosophic manifesto', in Hugh J. Silverman (ed.), *Philosophy and Non-Philosophy since Merleau-Ponty*, N.Y. and London, Routledge, 1988, p. 109.
25 Quoted in Caws, op. cit., pp. 111–12.
26 Ibid., p. 116.
27 Ibid., pp. 110–11.
28 Translated in Caws on p. 112.
29 Ibid.
30 Ibid.
31 Quoted in Robert Young, *White Mythologies: Writing History and the West*, London, Routledge, 1990, p. 28.
32 Caws, op. cit., pp. 112–13.
33 Ibid., p. 113.
34 Ibid.
35 Quoted in Caws, op. cit., p. 113. (*IF3*, p. 435.)
36 See, for example, the essays 'Balzac: *The Peasants*', 'Balzac: *Lost Illusions*' and 'The Zola centenary' in *Studies in European Realism*, London, Merlin Press, 1950. See also George Steiner, 'Georg Lukács and his devil's pact', *Language and Silence: Essays 1958–1966*, London and Boston, Faber & Faber, 1967.
37 Caws, op. cit., pp. 113–14.
38 Jean-Paul Sartre, *L'idiot de la famille*, part 3, p. 435, quoted in Caws, op. cit., p. 113.
39 Georg Lukács, *History and Class Consciousness: Studies in Marxist Dialectics*, trans. Rodney Livingstone, Cambridge, Mass., MIT Press, 1971.

CHAPTER 9

1 Donald G. MacRae, 'Adam Ferguson', in Timothy Raison (ed.), *The Founding Fathers of Social Science*, Harmondsworth, Penguin 1969, p. 19.
2 Julia Kristeva, *Strangers to Ourselves*, trans. Leon S. Roudiez, N.Y., Harvester Wheatsheaf, 1991.
3 George Steiner, *After Babel: Aspects of Language and Translation*, 2nd edn, Oxford, Oxford University Press, 1992, pp. 124–5.
4 Quoted in Edward W. Said, *Orientalism*, Harmondsworth, Penguin, 1985, p.78.
5 Ibid., p. 215.
6 George Steiner, *The Death of Tragedy*, London, Faber & Faber, 1961, p. 70.
7 Edwin A. Burtt, *The English Philosophers from Bacon to Mill*, N.Y., Modern Library, 1939, pp. xii-xiii.
8 Peter Winch, *The Idea of a Social Science and its Relation to Philosophy*, second edn, London, Routledge, 1990.

9 Richard Rorty, *Philosophy and the Mirror of Nature*, Princeton, N.J., Princeton University Press, 1979.
10 David Caute, *Fanon*, London, Fontana, 1970, pp. 14–15.
11 Ibid.
12 Ibid. Frantz Fanon's *Les Damnés de la terre* appeared in English in 1965 as *The Wretched of the Earth*.
13 Said, *Orientalism*, pp. 263–4.
14 Henry James, *Literary Criticism: French Writers, Other European Writers, The Preface to the New York Editions*, N.Y., The Library of America, 1984, p. 508.
15 Quoted in Said, *Orientalism*, p. 264.
16 Ibid.
17 Ibid., p. 265.
18 Ibid., pp. 276, 280.
19 Ibid., p. 274.
20 Ibid., p. 275.
21 Ibid.
22 Ibid., p. 276.
23 Ibid., p. 266.
24 Ibid.
25 Ibid., p. 266.
26 Ibid., p. 284.
27 Ibid., p. 267.
28 Ibid.
29 Louis Massignon, 'Africa (excluding Egypt),' in H. A. R. Gibb, *Whither Islam? A Survey of Modern Movements in the Moslem World*, London, Victor Gollancz, 1932, pp. 75–98.
30 Ibid., p. 84.
31 Ibid., pp. 77–8.
32 Said, *Orientalism*, p. 284.
33 Ibid., p. 267.
34 Edward W. Said, *Beginnings: Intention and Method*, N.Y., Columbia University Press, 1985, p. 6. Said asks us to:

Consider the general education brought to literary criticism by an individual today. Whatever else he may have been trained in, it was almost certainly not classical philology, the one discipline in Europe and America that was practically *de rigueur* for the literary scholar until World War II.

35 Quoted in Said, *Orientalism*, p. 106.
36 Friedrich Nietzsche, *The Birth of Tragedy out of the Spirit of Music*, 1872, trans. Walter Kaufmann in *Basic Writings of Nietzsche*, New York, The Modern Library, 1968, pp. 3–144. A concise background to the controversy between Nietzsche and Wilamowitz can be found in Kaufmann's 'Translator's Introduction', pp. 3–13, in Kirsti Simonsuuri's entry on Wilamowitz in *The Fontana Dictionary of Modern Thinkers*, ed. Alan Bullock and R. B. Woodings, London, Fontana, 1983, p. 822, and, in more detail, from the classical philologist's point of view, in Hugh Lloyd-Jones, *Blood for the Ghosts: Classical Influences in the Nineteenth and*

Twentieth Centuries, London, Duckworth, 1982, particularly but not exclusively in the article on 'Nietzsche'.

37 Karatani Kojin, *Nihon Kindai Bungaku no Kigen* (The Origins of Modern Japanese Literature), Tokyo, Kodansha, 1980.

CHAPTER 10

1 Alexandre Kojève, *Introduction to a Reading of Hegel: Lectures on the Phenomenology of Spirit*, assembled by Raymond Queneau, ed. Allan Bloom, trans. James H. Nichols, Jr., Ithaca and London, Cornell University Press, 1969.

2 Jacques Derrida, *Glas*, Paris, Editions Galilee, 1974. Published in English as *Glas*, trans. John P Leavy, Jr. and Richard Rand, Lincoln, Nebraska and London, University of Nebraska Press, 1986. 'The double session' appears in Jacques Derrida, *Dissemination*, trans. Barbara Johnson, London, Athlone Press, 1981, pp. 173–286.

3 Mishima Yukio, *Yukoku* (Patriotism), in *Hanazakari no Mori, Yukoku*, Tokyo, Shincho-sha, 1968; Maruyama Masao, *Gendai Seiji no Shiso to Kodo* (Thought and Behaviour in Modern Japanese Politics), Tokyo, Mirai-sha, 1957.

4 'Rethinking Japan', *Business Week*, 7 August 1989, pp. 44–52.

5 Alan, Lord Bullock, 'Eduard Bernstein', in Alan Bullock & R. B. Woodings (eds), *The Fontana Dictionary of Modern Thinkers*, London, Fontana, 1983, pp. 68–9.

6 Carol Gluck, 'The triumph of the East: "Lessons" to be learnt from Japanese success', *Times Literary Supplement*, 28 October 1994, p. 10. I began to formulate this view with a lecture that I delivered in Berlin and Oxford in 1983 titled 'Beyond political economy: a critique of issues raised in Chalmers Johnson's *MITI and the Japanese Miracle*', *Social and Economic Research on Modern Japan*, Occasional Paper No. 35, Berlin, East Asian Institute, Free University of Berlin, 1983.

   Johnson's stimulating role in this debate over economic positivism and area studies was affirmed in the article by Chalmers Johnson and E. B. Keehn, 'A disaster in the making: rational choice and Asian studies', which appeared in *National Interest*, no. 36, Summer 1994, pp. 14–22.

7 See Friedrich List, *The National System of Political Economy*, trans. S.S. Lloyd, London, Longmans, Green and Co., 1922, and Otsuka Hisao, *Otsuka Hisao Chosaku-shu, Dai-roku-kan, Kokumin Keizai* (The Collected Works of Otsuka Hisao, Volume 6, National Economics), Tokyo, Iwanami Shoten, 1969.

   The cardinal nature of the discussion about mercantilism versus positivism is alive in the recent writings of James Fallows, one of the most conspicuous voices in the first flowering of anti-Japanese Revisionism in the print media. In contrast with his earlier polemics, his *Looking at the Sun: The Rise of the New East Asian Economic and Political System*, N.Y., Pantheon, 1994, may, in a very welcome development, do much to create a large and informed readership for List.

8 Roland Barthes, 'Chateaubriand: *Life of Rancé*', *New Critical Essays*,

trans. Richard Howard, Berkeley and Los Angeles, University of Calif. Press, 1990, p. 41.

9 Joachim Pissarro, 'The broader picture', *Independent on Sunday*, 30 September 1990, p. 32.

10 Ibid.

11 Jonathan Culler, *Barthes*, London, Fontana, 1983, p. 105.

12 Roland Barthes, *Empire of Signs*, trans. Richard Howard, London, Jonathan Cape, 1983, p. 3.

13 Ibid.

14 Fredric Jameson, 'Foreword' in Jean-François Lyotard, *The Postmodern Condition: A Report on Knowledge*, trans. Geoff Bennington and Brian Massumi, Manchester, Manchester University Press, 1984, p. viii.

15 Ibid.

16 Ibid., p. ix.

17 Ibid., p. ix.

18 Ibid.

19 The Derrida–Searle exchange was contained in Jacques Derrida, 'Signature event context', *Glyph*, vol. I, Baltimore, Md., Johns Hopkins University Press, 1977, pp. 172–97; John R. Searle, 'Reiterating the differences', *Glyph*, vol. I, Baltimore, Md., Johns Hopkins University Press, 1977, pp. 198–208; Jacques Derrida, 'Limited Inc abc', *Glyph*, vol. II, Baltimore, Md., Johns Hopkins University Press, 1977, pp. 162–254. J.G. Merquior's critique is contained in his *Foucault*, London, Fontana Press/Collins, 1985.

20 Takeuchi Yoshimi, '*Kindai to wa Nani ka: Nihon to Chugoku no baai*' (What is modernity? The case of Japan and China), *Takeuchi Yoshimi Zenshu* (The Complete Works of Takeuchi Yoshimi), Tokyo, Chikuma Shobo, 1980, volume 4, p. 145.

21 W. Hegel, *The Philosophy of History*, trans. J. Sibree, London, The Colonial Press, 1899, p. 99.

22 Jacques Derrida, 'White mythology', *Margins – of Philosophy*, trans. Alan Bass, Chicago, University of Chicago Press, 1982, p. 213.

23 Claude Lévi-Strauss, *La Pensée sauvage*, Paris, Librairie Plon, 1962. For a left-wing postmodernist assessment of this prehistory, including both the French and Subaltern Schools, see Robert Young, *White Mythologies: Writing History and the West*, London, Routledge, 1990.

24 Marx's 'Eleventh thesis', as Engels edited it, forcefully states that 'The philosophers have only *interpreted* the world, in various ways; the point, however, is to *change* it'. Karl Marx and Friedrich Engels, *The German Ideology*, Moscow, Progress Publishers, 1968, p. 667. Lyotard's often severe criticism of Habermas, which is an updated version of French theory's general dissent from Hegel (to which Lyotard also subscribes), is in full cry in *The Postmodern Condition: A Report on Knowledge*, trans. Geoff Bennington and Brian Massumi, Manchester, Manchester University Press, 1984.

25 Quoted in Said, *Orientalism*, Harmondsworth, Penguin, 1985, p. 77.

26 Ibid.

CHAPTER 11

1 Chalmers Johnson, *MITI and the Japanese Miracle: The Growth of Industrial Policy, 1925–1975*, Stanford, Calif., Stanford University Press, 1982.

2 *Collins English Dictionary*, 3rd edn, Glasgow, HarperCollins, 1991.

3 Roland Barthes, 'Chateaubriand: *Life of Rancé*', *New Critical Essays*, trans. Richard Howard, Berkeley and Los Angeles, University of California Press, 1990, p. 41.

4 Quoted in Joachim Pissarro, 'The broader picture', *Independent on Sunday*, 30 September 1990, p. 32.

5 Quoted in George Steiner, *In Bluebeard's Castle: Some Notes towards the Redefinition of Culture*, New Haven, Conn., Yale University Press, 1971, p. 85.

6 Ibid., pp. 90, 91.

7 Ibid., p. 89.

8 From *The Third Pythian Ode*, as translated by Richmond Lattimore, quoted in Steiner, op. cit., p. 90.

9 Ibid., p. 91.

10 Ibid.

11 Maruyama Masao, '*Bunmeiron no Gairyaku*' o *Yomu* (Reading 'An Outline of Civilization'), Tokyo, Iwanami Shincho, 1986. Maruyama's case is set out in 'Koten kara do manabu ka', pp. 1–23.

12 Ibid., *jo*, pp. 10–13.

13 Ibid., pp. 13–23.

14 Isaiah Berlin, 'Does political theory still exist?', *Concepts and Categories: Philosophical Essays*, Oxford, Oxford University Press, 1980, pp. 143–72.

15 Mark Lilla, 'The trouble with the Enlightenment' (review of Isaiah Berlin's *The Magus of the North*), *London Review of Books*, 6 January 1994, pp. 12–13.

16 Ibid., p. 12.

17 Ibid.

18 Iain Hampsher-Monk, *A History of Modern Political Thought: Major Political Thinkers from Hobbes to Marx*, Oxford, Blackwell, 1992, p. ix.

19 Ibid.

20 See Patrick Riley, 'Social contract', in David Miller, Janet Coleman, William Connolly and Alan Ryan (eds), *The Blackwell Encyclopedia of Political Thought*, Oxford, Basil Blackwell, 1991, pp. 478–89.

21 See article by James Tully, 'Francisco Suarez', in David Miller, Janet Coleman, William Connolly and Alan Ryan (eds), *The Blackwell Encyclopedia of Political Thought*, Oxford, Basil Blackwell, 1991, p. 508–9.

22 Jonathan Culler, *Barthes*, London, Fontana, 1983, p. 62.

23 Quoted in Culler, ibid., p. 68. See Roland Barthes, *Critique et vérité*, Paris, Editions du Seuil, 1966. Also *Criticism and Truth*, trans. Katrine Pilcher Keuneman, London, Athlone Press, 1987.

24 Werner Marx, *Hegel's Phenomenology of Spirit: Its Point and Purpose – A Commentary on the Preface and Introduction*, trans. Peter Heath, N.Y., Harper & Row, 1975.

25 Ibid., p. xiv.

26 Ibid.

27 Ibid., pp. xii-xiii.

28 Ibid., p. xiii.
29 Ibid.
30 Ibid.
31 Ibid.
32 Ibid.
33 Ibid.
34 Richard Rorty, 'Lumps and texts', *Philosophical Papers, Volume 1: Objectivity, Relativism and Truth*, Cambridge, Cambridge University Press, 1991, p. 89.
35 Chalmers Johnson, *MITI and the Japanese Miracle*, p. 32.
36 Friedrich List, *The National System of Political Economy*, trans. S. S. Lloyd, London, Longmans, Green and Co., 1922.

CHAPTER 12

1 Ronald Dore, *British Factory – Japanese Factory: The Origins of National Diversity in Industrial Relations*, Berkeley and Los Angeles, University of California Press, 1973, and *Shinohata: A Portrait of a Japanese Village*, London, Allen Lane, 1978.
2 David Williams, *Japan: Beyond the End of History*, London, Routledge, 1994.
3 Ibid., pp. 191–3.
4 James E. Alt and Kenneth A. Shepsle (eds), *Perspectives on Positive Political Economy*, Cambridge, Cambridge University Press, 1990.
5 Mancur Olson, 'Toward a unified view of economics and the other social sciences', in James E. Alt and Kenneth A. Shepsle (eds), *Perspectives on Positive Political Economy*, Cambridge, Cambridge University Press, 1990, p. 212.
6 Peter C. Ordeshook, 'The emerging discipline of political economy', in James E. Alt and Kenneth A Shepsle (eds), *Perspectives on Positive Political Economy*, Cambridge, Cambridge University Press, p. 10.
7 Ibid.
8 Alexander Rosenberg, 'If economics isn't a science, what is it?', in Michael Martin and Lee C. McIntyre (eds), *Readings in the Philosophy of Social Science*, Cambridge, Mass. and London, MIT Press, 1994, pp. 661–74.
9 Immanuel Kant, *Critique of Pure Reason*, trans. Norman Kemp Smith, London, Macmillan, 1929 (second impression with corrections 1933), p. 540.
10 Edward W. Said, *Orientalism*, Harmondsworth, Penguin, 1985, p. 257.
11 Ibid.
12 Leszek Kolakowski, *Positivist Philosophy: From Hume to the Vienna Circle*, trans. Norbert Guterman, Harmondsworth, Penguin, 1972, p. 203.
13 See Edmund Husserl, *The Crisis of European Sciences and Transcendental Phenomenology*, trans. David Carr, Evanston, Ill., Northwestern University Press, 1970.
14 Quoted in John Hale, *The Civilization of Europe in the Renaissance*, London, HarperCollins, 1993, p. 3.
15 The tensions are unambiguously revealed in Edward W. Said, 'Raymond

Schwab and the romance of ideas' as well as 'Islam, philology, and French culture: Renan and Massignon', in *The World, the Text and the Critic*, London, Vintage, 1991, pp. 248–89.

16 For a valuable explanation of this distinction in the decorative arts, see Robin Reilly, *Wedgwood*, two volumes, London, Macmillan, 1989, vol. II, pp. 101–7. In essence, to confuse *japonisme* with *japonaiserie* is to fail 'to differentiate between genuine oriental work and European inventions in what were believed to be oriental styles' (p. 107).

17 In his *Rodin: A Biography*, N.Y., Henry Holt, 1987, Frederic V. Grunefeld quotes Rodin's conclusion that his rejection by the Ecole des Beaux-Arts was, in the end, 'Great good luck' (p. 31).

18 Frank Elgar, *Cézanne*, London, Thames & Hudson, 1974, p. 15. Elgar's analysis speaks to the point: 'Shy people often hide their weaknesses behind defiance and cynicism. In Cézanne's case, there was also the need to protect himself against possible [artistic] influences, and the more powerful the influences were, the more justified his self-protection' (pp. 28–9).

19 Maruyama Masao, '*Bunmeiron no Gyaraku*' *o Yomu* (Reading 'An Outline of Civilization'), Tokyo, Iwanami Shoten, 1986, *jo*, pp. 4–5.

20 Richmond Lattimore's translation from *The Third Pythian Ode* is quoted in George Steiner, *In Bluebeard's Castle: Some Notes towards the Redefinition of Culture*, New Haven, Conn., Yale University Press, 1971, p. 90.

21 Coppola's remarks are recorded in his wife's documentary film on the making of *Apocalypse Now*.

List of works cited

Adorno, Theodor W., Albert, Hans, Dahrendorf, Ralf, Habermas, Jürgen, Pilot, Harald and Popper, Karl R., *The Positivist Dispute in German Sociology*, trans. Glyn Adey and David Frisby, London, Heinemann, 1976.

Allison, Graham T., *Essence of Decision: Explaining the Cuban Missile Crisis*, Boston, Little Brown, 1971.

Alt, James E. and Shepsle, Kenneth A. (eds), *Perspectives on Positive Political Economy*, Cambridge, Cambridge University Press, 1990.

Althusser, Louis, 'From *Capital* to Marx's philosophy', in Louis Althusser and Etienne Balibar, *Reading Capital (Lire Capital)*, trans. Ben Brewster, London, Verso, 1979.

—*For Marx*, trans. by Ben Brewster, London, Allen Lane, The Penguin Press, 1969.

Angel, Robert C., *Explaining Economic Policy Failure: Japan in the 1969–1971 International Monetary Crisis*, New York, Columbia University Press, 1991.

Aoki, Tamotsu, '*Bunka no Hiteisei*' (Culture as negation), *Chuo Koron*, Tokyo, Chuo Koron-sha, 1987.

Appiah, Anthony K., 'African-American philosophy?', *The Philosophical Forum*, vol. XXIV, nos 1–3, Fall–Spring 1992–1993.

Asada, Akira, '*Rekishi no Owari*' to Seiki-matsu no Sekai ('The End of History' and a *Fin de Siècle* World), Tokyo, Shogakkan, 1994.

Ayer, A. J., *Hume*, Oxford, Oxford University Press, 1980.

Barry, Norman P., *An Introduction to Modern Political Theory*, London, Macmillan, 1981.

Barthes, Roland, *Critique et vérité*, Paris, Editions du Seuil, 1966; *Criticism and Truth*, trans. Katrine Pilcher Keuneman, London, Athlone Press, 1987.

—*Empire of Signs*, trans. Richard Howard, London, Jonathan Cape, 1983.

—'Chateaubriand: *Life of Rancé*', *New Critical Essays*, trans. Richard Howard, Berkeley and Los Angeles, University of California Press, 1990.

Begg, David, Fischer, Stanley and Dornbusch, Rudiger, *Economics*, London, McGraw-Hill, 1991.

Behler, Ernst, *Confrontations: Derrida/Heidegger/Nietzsche*, trans. Steven Taubeneck, Stanford, Calif., Stanford University Press, 1991.

Bell, Daniel, 'Weber, Karl Emil Maximillian (Max)', in Alan Bullock and

R.B. Woodings (eds), *The Fontana Dictionary of Modern Thinkers*, London, Fontana, 1983, pp. 806–7.

Bellah, Robert N., *Tokugawa Religion: The Values of Pre-Industrial Japan*, New York, The Free Press, 1957.

Benda, Julien, *The Treason of the Intellectuals* (*La Trahison des clercs*, 1927), trans. Richard Addington, New York, W. W. Norton, 1969.

Benton, Ted, *Philosophical Foundations of the Three Sociologies*, London, Routledge & Kegan Paul, 1977.

Berlin, Sir Isaiah, 'Does political theory still exist?', *Concepts and Categories: Philosophical Essays*, Oxford, Oxford University Press, 1980, pp. 143–72.

—'Verification', *Concepts and Categories: Philosophical Essays*, Oxford, Oxford University Press, 1980, pp. 12–31.

—'Nationalism: past neglect and present power', *Against the Current: Essays in the History of Ideas*, Oxford, Clarendon Press, 1989, pp. 333–55.

—'The pursuit of the ideal', *The Crooked Timber of Humanity: Chapters in the History of Ideas*, London, John Murray, 1990, pp. 1–19.

Bernal, Martin, *Black Athena: The Afroasiatic Roots of Classical Civilization, Volume I: The Fabrication of Ancient Greece 1785–1985*, London, Free Association Books, 1987.

Bernstein, Richard J., *The Restructuring of Social and Political Theory*, London, Methuen, 1979.

Bill, James A. and Hardgrave, Jr., Robert L., *Comparative Politics: The Quest for Theory*, Washington, D.C., University Press of America, 1981.

Bloom, Allan, *The Closing of the American Mind*, New York, Simon & Schuster, 1987.

Borradori, Giovanna, *Conversazioni americane con W. O. Quine, D. Davidson, H. Putnam, R. Nozick, A. C. Danto, R. Rorty, S. Cavell, A. MacIntyre, Th. S. Kuhn*, Milan, Guis. Laterza & Figli, 1991. *The American Philosopher: Conversations with Quine, Davidson, Putnam, Nozick, Danto, Rorty, Cavell, MacIntyre, and Kuhn*, trans. Rosanna Crocitto, Chicago, University of Chicago Press, 1994.

Bowie, Malcolm, *Lacan*, London, Fontana, 1991.

Buckley, Sandra and Mackie, Vera, 'Women in the new Japanese state', in Gavan McCormack and Yoshio Sugimoto (eds), *Democracy in Contemporary Japan*, Armonk, N.Y., M. E. Sharpe, 1986, pp. 173–85.

Bullock, Alan, Lord, 'Eduard Bernstein', in Alan Bullock and R. B. Woodings (eds), *The Fontana Dictionary of Modern Thinkers*, London, Fontana, 1983, pp. 68–9.

Burtt, Edwin A., *The English Philosophers from Bacon to Mill*, New York, Modern Library, 1939.

Butler, David and Stokes, Donald, *Political Change in Britain: Forces Shaping Electoral Choice*, revised edn, New York, St Martin's, 1976.

Calder, Kent E., *Crisis and Compensation: Public Policy and Political Stability in Japan, 1949–1986*, Princeton, N.J., Princeton University Press, 1988.

—*Strategic Capitalism: Private Business and Public Purpose in Japanese Industrial Finance*, Princeton, N.J., Princeton University Press, 1993.

Campbell, Angus, *The American Voter*, New York, Wiley, 1960.

Campbell, James, *Talking at the Gates: A Life of James Baldwin*, London, Faber & Faber, 1991.

Campbell, John Creighton, *Contemporary Japanese Budget Politics*, Berkeley, Calif., University of California Press, 1977.

—*How Policies Change: The Japanese Government and the Aging Society*, Princeton, N.J., Princeton University Press, 1992.

Caute, David, *Fanon*, London, Fontana, 1970.

Caws, Peter, 'Sartre's last philosophic manifesto', in Hugh J. Silverman (ed.), *Philosophy and Non-Philosophy since Merleau-Ponty*, New York and London, Routledge, 1988.

Chomsky, Noam, 'A review of B. F. Skinner's *Verbal Behaviour*', *Language*, vol. 35, no. 1, 1959, pp. 26–58. Reprinted in J. A. Fodor and J. J. Katz (eds), *The Structure of Language*, Prentice-Hall, 1964, pp. 547–8.

—*Aspects of the Theory of Syntax*, Cambridge, Mass., MIT Press, 1965.

Cicero, Marcus Tullius, *De finibus bonorum et malorum*, Book V, with a translation by H. Rackman, London, William Heinemann, 1971.

Cohen, Michael D., March, James G. and Olsen, Johan P., 'A garbage can model of organizational choice', *Administrative Science Quarterly*, vol. 17. no. 1, March 1972, pp. 1–25.

Collins English Dictionary, 3rd edn, Glasgow, HarperCollins, 1991.

Conrad, Peter, *Imagining America*, London and Henley, Routledge & Kegan Paul, 1980.

Cotton, James, 'James Harrington', in David Miller, Janet Coleman, William Connolly and Alan Ryan (eds), *The Blackwell Encyclopedia of Political Thought*, Oxford, Basil Blackwell, 1991.

Crawcour, E. Sydney, 'Industrialization and technological change, 1885–1920', in Peter Duus (ed.), *The Cambridge History of Japan, Volume 6: The Twentieth Century*, Cambridge, Cambridge University Press, 1988, pp. 385–450.

Culler, Jonathan, *Saussure*, London, Fontana/Collins, 1976.

—*Barthes*, London, Fontana, 1983.

Curtis, Gerald L., *The Japanese Way of Politics*, New York, Columbia University Press, 1988.

Dale, Peter, *The Myth of Japanese Uniqueness*, London and Oxford, Croom Helm and Nissan Institute of Japanese Studies, 1986.

de Bary, Wm. Theodore, *East Asian Civilizations: A Dialogue in Five Stages*, Cambridge, Mass., Harvard University Press, 1988.

— *The Trouble with Confucianism*, Cambridge, Mass., Harvard University Press, 1991.

Derrida, Jacques, *Glas*, Paris, Editions Galilee, 1974. *Glas*, trans. John P. Leavy, Jr. and Richard Rand, Lincoln, Nebraska and London, University of Nebraska Press, 1986.

—'Signature event context', *Glyph*, vol. I, Baltimore, Md., Johns Hopkins University Press, 1977, pp. 172–97.

—'Limited Inc abc', *Glyph*, vol. II, Baltimore, Md., Johns Hopkins University Press, 1977, pp. 162–254.

—'The double session', in *Dissemination*, trans. Barbara Johnson, London, Athlone Press, 1981.

—'White mythology', *Margins – of Philosophy*, trans. Alan Bass, Chicago, University of Chicago Press, 1982.

Dore, Ronald, *British Factory – Japanese Factory: The Origins of National*

Diversity in Industrial Relations, Berkeley and Los Angeles, University of California Press, 1973.

—*Shinohata: A Portrait of a Japanese Village*, London, Allen Lane, 1978.

—*Flexible Rigidities: Industrial Policy and Structural Adjustment in the Japanese Economy, 1970–1980*, London, Athlone Press, 1986.

—*Taking Japan Seriously: A Confucian Perspective on Leading Economic Issues*, London, Athlone Press, 1987.

—'An outsider's view', in Kozo Yamamura (ed.), *Japan's Economic Structure: Should It be Changed?*, Seattle, Society for Japanese Studies, 1990.

—'Function and cause', in Michael Martin and Lee C. McIntyre (eds), *Readings in the Philosophy of Social Science*, Cambridge, Mass., MIT Press, 1994, pp. 377–89.

Douglas, Mary, *Evans-Pritchard*, London, Fontana, 1980.

Duke, Benjamin, *The Japanese School: Lessons for Industrial America*, New York, Praeger, 1986.

Durkheim, Emile, *The Rules of Sociological Method and Selected Texts on Sociology and Its Method*, trans. W. D. Halls, London, Macmillan, 1982.

—*Suicide: A Study in Sociology*, trans. John A. Spaulding and George Simpson, London, Routledge, 1989.

Easton, David, *A Framework for Political Analysis*, Englewood Cliffs, N.J., Prentice-Hall, 1965.

Edwards, Paul (ed. in Chief), *The Encyclopedia of Philosophy*, New York, Macmillan and The Free Press, 1967.

Elgar, Frank, *Cézanne*, London, Thames & Hudson, 1974.

Fallows, James, *Looking at the Sun: The Rise of the New East Asian Economic and Political System*, New York, Pantheon, 1994.

Fanon, Frantz, *Black Skin, White Masks*, trans. Charles Lam Markman, New York, Grove Press, 1967.

—*Studies in a Dying Colonialism*, trans. Haakon Chevalier, London, Earthscan Publications, 1989.

—*The Wretched of the Earth*, trans. Constance Farrington, London, Penguin, 1990.

Fischer, David Hackett, *Historians' Fallacies: Toward a Logic of Historical Thought*, New York, Harper & Row, 1970.

FitzGerald, Frances, *Fire in the Lake: The Vietnamese and the Americans in Vietnam*, Boston, Little, Brown, 1973.

Flanagan, Scott C. and Richardson, Bradley M., *Japanese Politics*, Boston, Little, Brown, 1984.

Flanagan, Scott C., Kohei, Shinsaku, Miyake, Ichiro, Richardson, Bradley M. and Watanuki, Joji, *The Japanese Voter*, New Haven, Conn., Yale University Press, 1991.

Flaubert, Gustave, *Salammbo*, trans. A.J. Krailsheimer, Harmondsworth, Penguin, 1977.

Freud, Sigmund, 'The intepretation of dreams' (1900), in *The Penguin Freud Library*, Harmondsworth, Penguin, 1976, vol. 4.

Friedman, David, *The Misunderstood Miracle: Industrial Development and Political Change in Japan*, Ithaca, N.Y., Cornell University Press, 1988.

Fukuyama, Francis, 'The end of history?', *National Interest*, Summer 1989, pp. 3–18.

—*The End of History and the Last Man*, London, Hamish Hamilton, 1992.

Gardner, Howard, *The Quest for Mind: Piaget, Lévi-Strauss and the Structuralist Movement*, New York, Vintage, 1974.

Gluck, Carol, 'The triumph of the East: "Lessons" to be learnt from Japanese success', *Times Literary Supplement*, 28 October 1994, p. 10.

Gombrich, E. H., *Meditations on a Hobby Horse and Other Essays on the Theory of Art*, London, Phaidon, 1963.

Gordon, Scott, *The History and Philosophy of Social Science*, London, Routledge, 1991 (new paperback edn published 1993).

Grafton, Anthony, *New Worlds, Ancient Texts: The Power of Tradition and the Shock of Discovery*, Cambridge, Mass., The Belknap Press of Harvard University Press, 1992.

Griffin, Jasper, *Virgil*, Oxford, Oxford University Press, 1986.

Grunefeld, Frederic V., *Rodin: A Biography*, New York, Henry Holt, 1987.

Gunnel, John G., 'Political theory and political science', in David Miller, Janet Coleman, William Connolly and Alan Ryan (eds), *The Blackwell Encyclopedia of Political Thought*, Oxford, Basil Blackwell, 1991, pp. 386–90.

Habermas, Jürgen, *On the Logic of the Social Sciences*, trans. Shierry Weber Nicholsen and Jerry A. Stark, Cambridge, Polity Press, 1990.

Haddock, B. A., *An Introduction to Historical Thought*, London, Edward Arnold, 1980.

Hale, John, *The Civilization of Europe in the Renaissance*, London, Harper-Collins, 1993.

Halfpenny, Peter, 'Positivism' in David Miller, Janet Coleman, William Connolly and Alan Ryan (eds), *The Blackwell Encyclopedia of Political Thought*, Oxford, Basil Blackwell, 1991.

Hampsher-Monk, Iain, *A History of Modern Political Thought: Major Political Thinkers from Hobbes to Marx*, Oxford, Basil Blackwell, 1992.

Hardgrave, Jr., Robert L. and Kochanek, Stanley A., *India: Government and Politics in a Developing Nation*, 4th edn, San Diego, Harcourt Brace Jovanovich, 1986.

Hegel, W., *The Philosophy of History*, trans. J. Sibree, London, The Colonial Press, 1899.

—*Hegel's Philosophy of Right*, trans. T. M. Knox, Oxford, Clarendon Press, 1952.

Hiromatsu, Wataru (ed. and trans.), *Die Deutsche Ideologie, 1. Band, 1. Abschnitt* by Karl Marx and Friedrich Engels, Tokyo, Kawade Shobo, 1974.

Hofheinz, Jr., Roy and Calder, Kent E., *The Eastasia Edge*, New York, Basic Books, 1982.

Husserl, Edmund, *Phenomenology and the Crisis of Philosophy*, translations of *Philosophy as a Rigorous Science* and *Philosophy and the Crisis of European Man* by Quentin Lauer, New York, Harper Torchbooks, 1966.

—*The Crisis of European Sciences and Transcendental Phenomenology*, trans. David Carr, Evanston, Ill., Northwestern University Press, 1970.

Inoguchi, Takashi and Okimoto, Daniel I. (eds), *The Political Economy of Japan, Volume 2: The Changing International Context*, Stanford, Calif., Stanford University Press, 1988.

James, Henry, *Literary Criticism: French Writers, Other European Writers,*

The Prefaces to the New York Editions, New York, The Library of America, 1984.

Jameson, Fredric, 'Foreword', in Jean-François Lyotard, *The Postmodern Condition: A Report on Knowledge*, trans. Geoff Bennington and Brian Massumi, Manchester, Manchester University Press, 1984, pp. vii–xix.

Jansen, Marius, 'History of Japanese studies in the United States', in M.B. Jansen (ed.), *Japanese Studies in the United States, Part I: History and Present Condition*, Ann Arbor, Mich., Association of Asian Studies, 1988.

Johnson, Chalmers, *Japan's Public Policy Companies*, Washington, D.C. and Stanford, Calif., AEI–Hoover Policy Studies, 1978.

—*MITI and the Japanese Miracle: The Growth of Industrial Policy, 1925–1975*, Stanford, Calif., Stanford University Press, 1982.

Johnson, Chalmers and Keehn, E. B., 'A disaster in the making: rational choice and Asian studies', *National Interest*, no. 36, Summer 1994, pp. 14–22.

Johnson, Chalmers, Tyson, Laura d'Andrea and Zysman, John (eds), *Politics and Productivity: How Japan's Development Strategy Works*, New York, Harperbusiness, 1989.

Kahn, Herman, *The Emerging Japanese Superstate: Challenge and Response*, Englewood Cliffs, N.J., Prentice-Hall, 1970.

Kant, Immanuel, *Critique of Pure Reason*, trans. Norman Kemp Smith, London, Macmillan, 1929 (second impression with corrections 1933).

Karatani, Kojin, *Nihon Kindai Bungaku no Kigen* (The origins of modern Japanese literature), Tokyo, Kodansha, 1980.

—'One spirit, two nineteenth centuries', trans. Alan Wolf, in Masao Miyoshi, and H. D. Harootunian (eds), *Postmodernism and Japan*, Durham and London, Duke University Press, 1989.

—*'Kindai no Chokoku ni Tsuite'* (Concerning the overcoming of modernity), in *Shuen o Megutte* (Concerning endings), Tokyo, Fukutake Shoten, 1990.

—*Marukusu: Sono Konosei no Chushin* (Marx: on the possibilities of his thought), Tokyo, Kodansha, 1990.

—*'Rekishi to Tasha'* (History and the other), in *Shuen o Megutte* (Concerning endings), Tokyo, Fukutake Shoten, 1990.

Kelly, Aileen, 'Introduction', in Sir Isaiah Berlin, *Russian Thinkers*, London, Hogarth, 1978, pp. xiii–xiv.

Kermode, Frank, *The Classic*, London, Faber & Faber, 1975.

Keynes, John Maynard, *The Collected Works of John Maynard Keynes, Volume II: The Economic Consequences of the Peace*, London and Cambridge, Macmillan/Cambridge University Press, 1971.

Kojève, Alexandre, *Introduction to a Reading of Hegel: Lectures on the Phenomenology of Spirit*, assembled by Raymond Queneau, ed. Allan Bloom, trans. James H. Nichols, Jr., Ithaca and London, Cornell University Press, 1969.

Kolakowski, Leszek, *Positivist Philosophy: From Hume to the Vienna Circle*, trans. Norbert Guterman, Harmondsworth, Middlesex, Penguin, 1972.

—*Main Currents of Marxism: Its Rise, Growth and Dissolution, Volume I: The Founders*, trans. P. S. Falla, Oxford, Clarendon Press, 1978.

—*Bergson*, Oxford, Oxford University Press, 1985.

Kristeva, Julia, *Strangers to Ourselves*, trans. Leon S. Roudiez, New York, Harvester Wheatsheaf, 1991.

Kuhn, Thomas S., *The Structure of Scientific Revolutions*, Chicago, University of Chicago Press, 1970, second edition.

Kumon, Shumpei and Rosovsky, Henry (eds), *The Political Economy of Japan, Volume 3: Cultural and Social Dynamics*, Stanford, Calif., Stanford University Press, 1992.

Leavis, F.R., *The Great Tradition*, Harmondsworth, Penguin 1972.

Lévi-Strauss, Claude, *Les Structures élémentaires de la parente*, Paris, Presses Universitaires de France, 1949.

—*La Pensée sauvage*, Paris, Librairie Plon, 1962.

Lilla, Mark, 'The trouble with the Enlightenment' (review of Isaiah Berlin's *The Magus of the North*), *London Review of Books*, 6 January 1994, pp. 12–13.

List, Friedrich, *The National System of Political Economy*, trans. S. S. Lloyd, London, Longmans, Green & Co., 1922.

Lloyd-Jones, Hugh, *Blood for the Ghosts: Classical Influences in the Nineteenth and Twentieth Centuries*, London, Duckworth, 1982.

Lukács, Georg, *History and Class Consciousness: Studies in Marxist Dialectics*, trans. Rodney Livingstone, Cambridge, Mass., MIT Press, 1971.

—*Studies in European Realism*, trans. E. Bone, London, Merlin Press, 1972.

—*The Young Hegel: Studies in the Relations between Dialectics and Economics*, trans. Rodney Livingstone, London, Merlin Press, 1975.

Lyotard, Jean-François, *The Postmodern Condition: A Report on Knowledge*, trans. Geoff Bennington and Brian Massumi, Manchester, Manchester University Press, 1984.

McCormack, Gavan and Sugimoto, Yoshio (eds), *Democracy in Contemporary Japan*, Armonk, N.Y., M. E. Sharpe, 1986.

Macey, David, *The Lives of Michel Foucault*, London, Verso, 1994.

McKenzie, Richard B.and Tullock, Gordon, *Modern Political Economy: An Introduction to Economics*, Tokyo, McGraw-Hill/Kodansha, 1978.

MacRae, Donald G., 'Adam Ferguson', in Timothy Raison (ed.), *The Founding Fathers of Social Science*, Harmondsworth, Penguin, 1969.

Maruyama, Masao, *Nihon Seiji Shiso-shi Kenkyu*, Tokyo, Tokyo Daigaku Shuppan-kai, 1952. Translated by Mikiso Hane as *Studies in the Intellectual History of Tokugawa Japan*, Tokyo, University of Tokyo Press, 1974.

—*Gendai Seiji no Shiso to Kodo*, Tokyo, Mirai-sha, 1957. *Thought and Behaviour in Modern Japanese Politics*, ed. Ivan Morris, London, Oxford University Press, 1963.

—*Taiheisaku* (notes and commentary) in Yoshikawa Kojiro, Maruyama Masao, Nishida Taichiro and Tsuji Tatsuya (eds), *Ogyu Sorai, Nihon Shiso Taikei, Dai-36 kan*, Tokyo, Iwamani Shoten, 1973, pp. 447–86, 787–829.

—'*Bunmeiron no Gairyaku*' *o Yomu* (Reading 'An Outline of Civilization'), *jo, chu, ge*, Tokyo, Iwanami Shoten, 1986.

Marx, Karl, *The 18th Brumaire of Louis Bonaparte*, New York, International Publishers, 1969.

—*A Contribution to the Critique of Political Economy*, trans. S. W. Ryazanskaya, Moscow, Progress Publishers, 1970.

Marx, Karl and Engels, Friedrich, *The German Ideology*, Moscow, Progress Publishers, 1968.

Marx, Werner, *Hegel's Phenomenology of Spirit: Its Point and Purpose – A Commentary on the Preface and Introduction*, trans. Peter Heath, New York, Harper & Row, 1975.

Massignon, Louis, 'Africa (excluding Egypt)', in H. A. R. Gibb, *Whither Islam? A Survey of Modern Movements in the Moslem World*, London, Victor Gollancz, 1932, pp. 75–98.

Merquior, J. G., *Foucault*, London, Fontana Press/Collins, 1985.

Mill, John Stuart, *Auguste Comte and Positivism*, Ann Arbor, Michigan, University of Michigan Press, 1961.

Miller, David, 'Political theory' in David Miller, Janet Coleman, William Connolly and Alan Ryan (eds), *The Blackwell Encyclopedia of Political Thought*, Oxford, Basil Blackwell, 1991, pp. 383–5.

Miller, David, Coleman, Janet, Connolly, William and Ryan, Alan (eds), *The Blackwell Encyclopedia of Political Thought*, Oxford, Basil Blackwell, 1987 (paperback edn published, with corrections in 1991).

Miller, Roy Andrew, *Nihongo: In Defence of Japanese*, London, Athlone Press, 1986.

Milton, John, 'Lycidas' in John Barrell and John Bull (eds), *The Penguin Book of English Pastoral Verse*, Harmondsworth, Penguin, 1982, pp. 185–90.

Mishima, Yukio, *'Yukoku'* (Patriotism), in *Hanazakari no Mori, Yukoku*, Tokyo, Shincho-sha, 1968. A translation of 'Yukoko' appears in Yukio Mishima, *Death in Midsummer and Other Stories*, Tokyo, Charles E. Tuttle, 1987.

Miyoshi, Masao, *Off Center: Power and Culture Relations between Japan and the United States*, Cambridge, Mass., Harvard University Press, 1991.

Miyoshi, Masao and Harootunian, H. D. (eds), *Postmodernism and Japan*, Durham and London, Duke University Press, 1989.

Murakami, Yasusuke, *Hankoten no Seiji Keizaigaku* (Anti-classical political economy), Tokyo, Chuo Koron-sha, 1992.

Nagel, Ernest, *The Structure of Science: Problems in the Logic of Scientific Explanation*, New York, Harcourt Brace and World, 1961.

Naipaul, V. S., *In a Free State*, Harmondsworth, Penguin, 1973.

—*The Enigma of Arrival*, Harmondsworth, Penguin, 1987.

Najita, Tetsuo, *Japan: The Intellectual Foundations of Modern Japanese Politics*, Chicago and London, University of Chicago Press, 1974.

Newman, Robert P., *Owen Lattimore and the 'Loss' of China*, Berkeley, University of California Press, 1992.

Nietzsche, Friedrich, *The Birth of Tragedy out of the Spirit of Music*, trans. Walter Kaufmann, in *Basic Writings of Nietzsche*, New York, The Modern Library, 1968, pp. 3–144.

Nikkei Kinyu Shinbun, *Kogin no Henshin: Sangyo Kinyu no Yu wa Yomigaeru ka* (IBJ's Metamorphosis: Can the Hero of Industrial Finance Make a Comeback?), Tokyo, Nihon Keizai Shinbun-sha, 1994.

Okimoto, Daniel I., *Between MITI and the Market: Japanese Industrial Policy for High Technology*, Stanford, Calif., Stanford University Press, 1989.

Olson, Mancur, 'Toward a unified view of economics and the other social sciences' in James E. Alt and Kenneth A. Shepsle (eds), *Perspectives on Positive Political Economy*, Cambridge, Cambridge University Press, 1990.

Ordeshook, Peter C., 'The emerging discipline of political economy', in

James E. Alt, and Kenneth A. Shepsle, (eds), *Perspectives on Positive Political Economy*, Cambridge, Cambridge University Press, 1990.

Otsuka, Hisao, *Otsuka Hisao Chosaku-shu, Dai-roku-kan, Kokumin Keizai*, (The Collected Works of Otsuka Hisao Volume 6, National Economics), Tokyo, Iwanami Shoten, 1969.

Ouchi, William G., *Theory Z: How American Business Can Meet the Japanese Challenge*, Reading, Mass., Addison Wesley, 1981.

Parekh, B., 'The poverty of Indian political theory', *History of Political Thought*, vol. XIII, no. 3, Autumn 1992.

Patrick, Hugh, 'The future of the Japanese Economy: output and labor productivity', *Journal of Japanese Studies*, vol. 3, no. 2, Summer 1973.

Patrick, Hugh and Rosovsky, Henry (eds), *Asia's New Giant: How the Japanese Economy Works*, Washington, D.C., The Brookings Institution, 1976.

Pempel, T. J., *Policy and Politics in Japan: Creative Conservatism*, Philadelphia, Penn., Temple University Press, 1982.

Peters, Thomas J. and Waterman, Jr., Robert H., *In Search of Excellence: Lessons from America's Best-Run Companies*, New York, Harper & Row, 1982.

Pharr, Susan J., *Losing Face: Status Politics in Japan*, Berkeley and Los Angeles, University of California Press, 1990.

Pinguet, Maurice, *Le Texte japon*, trans. Tachiura Nobuo, Tamura Takeshi and Kudo Yoko as *Tekusuto Toshite no Nihon*, Tokyo, Chikuma Shobo, 1987.

Pissarro, Joachim, 'The broader picture', *Independent on Sunday*, 30 September 1990, p. 32.

Plamenatz, John, 'The use of political theory', in Anthony Quinton (ed.), *Political Philosophy*, Oxford, Oxford University Press, 1967.

Putnam, Robert D., *Making Democracy Work: Civic Traditions in Modern Italy*, Princeton, N.J., Princeton University Press, 1993.

Quinton, Anthony, Lord, 'Popper', in Alan Bullock and R. B. Reading (eds), *Fontana Biographical Companion to Modern Thought*, London, Collins, 1983, pp. 609–10.

Raison, Timothy (ed.), *The Founding Fathers of Social Science*, Harmondsworth, Penguin, 1969.

Ramseyer, J. Mark and Rosenbluth, Frances McCall, *Japan's Political Marketplace*, Cambridge, Mass., Harvard University Press, 1993.

Rawls, John, *A Theory of Justice*, Oxford, Clarendon Press, 1972.

Reich, Robert B., *The Next American Frontier*, New York, New York Times Books, 1983.

Reilly, Robin, *Wedgwood*, two volumes, London, Macmillan, 1989.

Richardson, Bradley M. and Flanagan, Scott C., *Politics in Japan*, Boston, Little Brown, 1984.

Riley, Patrick, 'Social contract', in David Miller, Janet Coleman, William Connolly and Alan Ryan (eds), *The Blackwell Encyclopedia of Political Thought*, Oxford, Basil Blackwell, 1991.

Roberts, John G., *Mitsui: Three Centuries of Japanese Business*, Tokyo, Weatherhill, 1973.

Rorty, Richard, *Philosophy and the Mirror of Nature*, Princeton, N.J., Princeton University Press, 1979.

—*Philosophical Papers, Volume 1: Objectivity, Relativism, and Truth*, Cambridge, Cambridge University Press, 1991.
Rosenberg, Alexander, 'If economics isn't a science, what is it?', in Michael Martin and Lee C. McIntyre (eds), *Readings in the Philosophy of Social Science*, Cambridge, Mass. and London, MIT Press, 1994.
Rosenbluth, Frances McCall, *Financial Politics in Contemporary Japan*, Ithaca, N.Y., Cornell University Press, 1989.
Russell, John, *Francis Bacon*, revised edn, London, Thames & Hudson, 1993.
Ryan, Alan, *J. S. Mill*, London, Routledge & Kegan Paul, 1974.
Sabine, George H. and Thorson, Thomas L., *A History of Political Theory*, 4th edn, Fort Worth, Texas, Dryden Press, 1973.
Said, Edward W., *Covering Islam: How the Media and the Experts Determine How We See the Rest of the World*, London, Routledge & Kegan Paul, 1981.
—*Beginnings: Intention and Method*, New York, Columbia University Press, 1985.
—*Orientalism*, Harmondsworth, Penguin, 1985.
—*The World, the Text and the Critic*, London, Vintage, 1991.
—*The Question of Palestine*, London, Vintage, 1992.
—*Culture and Imperialism*, London, Chatto & Windus, 1993.
Sakai, Naoki, 'Nihon Shakai Kagaku Hoho Josetsu' (Methods in Japanese social science: an introduction), *Iwanami Koza Shakai Kagaku no Hoho, III, Nihon Shakai Kagaku no Shiso* (Iwanami Course on Methods in Social Science, Volume III, Japanese Social Science as Thought), Tokyo, Iwanami Shoten, 1993, pp. 12–14.
Samuels, Richard J., *The Politics of Regional Policy: Localities Incorporated?*, Princeton, N.J., Princeton University Press, 1983.
—*The Business of the Japanese State: Energy Markets in Comparative and Historical Perspective*, Ithaca and London, Cornell University Press, 1987.
— 'Japanese political studies and the myth of the independent intellectual', in Richard J. Samuels and Myron Weiner (eds), *The Political Culture of Foreign Area Studies: Essays in Honor of Lucian W. Pye*, Washington, D.C., Pergammon-Brassey's, 1992, pp. 17–59.
—*'Rich Nation, Strong Army': National Security and the Technological Transformation of Japan*, Ithaca and London, Cornell University Press, 1994.
Samuelson, Paul A., *Economics*, New York, McGraw-Hill, 1948.
—*Economics*, 9th edn, Tokyo, McGraw-Hill Kogakusha, 1973.
Sartre, Jean-Paul, *Critique de la Raison Dialectique I*, Paris, Gallimard, 1960. Trans. Alan Sheridan Smith as *Critique of Dialectical Reason: Theory of Practical Ensembles*, London, New Left Books, 1976.
—*L'Idiot de la famille: Gustave Flaubert de 1821 à 1857*, Paris, Gallimard, 1971.
—*Critique de la Raison Dialectique II: L'intelligibilité de l'histoire*, ed. Arlette Elkaim-Sartre, Paris, Gallimard, 1985.
—*St Genet: Actor and Martyr*, trans. Bernard Frechtman, London, Heinemann, 1988.
Sayer, Andrew, *Method in Social Science: A Realist Approach*, 2nd edn, London, Routledge, 1992.

Scalapino, Robert A., *The Japanese Communist Movement, 1920–1966*, Berkeley and Los Angeles, University of California Press, 1967.

Scalapino, Robert A. and Masumi, Junnosuke, *Parties and Politics in Contemporary Japan*, Berkeley, Los Angeles and London, University of California Press, 1962.

Schama, Simon, *Dead Certainties (Unwarranted Speculations)*, London, Granta Books, 1991.

Searle, John R., 'Reiterating the differences', *Glyph*, vol. I, Baltimore, Md., Johns Hopkins University Press, 1977, pp. 198–208.

Simonsuuri, Kirsti, 'Wilamowitz-Moellendorff, Ulrich Friedrich Richard von', in Alan Bullock and R. B. Woodings (eds), *The Fontana Dictionary of Modern Thinkers*, London, Fontana, 1983, p. 822.

Skinner, Quentin (ed.), *The Return of Grand Theory in the Human Sciences*, Cambridge, Cambridge University Press, 1990.

Smith, Beverly, 'Democracy derailed: citizens' movements in historical perspective', in Gavan McCormack and Yoshio Sugimoto (eds), *Democracy in Contemporary Japan*, Armonk, N.Y., M. E. Sharpe, 1986, pp. 157–72.

Solman, Aaron, 'Behavioural sciences', in Alan Bullock and Oliver Stallybrass (eds), *The Fontana Dictionary of Modern Thought*, London, Fontana/Collins, 1977, p. 57.

Steiner, George, *The Death of Tragedy*, London, Faber & Faber, 1961.

—*In Bluebeard's Castle: Some Notes Towards the Redefinition of Culture*, New Haven, Conn., Yale University Press, 1971.

—*Extraterritorial: Papers on Literature and the Language Revolution*, London, Faber & Faber, 1972.

—'George Lukács and his devil's pact', *Language and Silence: Essays 1958–1966*, New York, Atheneum, 1974, pp. 325–39.

—*After Babel: Aspects of Language and Translation*, Oxford, Oxford University Press, 1975; 2nd edn, 1992.

—'After the book?', *On Difficulty and Other Essays*, Oxford, Oxford University Press, 1978, pp. 186–203.

—'Dante and the gossip of eternity', *On Difficulty and Other Essays*, Oxford, Oxford University Press, 1978, pp. 164–85.

—*Heidegger*, London, Fontana, 1978.

—'Text and Context', *On Difficulty and Other Essays*, Oxford, Oxford University Press, 1978, pp. 1–17.

—'The Archives of Eden', *Salmagundi*, Fall 1980–Winter 1981, pp. 57–89, 250–3.

Stockwin, J. A. A., *The Japanese Socialist Party and Neutralism: A Study of a Political Party and its Foreign Policy*, Carlton, Victoria, Melbourne University Press, 1968.

—*Japan: Divided Politics in a Growth Economy*, London and New York: W. W. Norton, 1982.

Stockwin, J. A. A. et al., *Dynamic and Immobilist Politics in Japan*, London, Macmillan Press, 1988.

Strauss, Leo, *Natural Right and History*, Chicago, University of Chicago Press, 1953.

Strauss, Leo and Cropsey, Joseph (eds), *History of Political Philosophy*, 3rd edn, Chicago, University of Chicago Press, 1987.

Takeuchi, Yoshimi, '*Kindai to wa Nani ka: Nihon to Chugoku no baai*'

(What is modernity? The case of Japan and China), *Takeuchi Yoshimi Zenshu* (The Complete Works of Takeuchi Yoshimi), Tokyo, Chikuma Shobo, 1980, volume 4.

Taubeneck, Steven, 'Afterword', in Ernst Behler, *Confrontations: Derrida/ Heidegger/Nietzsche*, trans. Steven Taubeneck, Stanford, Calif., Stanford University Press, 1991.

Tawney, R. H., *Religion and the Rise of Capitalism*, Harmondsworth, Penguin, 1938.

Taylor, Charles, 'Neutrality in political science', in P. Laslett and W. G. Runciman (eds), *Politics and Society*, 3rd series, Oxford, Basil Blackwell, 1967.

—'Understanding and ethnocentricity', *Philosophy and the Human Sciences, Philosophical Papers 2*, Cambridge, Cambridge University Press, 1985.

Trezise, Philip H. and Suzuki, Yukio, 'Politics, government, and economic growth in Japan', in Hugh Patrick and Henry Rosovsky (eds), *Asia's New Giant: How the Japanese Economy Works*, Washington, D.C., The Brookings Institution, 1976.

Tully, James, 'Francisco Suarez', in David Miller, Janet Coleman, William Connolly and Alan Ryan (eds), *The Blackwell Encyclopedia of Political Thought*, Oxford, Basil Blackwell, 1991, pp. 508–9.

Tyson, Laura d'Andrea, *Who's Bashing Whom: Trade Conflict in High-Technology Industries*, Washington, D.C., Institute for International Economics, 1992.

Unger, J. Marshall, *The Fifth Generation Fallacy: Why Japan is Betting Its Future on Artifical Intelligence*, New York, Oxford University Press, 1987.

Vattimo, Gianni, *The End of Modernity: Nihilism and Hermeneutics in Postmodern Culture*, trans. Jon R. Snyder, Cambridge, Polity Press, 1991.

—*The Adventures of Difference*, trans. Cyprian Blamires and Thomas Harrison, Cambridge, Polity Press, 1993.

Viner, Jacob, *The Long View and the Short: Studies in Economic Theory and Policy*, New York, Free Press, 1958.

Vogel, Ezra F., *Japan as No. One: Lessons for America*, Cambridge, Mass., Harvard University Press, 1979.

—*Comeback*, Tokyo, Charles E. Tuttle, 1985.

Wade, Robert, *Governing the Market: Economic Theory and the Role of Government in East Asian Industrialization*, Princeton, N.J., Princeton University Press, 1991.

Walcott, Derek, *Omeros*, London, Faber & Faber, 1990.

Ward, Robert E. *Japan's Political System*, Englewood Hills, N.J., Prentice-Hall, 1967.

Weber, Max, *The Protestant Ethic and the Spirit of Capitalism*, trans. Talcott Parsons, London, Unwin, 1930.

—*The Religion of China: Confucianism and Taoism*, trans. Hans H. Gerth, New York, The Free Press, 1951.

White, Edmund, *Genet: A Biography*, London, Chatto & Windus, 1994.

Whorf, Benjamin Lee, *Language, Thought and Reality: Selected Writings of Benjamin Lee Whorf*, ed. John B. Carroll, Cambridge, Mass., MIT Press, 1991.

Wilks, Stephen and Wright, Maurice (eds), *The Promotion and Regulation of Industry in Japan*, London, Macmillan, 1992.

Williams, David, 'A Triumph of Motivated Bureaucracy', (review of Tetsuo Najita's *Japan: The Intellectual Foundations of Modern Japanese Politics*), Chicago and London, University of Chicago Press, 1974), *The Japan Times*, 1981.

—'Beyond political economy: a critique of issues raised in Chalmers Johnson's *MITI and the Japanese Miracle*', *Social and Economic Research on Modern Japan*, Occasional Paper No. 35, Berlin, East Asian Institute, Free University of Berlin, 1983.

—*Provincial Police Training in Britain: Continuity and Reform 1947–1985*, Oxford D.Phil. dissertation.

—'Reporting the death of the Showa Emperor', *Nissan Occasional Paper Series*, University of Oxford, no. 14, 1990.

—*Japan: Beyond the End of History*, London, Routledge, 1994.

Winch, Peter, *The Idea of a Social Science and its Relation to Philosophy*, 2d edn, London, Routledge, 1990.

Wolferen, Karl van, *The Enigma of Japanese Power: People and Politics in a Stateless Nation*, London, Macmillan, 1989.

Wood, David and Bernasconi, Robert (eds), *Derrida and Différance*, Evanston, Ill., Northwestern Univerity Press, 1988.

Yamamura, Kozo (ed.) *Japan's Economic Structure: Should It Change?*, Seattle, Society of Japanese Studies, 1990.

Yamamura, Kozo and Yasuba, Yasukichi (eds), *The Political Economy of Japan, Volume 1: The Domestic Transformation*, Stanford, Calif., Stanford University Press, 1987.

Young, Robert, *White Mythologies: Writing History and the West*, London, Routledge, 1990.

Index

Note: Authors' works are organized alphabetically without reference to the definite and indefinite articles of the languages in which they are given, i.e. according to the word following the article.

sparked with 100; dominated by positivist law-making 20; economic behaviour and 59; foundations 120; tendency of students to yield to claims of 18 economic theory 78, 80; liberal 126, 233; neo-liberal 93; positivist 125; traditional 86
economics 153, 175; Anglo-American 24; capitalist 208; classic divide between political science and 122, 123; classical 206; elevation of 268; English-language textbooks on 51; importance of 125; mathematical approaches in 261; modern, methodology of 59; national 164; new classical 109; positive science in the classic sense 126; positivist xvi–xvii, 18, 19, 20, 59, 65, 78–89, 100, 120, 168, 236, 262, 264, 271; study of 263; 'theoretical advances' of 263; total absorption of political science by 262; *see also* economic positivism; economic theory
Economist, The 52
Edinburgh 70
Edo period 31, 34, 194
egalitarianism 93, 182, 186; commitment to 195
Egypt 5, 31, 58, 127
Einsteinian physics 263
Eliot, T. S. 40, 150, 154, 199, 203, 247
elitism 37, 38, 67
empiricism 10, 79, 97–139, 148, 159, 185–6, 146; abandoned spirit 11; ancient 205; antipositivist 22; ban on certain schools of 270; belief in xvi; British fiction 223; 'cautious activism' and 86; certain branches would urge to ignore Japan's canonic potential 8; classic 198, 239; commitment to dilute 225; common sense 198; corrective 172, 179, 182; description 93; dominant role of 269; fitful 225; focused 207; great weight assigned tradition to

accurate vision 218; grist to the mills of 206; gross distinction between statements 89; grounds for abandoning 264; guileless 226; inadequacy 94; involves no commitment to scientific law-making 62; logical 89; low-level generalizations 94; misdirected 8; naïve 198, 222; non-positivistic 85; not scientifically rigorous 63; ontology 211; overlapping definitions to positivism and 61; positivism and, merely alternative terms for the same school 73; positivism grounded in 58; post-medieval tradition 72; practical workaday 64; problems posed by some forms 153; proof of Japanese economic miracle found in 81; pure xvii, 75, 76, 78, 263, 264; quantitative 69; strengths and limitations 230; traditional Anglo-American, notion central to 222; uncritical awe of 95; unfruitful elision of positivism and 70; 'unthinking' 68; unwise equation of positivism with 59; weaknesses 220
Encyclopedia of Philosophy, The 52–3, 56
encyclopedias 55, 91, 151, 158
Engels, Friedrich 78, 204, 205, 210
English Civil War (1642–51) 7, 117
Enlightenment 52, 174–7, 180, 185, 194, 197, 269; cultural condescensions xii; Scotland 217; social theory 66; universal ambitions of the project 70
'epistemic break' 90, 100
epistemology 29, 99, 101, 116, 126, 231; certitude 110; consequences 265, 270; current retreat from concerns 261; demands 27; difficulties 225, 259; distinctions 90, 222; European 222; foundations, empirical political science 237; non- or post-referential 240; one-sided 198; realism 239; weaknesses 131
essentialism: embrace of totalities

Index compiled by Frank Pert